Women in IT in the New Social Era:

A Critical Evidence-Based Review of Gender Inequality and the Potential for Change

Sonja Bernhardt
ThoughtWare, Australia

A volume in the Advances in Human and Social Aspects of Technology (AHSAT) Book Series

BUSINESS SCIENCE Reference
An Imprint of IGI Global

Managing Director: Lindsay Johnston
Production Editor: Jennifer Yoder
Development Editor: Austin DeMarco
Acquisitions Editor: Kayla Wolfe
Typesetter: Michael Brehm
Cover Design: Jason Mull

Published in the United States of America by
Business Science Reference (an imprint of IGI Global)
701 E. Chocolate Avenue
Hershey PA 17033
Tel: 717-533-8845
Fax: 717-533-8661
E-mail: cust@igi-global.com
Web site: http://www.igi-global.com

Library of Congress Cataloging-in-Publication Data

Bernhardt, Sonja, 1959-
Women in IT in the new social era : a critical evidence-based review of gender inequality and the potential for change / by Sonja Bernhardt.
pages cm
Includes bibliographical references and index.
Summary: "This book aims to bring the topic of women in IT to the forefront of discussion about what can be done to correct this lopsided gender distribution by providing an essential guide for government professionals, students, and researchers in the ICT field looking to develop a solution to equalize the retention rate of women in these related fields"-- Provided by publisher.
ISBN 978-1-4666-5860-8 (hardcover) -- ISBN 978-1-4666-5861-5 (ebook) -- ISBN 978-1-4666-5863-9 (print & perpetual access) 1. Women in computer science. 2. Women in technology. 3. Sex discrimination in employment. 4. Information technology--Social aspects. I. Title.

QA76.9.W65B47 2014
004.082--dc23

2013051358

This book is published in the IGI Global book series Advances in Human and Social Aspects of Technology (AHSAT) (ISSN: 2328-1316; eISSN: 2328-1324)

British Cataloguing in Publication Data
A Cataloguing in Publication record for this book is available from the British Library.

For electronic access to this publication, please contact: eresources@igi-global.com.

Advances in Human and Social Aspects of Technology (AHSAT) Book Series

Ashish Dwivedi
The University of Hull, UK

ISSN: 2328-1316
EISSN: 2328-1324

Mission

In recent years, the societal impact of technology has been noted as we become increasingly more connected and are presented with more digital tools and devices. With the popularity of digital devices such as cell phones and tablets, it is crucial to consider the implications of our digital dependence and the presence of technology in our everyday lives.

The **Advances in Human and Social Aspects of Technology (AHSAT) Book Series** seeks to explore the ways in which society and human beings have been affected by technology and how the technological revolution has changed the way we conduct our lives as well as our behavior. The AHSAT book series aims to publish the most cutting-edge research on human behavior and interaction with technology and the ways in which the digital age is changing society.

Coverage

- Activism & ICTs
- Computer-Mediated Communication
- Cultural Influence of ICTs
- Cyber Behavior
- End-User Computing
- Gender & Technology
- Human-Computer Interaction
- Information Ethics
- Public Access to ICTs
- Technoself

IGI Global is currently accepting manuscripts for publication within this series. To submit a proposal for a volume in this series, please contact our Acquisition Editors at Acquisitions@igi-global.com or visit: http://www.igi-global.com/publish/.

The Advances in Human and Social Aspects of Technology (AHSAT) Book Series (ISSN 2328-1316) is published by IGI Global, 701 E. Chocolate Avenue, Hershey, PA 17033-1240, USA, www.igi-global.com. This series is composed of titles available for purchase individually; each title is edited to be contextually exclusive from any other title within the series. For pricing and ordering information please visit http://www.igi-global.com/book-series/advances-human-social-aspects-technology/37145. Postmaster: Send all address changes to above address.

Titles in this Series

For a list of additional titles in this series, please visit: www.igi-global.com

Women in IT in the New Social Era: A Critical Evidence-Based Review of Gender Inequality and the Potential for Change
Sonja Bernhardt (ThoughtWare, Australia)
Business Science Reference • copyright 2014 • 320pp • H/C (ISBN: 9781466658608) • US $195.00 (our price)

Gamification for Human Factors Integration Social, Education, and Psychological Issues
Jonathan Bishop (Centre for Research into Online Communities and E-Learning Systems, Belgium)
Information Science Reference • copyright 2014 • 362pp • H/C (ISBN: 9781466650718) • US $175.00 (our price)

Emerging Research and Trends in Interactivity and the Human-Computer Interface
Katherine Blashki (Noroff University College, Norway) and Pedro Isaias (Portuguese Open University, Portugal)
Information Science Reference • copyright 2014 • 580pp • H/C (ISBN: 9781466646230) • US $175.00 (our price)

Creating Personal, Social, and Urban Awareness through Pervasive Computing
Bin Guo (Northwestern Polytechnical University, China) Daniele Riboni (University of Milano, Italy) and Peizhao Hu (NICTA, Australia)
Information Science Reference • copyright 2014 • 440pp • H/C (ISBN: 9781466646957) • US $175.00 (our price)

Gender Divide and the Computer Game Industry
Julie Prescott (University of Bolton, UK) and Jan Bogg (The University of Liverpool, UK)
Information Science Reference • copyright 2014 • 321pp • H/C (ISBN: 9781466645349) • US $175.00 (our price)

User Behavior in Ubiquitous Online Environments
Jean-Eric Pelet (KMCMS, IDRAC International School of Management, University of Nantes, France) and Panagiota Papadopoulou (University of Athens, Greece)
Information Science Reference • copyright 2014 • 325pp • H/C (ISBN: 9781466645660) • US $175.00 (our price)

Uberveillance and the Social Implications of Microchip Implants Emerging Technologies
M.G. Michael (University of Wollongong, Australia) and Katina Michael (University of Wollongong, Australia)
Information Science Reference • copyright 2014 • 509pp • H/C (ISBN: 9781466645820) • US $265.00 (our price)

Innovative Methods and Technologies for Electronic Discourse Analysis
Hwee Ling Lim (The Petroleum Institute-Abu Dhabi, UAE) and Fay Sudweeks (Murdoch University, Australia)
Information Science Reference • copyright 2014 • 546pp • H/C (ISBN: 9781466644267) • US $175.00 (our price)

Table of Contents

Chapter 4

Chapter 5

Chapter 6

Foreword

by Dale Spender

The Internet was called "the superhighway" in 1995 when in I published the book, *Nattering on the Net: Women, Power, and Cyberspace*. As the superhighway at that time was dominated by many unruly men, many wise women chose to keep off it. Smart phones didn't exist and only 5% of women—20 years ago—used the Internet! Partly because it didn't connect with their lives, their living, or their imagination.

As a writer and a publisher, I was, however, concerned about women's position in this new medium; publishing houses had effectively been controlled by men and for centuries women had even resorted to using male pseudonyms in order to get into print. Would our reluctance to take our chances on the superhighway become a future limitation?

I knew of course that almost every technological invention was widely believed to be beyond women's capabilities. Even the telephone—which was designed for the businessman—was considered inappropriate for women when first introduced. They might be good at face-to-face talk, but they wouldn't be able to conduct a conversation in the abstract: without someone to look at, they wouldn't know what to say.

Well we all know how ridiculous that belief was; it didn't take women very long to work out that the telephone wasn't for business – it was for communication, the ideal means for keeping up with friends and family. Within a short space of time women took over the telephone and made it their own.

Maybe—I thought—this would happen again. In the meantime, I became a spruiker for women and the Internet. It was made for them:

- It can't hurt you
- You can't break it
- And there is no mess to clean up afterwards

And once the mobile phone appeared on the scene, it didn't take long for women to get the message.

Fast-forward to 2014, and what do you find? Anyone who has attended a "business chicks" event in Australia (or its equivalent overseas) would soon notice that there were hundreds (thousands sometimes) of thirty-something women in the room (some younger, not many older) and that they were all energized "women in business." Any conversations you might overhear—among the buzz—would include sales, Websites, social media, marketing, and security – online and off! They were digitally oriented to their fingertips.

Not much talk about coding, however.

These women are the living evidence of the revolution that has occurred at the workplace and its location. Many of them are online small businesses women—who work from home—like Mia Freedman of Mamamia, for example. Others have big accounting, legal, and fashion businesses, and are equally digitally savvy.

Some are climbing the established career ladders in the new IT industries – as Sheryl Sandberg (2013) makes clear in her book (*Lean In*). A past Vice President at Google and now the Chief Operating Officer of Facebook, she is a symbol of success in an IT business world.

And she wants other women to take up the challenge and join her – to "Lean In" rather than hold back! The women she is addressing need only the opportunity! They are keen to have their careers, to be in charge of their own lives, to own their own homes.

Real estate agents report that young women are more likely than young men to be in the property market; young men go for cars. The Westpac Home Ownership Report—September 2013—found that Generation Y young women have a better grasp of finances than their male counterparts, and that 75% of the women were planning to pay off their loans as quickly as possible. Many gave a higher priority to home ownership than to marriage! They seek to be financially independent. So much for the old stereotype of women waiting for their prince to come.

"Girls just wanna have funds" is a common pattern among young business women who are ambitious and competitive, as well as co-operative, and they are the women in IT. Their career counselors at school may not have advised them to take this path, and they may not have formal IT qualifications from a university, but they are more than likely to have a degree.

They will have been to workshops and courses related to IT and know how to get the best out of LinkedIn, Twitter, Facebook, etc., run by "business chicks" and other comparable organisations. If they aren't classified as IT workers with start-up businesses, it's a failure of our definitions, not of their occupation, skills, and attitudes. They are the workers of the 21st century, and they are doing very well. Better than the men.

For reasons that are not quite clear—in the Western world and in China—women are now better educated than men. They are 60% of the university students and graduates and generally get better grades.

The Mission Australia Youth Survey (2013) questioned 15,000 young people between the ages of 15 – 19 and found that while most intended to complete their formal education, young men were almost three times more likely than young women to say they didn't intend to complete Year 12.

This absence of males in higher education at a time when it is such a major requirement comes as something of a surprise given that men designed the education system in the early 19th century and only opened the doors to women not much more than one hundred years ago. However, male enrolments have declined throughout the Western world, and their drop-out rate also gives cause for concern. Campus surveys suggest that when female students are in the library working, males are watching porn and playing video games.

Female students on Australian campuses are more career-oriented than their male peers; they make plans, organize work experience, even arrange jobs before they graduate. In contrast, male students often express the view that something will come up, and the future can take care of itself (Mission Australia Youth Survey, 2013).

This does help to account for women having become the majority in everything including law and medicine (more than half the GPs), vet science, accounting and auditing, financial management, optometry, dermatology, medical genetics, forensic pathology, among hundreds of others: the US pharmacy industry stands out because 8% of students were female in 1960, and they are 60% today. The exceptions are that men still hold the fort in IT and Engineering, and because of their central and crucial role in today's world, this is generally viewed as something of a problem (Rosin, 2012, p. 118).

In China, India, and other Asian countries, IT in all its forms—including coding—is considered "a good job for a girl." In Brazil, women are also regarded as "excellent engineers." These are much less likely to be the expectations in Australia.

As Washington Correspondent Liza Mundy (2012) points out in her book *The Richer Sex*, "Globally, a generation of young women is entering the job market better educated than young men and poised to become the most financially powerful generation of women in history" (p. 6).

And all of these young women are IT literate. They have entered a new and open market place where there is much less entrenched power, and they have so many of the appropriate skills that they are making their mark. "For the first time in history the global economy is becoming a place where women are finding more success than men" (Rosin, 2012, p. 117).

Just for the record, 40% of wives in America now earn more than their husbands (It's 25% in Queensland). Only 18% of men in the US are breadwinners, and 1 in 5 men of working age is not working. Women are on the rise, changing the established sex roles and the nature of work and redefining the relationships for the entire society in an IT environment.

Women have done this for themselves. Choosing to "start up" an online business wasn't in their curriculum any more than the cultural changes brought about by social media. They spent their time outside school exploring every use of an app, but unless they attended an exceptional school, their lessons didn't cover how to create one; most of them certainly weren't introduced to coding.

Mathematics, which suffers from the false image that it's not for girls, isn't compulsory, and so most are put-off from taking it. When they are confronted with "choices," they sensibly seek subjects that will likely result in the highest marks. These factors then influence career options.

When it comes to the last school hurdle, a written exam, they weren't given the opportunity to show what they could do, what problems they could solve, what extraordinary online communication and verbal skills they possessed – all the basics for the digital world. Instead, they had to write with pen and paper!

For girls who can skim along a keyboard, find anything on their iPads in seconds, and send text messages from under their desks without looking, getting them to write an exam answer is like asking those who have a driving license to manage a horse and cart.

The information they were required to write down on paper was supposedly stored in their heads, when they thought that was what the save key was for! Even worse, their habits of cooperation, collaboration, and consulting each other were not tolerated; they were called cheating. Everyone had to do their own work – no sharing allowed. How would they cope?

Very well it seems, even though these old skills aren't the ones they need now.

In surveys in the United States and Australia, women have undergone a radical transformation. A generation ago, women shaped their lives around the needs of men; they generally had marriage as a goal and work as an interim measure. They gave up work after they were married (as late as 1966 in Queensland, Australia, women had to resign from the public service when they married).

But things have changed dramatically, as the traditional male jobs of the industrial revolution dwindle and the demands of the information economy expand. As Hanna Rosin says, "Women are knocking at the door of leadership at the very time their talents are especially well matched with the requirements of the day" (Rosin, 2012, p. 199). Where EQ is valued over IQ.

Education, childcare, aged care, health, financial management, retail, medical science, are all traditional women's occupations – and while they are also where the biggest gender pay gaps exist, the pattern is that men's wages overall have stagnated over the last decade, while those of women are trending up (in the United States the gap is closing, while over the past years the gap has grown in Australia, but this could well be about to change).

In an information environment, everyone is a learner as technology changes so rapidly. It is more a matter of keeping up with the new than learning the old. The secret to success is adaptation, and women are the experts in this field. Researchers report that many men when confronted with online job applications and forms that are required for employment benefits call on wives, mothers, girlfriends to help them find their way around in the digital world! Whether they have been blue-collar workers or stock market traders!

It is said that print democratized reading; once books were commercially available rather than the texts that were sacred manuscripts locked away for the few in religious institutions, the masses learned to read. And if the printing press opened up the world of reading to anyone who wanted to try it, the Internet has opened up "authorship," creativity, problem solving, and entrepreneurialism to anyone who wants to have a go.

It is gender neutral. And you can do it for yourself, as every toddler with an iPad or mobile phone already knows.

When I got my first iPhone, I revealed my age when I asked the young woman if there was a manual; No, she said quite slowly and patiently, "You just go home and play with it and find out what you want to do. Everyone does it differently." That's the change from the factory system to the realm of creativity.

The legacy education system we have inherited has worked against taking the initiative; it is a standardized system that was perfectly acceptable and even successful in an industrial age where creativity would have completely disrupted the ordered assembly line.

Like the products that were made at the factory, the ingredients that went into the school systems were also "standardized" – starting with what was expected of girls and boys! Everyone started school at the same age, usually had the same curriculum and lessons, passed through the same grade system, sat for the same exams, and had to get the same right answers to succeed.

The assembly line system is still there, and if girls think there is something about IT (and math and science and engineering) as they are currently taught that is a turn-off, they are likely to be stuck with it. They will have little opportunity to take charge and experiment for themselves, except in some rare progressive schools such as Pymble Ladies College (PLC), where they are allowed to take their mobile phones into their exams. However, in a textbook-based classroom they can't try these subjects out for themselves, to play with them and work out what is myth and what is magic, and what they can do once they start.

This is a problem. For while women and IT use have become almost inseparable, they don't build IT!

It was Bill Gates who said that they don't call it programming for nothing. Coding has become the underpinning of our entire lives, and there are many good reasons that women should be in there doing it, reflecting their view of the world, their values, and their skills, just as they should have been in publishing all these years ago, making the decisions about what was necessary or desirable, rather than having a lop-sided view from only one gender.

One of the findings that emerged from the research on the Global Financial Crisis was that women were better stock market traders than men. It was the men who traded vastly more frequently than women, out of a sense of bravado and authority. This pumped up confidence and competitiveness, which was once regarded as leadership and resulted in heavy losses, has since been redefined as a liability.

Women's caution in contrast, long seen as a failure to take risks, is now valued as a necessary skill, and the guidelines that have been issued for future use call for more women on the trading floor, as this will mean fewer pointless risks. There are implications here for our IT infrastructure. Women are the balance and the safety measure.

There are already predictions about algorithms that can start to operate independently (this has been a reality on the Stock Exchange where on more than one occasion a rogue computer "sold" the shares of a company and almost bankrupted it).

Recently, some serious scientists outlined three possibilities for the cataclysmic end of the world; they were a meteor, climate change, and being taken over by robots. Whether this is science fiction isn't the point; we need more women in IT, and that means we need to offer them the opportunity to explore, play with, create, and enjoy the satisfaction that coding can provide. Sonja Bernhardt's enthusiasm for IT and creating software for specific purposes can light up a room. Why should other women not enjoy the same experience? Currently, few of them get such an opportunity.

We will need a new breed of teachers for whom IT is a way of life and not just another subject; it will mean learning by exploring – and with different students coming up with different solutions. No more same answers that are the right ones! National curriculums that are saturated in print skills are not the best way to prepare for a digital society and workplace.

Some countries in the world have redesigned education for the 21st century, and kids in China, for example, are taught the excitement of coding from kindergarten to Grade 12 (perhaps I should rephrase that and say that they are given the chance to explore all the opportunities of coding from the day they start school). In the UK, Google provided 15,000 free Raspberry Pis (n.d.) for school kids.[1]

Once some schools got them, they all wanted them, and coding is spreading through the system.

At the same time, two fourteen-year-old boys in the United States who were convinced that every kid should learn to code, also recognized it wouldn't be their teachers who taught them. They set up their own business, Menlo App Academy (n.d.), and offered to teach any student between the age of 9 and 18 how to program mobile apps.

Their aim now is to teach 25 teachers who will in turn teach 2,500 other teachers so that the US can become a nation of coders: It's basic 21st century literacy. If school girls were offered such a chance, there would be those who would choose to explore the possibilities. They could even make it their IT business!

It might be a good idea to introduce it in Australia, better than spending days learning spelling, when there is an app for that!

Sonja Bernhardt has long known that women want to learn, adapt, change, and be inspired; that is one of the reasons she was the founder and inaugural president of WIT (Women in Technology) in 1997. Her enthusiasm was infectious, and many a young female students who had breakfast with Sonja at one of the WIT events went into IT.

They knew what they were doing because they had the chance to explore, and question, and watch, and listen, which wasn't every girls' good fortune. Maybe some of them didn't stay (I know a few doctors who don't practice, and a few lawyers who think they made the wrong choice), but there are a lot like Sonja Bernhardt who are in IT and who love it, as she does.

I have asked some young women at Business Chicks and other events for young entrepreneurs what started the passion, and the answer has often been, I went to WIT. Today, they use Business Chicks and other women's professional organisations as a "market square" where they can go to exchange skills, be sociable, make new contacts, and promote their businesses. They are the IT workers, they are financially independent, and they are changing the world. Not a bad achievement.

All girls should have the option and reward of making the model as well as knowing how to use it! However, this will mean an education revolution that is not on the horizon of the educational authorities.

This book will help to not only change minds and understandings about how we learn and work and live and play in the 21st century IT world. It is a crucial contribution to a better-planned and safer future. Sonja Bernhardt is to be congratulated for her long commitment to the importance of IT and her research, energy, and inspiration.

Dale Spender
University of London, UK

REFERENCES

MenloApp Academy. (n.d.). Retrieved from http://www.rizzarr.com/the-spreading-ripple-2/one-person-lots-of-ripples/2013/09/24/two-boys-create-app-that-is-changing-the-way-students-learn-digital-code/

Mission Australia Youth Survey. (2013). Retrieved from http://www.theaustralian.com.au/national-affairs/policy/job-worries-change-youth-focus/story-fn9hm1pm-1226773756676#sthash.lmarzkBF.dpuf

Mundy, L. (2012). *The richer sex: How the new majority of female breadwinners is transforming our culture*. New York: Simon and Schuster.

Raspberry Pis. (n.d.). Retrieved from http://en.wikipedia.org/wiki/Raspberry_Pi

Rosin, H. (2012). *The end of men and the rise of women*. New York: Riverhead Books.

Sandberg, S. (2013). *Lean in: Women, work and the will to lead*. New York: Random House.

ENDNOTES

1 The Raspberry Pi is a credit-card-sized single-board computer developed in the UK by the Raspberry Pi Foundation with the intention of promoting the teaching of basic computer science in schools.

Dale Spender *has been an author, feminist, educator, and public speaker most of her life. She began as a high school teacher, lectured at James Cook University, and received her PhD at the University of London, where she also taught teachers to teach. She has lectured at many universities internationally. Her book, Man Made Language, exposes the extent to which women's language supports that of men. She sent her first email in 1986 and has been hooked on digital ever since. A former chair of the CAL, she has served on numerous boards in the public and private sectors as well as working as a consultant with AOL, Microsoft, Apple, Fujitsu, the Commonwealth Bank, and DEEWR. She is a former deputy chair of the State Library of Queensland and the chair of Second Chance Program that raises money for homeless women; she is a past deputy chair of the Australian Society of Authors. She has written/edited more than 30 books and is currently completing one on women's status: Money Makes a Difference.*

Foreword

by Pia Waugh

Growing up as a female geek in Australia has been quite an experience. My mum was a techie and worked with software and networks, and there was a grand total of two people in my school interested in computers prior to university. So my enjoyment of computers in my early years was pretty organic and natural.

As a young woman, I was unfortunately told—repeatedly—that my enjoyment of gaming, bleeding edge technologies, fixing computers, and software somehow made me strange. An exception that proved some weird and illogical rule about women and technology.

After a while I started to believe that perhaps I might be an exception, or that maybe I did have a "male brain," or something else peculiar. Then I went overseas and discovered countries where women were 60% of the IT sector and I realised the idea that IT or technology is somehow a male thing was cultural. I, basically, decided then and there to do what I love regardless of what people tell me. I figured the best way to contribute to the IT gender debates that have raged in Australia for decades now was to be the change I wanted to see.

To do IT because I love it. To do awesome projects because they are fun and challenging. To give the men and women around me another example of a female geek to help break down the stereotype.

I am extremely pleased to say that I have seen a genuine change in the last decade. There are more technical women visible in Australia, a more positive attitude towards IT as an awesome industry that young people want to get involved in, and more young girls and boys are starting to identify as change agents with geek super powers throughout school and university.

Many people have contributed to this movement, and the Internet has bred a more socially literate breed of geek that can often transcend the limiting and unfounded biases of generations before. I feel proud now to identify as simply a geek, who happens to be female. After all, with almost everything in modern life depending on technology, the geek will inherit the Earth and all geeks—regardless of gender, age, beliefs, ethnicity, or any other traditional box—have an important role to play as the pioneers of the digital age.

Pia Waugh
GovHack, Australia

Pia Waugh *is an open government and open data ninja, working within the machine to enable greater transparency, democratic engagement, citizen-centric design, and real innovation in the public sector and beyond. She is passionate about improving the world by getting great technologies to people who need them and creating a well-connected global society where anyone can play and succeed. She has worked extensively in the IT sector, as a political adviser, has run her own business, and for both state/territory and federal government. Pia currently works as the Director of Coordination and Gov 2.0 for the Australian Government CTO. Pia was at various times also the President of Software Freedom International, the President (then VP) of Linux Australia, and on the linux.conf.au 2007 organising team. She speaks at technology, open source, and open culture events in Australia and around the world. Current projects include Gov 2.0 and open government, GovCamp and GovHack, Society5, the Distributed Democracy, and data.gov.au.*

Preface

I did not set out to have a career in IT. Rather, I fell into it sideways when a Human Resources job I took turned out to be an HR software support position. I had always been good at math, and the combination of interests made it a good fit for me. Over the years, my career evolved from employee, to consultant, to finally running my own software development company.

When I started in IT back in the 1990s, I looked around and saw how few other women there were. I started to think about the women in IT I knew, who did not know each other. I was determined to do something about it and hit on the idea of founding an organisation for women in IT, to provide a forum for networking, encouragement in a male-dominated field, publicising IT, and otherwise encouraging other women into what we knew was an interesting and well paid career. In 1997, Women in Information Technology (WIT) was born in Queensland, Australia, with a nucleus of ten women (the name has since changed to Women in Technology [WiT] to reflect a broadening of focus).

Over the years, WIT engaged in many programs to help women enter and progress their careers in IT and other scientific and technology fields. They ranged from interventions to encourage schoolgirls to consider IT all the way to board readiness programs to assist female entry onto company boards.

Through WIT, related organisations such as Australian Women in IT, Science, and Engineering (AWISE) and my personal initiatives, I voluntarily dedicated decades of my life to "the cause" of trying to increase the number of women taking up technology studies and careers, but what I observed was that not only were numbers actually declining but also the same arguments and intervention projects were being recycled and recycled across the years and around the world. Then in 2012, I had one of those "AH-HA" moments. I knew I wanted to write this book; I knew I needed to write this book, and I did.

OVERVIEW

"Attraction, Promotion, and Retention" has been the catch-cry of many passionate activists in this field around the globe for more than two decades. Yet to date the secret of attracting females to study technology and to enter technology careers, navigating suitable promotional pathways, and retaining women in technology industries has not been found. Without a doubt, this topic has attracted voluminous research over the past decades and continues to do so. Essentialist Theory, Social Construction Theory, Individual Differences Theory, Structuration Theory, Theory of Reasoned Action, and resulting Gender Modeling, Leaky Pipeline, Life Course Approach, Critical Mass, and Dualism Models have all been used over time to frame researchers' discussions regarding the lack and decline of females in technology studies and careers.

Despite the wide variety of theories proposed in efforts to frame and understand the issues, to date none have been accepted as a universally accurate framework, nor been applicable across varying cultures and ethnicities. However, the problem is deeper than that. As succinctly put by Mitchell (2013):

It's perplexing to make sense of some theories when one looks at the timeline. If social pressures and cultural attitudes were to blame, one would think the numbers would have been consistently low. On the other hand, if social attitudes had changed for the better over the last four decades, one would expect to see a gradual improvement over time. The same applies to changes in the market, such as negative perceptions of IT careers as outsourcing took hold in the '90s and '00s. The numbers also don't track with the unemployment rate, and even if they did, again, one would expect both men and women to be affected evenly.

The evidence presented in this book confirms that despite the reams of global research and decades of well-intentioned work by organizations, activists, and advocates to tackle the problem—including ad hoc, systematic, and comprehensive efforts, comprising career days, computer clubs, role modelling, mentoring, coaching, general promotional events and more—the attempts have been futile. A multitude of things have been done, but their goal of increasing the number of women in IT remains elusive. Yet, belief in the value of the programs persists, despite the lack of objective evidence. It is time to recognise that there has been a massive global failure to stem the decline of girls taking up technology studies and women entering technology careers. This failure has cost many millions of dollars around the globe, and it is time to seriously question the sense of continuing.

Ultimately when looking at the "issue or problem" of recruitment, promotion, and retention of women in technology fields, I propose that the chief problem is the topic is fundamentally flawed:

- It assumes that the "natural" state of the number of women engaged in technology studies and careers is a "problem" that needs "fixing or correcting"; and
- It layers a gender lens over the ensuing discussions, research, and actions.

This matters because the way we perceive a topic determines our responses to it. For example, if we believe artificial external factors are the main cause, it implies that artificial interventions to ameliorate those factors will have a significant benefit. For example, in her TEDx talk, Schiebinger (2013) states, "Fix the numbers of women…ought to shift to Fix the institutions.... We will not be successful in recruiting and retaining more women if we focus on women alone, we need to take the next step and that is transform institutions."

The hard fact is that neither the issue nor the proposals are new. For decades, we have been worried about how few women there are in IT and other technical fields. We have generated theories and interventions relating to surmised barriers that keep women out of IT or drive them from it after they enter it. We have achieved nothing – so why do we think more of the same will achieve more?

It is not that those past focuses were inherently unreasonable. Given the historical fight of women against bias in education and careers, it was not unreasonable to propose that persistently low numbers in a given field reflected the same causes and prejudices. Nor, given that the issue is gender disparity, was it unreasonable to view it through the lens of gender theory. However, when we see the number of women pursuing higher education rising to surpass the number of men, when intervention after intervention in one field has no real effect, while in other fields women come to equal or outnumber men without anybody pushing: it is surely time to question our theories.

In business, when an approach consistently fails to deliver expected outcomes either the approach is adjusted or the "issue" is dropped. In science, when experiments are not consistent with a theory we question the theory. However, when it comes to women in IT, the theories live on while reality is blamed for the results. Perhaps it is time to ask the questions, "Should we really care if fewer women are attracted to IT roles? If women aren't interested in IT careers there is no reason to hold a gun to their heads and force them to into work they don't want to do" (Cave, 2013), and "Why don't we just leave the situation alone and see what emerges, instead of collectively trying to engineer an artificial situation?"

It is notable that the overwhelming majority of respondents to a poll conducted for this book identified personal interest from a young age as their own greatest influence on choosing a career in IT, and a clear majority of the remainder nominated discovering an interest after being exposed to IT in their job. In other words, the vast majority of respondents simply chose according to their internal affinity for the field, whether discovered early or later in life. These results map to a more rigorously designed survey conducted by Lyons et al. (2012). These women neither sought out nor were converted by intervention programs, they just chose according to their personal interests. Women in IT or girls interested in STEM see themselves as interested, competent, and above all, as people who regard obstacles as a challenge to be met and overcome. It is that strength and uniqueness of the individual core that forms the central thesis of this book.

Similarly, the failure of interventions and the stagnant level of female participation in IT, while in other fields it has soared from a small minority to a large majority, point to the answer lying within women, not outside them. It is certainly not that women are not as good at the subject as men. It is not even the case that women are not interested in it: many girls are interested in STEM fields. However, career choice takes more than ability and interest. It takes being *more interested than in any of the other choices available.*

I believe that is the whole secret. Women are under-represented in some fields and over-represented in others because, statistically, their interests differ from those of men. It does not matter how much we tell girls how much *we* enjoy IT, all that matters to them is what *they* are interested in doing.

However, whilst personal interest is the main driver, not all girls have an equal ability to discover their interest, and whilst interest can drive someone to a career, there may still exist barriers such as prejudice that make it an unhappy experience.

That is where the seismic shifts happening within the field of IT itself bring both a challenge and a solution.

The challenge is to researchers and organisers. Our frequently changing technology landscape makes it difficult for a traditionally developed and distributed research framework to keep up with the rate of change and incorporate the current influencing factors. Technology and industry game changers that impact the relevancy of a model or theory are introduced frequently. And when it comes to disseminating information, we are in an era where "trending" and following the latest technology craze is fast becoming not only the norm, but the main source of information for society. Similarly, those engaged in women in technology activities—planning, coordinating, or funding—ought to take notice of the tectonic shift beginning in technology and society and shift accordingly. It would be ironic indeed to bemoan the status of women in a dynamic technology field if we did not embrace the new approaches that field enables.

Perhaps we need to widen our perspective, to step back further and ask ourselves even harder questions about the issue of increasing female participation in IT. If you looked with fresh eyes at this issue today and saw the increasing influence of social media and tools, the organic growth of self-help groups, projects, and programs, ever more disruptive technologies coming online, and the increasing prospect of life extension, what would you do if starting now? Would you even perceive there was an "issue"? Would you feel there was a pressing need to take action to address "the problem"?

The fundamental solution to the "problem" is the same as the fundamental cause: women are unique individuals. It is by promoting the idea that it is the individual who matters, the individual who thinks and has talent, which will one day mean people are judged as individuals on their own merits, not according to prejudices based on gender or ethnicity. It is not up to us to decide what other people should be interested in, but it is up to us to do what we can to empower all individuals, whoever they are and whatever their interests are.

Embracing the new technologies is about recognising that the world is entering an era of disruptive technologies that will empower the individual in ways we cannot predict, that old power bases will crumble and new things arise. Already, we have seen social media playing a leading and powerful influence, such as in the "Arab Spring." That is where the power of the model presented in this book—the STEMcell model and its #SocialIT aspect—comes in to break down old traditions and build new ones. We must tap into this shifting technological landscape and actively use its tools and platforms, and by doing so, to empower every individual to find and achieve the interests and goals that are uniquely hers.

CHAPTER ORGANISATION

This book is organised into 10 chapters. An introduction presents a detailed summary of the other chapters, of which a brief outline is given here.

Chapter 1 tells the story of pioneering women in the technology field and frames the background. It is not meant to be a complete history of women in technology. Its intent is to highlight some historical pioneers and their contributions, and at the same time draw out the social and cultural circumstances that have contributed to the "lack" of women in technology throughout history.

Chapter 2 discusses global impacts of the new social era, leading to the proposal of a new model for framing the topic. Whilst the new model absorbs the elements of past models, it adds the influence of pervasive technologies such as social media and changes perspective to the main driver being individual choice more than external forces. The layers within the model are presented later in the book, in chapters 5 – 8.

Chapter 3 debates the relative and perceived value of traditional intervention programs. It proposes a practical cost/benefit analysis for the reader to conduct to understand and measure their value. The chapter then looks at some recent interventions in Europe, UK, and the USA. Results of original research are presented and mapped to the topic. It is argued that inherent individual interest is the true driver of career choice today.

Chapter 4 reviews popular theories proposed to address the situation, with specific attention to the Leaky Pipeline model, Critical Mass theory, Life Course approach, Structuration and Dualism theory, and Gender Modelling. The relevance of the traditional theories in the new #SocialIT era is examined.

Chapter 5 is primarily a literature review of the social and cultural contexts. Factors such as popular culture, cultural norms, parental expectations, occupational culture, stereotypes, role models, mentoring, clubs, networking, media, peers, family, security, and social norms are deconstructed.

Chapter 6 is primarily a literature review of the structural context. Factors such as IT industry branding, access to information, access to facilities, education, support mechanism, and government policies are discussed.

Chapter 7 presents the individual context, the core of the model. It specifically addresses the influence of philosophy, values, rights, assumptions, strength, self-belief, interests, differences, ability, curiosity, creativity, and reality on female career decisions.

Chapter 8 describes #SocialIT, the newer social forces, and future driving forces impacting all layers of the model and thus the overall participation of females in technology studies and careers. This chapter discusses future developments such as life extension, wide adoption of augmented technology and increased smart devices, and their likely impact. This chapter is a key chapter to the overall model and is fundamental to adapting to the new era.

Chapter 9 looks at the similarities and differences of the situation for women in IT in other industries and cultures. It examines the fields of science, construction, and engineering, and looks at ethnic differences in countries such as Korea, India, Malaysia, the Middle East, and South Africa, plus subcultures within Europe and the USA.

Chapter 10 gives the conclusions and presents 3 overarching recommendations plus 35 detailed recommendations. The detailed recommendations are structured within a framework mapping to the book's overall thrust and new social era approach.

PURPOSE AND SCOPE

Whilst I fit at least some definitions of "geek," I am not a coder. However, my key interest for this book lies in technology core or "hard" skills: the coders, analysts, and architects, the designers and creators. As such in this book, except where quoted from others, I use the term IT instead of ICT. To me there is a clear difference, and mostly I never really "took to" ICT when it was first coined. I always felt that the "C" (Communication) implied more than optical cables and wireless networks, and softened and blurred the concept of "IT" to include mere users of the technology – but maybe that's just me ☺.

Specifically, I want to make the difference between adopting and using technology versus designing and building it very clear. Many times, I have read headlines and reports that confuse the issue: where quotes regarding use of technology are cited as evidence that there are plenty of women involved. There is a clear and distinct difference between using and building. It is that difference I want to target and where my burning passions to make a difference in this field lie.

Similarly, we have to stress the difference between working in IT and working in an IT *company*. Whilst including marketers and artists who work for IT companies might make the figures look better, someone whose career would be equally applicable in a software house or a clothing manufacturer does not have an IT career unless she is applying core IT skills. Indeed, this blurring of lines is a critical problem with recent headlines rather hopefully proclaiming that "more than half of tech hires this year are women" (Fortt, 2013; Neal, 2013).

That said, this book has been written for a diverse audience spanning many interest groups and individuals: feminists and gender theorists, researchers, governments and policy makers, educators (primary, secondary, trade, and tertiary), traditional women in IT associations, new social media-style women in tech associations and specialist groups, sponsors and supporters, parents, individual activists and advocates, recruiters, employers, the media, content developers, and taxpayers, and above all, for the individual women and men in technology. In large part, this is an academic book, but I am not an academic. I am an active industry participant, and I own and run a successful, multi-award-winning software development company in the growing areas of Governance, Risk Management, and Compliance. Thus, I hope this book is of value to academics and researchers – but also to those in industry and the wider community.

I thoroughly enjoyed the research component of this book and only wish I had so widely covered the literature during my very active earlier days in the field. Not only has the intensive research activity contributed to my body of knowledge, but also I was fascinated to see projects and groups I had been involved with discussed and analysed in the formal literature. In some instances, specific references were made to me by name, whereas at the time I had no idea this was occurring even though I knew and networked with the authors. Looking at it historically, I found it highly interesting, and I realise I ought to have been more on top of it earlier. Perhaps a robust debate would have ensued and some ideas in this book would have been launched already. The value of hindsight rings in my ears.

Beyond published research, the themes in this book have been informed not only by my experience as an activist for women in technology over the years, but by the exponential explosion of knowledge and technology during those years. In my lifetime, we've come from hundreds of wires, thousands of switches, and vacuum tubes to chips embedded into everyday devices and tiny multifunction computers; from where not every home had a phone to where your phone not only goes with you but will take photos and video, surf the Internet, and play games. Now the influence of social media has become increasingly pervasive. We cannot sensibly talk about the future of women in IT without considering how the future itself is going to be radically different from today.

Indeed, the increasingly intersecting areas of science and technology fascinate me, and in this book you will find analogies reflecting that intersection. I use language that is representative of science and the model I have developed is represented as a three-dimensional Earth globe, with Earth events and layers as descriptive areas of the overall model.

All authors have biases that inform their choices, evaluations, and interpretations of source material as well as their own conclusions. I declare my author bias up front: I am grounded in strong philosophical roots of reality and reason, and firmly believe that individuals are individuals and responsible for their decisions and lives. Philosophy underpins my company and home life – in fact, each month for the past 15 years my house has been opened up for philosophical salons, where "taboo" subjects such as politics, religion, and education are robustly discussed while we consume copious amounts of wine.

As that last sentence might indicate, I am unashamedly and fairly typically Australian. As such, amongst the expected USA, European, and Asian references, you will find many references to Australian researchers and characters that inhabit my Australian landscape and world. My role model interviewees are all Australian.

I believe that the analyses, conclusions, and recommendations in this book present a view that to date has not been enunciated. I have tried to look at the theories and the facts and present them with a dose of reality. In part, it may be seen as a brave move to have done so: entrenched memes do not like to be challenged. Perhaps this book's main contribution to the field will be shock value resulting in people rethinking, engaging in discussion outside the traditional frameworks, and redesigning approaches accordingly. If all this book achieves is making people think and examine their assumptions, I will consider it a success.

My style in both business and activism is to innovate, lead, build, and establish an environment for independent operation, without the absolute requirement for my continued physical presence or hands-on involvement. I believe in reality, and facing reality means acknowledging that one day my physical presence (and/or possibly mental presence) will not be around. I like to leave "things" behind that make a difference. It is my hope that this book will do exactly that. It is my hope that this book will be read broadly and thoroughly across all my target audiences, and that its recommendations will be enthusiastically adopted. It is my hope that people refer back to this book as the start of a change for the better.

I have taken the unusual path of inviting two Forewords, specifically to help represent the key thrust and theme of this book. One foreword is from Dale Spender, a widely published, high profile, and well respected Feminist, who initially approached this issue from a traditional viewpoint and viewing lens. The other, Pia Waugh, is from the emerging young, hacker, geek, "do awesome" culture. I met Dale in 1998 when we were both appointed to the Queensland State Government Ministerial Technology Advisory Board, and I met Pia in 2006 when we were both presenters at a Girls in Computing event in Western Australia. I highly respect both Dale and Pia and feel honoured they agreed to craft forewords for this book.

I have chosen to begin each chapter with a quote. They have all been carefully selected not only for what they say but also for who said them and their fit to the chapter contents. I hope you enjoy them.

Sonja Bernhardt, OAM
ThoughtWare, Australia

REFERENCES

Cave, K. (2013). Women in IT: Does the shortage matter? *IDG Connect Infographic*. Retrieved May 22, 2013, from http://www.idgconnect.com/abstract/1251/infographic-women-it-does-shortage-matter

Fortt, J. (2013, November 21). More women in technology jobs? If only it were true. *CNBC*. Retrieved December 13, 2013, from http://www.cnbc.com/id/101217146

Lyons, T., Quinn, F., Rizk, N., Anderson, N., Hubber, P., & Kenny, J. ... Wilson, S. (2012). *Starting out in STEM: A study of young men and women in first year science, technology, engineering and mathematics courses*. Armidale, Australia: University of New England. Retrieved August 13, 2013, from http://www.une.edu.au/simerr/pages/projects/132iris_report.pdf

Mitchell, R. L. (2013). *Women computer science grads: The bump before the decline*. Retrieved August 28, 2013, from http://blogs.computerworld.com/it-careers/21993/women-computer-science-visual-trendline

Neal, M. (2013). No, the tech sector didn't hire more women than men this year. *Motherboard: Business*. Retrieved December 13, 2013, from http://motherboard.vice.com/blog/no-the-tech-industry-didnt-hire-more-women-than-men-this-year

Schiebinger, L. (2013). *Gendered innovations: Londa Schiebinger at TEDxCERN*. [Video]. Retrieved November 8, 2013, from http://www.youtube.com/watch?v=JaYzdz9X3n4

Acknowledgment

The idea for this book and the need for a new model of why there are so few women in IT was mine, as was consuming and analysing the research and crafting the book, but there are three people without whom it would not have happened, plus three other acknowledgments I'd like to make.

I sincerely with all my heart and mind give my deepest thanks to Robin Craig, my life partner and editor. I thank you, thank you, thank you. In a way, this is our book, Robin: you were central to its completion. When I was having my "can't do it, can't fit it all in, I have other priorities" moments, and you wisely refocused me and got me back on track. When you so brilliantly decided your perfect role was my editor, because you know me so well and knew how to ensure my words were clear and purposeful. I thank you for being my sounding board, for flagging additional research areas, and for those early morning whiteboard sessions when you awoke and brought light and meaning to my previous hours of crafting and scribbling. For your brilliant scientific mind and helping construct the model that is so appropriate. For all the things you had to put up with and do without in your own life while this book consumed me. I thank you for knowing me. You are my Roark.

I am indebted to author Candice Lemon-Scott, who secured my publisher. When I had my "AH-HA!" moment in 2012, I was fortunate to be involved in a school community along with Candice. I approached her with my idea for a book and before I knew it she had sketched the outline, submitted it, and I had a publishing offer from IGI land in my email. Candice, I know you say you played a very small role, but without your interpretation of my "hey I have an idea for a book" and your knowledge of how and who to apply to, this would not have happened – thank you.

With a deep sense of gratitude, I thank Valerie O'Neill, who was roped into being my research assistant. After the excitement of receiving a publishing offer, I ran into time management issues and my energy was drawn into other areas. I even considered pulling out, until Valerie (a friend of Robin's) came along and got me organized. Valerie set up my research directories and scanned the environment for appropriate research; she had the fun of ploughing through my many notes, emails, and items I had marked up and organising them as well as sourcing new material. Valerie, without your fabulous efforts, I would have cancelled the project, so thank you for the great work and especially for the reinvigoration.

To my Australian technology role models, Jenny Barbour, Karen Bard, Jenny Beresford, Madeleine Sanders, Barbara Tobin, and Ann Uldridge, we've had an interesting ride the past decades, and between us contributed a significant amount to the Australian technology landscape and learnt so, so much. I value you and your contributions to the industry, but mostly your friendship and how you have helped me grow.

To my double-blind peer reviewers: whoever you are, thank you, your comments helped apply focus and strengthen my message.

Finally, I must thank a piece of technology, my Nespresso™ coffee maker. Seriously – I wasn't much of a coffee drinker before, but I needed additional hours in the day to be able to manage my company during a growth phase, my home life, and "the book." I enjoyed being a science experiment and proving that coffee really does stimulate you ☺.

Thank you all.

Sonja Bernhardt, OAM
ThoughtWare, Australia

Chapter 1
Women in IT:
Background

ABSTRACT

The historical context of women in technology is introduced through individual and collective tales of notable women in the field, from Hypatia of Alexandria through to World War II Code Breakers. The lives of these women show that while women in technology (and its ancestors philosophy and mathematics) have been present throughout history, for millennia the pervading social and cultural contexts formed strong barriers against them. These barriers were so pervasive that they not merely hindered but practically suppressed female involvement in such fields. Yet, some women leaped those barriers, often in creative and interesting ways, to not only pursue their interests but also positively contribute to the overall fields of technology, science, and engineering. However, it took exceptionally resilient, strong individuals to do so.

Life is an unfoldment, and the further we travel the more truth we can comprehend. To understand the things that are at our door is the best preparation for understanding those that lie beyond.

– Hypatia of Alexandria,
4th Century AD (attributed)
(BrainyQuote, 2013).

INTRODUCTION

Throughout history there have been women in technology (and its ancestors philosophy and mathematics) who have made key contributions (Alic, 1986). They have not been in abundance, but they have been there. But what has history captured, and what is really known? There was a time when women could only be published under male pseudonyms. There was a time when girls were not educated or not allowed to enter the halls of higher learning. The pervading social and cultural contexts hindered and practically suppressed female involvement in these key fields. However some enterprising, resilient females managed: some masquerading as men, some using male names or having work published via a male colleague; a few managing to become known in their own right. Reflecting our modern concerns where the issue is much broader than just IT, similar issues were faced by pioneering

DOI: 10.4018/978-1-4666-5860-8.ch001

Table 1. The most recognised female pioneers in computing

Era	Person	Role	Significant Contribution
1815 - 1852	Ada Lovelace	Analyst, Metaphysician and Founder of Scientific Computing	First computer programmer
1906 - 1992	Grace Hopper	Pioneer Computer Scientist	Compilers and machines understanding normal language

Table 2. High profile women in IT

Era	Person	Role	Significant Contribution
1913 - 2000	Hedy Lamarr	Actress and Inventor	Inventor of spread spectrum communications – frequency hopping
WWII	ENIAC Programmers	Programmers	Programmed ENIAC to perform a ballistics trajectory, a differential calculus equation important to the WWII effort

women in science as well. In both cases it took exceptionally resilient, strong individuals to know their interest areas, to pursue them and to achieve in the face of the prevailing cultural and social conditions.

The history of early computing is peppered with tales of the early computers and the pioneers behind them. Generally the first names people associate with them are Colossus (Alan Turing), ENIAC (John Mauchly and Presper Eckert), UNIVAC (Eckert and Mauchly), ILLIAC (John von Neumann) and CSIRAC (Trevor Pearcey). But as the information below demonstrates, women were involved as programmers and analysts across all of those early computers; though their involvement was relatively unreported and "below the line," it was there.

This chapter is not meant to be a complete history of women in technology, which would be a book in its own right. Rather its intent is to highlight some historical pioneers and their contributions, while drawing out the social and cultural circumstances that have contributed to the "lack of women in technology" throughout history. As you read you may begin to see that often these pioneers went unrecognised for their achievements, and certainly all of them had to overcome the barriers of their times.

Women are rarely mentioned in the technology history books, with the exception of Ada Lovelace and Grace Hopper. These two high profile pioneers are generally the first that are noted, spoken about, and presented as evidence that women have played a role in the technology fields (Table 1).

There are interesting and compelling tales behind both of these "IT Leading Ladies," such as Ada's rumoured affair(s) and gambling addition, and Grace's literal "computer bug." Elements of those stories are related below.

Both of those well-known and remarkable pioneers exhibited an ability to see the future directions of computer science, and deserve their place in the history books. But there are other women pioneers in computing who are occasionally mentioned and can serve as role models, such as those in Table 2.

Again there are fascinating stories behind these early role models, such as Hedy's driving motivation of seeking to spy on her despised husband's Nazi meetings, and elements of their stories are presented further below.

Table 3. Other noteworthy contributors

Era	Person	Role	Significant Contribution
WWII	Bletchley Park and General MacArthur Bureau cryptologists	Cryptologists and Analysts	World War II codebreakers helping to defeat the enemy
350 - 415	Hypatia of Alexandria	Philosopher	Contributions to the development of mathematics

Other worthy additions to this background of women in technology are shown in Table 3. Their stories are also related later in this chapter.

And then there are more, such as these USA pioneers:

- Fran Allen, a pioneer in compiler optimisation;
- Judy Clapp, a programmer of the world's first real-time control computer, the Whirlwind;
- Thelma Estrin, a pioneer in bioengineering at UCLA;
- Milly Koss, a programmer of the first commercial computer, the UNIVAC;
- Joyce Little, a developer of one of the first curriculums for computer science; and
- Ethel Marden, a programmer of one of the first stored program computers.

Within Australia, we have the pioneering women who worked on CSIRAC: Betty Laby, Kay Thorne (nee Sullivan), Belinda Pearson and Alison Doig.

Plus a journey through history reveals a number of females actively engaged in mathematical pursuits that have contributed to the world of technology, such as Maria Gaetana Agnesi, Marie-Sophie Germain, Mary Fairfax Somerville, Sofia Kovalevskaya and Emmy Noether.

An extensive list of famous women in computer science has been compiled by the Anita Borg Institute (2013). It is telling that this list includes not only pioneering and famous women but also high level company officers with technical backgrounds. Whilst there remains a perception that we need more and more role models, this reveals a healthy underlying fact. As computers have become more widespread and women more qualified in the field, and as the field has broadened to include more and more derivative technologies, there are fewer "firsts" and individual achievements have tended to become both less noteworthy and less captured. What might have been striking role models in past decades begin to blend into the quotidian.

Yet for all the progress, there remain proportionately fewer women than men engaged in technology careers, and in fact the ratio has been in decline for over twenty years. That stubbornly low, declining representation has been the driving force for numerous researchers and industry advocates addressing its reasons and possible solutions.

Later chapters in this book investigate today's specific influencing factors relating to cultural, social and structural contexts, along with the impact of the new social era and the unique central role of the individual. The rest of this chapter presents the stories, the facts and rumours, of the women pioneers noted above, in order to better understand the prevailing historical, social and cultural circumstances that these notable women lived under. Those circumstances have contributed to life today and influence the underlying forces and beliefs that we ourselves operate within.

ADA LOVELACE

The Facts

Born: December 10, 1815; London, England
Died: November 27, 1852; London, England

Augusta Ada Byron Lovelace is remembered for two things – she was the daughter of poet Lord Byron (who separated from Ada's mother when Ada was only a month old, though he wrote of her in his poetry) and her contributions to computing: she is considered the first computer programmer in the world. In honour of her work, in 1980 the ADA computing language was developed and given document number MIL-STD-1815 after the year she was born.

An interesting aspect of her computer programming is that the Babbage Analytical Engine she created it for was never built. The earlier Babbage Difference Engine was finally constructed in London in 2002, 153 years after it was designed. Difference Engine No. 2, built faithfully to the original drawings, consists of 8,000 parts, weighs five tons, and measures 11 feet long. An identical Engine completed in March 2008 is on display at the Computer History Museum in Mountain View, California (Swade, 2008).

Ada met Charles Babbage, a professor of mathematics at Cambridge, in 1833 when she was just 17, and they began a voluminous correspondence on the topics of mathematics, logic, and ultimately all subjects (Lewis, 2013a).

In 1835, Ada married William King and when King inherited a noble title in 1838, they became the Earl and Countess of Lovelace. Ada had three children – two sons and a daughter. Ada wanted to pursue her studies and explore ideas, becoming possibly the first documented case of a working mother as well. To enable Ada to do this, the rearing of her children was supervised by her mother and husband.

Babbage became Lovelace's mentor, and helped Ada begin mathematical studies with Augustus de Moyan in 1840 at the University of London.

In 1842, an Italian mathematician, Louis Menebrea, published a memoir in French on the subject of Babbage's Analytical Engine. Babbage enlisted Ada to translate this article into English for a British scientific journal. During a nine-month period in 1842-43, she added many notes of her own to the translation, since she was familiar with Babbage's work. Her additions showed how Babbage's Analytical Engine would work and gave a set of instructions for using it to calculate Bernoulli numbers. She published the translation and notes under the initials "A.A.L." to conceal her identity, as did many who published before women were more accepted as intellectual equals (Lewis, 2013a). These notes are the source of her enduring fame.

Her notes ended up being three times the length of the original translation, with insights and imagination that even Babbage said he had not considered. She rightly saw it as a general-purpose computer and explained how the machines could tackle general problems (even unsolved ones), e.g. astronomical tables, generating random numbers and computing complex sequences of numbers.

Ada called herself "an Analyst (& Metaphysician)," and the combination was put to use in the notes. She understood the plans for the device as well as Babbage but was better at articulating its promise. Her notes anticipate future developments, including computer-generated music (Maisel & Smart, 1997).

Ada died of uterine cancer in 1852 at the age of 37 and was buried beside the father she never knew.

The role Ada played in mathematics and more specifically computer programming did not come to full light until the mid 1900s, when her work was found by a researcher and biographies on Babbage's "Enchantress of Numbers" began to appear.

The Rumours

Ada lived in an age when it was considered that mathematics would "tax the fragile brains of women." However she was fortunate that her mother was not discouraged by this belief and also wished her daughter to be unlike her poetical father. So she saw to it that Ada received tutoring in mathematics and music, as disciplines to counter dangerous poetic tendencies. Due to her family's prominent position, Ada was able to converse and study with a variety of talented people including Mary Fairfax Somerville and Charles Dickens.

Yet despite her intellect and advantages, Ada's personal life was turbulent. Her relaxed relationships with men led to rumours of affairs, a notable one being with scientist John Crosse, who shared her addiction to gambling (Wikipedia, 2013a). Some biographies even claim that Ada's mathematical pursuits were fired by her addiction to gambling and desire to develop a foolproof horse betting system.

By 1848, Ada was in great debt and sought to borrow funds. These were soon lost and she was in debt again. Her husband cleared her debts and decided to take her on a vacation and, unaware of her addiction – he believed her debt was due to excessive spending on books and music – he encouraged her to go to the Doncaster races with him. She became hooked again and her debts skyrocketed.

Not in good health for some time, her condition deteriorated and her gambling became frantic and drastic. She arranged for a number of money seeking schemes including pawning the Lovelace Diamonds and replacing them with fakes. She eventually confessed this to her mother who retrieved them for her – only for Ada to "lose" them again.

On her deathbed she confessed her affair with Crosse and the volume of family items and jewellery she had lost due to gambling. It is reported that her pain was controlled with morphine and opium but that upon hearing the waste and loss of her life, medication was withheld so that Ada's pain would redeem her soul (Wikipedia, 2013a; Lewis, 2013a).

GRACE HOPPER

The Facts

Born: December 9, 1906; New York, New York, USA
Died: January 1, 1992; Arlington, Virginia, USA

Grace Brewster Murray Hopper was one of the first programmers to transform large digital computers from oversized calculators into relatively intelligent machines capable of understanding "human" instructions. Hopper invented the first computer "compiler" in 1952 (Beyer, 2009).

A compiler is software that makes other computer software called programming languages easier to write. Until then computer programmers had been required to write programming instructions in binary code, a series of zeroes and ones. Hopper's compiler allowed programmers to use more human-sounding language commands to replace repetitive commands. She did this, she said, because she was lazy and hoped that "the programmer may return to being a mathematician" (Beyer, 2009).

In an era when few women went to college, she graduated Phi Beta Kappa with a degree in Mathematics and Physics from Vassar College, and went on to earn a Master's degree and then a PhD in Mathematics from Yale University. She married Vincent Hopper while still in her twenties and joined academia, rising from math instructor to associate professor at Vassar before the start of World War II (Maisel & Smart, 1997).

Hopper had come from a family with military traditions, and when World War II broke out she overcame obstacles of age (34), size (too small) and a career crucial to the war effort and joined the Navy. She was commissioned a lieutenant in

July 1944 and reported to the Bureau of Ordnance Computation Project at Harvard University, where she was the third person to join the research team of professor (and Naval Reserve lieutenant) Howard H. Aiken. She recalled that he greeted her with the words, "Where the hell have you been?" and pointed to his electromechanical Mark I computing machine, saying "Here, compute the coefficients of the arc tangent series by next Thursday" (Beyer, 2009).

Hopper plunged in and learned to program the machine, putting together a 500-page Manual of Operations for the Automatic Sequence-Controlled Calculator in which she outlined the fundamental operating principles of computing machines. By the end of World War II in 1945, Hopper was working on the Mark II version of the machine. Although her marriage was dissolved at this point, and though she had no children, she did not resume her maiden name. Hopper was appointed to the Harvard faculty as a research fellow, and in 1949 she joined the newly formed Eckert-Mauchly Corporation.

Hopper never again held only one job at a time. She remained associated with Eckert-Mauchly and its successors (Remington-Rand, Sperry-Rand, and Univac) until her official "retirement" in 1971. Her work took her back and forth among institutions in the military, private industry, business and academia.

She was one of the first software engineers and, indeed, one of the most incisive strategic "futurists" in the world of computing. In addition to her well-known development of compilers, Hopper changed the lives of everyone in the computer industry by developing the Bomarc system, later called COBOL (Common Business-Oriented Language). COBOL made it possible for computers to respond to words rather than numbers. COBOL enabled firms large and small to compile computerized payroll, billing, and other records. Hopper often jokingly explained, "It really came about because I couldn't balance my checkbook." (Dickason, 1992).

Among her many honours was the 1991 receipt of the National Medal of Technology, which honoured her as: .".."the first woman to receive America's highest technology award as an individual. The award recognizes her as a computer pioneer, who spent half a century helping keep America on the leading edge of technology" (Maisel & Smart, 1997).

Appropriately, Admiral Hopper was buried with full Naval honours at Arlington National Cemetery on January 7, 1992. Her beloved Navy named a ship in her honour, the *USS Hopper*.

Grace Hopper's work was never patented; her contributions were made before computer software technology was even considered a "patentable" field.

The Rumours

Grace Hopper is credited with coining the term "bug "when she traced an error in the Mark II to a moth trapped in a relay. The moth was carefully removed and taped to a daily log book with a note "First actual case of bug being found." However there is debate about coining the phrase "bug" in terms of an issue halting a computer program from running, as the term at least in other engineering contexts existed prior to this diary entry (Computerworld, 2011).

Grace Hopper was raised by a mother who shared her love of mathematics, and a father who felt that his daughter should not be held back by the fact that she was a girl.

Hopper's love of gadgets caused her to immediately fall for the biggest gadget she'd ever seen, the fifty-one foot long, 8 foot high, 8 foot wide, glass-encased mound of bulky relays, switches and vacuum tubes called the Mark I. It's an amusing aside to note that this miracle of then-modern science could store 72 words and perform three additions every second (Dickason, 1992).

HEDY LAMARR

The Facts

Born: November 9, 1913; Vienna, Austria-Hungary
Died: January 19, 2000; Casselberry, Florida

Hedy Lamarr was awarded Patent Number 2,292,387 on August 11, 1942, under the name Hedy Keisler Markey and George Antheil for a "Secret Communications System." This was for spread spectrum, also known as frequency hopping.

Lamarr and Antheil donated the patent as their contribution to the war effort, but the invention was not implemented during World War II. It only came into use 20 years later during the 1962 Cuban Missile Crisis, when it was installed on ships sent to blockade Cuba – three years after the patent expired. Neither of them ever received any compensation for their patent. The "Secret Communications System" has since seen extensive use in military communications. But most importantly, their patent also catalysed the use of Spread Spectrum, which is a highly efficient way of using multiple radio frequencies at the same time without interfering with each other. Thus Spread Spectrum is the technical basis that makes wireless communications work in cellular phones, faxes, and other wireless communications systems (National Congress of Inventor Organizations, 1997). It has been or is currently utilised in "wireless" LANS, integrated barcode scanners, palmtop computers, radio modem devices, digital cellular telephone communications, and city/state or country networks for passing faxes, computer data, email or multimedia data. And its use is on the verge of potentially explosive further development, especially in relation to the Internet.

Lamarr was known as an incredibly beautiful and talented actress of the 1940's, indeed as "The Most Beautiful Girl in The World." She starred with Clark Gable, Spencer Tracy and Judy Garland, appearing in approximately 25 films during her film career. It is unfortunately symptomatic of human nature that her beauty and acting brought her vastly more money, fame and adoration than her technological talents.

The Rumours

Ironically, Hedy Lamarr's real life, one of unusual twists and turns, was the stuff that movies are made of (National Congress of Inventor Organizations, 1997). She was born Hedwig Eva Maria Kiesler, of Jewish faith, which her own children found out about only on her death. She grew up in Vienna, Austria and married millionaire Fritz Mandl, a Nazi sympathizer who dealt arms to Hitler. During her four-year marriage to Mandl, she listened and learned about advanced weaponry when he took her to his business meetings as his showpiece wife.

It is rumoured that she grew to hate the Nazis – as well as her husband – and escaped to London, where she met Louis B. Mayer. He brought her to the United States and gave her a shot in Hollywood by giving her a movie contract, a new name, and a new life – though she never forgot about the war that was brewing back in Europe.

She met American composer George Antheil, dubbed "the bad boy of music," and with his help devised a plan to help the war effort. What they came up with was an idea for a sophisticated anti-jamming device for use in radio-controlled torpedos. But it is rumoured that her motivation was to invent something to enable spying on her husband and the Nazis.

ENIAC PROGRAMMERS

ENIAC (Electronic Numerical Integrator And Computer) was designed to calculate artillery-firing tables for the US Army's Ballistic Research Laboratory.

The first programmers of the ENIAC were six women: Kay Antonelli (nee McNully), Jean Bartik (formerly Betty Jennings), Betty Holberton (nee Snyder), Marlyn Meltzer (nee Wescoff), Frances Spence (nee Bilas), and Ruth Teitelbaum (nee Lichterman). These six women joined the World War II effort as "computers" for the Army's Ballistics Research Laboratories in a Philadelphia project where they worked on a new, top-secret machine.

The programmers were handed the schematics of the machine and told to make it perform numerical calculations for the war effort. This is exactly what they did, with no manuals or instruction set or even the concept of how to program such a machine. The programmers had to hardwire their programs using hundreds of cables, dozens of digit trays and 3,000 switches.

ENIAC could be programmed to perform complex sequences of operations, which could include loops, branches, and subroutines. The task of taking a problem and mapping it onto the machine was complex, and usually took weeks. After the program was figured out on paper, the process of getting the program "into" ENIAC by manipulating its switches and cables took additional days. This was followed by a period of verification and debugging, aided by the ability to "single step" the machine (Wikipedia, 2013b).

Light (1999) documents and describes the role of the women of ENIAC and outlines the historical omission or downplay of women's roles in computer science history. She notes that Eckert and Mauchly, the engineers who developed ENIAC, "dominate the story as it is usually told, but they hardly worked alone. Nearly two hundred young women, both civilian and military, worked on the project as human 'computers,' performing ballistics computations during the war. Six of them were selected to program a machine that, ironically, would take their name and replace them, a machine whose technical expertise would become vastly more celebrated than their own." Light (1999) points out that "The omission of women from the history of computer science perpetuates misconceptions of women as uninterested or incapable in the field."

COLOSSUS CODE BREAKERS

It was widely believed that ENIAC in the U.S.A. was the first electronic digital computer, but evidence now reveals that Colossus in the U.K. was the first. Colossus was located at Bletchley Park – headquarters of the British Military Intelligence Government Code and Cipher School during World War II. It was here that Colossus cryptologists/code breakers deciphered communications during wartime. Decrypts contained intelligence that changed the course of the war in Europe, saving an incalculable number of Allied lives.

A large number of women were trained for employment at Bletchley Park. At the height of the war, three-quarters of Bletchley Park staff were women (Lerner, 2013). Not all of the women at Bletchley Park were code breakers. Many of them were WRENS, a women's branch of the Navy, working in radio communications and clerical work; a number worked in the WAAF, the Women's Auxiliary Air Force; and some were cooks and cleaners. Very few of the women are formally recognised as cryptanalysts working at the same level as their male peers (Howard, 2013).

Research projects are now being undertaken to collate information about those female code breakers. A few notable names are: Jean Valentine, Ruth Bourne, Mavis Batey (nee Lever), Margaret Rock, Joan Murray (nee Clarke), Ruth Briggs and Sheila Lawn (nee Mackenzie), with more under research. Until recently, much about the Colossus machine was shrouded in secrecy, largely because the codes used remained in use by the British security services until a short time ago, and research had to wait until declassification in the US of wartime documents (Copeland, 2006).

The role these women played was mostly neither known nor spoken about. As expressed by Smange (2013), "these girls helped the war effort at the highest possible level and they were happy to stay quiet about their achievements for the rest of their lives." Additionally, in Bletchley Park success and recognition were assigned for the overall work and not for individuals. As Jean Valentine, one of the cryptologists said, "a message would come into it saying 'job up.' That meant that somebody somewhere had managed to break into it (the code), but we were not ever told it was us... it was a team effort... the job was done by a team of people. Nobody got the kudos for having done it" (Mkbschmid, 2009). But finally recognition is beginning, and as Sheila Lawn, who worked in Hut 3 Intelligence, said in 2009: "it's very nice to be recognised... like many other people who did similar quiet jobs, and just got on with the job" (HEXUStv, 2009).

Similarly, the involvement of Australian female code breakers, based in General MacArthur's Central Bureau in Brisbane in 1942, also had to await declassification of war archives. These women, Eve Scott (nee Hicks), Jean Robertson, Dorothy Morrow, Nancy Goldsteen, Joyce Morrison, Sybil Brady, Betty Chessell and Margaret Raymond, played a critical role in the Central Bureau. Ultimately, like their Bletchley Park counterparts, they played a significant role in the defence of the nation and the eventual defeat of the enemy.

The Central Bureau, a combined unit of Australian, American, Canadian and New Zealand personnel, played a major role in breaking Japanese communication codes, also working in conjunction with Bletchley Park and Colossus. An interesting aside is that due to classified records the women were not allowed to disclose the nature of their work. Most claimed they were secretaries, and their entire families and grandchildren grew up thinking that is all they were. It wasn't until the information was released from archives more than 50 years after World War II that they were able to admit any involvement (personal communication to WIT, Qld: 8 March, 2002).

HYPATIA OF ALEXANDRIA

Born: c. 350-370 in Alexandria, Egypt
Died: March 415 in Alexandria, Egypt

I conclude these stories of pioneering women in technology with that of Hypatia of Alexandria, as not only the first famous female mathematician but also archetypal of the issues that have cropped up through the following centuries in the tales of the women who followed. Her talents show what women are capable of; and to me her spirit, tenacity, resilience, individual strength and drive epitomise the underlying elements of what it took for a woman to "poke her head" up in a field of men.

Like many figures from antiquity, biographical details about Hypatia are sparse and tainted by partisan legend and speculation. Hypatia was the daughter of Theon of Alexandria, a teacher of mathematics with the Museum of Alexandria in Egypt. A centre of Greek intellectual and cultural life, the Museum included many independent schools and the great Library of Alexandria.

Her father was an enlightened man. Recognising his daughter's talents, will, and desire to learn, he took charge of her education even though the times were not favourable or encouraging for women to be educated. Hypatia came to symbolise learning and science, which the early Christians identified with paganism. She considered herself a neo-Platonist, a pagan and a follower of Pythagorean works. She was the first female mathematician and philosopher to be widely recognised in history. And unfortunately for history she was the last significant mathematician in the West until the late Middle Ages (Alic, 1986; Wikipedia, 2013c).

It is remarkable that Hypatia became head of the Platonist school at Alexandria, in about 400 AD, where she lectured on mathematics and philosophy, in particular teaching the philosophy of Neoplatonism (O'Connor & Robertson, 1999). According to historical accounts left by Socrates Scholasticus (c. 379-450), a contemporary of Hypatia, she was a charismatic teacher who attracted the best students from Asia, Africa, and Europe. They were drawn to her intelligence, her legendary beauty, and her reputation as an oracle (Salowey, 2004). She was not a mere repeater of the known: in addition to presenting classic problems, she developed new solutions and new problems for her students.

When the Library of Alexandria was destroyed, all of Hypatia's work was lost except for its titles and some references to it. Based on this small amount of evidence, historians argue that Hypatia was an excellent compiler, editor, and preserver of earlier mathematical works (Lewis, 2013). Though few of her writings survive, much of her thought is known because descriptions of her work survive in the form of letters and histories written by her students and followers. Hypatia assisted her father in writing his eleven-part commentary on Ptolemy's *Almagest.* It is also thought she assisted him in producing a new version of Euclid's *Elements,* which has become the basis for all later editions of Euclid. In addition to the joint work with her father, we are informed by Suidas that Hypatia wrote commentaries on Diophantus's *Arithmetica,* on Apollonius's *Conics* and on Ptolemy's astronomical works (Salowey, 2004).

Hypatia became a legend in her own right. She dressed in the clothing of a scholar or teacher rather than in women's clothing. She moved about freely, driving her own chariot, contrary to the norm for women's public behaviour. She exerted considerable political influence in the city (Lewis, 2013b). There are differing accounts of her death, but it is indisputable that the political and religious unrest of the times were the cause. One day during March in 415, as she made her way through the city in her chariot, Hypatia was surrounded by a mob of Christian fanatics, dragged to a nearby church, stripped naked, tortured, and killed. Her body was taken outside the city and burned. The nature of her death had a profound negative impact on educational freedoms in the exploration and expression of ideas during the years that followed (Salowey, 2004). Her death coincided with rise of mysticism and fall of scientific investigation in the West (Alic, 1986) and is symbolic of the fall into the "Dark Ages."

In our modern age where we worry about "not enough" women in technology careers and the perils of "positive sexism," the life and death of Hypatia, and the struggles of the other female pioneers throughout history, show us how far we have truly come.

REFERENCES

Alic, M. (1986). *Hypatia's heritage: A history of women in science from antiquity to the late nineteenth century*. London, UK: The Women's Press.

Anita Borg Institute. (2013). *Famous women in computer science*. Retrieved November 15, 2013, from http://anitaborg.org/news/profiles-of-technical-women/famous-women-in-computer-science/

Beyer, K. W. (2009). *Grace Hopper and the invention of the information age*. Cambridge, MA: MIT Press.

BrainyQuote. (2013). *Hypatia quotes*. Retrieved August 2, 2013, from http://www.brainyquote.com/quotes/authors/h/hypatia.html

Computerworld. (2011). *Moth in the machine: Debugging the origins of 'bug'*. Retrieved November 11, 2013, from http://www.computerworld.com/s/article/9183584/Moth_in_the_machine_Debugging_the_origins_of_bug_

Copeland, J. (Ed.). (2006). *Colossus: The secrets of Bletchley Park's codebreaking computers*. Oxford, UK: Oxford University Press.

Dickason, E. (1992). *Remembering Grace Murray Hopper: A legend in her own time*. Retrieved November 11, 2013, from http://www.history.navy.mil/bios/hopper_grace.htm

HEXUStv. (2009). *Bletchley Park code breakers – Mr and Mrs Lawn*. [Video]. Retrieved November 12, 2013, from http://www.youtube.com/watch?v=FVE5K89EMe0

Howard, K. (2013). *Women codebreakers*. Bletchley Park Research. Retrieved November 12, 2013, from http://www.bletchleyparkresearch.co.uk/research-notes/women-codebreakers/

Lerner, A. W. (2013). *Bletchley Park*. Espionage Encyclopaedia. Retrieved November 12, 2013, from http://www.faqs.org/espionage/Bl-Ch/Bletchley-Park.html

Lewis, J. J. (2013a). *Ada Lovelace*. About.com Women's History. Retrieved November 11, 2013, from http://womenshistory.about.com/cs/sciencemath1/a/bio_lovelace.htm

Lewis, J. J. (2013b). *Hypatia of Alexandria*. About.com Women's History. Retrieved November 11, 2013, from http://womenshistory.about.com/od/hypati1/a/hypatia.htm

Light, J. S. (1999). When computers were women. *Technology and Culture*, *40*(3), 455–483.

Maisel, M., & Smart, L. (1997). *Women in science*. San Diego, CA: San Diego Supercomputer Centre. Retrieved November 11, 2013, from http://www.sdsc.edu/ScienceWomen/GWIS.pdf

Mkbschmid. (2009). *Jean Valentine explains the Bombe*. [Video]. Retrieved November 12, 2013, from http://www.youtube.com/watch?v=oex-9IkQRcg

National Congress of Inventor Organizations. (1997). Great inventors: 1940's film goddess Hedy Lamarr responsible for pioneering spread spectrum. *America's Inventor Online Ed*. Retrieved November 30, 2013, from http://inventionconvention.com/americasinventor/dec97issue/section2.html

O'Connor, J. J., & Robertson, E. F. (1999). *Hypatia of Alexandria*. University of St Andrews Scotland. Retrieved November 12, 2013, from http://www-history.mcs.st-and.ac.uk/Printonly/Hypatia.html

Salowey, C. A. (2004). *Great lives from history: The ancient world, prehistory-476 C.E. Hypatia – Egyptian scientist*. Pasadena, CA: Salem Press. Retrieved November 15, 2013, from http://salempress.com/store/samples/great_lives_from_history_ancient_world/great_lives_from_history_ancient_world_hypatia.htm

Smange. (2013). *The women of Bletchley Park*. Retrieved November 12, 2013, from http://www.squidoo.com/women-bletchley-park

Swade, D. (2008). *The Babbage engine*. Computer History Museum. Retrieved November 11, 2013, from http://www.computerhistory.org/babbage/

Wikipedia. (2013a). *Ada Lovelace*. Retrieved November 11, 2013, from http://en.wikipedia.org/wiki/Ada_Lovelace

Wikipedia. (2013b). *ENIAC*. Retrieved November 12, 2013, from http://en.wikipedia.org/wiki/ENIAC

Wikipedia. (2013c). *Hypatia*. Retrieved November 12, 2013, from http://en.wikipedia.org/wiki/Hypatia

KEY TERMS AND DEFINITIONS

Analytical Engine: A proposed 19th Century mechanical general purpose computer.

COLOSSUS: The world's first programmable electronic digital computer.

CSIRAC: Council for Scientific and Industrial Research Automatic Computer, originally known as CSIR Mk 1, was Australia's first digital computer.

Difference Engine: An automatic mechanical calculator designed in the 19th Century to tabulate polynomial functions, never built at the time.

ENIAC: Electronic Numerical Integrator And Computer: one of the first Turing complete (computationally universal) electronic general purpose computers.

ILLIAC: Illinois Automatic Computer. A series of supercomputers built between 1951 and 1974.

IT: Information Technology. Synonymous with ICT.

MARK I and II: A series of electromechanical computers at Harvard University.

SILLIAC: The Sydney version of the ILLIAC.

UNIVAC: Universal Automatic Computer. An electronic digital stored-program computer considered to be the first general purpose computer for commercial use.

Chapter 2
A New Approach

ABSTRACT

We are in new times that call for new ways of thinking. Digital disruption is almost the norm, and the power of social media has shaken governments. The emergence of this new disruptive Social Era demands a new model for framing the cultural, social and structural contexts, and influences on women in IT. Such a model is presented in the "STEMcell" Model, a unique 3D Earth-style visualisation that incorporates the influence of social media in its #SocialIT layer and brings new recognition to the central role of the individual at and as its core. The rules have changed, so when viewing women in technology, it is time to adapt and adopt the new model. It is time to consider the core significance of the individual and the seismic digital disruptions and tectonic technological changes we are experiencing and move towards a new approach. The rules of the new social era are translated into new rules of encouraging women in IT in this chapter. The key is that small, fast, fluid, and distributed will prevail over large, stable, and centralised.

You never change things by fighting the existing reality. To change something, build a new model that makes the existing model obsolete.

– Buckminster Fuller: architect, inventor and futurist. (Goodreads, 2013)

INTRODUCTION

"Over the last 20 years much has been done to encourage female students to choose computing courses and computing careers. Some instances of positive effects have been reported, yet the proportional disparity in gender in this discipline continues to grow" (Ashcraft, Eger & Friend, 2012).

DOI: 10.4018/978-1-4666-5860-8.ch002

"Attraction, Promotion and Retention" has been the catch cry of many passionate activists in this field around the globe for more than two decades. Yet to date the "secret" of:

1. attracting females to study technology and to enter technology careers;
2. navigating suitable promotional pathways; and
3. retaining women in technology industries

has not yet been discovered despite significant global efforts. Why is this? What has been done and what can be done? What is at the core of this issue?

A NEW ERA

We are in a new era where every Facebook post, Tweet, Pinterest, meme, Instagram upload, Tumblr share, Digg, YouTube video, Hangout, crowdsourcing project and social media group and/or community can make a difference. And if that list of examples is already outdated by the time you read this, it simply stresses how quickly this new era is evolving.

Social media have grown from the early Internet days of people connecting via CompuServe and bulletin boards to the first blogs and forums to the development of multiple social networking sites, news aggregators and crowdsourcing platforms (Curtis, 2013), through to the formation of digital revolutions that have been super-charged by social tools.

Two examples of recent seismic digital revolutions are:

- It is widely reported (Mainwaring, 2011; Boyd 2011) that social media had a powerful influence before and after the 2011 Egyptian revolution. That revolution, which resulted in the overthrow of Mubarak's government, is known as both the "Arab Spring" and "Facebook revolution" (Bogart, 2013). Social networks quickly sprung up as both a source of news and a means for organization of protests and rallies. In 2013 Egypt faced similar circumstances concerning the first democratically elected president, however "no longer is social media in Egypt used just by activists, politicians have now joined the conversation as they have understood the importance and the power of social media" (Bogart, 2013).
- Similarly, fed by deregulation of the telecommunications industry there is a digital revolution change occurring in the Pacific Islands. "The Pacific Islands region is in the midst of an information and communications technology (ICT) revolution that could have major implications, particularly for democratic governance and the region's development. In urban, and increasingly in rural settings, Pacific Islanders are using new digital tools to communicate, form online networks and coordinate" (D. Cave, 2012). Cave notes the importance of social media in this phenomenon: "This influx of mobile phones in the Pacific Islands has occurred at the same time as another global phenomenon sweeping the world, the rise of social media, and the Pacific's growing mobile phone penetration has helped fuel social media uptake. Access to social media communities is enabling Pacific Islanders to connect with one another, form online networks, share content, project opinion, promote debate and coordinate activities in ways that were unimaginable just a few years ago. This has resulted in the emergence of a Pacific 'digital generation' of activists, thinkers, informers and influencers." As a result, "In particular, the combination of these powerful digital tools has given Pacific Islanders greater opportunity to harness, influence and promote political and social change in the region. Led by bloggers, digital entrepreneurs and social media groups in Papua New Guinea, a Pacific 'digital generation' is emerging that is playing an increasingly influential role in society" (D. Cave, 2012).

These are not new phenomena. Fang (1997) argues that there have been six information revolutions, from writing and printing through to the "Information Highway," and that in each one "The tools of communication gave social and political changes added dynamism and were themselves given a forward thrust by those other changes, a symbiotic relationship of cause and effect. Information revolutions tended toward some levelling of conditions for those who participated in them. Their results tended to be egalitarian. They pointed toward a greater degree of democratization or sharing of influence than previously existed. Where the use of the tools has been limited, both in ancient times and now, human beings have been less free." He goes on to point out "As to the belief that the average citizen lies increasingly helpless under the heel of political and economic tyrants who dominate the media and suppress freedom of thought, history tells the opposite story. The dissemination of the tools of mass communication has increased the potential for social protest, and to that extent it has made humankind more free, not less."

However, as with each previous advance in mass communication, compared to what was available before the advent of social media (along with enabling hardware like smartphones) has greatly increased the ability of average people to communicate, and greatly decreased the ability of entrenched powers to control, censor or suppress information.

With the widespread adoption of recent disruptive and enabling technologies and the low barriers to entry, social media have rapidly become an integral part of life. There are general social networks with user bases larger than the population of many countries. At the other end of the scale, there are niche sites for virtually every special interest out there and even niches of niches, ensuring that a granularity of interest topics/areas is covered. Based on the Pacific Islands example above it is possible to speculate that in other countries that may have issues of digital divide/access to technology, if telecommunications are deregulated we would see rapid uptake of digital technologies, more communities online and the growth of niche groups from those countries.

Consequently, events where social media have had a leading and powerful influence, such as the digital revolution examples above, are increasing. Mainwaring (2011) writes "The role of social media is critical because it helps to spread cognitive dissonance by connecting thought leaders and activists to ordinary citizens, rapidly expanding the network of people who become willing to take action."

This becomes even more powerful when combined with other tools of the new era such as "open data." For example this is being used in Africa to track and expose government corruption and monitor politicians' behaviour, including easier access to and visualization of public records (Firth, 2013).

The United Nations, through the UNESCO (2012) report, notes the importance of technologies not only for advocacy and activism but also economic growth, by saying "ICTs propel the world economy, inform our lives, shape the world of work and play (the latter often via social media), and set the stage for future innovation. They play a fundamental role in supporting human rights and reducing labour burdens, while serving as stepping-stones out of poverty. And both men and women are beneficiaries of ICT innovations across a range of areas: in health and reproductive rights, employment opportunities, natural resources management, transportation, energy, personal security, and food security.

"In fact, ICTs touch almost every aspect of our lives. They offer a means for social connection, serve as vehicles for cultural expression and help tie us to time-honoured traditions. Information and communication technology are also employed as vehicles for participation, advocacy, and activism, and as a means to hold government accountable to the publics they serve.

"Our social and economic progress depends on these technologies, in part because the potential for economic development is linked to access to broadband Internet and to a nation's capacity to function as a knowledge-based society. In China there's an estimated 2.5% increase in GDP for every 10% increase in broadband penetration and World Bank research indicates a 10 percentage point rise in broadband penetration adds a 1.38%

rise in economic growth for low and middle income countries."

As suggested by the simultaneous penetration of social media into both broad and niche groups, this powerful influence is not limited to political upheavals. Of particular relevance here, social media are tools that women in technology activists could and should use: to mobilize the wider community of politicians, educators, students, those in the industry and women in general into action, and engage their energy, interests, sponsorship and support. The Egypt and Pacific Islands examples are indicators of the immense influence social media can have and are gaining amongst communities.

In the women in technology field there are already many niche arms including a multitude based on a variety of sub cultures: twitter groups based on platforms, such as @linuxchixperu and @Webgrrls; communities based on geography and/or ethnicity, e.g. Latinas in Computing @LatinasinC, Black Girls Code @BlackGirlsCode, and Girls in Tech NYC @GITnyc; groups based on stage of life, e.g. @GirlGeekCoffees and TechGirls @TeenTechGirls; as well as more general gatherings, e.g. @WomenWhoCode, Women in Technology @MCWT and many, many more.

We are in an era of digital disruption, with industry experts proclaiming a process of deep change. Gorbis (2013) notes that being "in a time of rapid innovation, signals of change are all around us," whilst Scoble & Israel (2013) describe it as an "age of context," in which social media is one of five "converging forces that promise to change virtually every aspect of our lives." The other forces – mobile, data, sensors and location-based technology – combined with social media are forming a new generation of personalized technology, bringing with it sweeping changes.

This is the age neatly coined by Nilofer Merchant as the "#SocialEra" (Merchant, 2012a, 2012b). This is more than an opportunity for extending traditional activities. In her thought provoking book on the coming societal deep shift, *11 Rules for Creating Value for the #SocialEra*, Merchant begins with an obituary for "traditional strategy" and points out that to progress in the new #SocialEra traditional beliefs and practices need to be discarded.

Merchant describes #SocialEra as: "Social Era is about the power of communities, of collaboration and co-creation. In the industrial era, power was from holding what we valued closed and separate; in the Social Era, there is another framework for how we engage one another — an open one." She identifies several practices and beliefs as the ones that need to be discarded, including "right strategy reigns supreme," "size matters," "stability rules," "sustainable advantages exist" and "the customer is the guy at the end of the value chain."

AN OLD SHORTFALL

Whilst Merchant's *11 Rules* was primarily written to describe business strategy, the same arguments are applicable to the oft discussed and much researched issue of the lack of women in information technology across the whole spectrum of studies, careers and leadership. Merchant flags that the death of traditional strategy has "left management thinkers ... struggling to fit relatively newer concepts like crowdsourcing, open innovation, transparency, co-creation, and collaboration into its classic models." Women in technology activists and advocates must now make the leap over this struggle too. Closer embedding of "tools of the trade" such as crowdsourcing and social media tools into women and technology activities is now required. This will enable progress to a new approach towards strategies and activities for promoting attraction, promotion and retention of women in IT.

That there are disproportionately few women in IT careers has been recognized and agonized over since the topic was first considered. Evidence of the long history and significant research efforts in the study of this shortfall includes:

1. The field is prolific, with respected, well published and much cited references from authors such as Trauth, Nielson & von Hellens (2003), Ahuja (2002), von Hellens, Pringle, Nielson & Greenhill (2000), Anderson, Timms & Courtney (2006) and Anderson, Lankshear, Timms & Courtney (2008b), and especially the seminal works of Margolis & Fisher (2003) and Adya & Kaiser (2005, 2006).
2. In editorial comments, von Hellens, Trauth & Fisher (2012) note, "the first papers in the area of women and computing, as it was then called, were being published in the early 1980s. The focus, not surprisingly, was on why so few women studied or worked in IT. This question has continued to dominate the literature and the debate." Later they note that "In response to the decline in women's participation in ICT education and the workforce, many initiatives have been launched and programs developed (Craig, Dawson, & Fisher, 2009; Klawe, Whitney, & Simard, 2009). These attempts to address this problem are labelled as 'intervention programmes'." (This book specifically discusses intervention programmes in the next chapter.)
3. Castano & Webster (2011) state "the low and declining proportion of women in computing has been widely noticed and much lamented (Cohoon & Aspray, 2006; OECD, 2007; Kirkup, Zalevski, Maruyama, & Batool, 2010; Misa, 2010)… Considerable effort has been devoted to reaching a gender balance in ICT professions, apparently to little effect. Women still make up fewer than 20% of ICT professionals in most OECD countries, and there is little sign of any substantial increase in their presence. Perhaps we have failed to properly understand the factors involved in women's absence, or to design appropriate remedial measures. We may need to reconsider our approach to the issue."
4. A review of the literature on research into girls and IT from 1994 to the early 2000s is presented by Barker & Aspray (2006), who extend work done by Dryburgh (2000) on girls in IT in the 1990s.
5. Ashcraft, Eger & Friend (2012) provide a summary of literature from the early 2000s.
6. Any Web search will reveal literally thousands of others.

In addition to those examples, I argue that the mere existence of publications such as *The Encyclopedia of Gender and Information Technology* edited by Eileen Trauth (2006) provides objective proof of an issue regarding women in technology. The encyclopaedia comprises 1,451 pages across two volumes, with 213 entries from 295 international specialists/researchers, including this author (Bernhardt, 2006). The encyclopaedia also includes over 4,700 references to additional works on gender and information technology in order to stimulate further research.

The sheer volume of global effort, interest, passion and focus of the authors and their readers is worthy of note. However that very volume of work and the decades over which it has been pursued stress that despite all the activity no "solution" has yet been found. That leads to the following questions:

- Why bother: Is a solution actually required?
- What has been the cumulative impact of the past efforts?
- Are the women who want to be in IT already in IT?
- What does the future look like?

Cave (2013) presents similar issues/questions: "Cynics argue this is inevitable… Whilst equality zealots maintain that any imbalance is unfair and should be stamped out at all costs. But should we really care if fewer women are attracted to IT roles? If women aren't interested in IT careers there is no reason to hold a gun to their heads and force them to into work they don't want to do." We will revisit this and related controversies in the next chapter.

A NEW MODEL FOR A NEW ERA

I will go further and postulate that anecdotal evidence and documented research, the existence of a whole two-volume encyclopaedia on the issue and the repeated themes and programs across nations, are undeniable proof not only that the issue exists but there has been a massive global failure to solve it. The attraction, promotion and retention models, methods, intervention projects and programs identified throughout the encyclopaedia and in the primary literature have not helped prevent the decline, let alone the lack, of females in technology studies and careers, nor the departure of women from a technology career once they choose one. And it is certainly not for lack of trying. This failure is dissected further in the next chapter.

In light of the failure and ongoing decline, despite the area being well-researched and the significant effort applied to intervention activities, I agree with Castano & Webster (2011): it is time to reconsider the approach to the issue, and I propose a new look at this old issue by presenting a new model. A high level overview is shown in Figure 1, with more detailed breakdown in subsequent Figures. While this model is intended to represent a new approach to map to the changing environment, it builds on the prior research, theories and models of many academics and industry participants, extending them to focus on the true drivers and take into account the impacts and influences from the disruptive technologies of #SocialEra.

The model is used as the skeleton of this publication and is referenced throughout it, with the details of the various contexts and factors deconstructed in later chapters. However the basic model is summarized here to provide a conceptual overview and to aid visualization of the constructs, context and factors from this early stage.

THE MODEL

Conceptual Framework

The model is called the "STEMcell" model. "STEM" reflects that IT is part of the broader STEM fields (Science, Technology, Engineering and Mathematics), which encounter much the same issues, and "cell" reflects the central role of the individual in the model. The combination "STEMcell" reflects the power of the individual to become whatever she wishes, albeit constrained by her environment.

The conceptual framework of the STEMcell model is illustrated in Figure 1 and works in this way:

- Cultural, Social and Structural contexts and factors may encourage or discourage participation or present obstacles that inhibit incentives or enhance disincentives.
- Individual context determines how individuals react to their environment. Individuals accept, react to or may overcome/override the Cultural, Social and Structural contexts, influencers and obstacles.
- #SocialIT represents #SocialEra, the current disruptive technology, in its application as an influencing platform/environment for women in IT. It can enhance the positive and reduce the negative aspects of the Cultural, Social, Structural and Individual contexts, thus promoting attraction, promotion and retention of women in IT.

The model relates to previous work in these ways:

Figure 1. Conceptual framework of the STEMcell model

- That Individuals are core and experience societal influences in different ways and may vary in their response to gender group biases was pointed out by Trauth (2002) and Castano & Webster (2011). Additionally, Ham, Junankar & Wells (2009) confirmed that personality has a significant effect on occupational choice outcomes, in particular for females. Trauth, Quesenberry & Huang, (2009) proposed a number of constructs that enable theorizing on within-gender variation. A snapshot poll conducted for this publication supports these more substantive research results on the centrality of individual choice. Results of the poll are described in the next chapter and a discussion specifically on the individual context is presented in Chapter Eight.
- Cultural influence encloses and contains the other components like a crust. The influence of cultural aspects has been noted by Ashcraft et al. (2012), Adya & Kaiser (2005), Castano & Webster (2011), Gras-Velazquez, Joyce & Debry (2009), Miliszewska & Moore (2011) and Lang & McKay (2006). A review of the literature relating to cultural influence is presented in Chapter Six, with specific factors relating to ethnic differences discussed in Chapter Ten.
- Social and Structural aspects of the model wrap around the individual like a mantle. These have been previously outlined in the literature by a variety of authors, e.g. Adya & Kaiser (2005, 2006), Clayton (2007), Clayton, Beekhuyzen, & Nielsen (2012) and Miliszewska & Moore (2011). A review of the literature relating to social context is in discussed in Chapter Six while structural context is discussed in Chapter Seven.
- # SocialIT is added as a disruptive penetrating force. Its influence and the future

Table 1. Cultural context and their influencers

Influencing Factor	Reference
Popular culture	Ashcraft, Eger & Friend (2012); Hayes (2005, 2008)
Cultural norms	Castano & Webster (2011); Gras-Velazquez, Joyce & Debry (2009); UNESCO (2012)
Parental expectations	Ashcraft et al. (2012)
Occupational culture	Ahuja (2002); Guzman, Stanton, & Eischen (2006); Guzman & Stanton (2009); Modi, Schoenberg & Salmond (2012)

influence of other disruptive technologies is an addition to the prior models. Chapter Nine describes #SocialIT factors in more detail. It is worth noting that living and breathing what she proposed, when asked if the #SocialEra naming could be used as part of this model or if IP/Trademark applied, Merchant's reply was: "As long as you quote me as the authoritative source, you're covered. I'm doing *open*, cause that's the ethos of the SocialEra. ;-)" (N. Merchant, personal communication, July 19, 2013).

Within each segment of the model there are specific influencing factors that come into play. These may be positive influencers or may act as obstacles to either inhibit incentives or amplify disincentives. Factors that have been identified in the literature are noted below and that segment of the model expanded to incorporate them.

Cultural Context Influencing Factors and Potential Obstacles

To use the Earth globe's crust, mantle and inner core analogy, the Cultural context and factors operate like a crust: they surround the other areas, and in some instances may be so strong that their influence may cover/smother all other aspects and become the dominant context. Figure 2 focuses on the Cultural segment, itemizing that context and its influencing factors. These are as described in the existing literature as detailed in Table 1.

Social Context Influencing Factors and Potential Obstacles

Continuing the Earth analogy, Social context and factors operate like part of the mantle surrounding the core, and may be impacted by the overlaying Cultural crust. The Social context is expanded in Figure 3 to show its influencing factors. As with the Cultural segment these are derived from a review of the literature, detailed in Table 2.

Structural Context Influencing Factors and Potential Obstacles

Again continuing the Earth analogy, Structural context and factors operate like another part of the mantle surrounding the core and impacted by the overlaying Cultural crust. In addition, both "mantle" components interact: Social and Structural issues may shift to adjust the impact and relationship between them. For example, some Social factors may diminish structural issues and vice versa.

Figure 4 focuses on the Structural context and lists its influencing factors. As with the Cultural and Social segments these are derived from the literature, summarized in Table 3.

Individual Context Influencing Factors and Potential Obstacles

The final and central part of the Earth analogy is the Individual context and factors that comprise the core. The size of that core varies with the individual, who may shrug off the Social and Structural

Figure 2. Cultural context breakdown: Types of cultural influences and potential barriers

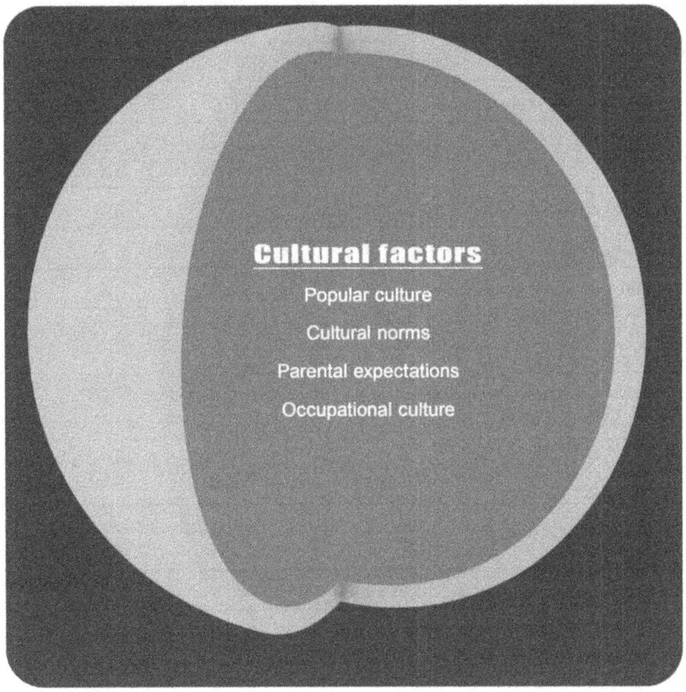

Figure 3. Social context breakdown: Types of social influences and potential barriers

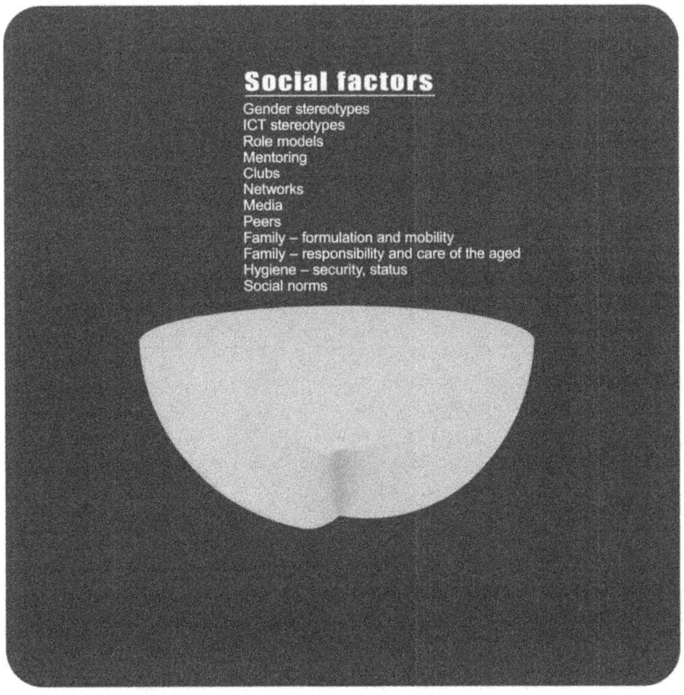

Table 2. Social context and their influencers

Influencing Factor	Reference
Gender stereotypes	Denner (2011); Gras-Velazquez et al. (2009); UNESCO (2012)
ICT stereotypes	Clayton, Beekhuyzen & Nielsen (2012); Denner (2011); UNESCO (2012)
Role models	Ahuja (2002); Ashcraft et al. (2012); Barker & Aspray (2006); Clayton et al. (2012); Cozza (2011); Gras-Velazquez et al. (2009); Miliszewska & Moore (2011)
Mentoring	Craig, Fisher & Lang (2007); Trauth et al. (2009)
Clubs	Lang, Fisher & Craig (2007); Miliszewska & Moore (2011)
Networks	Margolis & Fisher (2003); UNESCO (2012)
Media	Adya & Kaiser (2005); Ashcraft et al. (2012); Barker & Aspray (2006); Clayton et al. (2012); Cozza (2011); Lyons et al. (2012)
Peers	Adya & Kaiser (2005); Barker & Aspray (2006); Clayton et al. (2012); Cozza (2011); Denner (2011); Margolis & Fisher (2003)
Family – formulation and mobility	Adya & Kaiser (2005); Barker & Aspray (2006); Castano & Webster (2011); Clayton et al. (2012); Griffiths & Moore (2010); Margolis & Fisher (2003)
Family – responsibility and care of the aged	Adya & Kaiser (2005); Castano & Webster (2011); Clayton et al. (2012); Lang & McKay (2006); Trauth et al. (2009)
Hygiene – security, status	Beekhuyzen, Nielsen, & von Hellens (2006); Nielsen, von Hellens, Pringle & Greenhill (1999)
Social norms	UNESCO (2012)

Figure 4. Structural breakdown: Structural factors influencing female participation in IT

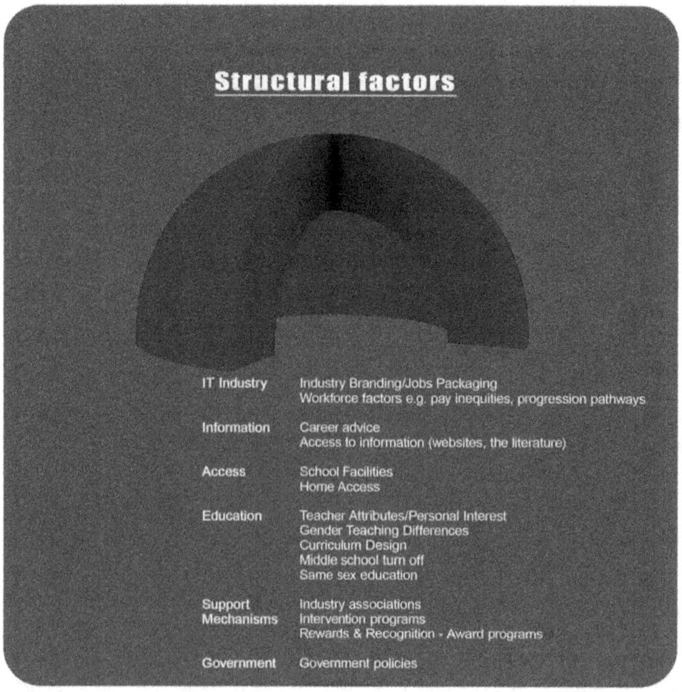

Table 3. Structural context and influencers

Structural Context		
Area	**Influencing Factor**	**Reference**
IT Industry	Industry Branding/Jobs Packaging	Bateman (2013); UNESCO (2012)
	Workforce factors, e.g. pay inequities, progression pathways	Bateman (2012); Blair, Gill & Benson (2013); Kirkup (2011); Tandon, Pritchard, Savelieva, Smith & Vogt (2012).
Information	Career advice	Gras-Velazquez et al. (2009)
	Access to information (websites, the literature)	Ashcraft et al. (2012); Baker (2012); Clayton et al. (2012); Gras-Velazquez et al. (2009); Miliszewska & Moore (2011)
Access	School Facilities	Cheeseman Day, Janus & Davis (2005); Clayton (2007); Clayton et al. (2012); Gras-Velazquez et al. (2009); Heemskerk, Brink, Volman & ten Dam (2005); Lang & McKay (2006); Miliszewska & Moore (2011)
	Home Access	Clayton (2007); Clayton et al. (2012); Gras-Velazquez et al. (2009)
Education	Teacher Attributes/Personal Interest	Adya & Kaiser (2005); Baker (2012); Clayton (2007); Clayton et al. (2012); Goode, Estrella & Margolis (2006); Gras-Velazquez et al. (2009)
	Gender Teaching Differences	Ashcraft et al. (2012); Barker & Aspray (2006); Castano & Webster (2011)
	Curriculum Design	Ashcraft et al. (2012); Bateman (2012); Barker & Aspray (2006); Clayton, von Hellens & Nielsen (2009); Clayton et al. (2012); Gras-Velazquez et al. (2009); Liston, Peterson & Ragan (2009); Margolis & Fisher (2003); Newmarch, Taylor-Steele & Cumpston (2000); Palmen (2011); Timms, Courtney & Anderson (2006)
	Middle school turn off	Anderson, Lankshear & Courtney (2008a), Gras-Velazquez et al. (2009); Modi et al. (2012)
	Same sex education	Adya & Kaiser (2005); Ashcraft et al. (2012); Goode et al. (2006)
Support Mechanisms	Industry associations	Berry & Kalessi (2011); Personal observation of the establishment and growth of niche associations (globally)
	Intervention programs	Lyons et al. (2012); Miliszewska & Moore (2011)
	Rewards & Recognition - Award programs	Kroes (2013); Modi et al. (2012); Tandon et al. (2012)
Government	Government policies	Barker & Aspray (2006); Gras-Velazquez et al. (2009); Miliszewska & Moore (2011); Palmen (2011); Personal observation of government established taskforces and resulting papers

contexts and even expand to weaken the impacts of the Cultural crust. Or the individual core may comfortably accept her environmental influences or in the worst cases, be crushed by them.

The impact of the individual has been examined in the literature by many researchers including Castano & Webster (2011), Ham et al. (2009), Trauth (2002) and Trauth, Huang & Quesenberry (2006). However to date it has been done from the perspective of the individual as just another societal factor. It has been under a genderised view where generally the individual is assumed to be almost entirely malleable, a near blank slate absorbing cultural, social and structural influences without any free will of her own. The problem with that approach is it ignores the fundamental strength, philosophy, values and will of the individual. This is especially ironic when one thing that characterizes girls interested in STEM is strong self-will and confidence (Modi et al., 2012). It is those philosophical and individual strength factors that I highlight in Figure 5.

It is notable that the overwhelming majority of over 100 respondents to a July 2013 poll con-

Figure 5. Individual breakdown: Individual factors affecting career choices

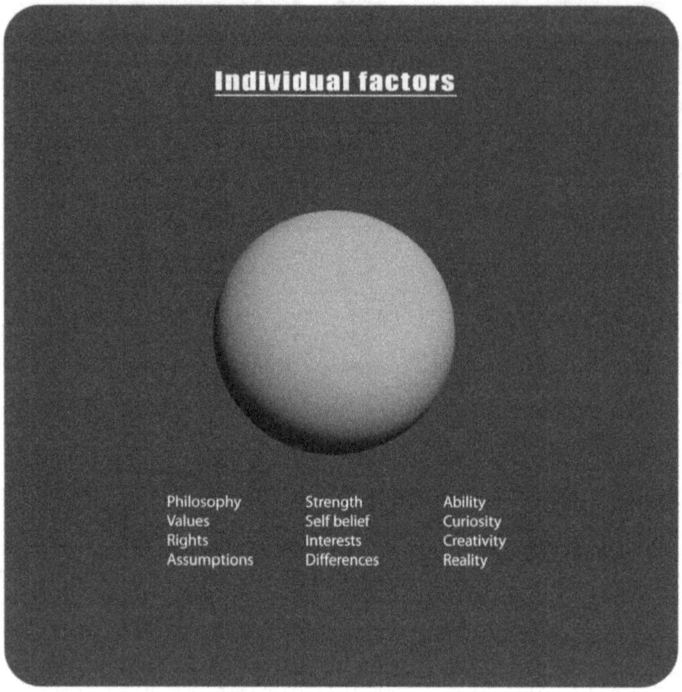

ducted as part of this publication identified personal interest from a young age as their own greatest influence on choosing a career in IT, and a clear majority of the remainder nominated discovering an interest after being exposed to IT in their job. In other words, the vast majority of respondents simply chose according to their internal affinity for the field, whether discovered at an early age or later in life. Whilst this was an informal poll it is interesting that very similar, and if anything more striking, results are reported by Lyons et al. (2012: Figure 13). The survey results are detailed in the next chapter.

#SocialIT Context and Influencing Factors

Wrapping around and disrupting the Earth model are the #SocialIT context and factors. This layer is affected by the others but has the potential to not only bypass them by directly reaching the core but also transform them. #SocialIT factors are tagged in Figure 6.

K. Cave (2012) describes recent disruptive trends as technology moving from tool to cool and exciting: "the industry is starting to get 'cool': Tablets and smartphones are the definitive accessory; the iPad is so sexy that if you want, you can pay $6,900 to dress it up in a designer David August case; Facebook founder Mark Zuckerberg had a film made about him (even if it wasn't that flattering); and each new Apple product launch causes a quasi-religious frenzy in consumers and journalists alike. What's more, the 'Apple effect' is starting to touch other companies and products in the space. How many people got excited about Samsung ten years ago?"

The Detailed STEMcell Model: Context and Factors

Putting together the sum of those parts results in the total STEMcell model. The overall contexts and their interactions are outlined in Figure 1 and shown with their detailed factors in Figure 7.

Figure 6. # SocialIT breakdown: Qualities of the new social era

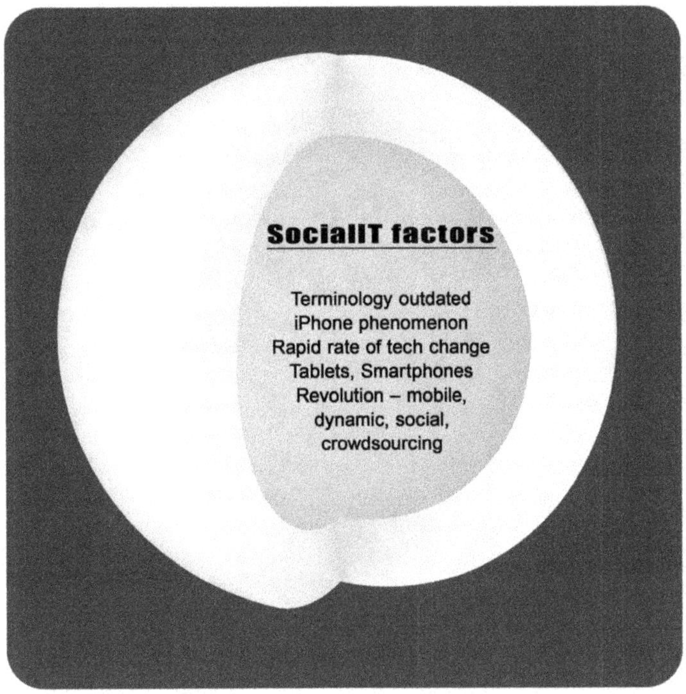

IMPLICATIONS OF THE NEW ERA

The rise of the new era inspired the creation of the #SocialIT layer of the STEMcell model. If this new era can help bring down governments and transform societies, what might it achieve for our other goals, including the question of women in IT? We will now delve more deeply into the qualities and implications of this era.

Stow Boyd, who coined the terms social tools and hashtag, describes his focus areas as "the tectonic shift pushing business, media, and society into an unclear and accelerating postnormal future" (Boyd, 2011). Similarly, I believe that #SocialEra and #SocialIT are the beginning of a tectonic shift and those engaged in women in technology activities – researching, planning, coordinating or funding – ought to take notice and shift accordingly. That is, we need to move away from the old traditional approaches and shift to be in line with the dynamic industry we inhabit by moving towards dynamic new approaches. It would be deeply ironic to fail to do so.

Researchers too need to adapt to this future. As Fitzpatrick (2011) argues, academic publishing is facing its own crisis and needs "reconceiving its future in more communally-oriented ways … Fitzpatrick focuses on the technological changes—especially greater utilization of Internet publication technologies, including digital archives, social networking tools, and multimedia—necessary to allow academic publishing to thrive into the future."

There are two key areas to consider for women and technology that map under Merchant's #SocialEra:

1. What are the alternatives to the traditional strategies?
2. How are the 11 rules applied?

These are explored in more detail below.

Figure 7. Conceptual framework of the STEMcell Model including detailed factors

Alternatives to Traditional Strategies

In order to make the #SocialEra shift to adopt the STEMcell model, the "traditional strategy" concepts identified by Merchant (2012a) need to be cast aside. Specifically for Women in Technology activists and advocates, the five old strategies and their translation into the new era may be analyzed as follows.

1. Right Strategy Reigns Supreme

Merchant (2012a) relates this to a historical group of executives determining a strategy and it becoming the key executed approach over time. She flags that "This worked well in a simpler time when markets were stable, and when information was scarce… Back then, mobilizing the talent and creativity of all members was not required to be competitive."

The implication of throwing out the "right strategy reigns supreme" strategy in the #SocialIT era for women and technology is: *Existing assumptions (strategies) of activities to address the issue are to be challenged.* It is time to review the traditional strategies – meaning not only the kinds of organizations that define the strategies (researchers and industry associations) but even the specific activities arising from those strategies such as intervention activities (e.g. career days, role models and mentoring). These activities or at least their organization and structure may no longer be applicable in the #SocialIT era.

Perhaps it is even time to consider halting activities organized by large overarching industry groups and associations altogether. Instead let the #SocialIT community evolve and adapt to current and future circumstances according to its own internal dynamics and the needs and drives of its participants.

The question to ask here is: If you arrived today without the "benefit" of historical research, prior strategies and traditional programs; if you looked at the world as it is with fresh eyes – what would you do?

2. Size Matters

Merchant (2012a) describes this as "Size created competitive barriers and correlated with market power… This meant some dominant firms could reach consumers when others could not… Being big had many advantages and no meaningful disadvantages. Size came to be its own measure of success."

The implication for women in IT strategies is: *Large scale industry associations, organisations and events are no longer to be considered the dominant "force" or the measure of success.* An activity in 2008 discussed by Craig, Lang & Fisher (2008) was a one day "Girls in Computing" event for 1400 secondary school girls, which was a year in the planning, involved 68 volunteers and attracted more than $150,000 in corporate cash sponsorship and in-kind support. Events of that scale may be a thing of the past.

In #SocialEra purpose surpasses size. It brings an alternative in which individuals may take action that impacts across wide community areas and seamlessly brings diverse groups together under a united purpose.

3. Stability Rules

Merchant (2012a) outlines this strategy by flagging that "economic disruptions were thought to be exceptions. It thus made sense to invest in building organizational structures to last. Although the idea that disruptions are rare may seem quaint in today's world, vast numbers of organizations are still functioning under the assumption that change is the anomaly, rather than the norm."

The implication is: *Change is the norm in the IT industry*. The new way is like the industry itself, where dynamic fluid rules that are able to adjust according to circumstances are more suitable. In the past researchers and industry groups provided a stable base and an umbrella to formally link like interests together. However these formal structures themselves make them slow to move and adapt – in the #SocialEra almost instantaneous real time fluidity is required.

4. Sustainable Advantages Exist

Merchant (2012a) describes this as "industries consist of relatively enduring and stable competitive forces… We set an annual strategy and then spend most of the year executing against that strategy. Reviewing Traditional Strategy before the appropriate next cycle is then interpreted by corporate boards as an execution problem—such as trying to move the goal posts… do we focus on the current business and market, or do we build the capacity to identify and tap into the next?"

The implication for #SocialIT is: *What worked yesterday may not work tomorrow, and it is OK to recognize that and move on.* Being the longest surviving, largest or strongest organization is no longer a requirement and might not even be an advantage. Agile and dynamic approaches that can shift with the prevailing trends and interests are more important.

Instead of traditional targets and goals for intervention programs such as number of attendees at events, percentages of course enrolments and career representation, acceptance of fast paced change may mean focusing on rapid small gains where even the goals may dynamically adjust according to current trends.

Table 4. The shift from traditional strategy to the #SocialIT approach

Traditional Strategy		Shift in #SocialIT Era
Right strategy reigns supreme	=>	Challenge assumptions, review structures and programs
Size matters		Individuals may act and impact
Stability rules		Dynamic, fluid style
Sustainable advantages exist		It is OK to discard and start again/move on
The customer is the guy at the end of the value chain		Communities will and ought to be the creators

5. The Customer is the Guy at the End of the Value Chain

Merchant (2012a) explains this as "The organization made things and told the buyer that it was good, and the buyer bought. But by the 1980s, buyers became customers with cynicism, opinions, and expectations, and by the 1990s, the old approach was starting to show the strain. Then in the early twenty-first century, so-called 'customers' began to exert co-creative tendencies… the idea that products can be co-created is still often treated as an anomaly. Even in these enlightened times, most organizations have a hard perimeter wall between the company and its employees, and the customers."

The implication of this new view of the customer in #SocialIT is: *The "customers" for research and activities targeting the issue of women in technology are the individuals in the wider community. Their inputs at the start are now vital, rather than them being either the subject of research or passive attendees receiving intervention projects and programs.* The "customers" in #SocialIT will generate their own research, activity and action. The fast paced, small gains referred to above will derive more from assisting individuals to find their own way and achieve their own goals than from the theories or goals of the organizations aiming to help them.

Summary of the Strategy Shifts

These five tectonic shifts in #SocialIT are summarized in Table 4.

Applying the 11 Rules

Merchant (2012a, 2012c) states that the social era is more than social media. It implies and requires new ways of doing things, and to support that she provides 11 rules that will allow people and organizations to survive and thrive. The meaning of those rules and their application to women in technology researchers, activists and advocates are analyzed as follows.

1. Connections create Value

Merchant (2012a) explains this as "The social era will reward those organizations that realize they don't create value all by themselves."

The implication for #SocialIT is that traditional industry associations for women in technology need to review their structure, purpose and relevancy. The smarter and more passionate you are and the prouder your organisation's achievements have been, the harder it can be to "let go." But the era of organisations distributing value to the masses is passing, in favour of a new era of plugging into the passion and brains of everyone involved. This is especially so when the most valuable connections can cross traditional, including geographical and industry, boundaries.

2. Power in Community

Merchant (2012a) outlines this as "Power used to come largely through and from big institutions. Today power can and does come from connected individuals in the community."

As with value, so with power, and the implication of #SocialIT is similar: we need to extend beyond industry groups as knowledge holders and interventionists to individuals and smaller groupings in the community. There is a need to develop greater ties and open communication between researchers, campaign activists and individuals; to make knowledge accessible to all and transfer the power to individuals to follow their own paths.

3. Collaboration Control

Merchant (2012a) explains this as "Organizations that 'let go at the top' – forsaking proprietary claims and avoiding hierarchy – are agile, flexible, and poised to leap from opportunity to opportunity."

With value and power recognised as decentralised rather than best held by traditional organisations, control must follow. Again the implication for #SocialIT is that it is time to seriously review traditional industry associations to assess their relevancy, and if necessary accept that it is best to move on.

It may be time to tear down traditional industry association walls and rebuild on #SocialEra methods, allowing everyone to be part of the bigger picture. The core of the old organisations – the people in them – would remain, but as part of flexible, fluid networks spanning industries and countries, applying old and learning new knowledge in collaboration with all interested parties. This is already beginning with the proliferation of web based niche groups and niches of niches. It is time to embrace that trend.

4. Celebrate Onlyness

The foundational element that #SocialEra starts with is celebrating each human and, more specifically, *onlyness*: a term coined by Merchant (2012a) and defined as the thing that only one particular person can bring to a situation. It includes the skills, passions, and purposes of each human.

Onlyness ties into the proposed Model's identification of the individual as core to the whole thing. Not only is the individual the core driver of female participation in IT, she is the essential component of #SocialIT and its ability to penetrate the social, cultural and structural issues to empower herself and other individuals.

Existing organisations and activists already have aligned purpose and passionate volunteers, but traditional activities often involve centrally controlled, large-scale intervention activities needing dozens or even hundreds of coordinated volunteers. In #SocialIT those volunteers can have a greater impact while requiring less, and in many cases no, central coordination. They do not even have to agree: the celebration of onlyness allows all to participate in their own way, with the value of their inputs decided by the "marketplace" rather than the opinions or votes of a committee.

5. Allow All Talent

Merchant (2012a) states, "this is essential for solving new problems as well as for finding new solutions to old problems."

This rule is an implication of the concept of "onlyness" and the power of the individual to contribute via #SocialEra tools. The implication for #SocialIT is similar: it is time to consider extending beyond the boards and committees of traditional associations to instead utilise social media connections, thus expanding the pool of ideas and the numbers and networks of engaged community members.

6. Consumers Become Co-Creators

Merchant (2012a) outlines this as "Consumers are now seen as a source of value creation and competitive advantage. This collaboration shares power between the participants as we start to recognize value creation as an act of exchange, not simply a one-way transaction."

The implication for #SocialIT is that the subjects of research and participants in intervention activities can now become the creators of research and activities and the source of ideas. They can become the nucleus of or participants in their own unique networks, which feed back into the wider community.

7. Mistakes Can Build Trust

Merchant (2012a) explains "Reach and connection in the social era start to be understood as a relationship similar to falling in love, following an arc of romance, struggle, commitment, and co-creation."

The implication for #SocialIT is that sharing lessons learned and knowledge of past errors may lead to new, enhanced ways to approach activities. With the consumer being the creator, more things will be tried and more errors will occur, but in the long term this means more will be achieved.

8. Learn. Unlearn. (Repeat)

Merchant (2012a) states, "Instead of viewing strategy as a set end point, it becomes a horizon to aim for. Instead of perfection and getting it right the first time, innovation can be continuous."

The flip side of knowing mistakes have value is that learning is a process of change. We need to start by unlearning the things we thought we knew which haven't worked. #SocialIT starts by stopping repeating the same programs that have to date produced little to none of the desired outcomes. #SocialIT is not a new way to carry on business as usual, but a way to learn new ways of working, new activities and new ways of implementing them.

9. Bank on Openness

Merchant (2012a) describes this as "Protecting intellectual property allowed organisations to keep their edge, to erect barriers to entry from competitors. Then along came the social era, with its networks through which open, connected ideas became powerful, even catalytic."

In the past, organisations would develop their own intellectual property and either keep it to themselves by default or intent, or share it with a limited number of affiliated organisations. But this is changing. Shadbolt (2013) argues for the many benefits of open data compared to keeping it secret, and its value is already being seen in Africa, where open data combined with free analytical tools is changing society by empowering ordinary people (Firth, 2013).

#SocialIT will initially make it easier to share such ideas globally so everyone knows what worked and what did not, while ultimately such knowledge sharing will be inherent in the activities themselves. As a result #SocialIT will reduce duplicated efforts by groups across the world and harness the collaborative tools of the technology trade for all to share.

10. Social Purpose Unleashes Ownership

Merchant (2012a) explains "The social object that most unites people is a shared value or purpose. With social purpose, alignment happens without coordination costs."

Community of purpose, drive and passion already runs strong and deep in the Women in Technology communities. With #SocialIT we should aim to tap into this to ensure ongoing collaboration. As the #SocialEra progresses we will see more and more targeted networks springing up of their own accord and we can envisage networks of networks forming along their natural lines of alignment. While we should do what we can to encourage that – we will not be able to, nor should we want to, control it.

11. (There are No Answers)

Merchant (2012a) simply states: "Listen, learn, adapt."

The implication for #SocialIT is listen to the past history, learn new ways, adapt and change to map closer to where the industry has shifted and will continue to shift. We do not need to know the answers in advance, all we need is to hop on the train. Change can only accelerate in the future.

Summary of #SocialEra impacts

The implications of the 11 #SocialEra rules for the #SocialIT aspect of the overall STEMcell Model are summarised in Table 5.

As well stated by Merchant (2012b), "These changes are not transitory or reversible, but fundamental and irrevocable. The social-era models are inherently more fast, fluid, and flexible than the models that preceded them. The big question is: how are we actually going to *do* this thing?"

So How Do We Do This?

In the past few years the dynamic, fast changing technology industry, disruptive technologies and #SocialEra have brought with them many platforms and tools that can be used for activities previously part of traditional schooling or intervention programs. Two examples below illustrate ways in which #SocialEra is already reducing obstacles: in teaching how to code and profiling role models. And the third example illustrates why in the broad sweep of things, we might not have to "do" anything: it will do itself without our driving it.

Table 5. #SocialEra Rules and their Impact on Women in IT Activities

#SocialEra Rule		Women in Technology Impact
1. Connections create value	#SocialIT Transforms to	Review relevancy, structure and programs and dissolve old boundaries.
2. Power in community		Develop greater ties and open communication between researchers, campaign activists and individuals.
3. Collaboration control		Tear down the traditional industry association walls and reform into an open, fluid, collaborative model.
4. Celebrate onlyness		Large, centrally planned intervention activities requiring many coordinated volunteers may no longer be required nor desirable. The individual is core.
5. Allow all talent		Utilise social media connections to expand the pool of ideas and engaged community members: as contributors as much as participants.
6. Consumers become co-creators		The subjects of research and participants in intervention activities can now become the creators of research and activities and the source of ideas.
7. Mistakes can build trust		Past and future mistakes to be learned, shared and lead to new, enhanced ways to approach activities.
8. Learn. Unlearn. (Repeat)		Unlearn traditional interventions and learn new ways of working and new activities and ways of implementing them.
9. Bank on openness		Share IP globally to reduce duplicated efforts; harness collaborative tools.
10. Social purpose unleashes ownership		Tap into this to ensure ongoing collaboration.
11. (There are no answers)		Learn new ways, adapt and change to map closer to where the industry has shifted and will shift – continuously.

Now, ten years on from Margolis & Fisher (2003), instead of thinking about the "Clubhouse" it is time to rethink and reconstruct the environment to be more like, for example, the "Treehouse."

Online Learning Tools

Treehouse is a coding platform launched in November 2012 with the goal "To teach the world how to design and develop for the Web, iOS, and Android" (Empson, 2012). It is an educational platform employing video, quizzes, and a little gamification to help aspiring programmers and app developers learn the trade — regardless of their gender or prior experience.

Here is some feedback on the Treehouse website that indicates not only its value but that the area is growing, with similar resources being also available elsewhere:

- "The Treehouse team are fantastic and work closely with teachers like me in Australia – they're even willing to speak to the kids from the other side of the world in real time on occasion. What they offer is a great tool that supports what I do in the classroom with kids as young as 14. Keep up the good work guys!" (Bruce Fuda, University of Canberra)
- "Good to know there are good education resources out there. Codeavengers.com, like Treehouse is aimed at students, with FANTASTIC teacher helps. The interactive tutorials incorporate the NZ high school curriculum. I have found the lessons very fun and very effective. If you are a teacher... take 5 minutes and take a look." (Lynnell Keung Walmsley)
- "16 months in a Canadian private college: $16000. 16 months in Treehouse will cost: $400 to $800... and university takes too long... 4 years... I will get a shot at Treehouse." (Joaquim l'Antonio)

Ryan Carson, CEO of Treehouse, said that a key motivator for establishing Treehouse was because he "believes education and specifically the way institutions teach programming is broken." This style of comment is also threaded throughout the women in technology literature (Empson, 2012) and is included in the Model's structural context as part of issues impacting the industry (Figure 4).

With platforms such as Treehouse, many coders learn applicable skills and techniques without going through a degree program. Instead they use smart, interactive online tools. Using Scratch (a free Web based coding tool), even young and very young children can learn how to code stories, games and animations and share them with friends and communities. Another example is org.code (launched by Bill Gates and Mark Zuckerberg) for people in the USA to learn to code.

In this #SocialEra of tectonic change, sadly it is still likely that online educational resources like Scratch, Treehouse, Learnable, Udacity, Khan, Coursera, etc. will be disparaged by educators as replacing teachers with technology and part-time "experts" who lack real pedagogical training. I suggest this is another example of traditional strategy beliefs that need to be put aside in this new era. Such tools are part of the new approach. Educators will not be able to stop it: rather, they should concentrate on using and improving it.

Role Models

Reducing barriers to learning is part of the battle. Another part is proving to girls, by showing them real life examples, that women are as capable as anyone else. In November 2012, Google commenced using Hangouts for a series of talks titled "Women Techmakers" to specifically profile female technology role models (Gutelle, 2012). Using the free Hangout platform brings the role models to life across the world and the conversation into the community. Google aren't the only company highlighting powerful women. Throughout most of 2012, PBS and AOL teamed up to create *Makers*, a series that profiled women who have made a difference in the world. Whilst *Makers* was not specifically about women in technology, it is presented here as an example of using social media to profile stories. The more recent Girls in ICT Portal (http://girlsinict.org) provides another series of role model videos.

In this #SocialEra, cries of lack of role models are no longer realistic. The tools, often free, are readily available to profile successful women in technology. Perhaps what is required as a bridge between the old and the new is a crowdsourcing project to bring the wealth of existing role model information out of storage into public view. Such a project could fund pulling together past role model material from the multitude of organisations that have run such programs and projects, and make them readily and freely available in the public space.

Changing Attitudes

Another shift that is occurring and worth figuring into the changing landscape is the change in women's attitude to careers. "Over the last decade, a new generation of women have become more ambitious and career-minded than ever before. In fact, careers are now so fundamental to many young women, that a *Marie Claire* survey published this month showed that three quarters of twenty and thirty something respondents cite work as either 'very important' or the 'single most important thing' in their lives. On top of this, Citi reported that 36% of women it polled recently didn't factor marriage into their definition of 'having it all', and 27% didn't include children" (K. Cave, 2012).

Whilst such a shift could not take place without cultural and social factors that allow and encourage it, those factors are changing far more as a result of the natural evolution of society than because of an elite attempting to change society from above. There is a clear analogy here to trends in the prime historical cause for under-representation of women in many professions, mentioned in that quote: childbirth and the raising of children, traditionally female roles for obvious reasons. Ever since Malthus, people have agonised over population growth rates exceeding our capacity to feed all those people. Yet as countries develop and become richer and more technologically advanced, birth-rates drop dramatically as part of the natural course of events, or to put it in terms of the STEMcell Model, as a consequence of the sensible decisions of individuals responding to their circumstances. As Soubbotina (2004: p.18) states, "The reasons for lower fertility are varied, but most are related to developing countries' economic growth and development... Parents choose to have smaller families when health conditions improve because they no longer have to fear that many of their babies might die, and when they do not have to rely on their children to work on the family farm or business or to take care of them in their old age. In addition, more parents are sending their daughters to school, which is important because women with basic education tend to produce healthier children and smaller families. More women now have opportunities to work outside the home, so they are starting their families later and having fewer children. On top of all that, access to modern contraceptives for family planning is improving, making it easier for parents to control the number and spacing of their children."

Thus the decline in birth-rate in developing countries is not primarily a result of birth-control enthusiasts running intervention programs or parading role models of successful single women. It is simply the aggregate of individual choices as the society becomes wealthy enough and advanced enough to make options other than constant motherhood both possible and desirable.

I argue that in a similar manner, women's attitudes to careers in general are changing all by themselves in response to changes in society as we become richer, healthier, more long-lived and more technologically aware (how many teenagers now *don't* have a smartphone, which is a computer in their pocket more powerful than the personal computers of a decade ago and the mainframes before that?). We can jump on that train, join in the conversation, add our knowledge and thoughts to the mix: or become irrelevant.

The Core of the STEMcell Model

#SocialIT will be organically evolving, and in its turn is likely to be replaced in the future by other disruptive forces and technologies. However the core (the individual cell) that will remain is the individual and the choices she makes from the primary drivers of innate interests or talents. All that will and can change is how much those interests and talents will be enabled by each individual's ability to tap into whatever disruptive technologies exist at the time. And as with past information revolutions, that enabling can only get better.

However the flip side of empowering individuals through the STEMcell Model is we need to remember that the individual *is* the core. We need to face the possibility that this might mean women will always represent the minority in IT: not because of external barriers or impediments but simply because most women are interested in other fields. Nevertheless we know barriers still exist that inhibit access to information, realisation of what is possible or opportunities to pursue them. We know that some women do respond to intervention programs, despite their overall ineffectiveness. Thus the number of women who actually choose IT will be maximised if relevant information and especially experiences are readily available (so that they discover their interests) and obstacles that otherwise would make them give up are reduced. #SocialIT can play an important role in achieving that.

Beyond isolated individual cases, traditional programs have failed to make a measurable and/or significant impact on improving attraction, promotion and retention of females into technology studies and careers; these failures are discussed further in the next chapter. The new #SocialIT era provides the potential for maximising women's participation in IT by increasing visibility and reducing barriers (e.g. making it more "acceptable" and increasing social support and the feeling of belonging rather than isolation), while avoiding the errors of the past: poor cost/benefit ratio, volunteer burnout, frequent loss of knowledge and "reinventing the wheel" etc. #SocialIT is already starting and should be embraced.

Here are some examples of activities that are indicators that #SocialIT is already starting: "Kimberley Bryant … an electrical engineer, founded Black Girls CODE @BlackGirlsCode in October 2011 … Her goal: To train one million girls to code by 2040" (Stirland, 2013). In July 2013, Black Girls CODE ran a crowdsourcing campaign to secure funding, where their invitation was, "Imagine the impact if more girls grew confident in learning computer programming and planned to pursue careers as creators instead of being mere consumers of tech. This is exactly the type of confidence and change Black Girls CODE wants to ensure all girls experience, so we have recently launched a crowd funding campaign to raise $100,000 to educate 2,000 more girls in computer programming and seed eight chapters across the nation" (Bobe, 2013). This was not their first crowdsourcing project: in 2012 they ran a successful crowd funded campaign to teach programming to 200 girls of colour in seven USA cities.

Even at this early evolving stage there are some lessons from recent #SocialEra style campaigns. The European Union *Science It's a Girl Thing* launch in 2012 imploded due to a viral video. Rice (2012a) explained, "This campaign – designed to convince high school girls to pursue careers in science – had such a badly bungled launch. The problem lies in the 'teaser' video, which went viral last week for all the wrong reasons. It was put up on the campaign website, disliked, criticised, mocked and then pulled down."

Rice, who was part of the advisory group, acted swiftly and utilised crowdsourcing to come to the rescue. Rice (2012a) thought "Maybe crowdsourcing the creation of a teaser – based on the campaign's website – would be the best way to find out what could tempt teenage girls to study science."

The response was tremendous and the winners were announced in late November. The second key development was when the European Science Foundation came on board as a co-organizer of the contest. Even with something as anarchistic as a crowdsourcing contest, there is a lot of work to be done — setting up a good website, organizing the submissions, getting sensible materials to the jury members, and organizing the announcement of the winners. ESF took on these tasks and made the contest a much better experience than I ever could have done myself. ESF Chief Executive Martin Hynes also added considerable status to the event by joining the award ceremony and mentioning the contest in his remarks at the European Gender Summit. The contest got prize money, status, and excellent organizational support, but none of that would have mattered without the investment of the participants and other supporters. The decisions of many individuals to engage is the final crucial component (Rice, 2012b).

So the new era of #SocialIT will bring with it its own issues that will need to be considered along the way. In crafting this publication I seek to challenge the false/failed ideas of the past. However passionate and well intended the efforts of the traditionalist researchers, groups and individual activists and advocates who have taken up the goal of the attraction, promotion and retention of women in technology (studies and careers) are, *it has not worked*. Instead of an increase we have seen a continuing lack and actual decline of women in technology. It is time to pave the way for a new approach, one pivotal in connecting with a wider community of people and adopting new methods more suited to our new era.

Taking the words of Nilofer Merchant (2012a) and translating them to apply to the specific circumstances of women and technology, we can say (italics indicate my interpolations): "The Social Era unlocks new doors of both who can contribute – *to the body of knowledge about girls and women in technology* – and what can be created – *in terms of research and activities and projects instead of traditional intervention programs* – and thus changes the very source of power itself – *from traditional researchers, historical literature and industry associations to the global community of interest*."

In an interview with Deanna Zandt (2013) from Forbes.com, Nilofer Merchant said, "Let's face it, non-believers are committed to their non-believerness. We might never change them. Or as Geoffrey Moore would say, laggards wait until there is no choice other than to act. Laggards are the ones still using fax machines instead of email." The message to those reading this publication is: don't let yourself be a laggard – adapt now – STEMcell and #SocialIT here you come.

But before we head into the future, we will step back to see where we have come from. Our next chapter takes an inside view of the passionate believers and activists who have designed and delivered countless traditional intervention programs and projects. It looks at the outcomes of those efforts compared to their stated goals, and raises questions regarding their value and future in this new social era.

REFERENCES

Adya, M., & Kaiser, K. M. (2005). Early determinants of women in the IT workforce: A model of girls' career choices. *Information Technology & People*, *18*(3), 230–259. doi:10.1108/09593840510615860

Adya, M., & Kaiser, K. M. (2006). Factors influencing girls' choice of information technology careers. In E. M. Trauth (Ed.), *Encyclopaedia of gender and information technology* (Vol. 1, pp. 282–288). Hershey, PA: Idea Group Reference. doi:10.4018/978-1-59140-815-4.ch044

Ahuja, M. K. (2002). Women in the information technology profession: A literature review, synthesis, and research agenda. *European Journal of Information Systems*, *11*(1), 20–34. doi:10.1057/palgrave.ejis.3000417

Anderson, N., Lankshear, C., & Courtney, L. (2008a). *Girls and information communication technology (ICT) career pathways: Tackling the upper middle school 'turn off'*. Retrieved July 21, 2013, from http://www.neilrobertanderson.com/girlsict/current%20research.html

Anderson, N., Lankshear, C., Timms, C., & Courtney, L. (2008b). 'Because it's boring, irrelevant and I don't like computers': Why high school girls avoid professionally-oriented ICT subjects. *Computers & Education*, *50*(4), 1304–1318. doi:10.1016/j.compedu.2006.12.003

Anderson, N., Timms, C., & Courtney, L. (2006). If you want to advance in the ICT industry, you have to work harder than your male peers: Women in ICT industry survey: Preliminary findings. In *Proceedings of the 2006 Australian Women in IT Conference AusWIT 2006 10th Australian Women in IT Conference: Participation One Year On*. Adelaide, Australia: AusWIT.

Ashcraft, C., Eger, E., & Friend, M. (2012). *Girls in IT: The facts*. Boulder, CO: National Centre for Women & Information Technology (NCWIT). Retrieved August 6, 2013, from http://www.academia.edu/2283166/Girls_in_IT_The_Facts

Baker, T. (2012). *Enhancing STEM education with GIS ebook released*. Retrieved July 2, 2013, from http://blogs.esri.com/esri/gisedcom/2012/09/06/advancing-stem-education-with-gis-ebook-released/

Barker, L. J., & Aspray, W. (2006). The state of research on girls and IT. In J. M. Cohoon, & W. Aspray (Eds.), *Women and information technology: Research on underrepresentation* (pp. 3–54). Cambridge, MA: MIT Press. doi:10.7551/mitpress/9780262033459.003.0001

Bateman, K. (2012). *Men and women disagree on reasons why IT is less attractive to women.* Retrieved July 20, 2013, from http://www.computerweekly.com/news/2240159441/Men-and-women-disagree-on-reasons-why-IT-is-less-attractive-to-women

Bateman, K. (2013). *Is outdated terminology deterring females from roles in IT?* Retrieved July 2, 2013, from http://www.computerweekly.com/feature/Is-outdated-terminology-deterring-females-from-roles-in-IT

Beekhuyzen, J., Nielsen, S., & von Hellens, L. (2006). *Making IT fit: Research and action in Queensland*. Paper presented at the AusWIT Australian Women in IT Conference. Adelaide, Australia.

Bernhardt, S. (2006). Boards need women with IT. In E. M. Trauth (Ed.), *Encyclopedia of gender and information technology* (Vol. 1, pp. 70–76). Hershey, PA: Idea Group Reference. doi:10.4018/978-1-59140-815-4.ch012

Berry, M., & Kalessi, T. (2011). *Women's careers in the technology industry*. London, UK: Intellect and Women in Technology (Report). Retrieved August 1, 2013, from http://sciencewithart.ijs.si/pdf/Women's_Careers_in_the_Technology_Industry_2011_Report.pdf

Blair, R., Gill, K., & Benson, M. (2013). *Focus on the pipeline*. Alexander Mann Solutions and Everywomen. Retrieved August 1, 2013, from http://info.everywoman.com/women-in-management-focus-on-the-pipeline/

Bobe, A. (2013). *Meet a 13 year old programmer excited to change the world*. Black Girls CODE. Retrieved July 17, 2013, from http://women2.com/meet-a-13-year-old-programmer-excited-to-change-the-world/

Bogart, N. (2013). *How the role of social media has evolved since Egypt's last upheaval*. Retrieved July 18, 2013, from http://globalnews.ca/news/693614/how-the-role-of-social-media-has-evolved-since-egypts-last-upheaval/

Boyd, S. (2011). *Revolution – Messiness at scale, again*. Retrieved July 18, 2013, from http://stoweboyd.com/post/3105227293/revolution-messiness-at-scale-again

Castano, C., & Webster, J. (2011). Understanding women's presence in ICT: The life course perspective. *International Journal of Gender, Science and Technology, 3*(2), 358-363.

Cave, D. (2012). *Digital islands: How the Pacific's ICT revolution is transforming the region*. Sydney, Australia: Lowy Institute.

Cave, K. (2012). Women: Why doesn't IT have iPad appeal? *IDG Connect Business Management*. Retrieved May 22, 2013, from http://www.idgconnect.com/blog-abstract/654/kathryn-cave-global-women-why-doesn-t-it-have-ipad-appeal

Cave, K. (2013). Women in IT: Does the shortage matter? *IDG Connect Infographic*. Retrieved May 22, 2013, from http://www.idgconnect.com/abstract/1251/infographic-women-it-does-shortage-matter

Cheeseman Day, J., Janus, A., & Davis, J. (2005). *Computer and Internet use in the United States: 2003*. U.S. Census Bureau. Retrieved August 10, 2013, from http://www.census.gov/prod/2005pubs/p23-208.pdf

Clayton, K. (2007). *The influence of metropolitan Brisbane middle-school ICT experiences on girls' ICT study and career choices*. (Unpublished doctoral dissertation). Griffith University, Queensland, Australia.

Clayton, K., Beekhuyzen, J., & Nielsen, S. (2012). Now I know what ICT can do for me? *Information Systems Journal, 22*(5), 1–16. doi:10.1111/j.1365-2575.2012.00414.x

Clayton, K. L., von Hellens, L. A., & Nielsen, S. H. (2009). Gender stereotypes prevail in ICT: A research review. In *Proceedings of the Special Interest Group on Management Information System's 47th Annual Conference on Computer Personnel Research* (SIGMIS CPR) (pp. 153-158). ACM.

Cohoon, J. M., & Asprey, W. (Eds.). (2006). *Women and information technology: Research on underrepresentation*. London: MIT Press. doi:10.7551/mitpress/9780262033459.001.0001

Cozza, M. (2011). Bridging gender gaps, networking in computer science. *Gender, Technology and Development, 15*(2), 319–337. doi:10.1177/097185241101500207

Craig, A., Dawson, L., & Fisher, J. (2009). *Measuring the success of intervention programmes designed to increase the participation rate by women in computing*. Paper presented at the European Conference on Information Systems 2009. Verona, Italy.

Craig, A., Fisher, J., & Lang, C. (2007). *ICT and girls: The need for a large scale intervention programme.* Paper presented at the Association for Information Systems ACIS 2007. Toowoomba, Australia.

Craig, A., Lang, C., & Fisher, J. (2008). Twenty years of girls into computing days: Has it been worth the effort? *Journal of Information Technology Education, 7*, 339–353.

Curtis, A. (2013). *The brief history of social media.* Retrieved July 12, 2013, from http://www.uncp.edu/home/acurtis/NewMedia/SocialMedia/SocialMediaHistory.html

Denner, J. (2011). What predicts middle school girls' interest in computing? *International Journal of Gender. Science and Technology, 3*(1), 53–69.

Dryburgh, H. (2000). Underrepresentation of girls and women in computer science: Classification of 1990s' research. *Journal of Educational Computing Research, 23*(2), 181–202. doi:10.2190/8RYV-9JWH-XQMB-QF41

Empson, R. (2012). *Learn to code, get a job: Treehouse offers free courses to 2,500 college students.* Retrieved January 10, 2013, from http://techcrunch.com/2012/09/14/learn-to-code-get-a-job-treehouse-offers-free-courses-to-2500-college-students/

Fang, I. (1997). *A history of mass communication: Six information revolutions.* Boston: Focal Press.

Firth, N. (2013). Power at their fingertips. *New Scientist, 220*(2943), 22–23. doi:10.1016/S0262-4079(13)62682-2

Fitzpatrick, K. (2011). *Planned obsolescence: Publishing, technology, and the future of the academy.* New York: New York University Press. Abstract retrieved November 23, 2013, from http://www.amazon.com/gp/product/0814727883

Goode, J., Estrella, R., & Margolis, J. (2006). Lost in translation: Gender in high school computer science. In J. Cohoon & W. Aspray (Eds.), *Women and information technology: Research on underrepresentation* (pp. 89-114). Cambridge, MA: MIT Press.

Goodreads. (2013). *Richard Buckminster Fuller > Quotes.* Retrieved August 2, 2013, from https://www.goodreads.com/author/quotes/165737.Richard_Buckminster_Fuller

Gorbis, M. (2013). *The nature of the future: Dispatches from the socialstructured world.* New York: Free Press.

Gras-Velazquez, A., Joyce, A., & Debry, M. (2009). *Women and ICT: Why are girls still not attracted to ICT studies and careers?* (White Paper). Brussels: European Schoolnet (EUN Partnership AISBL).

Griffiths, M., & Moore, K. (2010). 'Disappearing women': A study of women who left the UK ICT sector. *Journal of Technology Management and Innovation, 5*(1), 95–107. doi:10.4067/S0718-27242010000100008

Gutelle, S. (2012). *Google to profile powerful women in the tech industry via hangout.* Retrieved July 10, 2013, from http://www.tubefilter.com/2012/11/01/google-developers-live-women-techmakers/

Guzman, I., & Stanton, J. (2009). IT occupational culture: The cultural fit and commitment of new information technologists. *Information Technology & People, 22*(2), 157–187. doi:10.1108/09593840910962212

Guzman, I., Stanton, J., & Eischen, D. (2006). Female perceptions of the information technology culture. In E. M. Trauth (Ed.), *Encyclopedia of gender and information technology* (Vol. 1, pp. 304–309). Hershey, PA: Idea Group Reference. doi:10.4018/978-1-59140-815-4.ch047

Ham, R., Junankar, P. N., & Wells, R. (2009). *Occupational choice: Personality matters* (IZA Discussion Paper No. 4105). Bonn: IZA. Retrieved August 23, 2013, from http://www.econstor.eu/bitstream/10419/35680/1/599093404.pdf

Hayes, E. (2005). Women, video gaming, and learning: Beyond stereotypes. *TechTrends, 49*(5), 23–28. doi:10.1007/BF02763686

Hayes, E. (2008). Girls, gaming and trajectories of IT expertise. In Y. B. Kafai, C. Heeter, J. Denner, & J. Y. Sun (Eds.), *Beyond Barbie and Mortal Kombat: New perspectives on gender and gaming* (pp. 217–230). Cambridge, MA: MIT Press.

Heemskerk, I., Brink, A., Volman, M., & ten Dam, G. (2005). Inclusiveness and ICT in education: A focus on gender, ethnicity and social class. *Journal of Computer Assisted Learning, 21*, 1–16. doi:10.1111/j.1365-2729.2005.00106.x

Kirkup, G. (2011). Preparing women for dead-end jobs? Vocational education and training (VET) for information and communication technology (ICT) jobs. *International Journal of Gender Science and Technology, 3*(2), 460–482.

Kirkup, G., Zalevski, A., Maruyama, T., & Batool, I. (2010). *Women and men in science, engineering and technology: The UK statistics guide 2010*. Bradford: UKRC.

Klawe, M., Whitney, T., & Simard, C. (2009). Women in computing – Take 2. *Communications of the ACM, 52*, 68–76. doi:10.1145/1461928.1461947

Kroes, N. (2013). *ICT and women speech – European commission*. Retrieved July 21, 2013, from http://europa.eu/rapid/press-release_SPEECH-13-366_en.htm

Lang, C., Fisher, J., & Craig, A. (2007). *Digital divas: Computer clubs for girls trial*. Brentwood Secondary College, Swinburne University of Technology Women in ICT Group and Victorian ICT for Women Network. Retrieved August 1, 2013, from http://www.swinburne.edu.au/ict/wict/documents/Report%20on%20Brentwood%20Computer%20Club%20Trial.pdf

Lang, C., & McKay, J. (2006). Australian IT enrolment trends and model of contributing factors. In E. M. Trauth (Ed.), *Encyclopedia of gender and information technology* (Vol. 1, pp. 50–56). Hershey, PA: Idea Group Reference. doi:10.4018/978-1-59140-815-4.ch009

Liston, C., Peterson, K., & Ragan, V. (2009). *Promising practices in informal information technology (IT) education for girls*. Paper prepared for AERA Meeting. San Diego, CA. Retrieved July 21, 2013, from http://www.eraeval.org/sites/default/files/files/PromisingPractices-Informal-IT-Education-Girls.pdf

Lyons, T., Quinn, F., Rizk, N., Anderson, N., Hubber, P., Kenny, J., et al. (2012). *Starting out in STEM: A study of young men and women in first year science, technology, engineering and mathematics courses*. Armidale, Australia: University of New England. Retrieved August 13, 2013, from http://www.une.edu.au/simerr/pages/projects/132iris_report.pdf

Mainwaring, S. (2011). *Exactly what role did social media play in the Egyptian revolution?* Retrieved July 18, 2013, from http://www.fastcompany.com/1727466/exactly-what-role-did-social-media-play-egyptian-revolution

Margolis, J., & Fisher, A. (2003). *Unlocking the clubhouse: Women in computing*. Cambridge, MA: MIT Press.

Merchant, N. (2012a). 11 rules for creating value in the #SocialEra. Boston, MA: Harvard Business School (HBR Singles).

Merchant, N. (2012b). Stop talking about social and do it. *HBR Blog Network*. Retrieved September 16, 2012, from http://blogs.hbr.org/cs/2012/03/stop_talking_about_social_and_do_it.html

Merchant, N. (2012c). The social era is more than social media. *FastCompany*. Retrieved September 24, 2012, from http://www.fastcompany.com/3001505/social-era-more-social-media

Miliszewska, I., & Moore, A. (2011). Attracting girls to ICT studies & careers – A snapshot of strategies. *Redress*, *20*(3), 10–14.

Misa, T. J. (Ed.). (2010). *Gender codes: Why women are leaving computing*. Hoboken, NJ: John Wiley. doi:10.1002/9780470619926

Modi, K., Schoenberg, J., & Salmond, K. (2012). *Generation STEM: What girls say about science, technology, engineering, and math*. Girl Scouts of the USA. Retrieved August 10, 2013, from http://www.girlscouts.org/research/pdf/generation_stem_full_report.pdf

Newmarch, E., Taylor-Steele, S., & Cumpston, A. (2000). *Women in IT – What are the barriers?* Paper presented at the Network of Women in Further Education Conference Showcase of Strategies for Women in Education on Information Technology Conference. Adelaide, Australia.

Nielsen, S., von Hellens, L., Pringle, R., & Greenhill, A. (1999). Students' perceptions of information technology careers: Conceptualising the influence of cultural and gender factors for IT education. *GATES Journal*, *5*(1), 30–38.

OECD. (2007). *ICTs and gender, working party on the information economy report, DSTI/ICCP/IE(2006)9/final*. Paris: Organisation for Economic Co-Operation and Development.

Palmén, R. (2011). Girls, boys and ICT in the UK: An empirical review and competing policy agendas. *International Journal of Gender. Science and Technology*, *3*(2), 407–423.

Rice, C. (2012a). *Science: It's a girl thing! A viral fiasco*. Retrieved July 14, 2013, from http://curt-rice.com/2012/07/28/science-its-a-girl-thing-a-viral-fiasco/

Rice, C. (2012b). *Science: It's your thing! 3 steps to a crowdsourcing success*. Retrieved July 14, 2013, from http://curt-rice.com/2013/01/03/science-its-your-thing-3-steps-to-a-crowdsourcing-success/

Scoble, R., & Israel, S. (2013). *Age of context: Mobile, sensors, data and the future of privacy*. CreateSpace Independent Publishing Platform.

Shadbolt, N. (2013). Time to let it all out. *New Scientist*, *220*(2943), 29.

Soubbotina, T. P. (2004). *Beyond economic growth: An introduction to sustainable development* (2nd ed.). Washington, DC: The World Bank. doi:10.1596/0-8213-5933-9

Stirland, S. L. (2013). *Kimberly Bryant wants black girls code to be girl scouts of technology*. Retrieved July 24, 2013, from http://techpresident.com/news/23974/kimberly-bryant-wants-black-girls-code-be-girl-scouts-technology

Tandon, N., Pritchard, S., Savelieva, V., Smith, G., & Vogt, E. (2012). *A bright future in ICTs: Opportunities for a new generation of women*. Geneva, Switzerland: International Telecommunication Union.

Timms, C., Courtney, L., & Anderson, N. (2006). Dimensions of 'boring': Secondary girls' perceptions of advanced ICT subjects. In *Proceedings of the Australian Computers in Education Conference 2006*. Cairns, Australia: ACEC.

Trauth, E. M. (2002). Odd girl out: An individual differences perspective on women in the IT profession. *Information Technology & People*, *15*(2), 98–118. doi:10.1108/09593840210430552

Trauth, E. M. (Ed.). (2006). *Encyclopedia of gender and information technology*. Hershey, PA: Idea Group Reference. doi:10.4018/978-1-59140-815-4

Trauth, E. M., Huang, H., & Quesenberry, J. L. (2006). Cross-cultural influences on women in the IT workforce. In *Proceedings of ACM SIGMIS Conference on Computer Personnel Research* (pp. 12-19). Claremont, CA: ACM.

Trauth, E. M., Nielsen, S. H., & von Hellens, L. A. (2003). Explaining the IT gender gap: Australian stories for the new millennium. *Journal of Research and Practice in Information Technology*, *35*(1), 7–20.

Trauth, E. M., Quesenberry, L. L., & Huang, H. (2009). Retaining women in the U.S. I.T workforce: Theorizing the influence of organizational factors. *European Journal of Information Systems*, *18*(5), 476–497. doi:10.1057/ejis.2009.31

UNESCO. (2012). *Girls in STEM and ICT careers: The path toward gender equality*. New York: UNESCO.

von Hellens, L., Trauth, E., & Fisher, J. (2012). Editorial. *Information Systems Journal*, *22*, 343–353. doi:10.1111/j.1365-2575.2012.00412.x

von Hellens, L. A., Pringle, R., Nielsen, S. H., & Greenhill, A. (2000). People, business, and IT skills: The perspective of women in the IT industry. In W. Nance (Ed.), *Proceedings of the ACM SIGCPR Special Interest Group on Computer Personnel Research* (pp. 152-157). Chicago, IL: Association for Computing Machinery.

Zandt, D. (2013). *Top reasons why the #SocialEra changes everything*. Retrieved July 18, 2013, from http://www.speakers.ca/2013/07/top-reasons-the-socialera-changes-everything/

KEY TERMS AND DEFINITIONS

ICT: Information and Communication Technology. Synonymous with IT.

#SocialEra: A term (coined by Nilofer Merchant) to describe a shift in focus from traditional methods to a more social movement, which has profound implications for business and how people work and lead.

#SocialIT: A term coined for the layer of the STEMcell Model derived from #SocialEra concepts. It is a disruptive, penetrating force that can enhance the positive and reduce the negative aspects of the Cultural, Social, Structural and Individual contexts affecting women in IT.

Social Media: Internet tools and sites where people interact freely, creating, sharing and discussing content and information about each other and their lives, using a multimedia mix of words, pictures, videos and audio. There are many forms including blogs, forums, social networks, wikis, virtual worlds and places to share content such as data, images and videos. See http://www.uncp.edu/home/acurtis/NewMedia/SocialMedia/SocialMediaHistory.html

STEM: Science, Technology, Engineering and Mathematics; conceptually related fields that share issues of under-representation of women. An extension of SET to include maths.

STEMcell Model: A model designed by Sonja Bernhardt that provides a conceptual framework for viewing contexts and layers impacting STEM fields.

Chapter 3
The Old Approach

ABSTRACT

For decades, governments, associations, and individuals have enthusiastically jumped to "solve the women in IT issue" with a variety of intervention programs aimed at increasing recruitment and retention of women in IT. But beyond a few individual career choices and anecdotal "feel good" results on the day, these traditional programs have failed utterly. An estimate of the cumulative effort and spending on these programs demonstrates the sheer size of the exercise and underlines the depth of the failure. We do not need more of the same, but rather, we need to work out why we have failed. New informal research is presented in this chapter on the key influences on women choosing IT careers, delivering a key result that women in IT have always known they liked technology or they discovered (by an accident of their job) they liked IT. Interventions have had minimal effect but the importance of adapting to the Social Era for future interventions is recognised. The conclusion is that there is little value in the traditional approaches and further massive spending is unwarranted. Rather, we need to recognise that the primary driving issue is individual interests and talents, whilst the remaining barriers are best overcome by embracing the new era and using the disruptive technologies, platforms, and tools of #SocialIT.

Insanity is doing the same thing over and over again – and expecting different results

– Albert Einstein (rumoured)
(BrainyQuote, 2013)

WHAT'S THE PROBLEM?

For more than two decades it has been noted by government employment statistics reports, researchers and the general industry that there are noticeably fewer females in technology than there are males. Having been identified as a problem, it has been subject to numerous theories regarding its cause and effect. Additionally researchers, educators and those in the industry have banded together via the formation of industry associations and groups, or acted individually, to design and implement solutions to solve the problem. These solutions have comprised a variety of projects and activities designed to correct what has been assumed to be the underlying cause(s). Their intent has been to intervene and artificially adjust the naturally occurring statistics of females attracted to and working in IT. These projects and activities have become known as intervention programs (von Hellens, Trauth & Fisher, 2012).

DOI: 10.4018/978-1-4666-5860-8.ch003

With the obvious exception of circumstances that limit access, such as poverty or strong cultural bias, there have been no noted issues or problems for female participation in the use of technology, and in fact in a number of areas females are avid users of new and emerging technologies (Ashcraft, Eger & Friend, 2012). Instead the problematic areas noted have been in educational and career choice: the number of girls undertaking technology studies at school, TAFE/VET and tertiary levels, and the number of women then entering, being promoted within and remaining in technology based careers. As such the design of intervention programs has been multi-pronged, both delivering differing activities and tailoring projects for the numerous target groups. All aim to *make a difference* to the attraction, promotion and retention of females in technology studies and careers, and more specifically to make a positive improvement in the participation rate.

WHAT'S THE HALF TIME SCORECARD?

The short answer is "Good Intentions – no Outcomes" (Barbara Tobin: industry participant, former president of Queensland's Women in Technology [WiT] and former chair of Australian Women in IT Science and Engineering [AWISE], personal communication, August 5, 2013).

A review of the literature reveals that across Western cultures similar kinds of projects and activities sprang up and were enthusiastically adopted. An example is NCWIT: "The National Centre for Women & Information Technology (NCWIT) is a coalition of more than 250 corporations, academic institutions, government agencies, and non-profits working to strengthen the computing workforce and promote technology innovation by increasing the participation of women and under-represented groups. NCWIT's national programs and alliances focus on reforming the entire pipeline, from K-12 through higher education to corporate, academic, and entrepreneurial careers. We believe that inspiring more women to choose careers in computing isn't only about equity, it's also about innovation, competitiveness, and workforce sustainability. In a global economy driven by innovation, gender diversity in IT means a larger and more competitive workforce and the ability to create technology that is as broad and creative as the people it serves" (DuBow, 2011). One look at the comprehensive NCWIT Scorecard (available at www.ncwit.org/scorecard) reveals its broad reach; yet it is more about compelling arguments for "making a difference" and highlighting intervention programs than evidence of having had a statistically significant difference since NCWIT's establishment in 2004.

Being able to understand that difference and measure it in a consistently objective way may be part of the solution, as hinted at by the following comment: "Many intervention programs to increase the number of women in the Information and Communications Technology (ICT) profession have been implemented over the last twenty years. Detailed evaluations help us to determine the effectiveness of these programs yet few comprehensive evaluations appear in the literature" (Craig, Fisher & Dawson 2011).

A similar thread regarding evaluations of such programs was noted earlier by Beekhuyzen, Nielson & von Hellens (2006): "There are many strategies to reverse the downward trend of female participation in information technology education and industry, but to date there has been little evidence of their success. There are many intervention programs aimed at encouraging women and girls into the IT industry, and supporting them in their IT work. There is also a large body of research discussing the reasons for declining female participation in the industry. However, to a large extent, these two domains still operate independently… The intervention programs may appear piecemeal but this approach may be more effective when dealing with a fragmented and dynamic industry."

These comments represent an emerging theme in the published literature that generally the success of intervention events has not been evaluated (Beekhuyzen et al., 2006; Craig, Lang & Fisher, 2008; Craig et al., 2011). However I argue that the real issue regarding evaluation is more about the differing expectations of academic researchers versus the industry participants and association leaders who manage the events. Whereas academic researchers understandably like to see formal publication of results, organizations running the events generally wish to evaluate their programs but have little incentive or resources to publish the results. In my experience across a multitude of intervention programs, evaluations have been considered and do exist (Bernhardt, 2001, 2006; Carbone & Sheard, 2001, 2006). There are some basic drivers embedded in the funding and management of intervention programs that provide a motive and mechanism for producing evaluation reports.

For example, in Australia and presumably other countries, when Government funding has been involved in sponsoring an event, evaluating outcomes and reporting against the funds' expenditure is generally a mandatory stage of the process. Similarly, when commercial enterprises support an event the production of a post-event report is usually part of the sponsorship agreement. Additionally, even without such external drivers, the voluntary boards and committees involved tend to craft review/evaluation reports for presentation to their own officeholders and members for post-event analysis, often accompanied by reports on lessons learned. As this material is mostly crafted by voluntary associations it is invisible to the formal publishing world, and in the pre #SocialEra usually exists in "paperwork" form or in private directories, so is not visible via a Web search either.

As such I argue that the real issue with our scorecard is not lack of evaluation (formally published in the literature or not) but is more about what has been evaluated, what have been the measures and what factors were measured against. Typically these have been attendance levels (not necessarily a measure of active participation), amount of funding received and size of the event including how many volunteers participated; and where a common thread has been to consider a large scale event as a success (Craig, Fisher & Lang, 2007). But what really matters is not how many resources were put into it or how many people came, but whether there was any lasting impact or flow-on effects. Unfortunately as noted below there is a lack of longitudinal studies to assess this.

WHAT IS THE END GAME SCORECARD?

A key piece of the historical issue jigsaw is summarized by Beekhuyzen, Nielson & von Hellens (2003): "Structuration theory illuminates two problems in studying female participation in the IT industry. Firstly, to understand the production and reproduction of social structure requires a longitudinal study but the rapid rate of change in the industry including high staff turnover make this difficult. Secondly the rapid rate of change makes it difficult to conceptualize in a meaningful way what constitutes the IT industry."

Formal definitions provided in the literature or by Government organizations do not necessarily reflect the reality of life inside IT. The rapidly changing landscape of technologies and platforms means that jobs that did not exist a short while ago have now come into existence while others have faded out of existence. For example, it is almost unheard of to see a role seeking Cobol skills today, whereas a proliferation of other programming languages that were not around when Cobol was popular are now sought, e.g. Java, Ruby on Rails, and Ajax. And in the near future, skills such as Dart, Go and Fantom are likely to be in demand. Or might disappear. Or both.

It is not all about the programming language though. The example above could be defined as a coder, programmer or analyst role regardless of the tool(s) used. But there are also entirely new segments and roles being carved out as a result of the landscape shifts. Now in 2013 the addition of crowdsourcing experts and social media educators and gurus to organisations' marketing or governance areas is becoming commonplace, whereas in 2010 it was unusual if not unheard of. And as the Internet becomes increasingly just another commodity like electricity, and apps for mobile devices have become cheap and ubiquitous, more and more organisations are moving to the cloud and mobile networking. So it is not just software: even traditional in-house IT hardware jobs are changing radically.

This lack of clarity about what is IT, how it is defined and what roles exist has contributed to hampering the understanding of why women are not attracted to IT. Combined with the lack of longitudinal studies to map the influence and impacts of traditional intervention activities, this has added layers of complexities to the problem. (Structural issues such as industry definition and packaging are covered in Chapter Seven: *Structural Context and Influencing Factors*, in more detail.)

Nevertheless, these issues of clarity and definitions cannot change the underlying facts. They might make it difficult to do longitudinal studies of particular intervention programs, but they don't make the industry-wide statistics any better. They cannot hide the fact that the participation of women in IT, however you define it, is low and falling. As noted by Misa (2010), "Today, fewer women enter computing than anytime in the past 25 years." His collection tells of women programmers, systems analysts, managers, and IT executives who flooded into technology fields in the 1960s and '70s, until "something unprecedented in the history of the professions hit computing in the mid 1980s: not merely did women stop entering computing in large numbers, but the proportion of women studying computing actually began falling – and it has continued to fall, steadily."

Let the Games Begin

In spite of this lack of clarity, for more than three decades passionate academics, educators, industry associations and individuals have put their energies into researching, planning, developing, administering, running, funding, supporting and assessing a plethora of projects and programs (Craig et al., 2011; Suriya & Craig, 2003).

The following Table 1 was presented by Craig et al. (2011: page 4) and, whilst not all-inclusive nor taking into account the new social era, it is indicative of the wide variety of projects and activities that fall under the umbrella of classic women in technology intervention programs. Those for Students may generally be classified under attraction (studies and careers), where Higher Education may be young or mature age students or VET courses. The programs for Women in Industry may be generally classified under promotion and retention categories as well as attraction. Note that some activities in this area may include women from outside the technology industries.

Table 1 runs the gamut from single individuals speaking at schools and universities to enormous IT career days with more than 1,000 girl attendees. The implicit assumption of these styles of intervention events has been that, as a direct result of the short intervention experience, girls' expectations and career plans may shift toward the uptake of information technology. Often this assumption is explicitly stated as the goals or aims of the event, for example Bernhardt (2001) noted that the objectives of the *Real Women - Unreal Jobs* career day/role model event held in 2000 were "having a positive impact on the media and community perceptions regarding women in the IT industry; positively impacting the number of girls entering IT studies; and positively impacting the number of women entering the IT industry."

Yet despite significant efforts across the globe, with the exception of some cultural/ethnic differences outlined in Chapter Ten: *Differences – Industries and Ethnicity*, statistics continue to

Table 1. Intervention programs per participant grouping (from Craig et al., 2011).

School Students	Higher Education Students	Women in Industry
Education initiatives: e.g. changing teaching styles, developing inclusive curricula, single-sex classes, and providing equal access or affirmative action.	Providing support communities, extra or peer tutoring, bridging courses, role models and orientation sessions. Supporting single-sex classes.	Encouraging and supporting women through board readiness programmes and professional development.
Running activities such as "Girls in Computing Days," computing workshops / camps / clubs.	Providing accurate information. Establishing mentoring and telementoring programs.	Creating support communities / social networking, mentoring, telementoring programs.
Raising teacher and/or parental awareness. Providing girls with accurate information.	Improving the curriculum and learning environment. Using pair-programming.	Promotion of workforce strategies and work-family balance.
Profiling successful women.	Scholarship or awards programmes.	Recognition and awards.
Creation of engaging resources such as videos or websites.	Supporting women returnees.	Developing women-only lists.
Mentoring high school students.	Providing gender and ICT courses.	Conferences for women in ICT.

show declining attraction and retention of girls and women in technology studies and careers. Whilst various reports present these statistics in different ways, countries and time periods, the overarching trend is a decline that has been consistently occurring since studies began in 1980. Here are some examples:

- Craig et al. (2011) states "Australian statistics, consistent with those from other western developed nations, indicate that participation levels by women in ICT education and training have been low since the 1980s (DEST, 2002)."
- Ashcraft et al. (2012) summarise the historical research and present statistics.
- Tandon, Pritchard, Savelieva, Smith & Vogt (2012) note "The lack of trained female professionals means that in OECD countries, women now account for less than 20 per cent of ICT specialists... On average, this research found that women accounted for 30 per cent of operations technicians, only 15 per cent of managers and a mere 11 per cent of strategy and planning professionals."
- Chi Onwurah MP's website notes that between 2001 and 2011 the percentage of tech jobs held by women declined from 22% to 17% in the UK (Simmonds, 2013). This kind of statistic is very interesting when overlaid with that decade being one of intense activity of intervention programs.
- Simmonds (2013) noted that after Chi Onwurah wrote to the top ten technology companies in the UK asking how many women they employ and what they are doing to attract more girls into the sector, "Google and Microsoft will not even say how many women they employ ... One company [IBM] did not reply to repeated enquiries."

Based on a review of the literature, industry experience and anecdotal evidence, I take the brave and potentially controversial step of saying that: there has been a massive global failure of significant girl and women in IT programs and projects. They have failed to meet their stated goals of attracting more girls into technology studies and women into technology careers. No activity to date has revealed the secrets of attraction, promotion and retention strategies and the actions required.

This step is brave because I have personally been responsible for designing, sourcing funding, leading, presenting at and advising a significant proportion of Australia-based intervention programs. These include the first documented large scale, industry association managed role model/ career day in Australia, *Real Women, Unreal Jobs* in 2000 (Craig et al., 2008). The IP and lessons learned from that program were passed from WIT (Women in Technology (Qld) – of whom I was the president at that time) to Women are IT in Victoria, and subsequently remoulded into the *Go Girl Go For IT* program that has been running since 2001. Later, under the leadership of AWISE (Australian Women in IT, Science & Engineering) with collaboration from Women are IT, we trademarked the IP for *Go Girl Go For IT* so that under the collaborative umbrella of AWISE, other groups and associations could tap into the IP and run similar events, without needing to start from scratch or duplicate efforts.

Within Queensland the initial WIT *Real Women – Unreal Jobs* event was repeated under its transformation into *Build the Future* and *Pathways to Technology*, and was subsequently remoulded with university representatives into the *Technology Takes You Anywhere* events. Craig et al. (2008, p.6) present statistics of event dates and attendances from 2000-2008 that is an interesting read through some Australian history in this area.

Another significant industry based program I initiated is the *WIT Board Readiness Program*. This program informs and mentors women with technology skills who are on boards or seeking board appointments, and over the course of its history has been successful in placing graduates of the program onto boards. This program was named in 2010 by the EU funded PRActising Gender Equality in Science (PRA.G.E.S.) project as a benchmark project (WIT, 2010).

Additionally, I personally, as a passionate individual activist for women in technology, have undertaken one high profile global and two media-noticed role model intervention projects:

- The controversial Screen Goddess IT Calendar 2007 (www.itgoddess.info) featured sixteen Australian women in IT, posing in famous scenes from movies;
- Doing IT Around the World (www.passionit.info) profiled 36 women across the globe, and included diary entries describing a day in their life in 2008, captured on 11 August (in honour of the date actress Hedy Lamarr was awarded the spread spectrum patent);
- IT's Million $ Babes competition (2007-2008) recognised female technology entrepreneurs who owned organisations earning more than AUD 1 million. This ran for 2 years until with the first global financial crisis I halted the program.

As such this statement of global failure is a self-included, reality-based statement born from practical hands on experience. It comes from consideration of the sphere of influence across a wide field of active involvement spanning 20 years, and taking impacts and outcomes into account.

Labelling the old approach a failure is potentially controversial because the topic alone is highly divisive and so many people have been keenly involved. By the nature of these projects and programs, thousands of passionate believers have been actively engaged in them and many believe that the programs were successful – and I was one of them. Another passionate advocate for women in IT expressed a common view when she said, "I believe that gender based programs have had a significant purpose and that was to raise awareness for the assortment of opportunity available within the IT industry for females and to create an understanding of the benefit diversity can bring to the workforce" (Jenny Barbour, Director, Jenny Barbour IT & Project Recruitment Pty Ltd and co founder of Women are IT {Victoria, South Australia and Western Australia]; personal communication, July 21, 2013). Those things may well have been achieved, but their goal of increasing the number of women in IT remains elusive. Yet belief in the value of the programs persists, despite the lack of objective evidence. People have been holding onto small pieces of anecdotal evidence to claim success, such as:

- "even if it only encourages one person to take up technology studies";
- "look, it changed the life of this person";
- or showing slightly more impact, as reported by Craig (2008): "In 2001 among the 1200 girls who participated in the Go Girl Go For IT event at Monash University was a group of twelve girls from a regional Catholic girls secondary school. Four of these twelve girls now work in the IT industry. Furthermore, two of the four girls participated in the organization of the 2006 Go Girl Go For IT event as they wanted to give other girls the opportunity that they had had in 2001."

Looking at this from the opposite end of the spectrum, Craig et al. (2008) ask "Were the promotional days just not successful or would the number of women selecting IT degrees have been even less without the occurrence of these days?" Unfortunately, in the absence of actual evidence the latter suggestion is just begging the question. The problem is that without evidence, any claims are arbitrary and we would be just as (un)justified proposing the opposite. For example, given the continued declining rates of female participation over the same period as intense intervention programs, we could argue that the intervention programs have in fact contributed to the decline and damaged the situation rather than assisted it.

In reality, facing the uncomfortable truth that something you did full of good intentions and where you put your mind, heart, soul, passion and money into has been declared a failure is, well … uncomfortable. But identifying the reality is more important than avoiding discomfort and controversy. And the fact is that while every individual success is worthwhile, if our only sign of success *is* those few individuals then we have to question whether all the effort required to achieve it has been well spent.

But if we have failed, it naturally raises the questions: Why? What have we been doing wrong? What can we do about it or is it too late? What are the real reasons/causes behind this?

What is Failure and How Do We Measure It?

To explore this further a starting point is the dictionary definition of failure:

1. The condition or fact of not achieving the desired end or ends;
2. An event that does not accomplish its intended purpose (thefreedictionary.com).

In this context the intended purpose of the traditional-style intervention programs run around the world such as those presented in Table 1, i.e. Mentoring, Role Modelling, Career Events, Hands on Sessions, Guest Presentations and Company Visits etc., has been not only to stem the decline in enrolments of girls into ICT studies but to reverse that and increase the number of females entering ICT careers. At the centre of these programs has been a drive to positively influence attraction, promotion and retention.

In the past we have had: WIT, FITT, GIDGITS, CC4G, NCWIT, WIC, AWISE, GKP, ACM-W, IFIP … a veritable acronym nightmare of organisations around the world running a multitude of programs. Tandon et al. (2012) outline the newly created *Girls in ICT Portal* (http://girlsinict.org/), launched in 2012. It has its own impressive list of groups from around the world with associated website links, proving that the "nightmare of organizations is growing and growing": mostly separately and all looking at the same issue, not necessarily connecting to each other, and operating more as a band-aid approach.

In order to understand the scale of the failure it makes logical sense to be able to measure programs against the stated goals/intended purpose. Craig (2008) said "it is always a challenge to measure the success of a program of this type, particularly one run without a central organizational base and by volunteer organizers. Limited sponsorship also meant that funds to conduct a full-scale evaluation of the event were unavailable." Craig's (2008) research argued that having a clear goal for the intervention makes it easier to evaluate its success. The suggestion of including funding for full-scale evaluations is a point worth tagging and ensuring that it carries over to any proposed new approach.

However we can get valuable clues by looking at what we do have. The following examples from the Australian experience are typical.

The *Real Women - Unreal Jobs* one-day event in 2000 was broken into three sections. The morning sessions were aimed at girls in lower secondary school, afternoon sessions at senior secondary and first year university students, with later afternoon sessions for other university students. A total of 825 girls attended over the day. The event was evaluated via a post-event survey completed on the day. A resounding 91% of participants indicated that they received a positive feeling about careers in IT, with 92% noting a positive feeling about women in IT (Bernhardt, 2001). This reflected a short-term attitudinal change that for the organizers fuelled perceptions of success.

Similar short-term attitudinal, feel-good responses were received in evaluation of the *Go Girl Go For IT* 2001 event (Carbone & Sheard, 2001). Similarly for the *Go Girl Go For IT* 2006 event, Carbone & Sheard (2006) report from 1168 student and 118 teacher responses:

- "strong consensus [from the participants] that the event was worthwhile, extremely informative and an exciting experience.
- 63% of the girls stated after the event that they would consider a career in computing
- 34% having considered such a career prior to the event
- 90% of the girls reported that the event gave them a positive feeling about computing
- 56% were interested enough to claim they would investigate more about computing;
- 57% would now consider selecting a computing subject at school."

A similar response pattern is reflected in the March 2006 Role Model event *Go Girl Go For IT* that was held in Perth (Bernhardt, 2006). Results from 938 students and 79 teachers were:

- 93% left the event with a positive feeling about careers in IT;
- Results showed a jump from 53% currently studying IT to 84% intending to include IT studies in the future, as a direct result of the Go Girl Showcase;
- Prior to the *Go Girl* event 33% of the responders were considering a career in IT, while after the event 76% indicated that they would now consider a career in IT.

Supporting these individual evaluations, wider research by Anderson, Lankshear, Courtney & Timms (2006) also indicates that girls who attend these types of intervention programs (large or small) are positively affected. More specifically they were more positive about careers in IT, whether they undertook higher-level IT subjects or not, and were *more likely* to consider enrolling in tertiary IT degree.

When you look more closely at the traditional intervention programs run by researchers or industry groups, you see that whilst each program and project may have its own merits and success at a local level, they can be costly, time consuming and require a vast quantity of volunteer resources and energy. For example, Craig et al. (2008) relate that "a one day 'Girls in Computing' event in 2008 for 1400 secondary school girls was a year in the planning, involving 68 volunteers. Corporate sponsors contributed more than $150,000 AUD in cash and in-kind support." But without the longitudinal studies to know if an immediately post-event "*more likely to*" translates into actual long-term *doing*, we are left not really knowing if all that investment was worthwhile or could have been better applied elsewhere.

In fact what we do know is that despite these local successes captured via comments and "feel good" on the day, there has been a massive failure of these intervention programs to reverse the overall picture of declining participation of women in IT and therefore a failure to accomplish their intended purpose. Due to a lack of longitudinal studies in following the event participants over an extended time span, it is not possible to identify whether such events have a statistical benefit that is swamped by factors in society at large. But we can certainly say that they have failed to measurably affect large-scale trends. It appears that the post-event glow is more a "sugar hit" than a fundamental shift that translates into affirmative action. Or to refer back to Merchant's (2012) #SocialEra Rule 7 that reach and connection are like falling in love: a fun first date doesn't make a marriage.

A clue to why this is so might be found by comparing the above figures with those of Kaskey (2012), who reports similar effects for high school students attending a university career day for accounting: 94% said they gained a better understanding of the field and the percentage considering a career in accounting rose from 27% before the event to 69% after. Yes, immediately after an event that exposes children to a field there is a jump in reported interest. But whether that survives the next interesting experience or even the next week is another question. As is whether much less expensive (in time and money) ways to simply present the options of what is available would achieve much the same results in the long term. It is notable that the event studied by Kaskey (2012) was described as "did not expend considerable time, money and effort" despite achieving similar short-term outcomes as major IT interventions.

These results highlight that short-term measurements of "reactive" interest don't tell us much about the real success of programs in achieving their long-term goals. Perhaps if something similar to Gillian Armstrong's films in the style of the popular "Up Series" had been commissioned, a better picture would be known. In Armstrong's film series she interviews three 14 year old girls then tracks their lives through a 5-part documentary in which they are re-interviewed at 18, 26, 33 and 48 years of age (Sexton, 2010). Imagine the richly detailed data we would have from a similar program with more participants. We revisit that idea later in this publication.

The continued voluminous research proves, and most readers of the publication know from their own awareness and experience, that there is an issue in attracting, retaining and promoting females in technology studies and careers. Yet the decades of interventions have had no measurable effect. I am proposing that in light of that evidence it is time to halt and seriously review the old approach before too many organisations in too many places around the globe continue to repeat the same thing over and over with no more to show for it.

I propose the following small activity to help quickly grasp an indication of financial impacts. If you add up the global spending by all of these projects, programs and research over just the past 5 years, it is likely that the funds and efforts spent would have been enough to establish a major university focused solely on IT courses for women and a corporation to hire them.

Think about it for a minute – consider how much money (including time and effort) governments, industry associations, corporations, educational institutions and volunteers have spent in the past 5 years trying to address this issue. Think of your own experience and multiply that out to your region, state, nation and the world. Then do the exercise again for a 10 year period, a 20 year period and so on.

Here is small calculation based on one of my own experiences.

Bernhardt (2002) presents a 16-page report on the i-STAR (ICT, Skills, Training and Role Model) program, including details from a spreadsheet calculating cash and in kind contributions. More specifically it shows the contributions towards the intervention activities run under the Women to Stars (W2*) program that was designed, managed and implemented by Women in Technology in Queensland, Australia.

The report describes the program as "W2* is about:

1. Providing tools for structured **mentoring**
2. Identifying, skilling and promoting women with ICT skills onto boards - (**board readiness**)
3. Providing a series of **role model** and careers events

The aim was to run mentoring, board readiness and role modelling activities in South East Qld and for rural and regional Queensland."

These activities were explained as:

- **Mentoring:** Development of an online mentoring kit and delivery of training into regional Queensland;
- **Board Readiness:** Awareness raising, skilling and provision of opportunities to board-ready women;
- **Role Modelling:** Visibility of ICT role models to a vast audience in regional Queensland as well as SEQ.

Section 9 of the report (Summary of Success) notes that the activities:

1. Attracted over 1,600 participants – with significant numbers in all streams:
    - *Mentoring: 105 plus more via Web visits and downloads.*
    - *Board Readiness: 365 (possibly more)*
    - *Role Modelling: 1,143 (possibly more)*
2. Reached beyond South East Queensland to regional cities (Rockhampton, Townsville and Cairns)
3. Reached other regional and rural areas via Web and emails.
4. Established a working model for ongoing activities.
5. Left behind tools and guides for ongoing use – e.g. video streaming and mentoring kit.
6. Helped cement that WIT is an organisation of real value that provides opportunities across the State and managed projects in an efficient productive way that delivers results.

Financially the report identifies cash contributions of $25,000 via a state government grant, $7,500 via other sources, and in kind contributions of $115,800. The in kind value was a logically calculated figure detailing the people, specific activities and dates and time spent. The formula used for volunteer time was calculated as 50% of the commercial rate, so in fact is actually lower than the real dollar value. The total W2* figures are shown in Table 2.

Thus the calculation shows an investment of approximately $150,000 across 4 projects driven by one state-based industry association over a few months. If that had been the only activity, with Queensland having approximately 15% of Australia's population it extrapolates to $1M for all of Australia (note that in at least one other state, Victoria, significantly more was spent pro rata in that same year). That gives us a rough and I would say conservative estimate of $5M over five years in Australia, and Australia is tiny compared to the rest of the industrialised world. Here is an example of the magnitude of the spending from the UK. When reporting in 2011 on funding cuts to the UKRC, previously the UK government's lead

Table 2. Dollar Value of W2 Intervention Program*

Program Activity	Cash	In Kind
Regional Tour (hands on activities e.g. robotics)	5,000	21,200
Mentoring	4,500	14,000
Board readiness	5,000	24,000
Role Model ICT Career day	18,000	51,600
Additional		5,000
TOTAL	$32,500	$115,800
GRAND TOTAL - $148,300		

organisation for supporting women in science and engineering, the report identifies that £2.5m annual funding had previously been given to the UKRC (The Engineer, 2011): and that's one organisation in one country.

Additionally, on top of any specific project calculations there are the many hidden costs of volunteer contributions. These are hard to estimate in the absence of records. Fortunately for this exercise, as a passionate activist in this area in 2001 I used a spreadsheet to track my personal volunteer contributions. It recorded how much time I spent on industry associations and intervention programs, such as attending meetings, preparing documentation, generating ideas, designing programs etc. Over a period of a year it calculated out to "giving up" three months of income earning capacity a year along with half of every weekend! Imagine what the size of the total community contribution would be if it was calculated across the thousands of people globally who voluntarily contribute to assisting women and technology associations and intervention programs.

Between direct and hidden costs and countries' different wealth and priorities, it is difficult to provide a precise global estimate, but you can see the point. If this were a commercial IT project and that many millions of dollars had been invested *without even coming close to achieving the stated aim* despite sincere and extended efforts: it would be called not only a failure but a catastrophe. If the CEO responsible assured you that despite no measurable increase in sales it had been a great success because of all the free samples given away, the favourable PR and the number of Facebook "Likes" – would you nod your head, or have her head?

If you are involved in organising or funding/supporting such traditional intervention programs, I ask you this: when has it ever been acceptable for a project to continue to fail to deliver year after year, milestone after milestone, country after country? It is not that the people involved are to blame – because it *is* year after year, country after country. So it has to be a fundamental flaw in the attempt itself.

Another factor to consider here is that anecdotally there seems to be a significant rate of "burnout" among the dedicated volunteers. This is reflected in the following comments made from personal interviews:

Speaking personally, my burn out occurred after I'd been involved with programs for over 12 years. I think the reason for this, is the absence of motivation as the number of female University admissions to IT, Science or Engineering have remained static. Speaking with colleagues, my feelings are shared. Fortunately there's always more wonderful passionate women who are keen to try to change this situation!! (Madeleine Sanders: co-founder of Women are IT [Victoria, South Australia, Western Australia] founding board member Australian Women in IT, Science and

Engineering [AWISE], personal communication, August 12, 2013).

I would not say burn out more likely Disillusionment (Barbara Tobin: Industry participant, former President of Queensland's Women in Technology [WiT], former Chair of Australian Women in IT, Science and Engineering [AWISE], personal communication, August 5, 2013).

The result is spikes of activity driven over a few years by individuals who then drop out, to be replaced by fresh-faced new victims. Anecdotally this appears to be due to a mixture of burn-out and personal reasons. Whatever the reasons, the result is that too often the knowledge and lessons learned go with them. Then a new crop of passionate volunteers begins almost from scratch and the pattern is repeated. Even if the organisation they belong to ran programs in the past, with the changes in people there may be no "institutional memory" and the new crop have no knowledge at all of the prior work and efforts. They feel it is a new issue they are attempting to address, and they fall into the same traps.

If addressing the low and declining rate of girls in technology studies and women in IT careers was a business, it would have been declared bankrupt years ago or the "product line" would have been discontinued: it just does not make commercial sense. As the objective measurable results currently stand it does not stack up!

Yet we keep doing it... Why?

My answer is because we who do it so passionately believe in what we are doing that we are blind to the facts and do not see the failures.

We need to take on board what Albert Einstein is rumoured to have said: "Insanity is doing the same thing over and over again – and expecting different results." Instead of staying in a cycle of doing the same thing using the same old approach over and over, for little impact and actually a reduced sphere of influence, we need to analyse this to find out what has worked and more importantly what has not and why, so that we can work out a pathway for the future. Given that many women do choose careers in IT but we feel the numbers are too low: why did the ones who are in IT choose it, and what can we learn from them? In other words, if we have learnt nothing from our failures what can we learn from the successes?

In order to understand what leads women into IT and the impact of the old approach, in July 2013 I polled 119 women with technology careers and asked 4 questions about what influenced their decisions and 3 biographical data questions. The survey was an opt-in, online survey posted to limited social media sites for approximately one week. The questions are listed below with the analysis of the results.

SNAPSHOT POLL RESULTS

The chief purpose of the poll was to capture key influencing aspects on women in IT, including intervention programs. The survey included an explanation of intervention programs being "like career days, role modelling or mentoring events specifically (in whole or in part) seeking to interest girls and women in IT careers."

Although responders were opt-in not randomised, I believe that the known weakness of opt-in polls was not a real disadvantage in this case: the people most likely to respond were women in IT who care about the question, i.e. the target audience. In addition, their responses on the things they expect would be effective (Figure 6) strongly indicate that there was no strong "anti-interventionist" bias in the sample.

Biographical information is summarized in Figures 1 and 2. The commonest age group was 25-35 (42%) and the majority of survey participants were from Australia/NZ (62%) – presumably as the survey was sent out via social media networks (Google+, Facebook, Twitter and LinkedIn) where most of my primary contacts are Australian.

Figure 1. Snapshot poll: Demographics

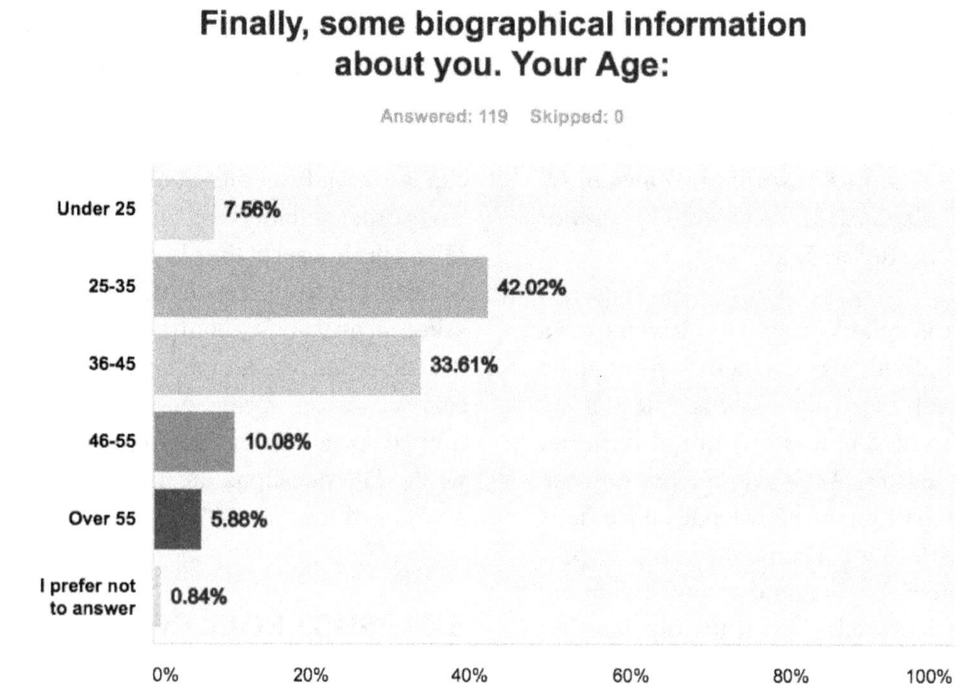

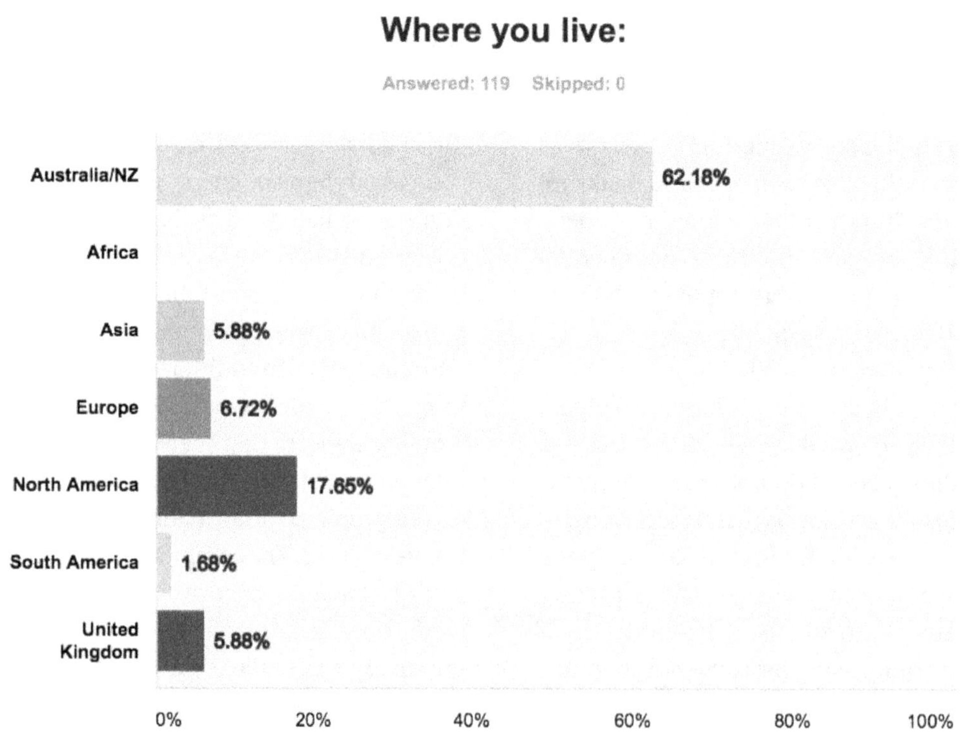

Figure 2. Snapshot poll: IT career classification

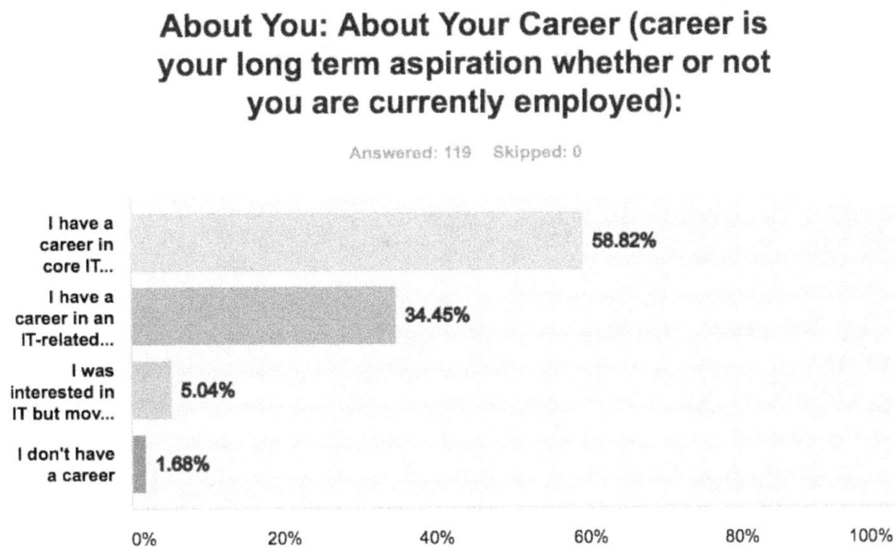

It is worth noting the career breakdown of the responders (Figure 2). A majority was in "hard" roles, with 59% self-identifying with core IT (programmer, analyst, architect) versus 35% identifying with IT-related "soft" roles (e.g. Web or graphics, IT project manager, support or marketing).

When asked specifically about their experiences of intervention programs (Figure 3), almost 80% of those who were currently engaged in technology careers were never offered one or had never heard of them. Only 6% replied that attending an intervention program was the critical factor in their having a career in IT, about equally split between the hard and soft classifications. This does confirm some success of these programs, though we cannot say to what extent it would hold in a randomised sample. Nor, given the findings of Kaskey (2012), can we say it represents a better result than simply presenting IT as a career in more generic career programs.

Note that the true percentage is probably higher than 80%, as 8% of responders skipped this question. While their reasons are unknown, it seems more likely that they would skip the question because they had no knowledge of intervention programs and it did not seem relevant to them, rather than they had experience but chose not to answer.

The responses show a marked trend. While the survey was a snapshot poll and as such must be interpreted with caution, its results are consistent with the extensive research conducted by Lyons et al. (2012), which found "while a number of dedicated 'Girls in STEM' type outreach programs have been operating in Australia, only around 1% of the 1565 females in this study recalled having participated in one of these." Thus given the comparatively low number of women in IT and the very high percentage of them who report no intervention involvement, it is fair to extrapolate that: *The great majority of women who take up IT careers do so without any formal intervention.*

Comments to the question show mixed thoughts about intervention programs, from very positive through neutral to very negative:

Figure 3. Snapshot poll: Experience of intervention programs

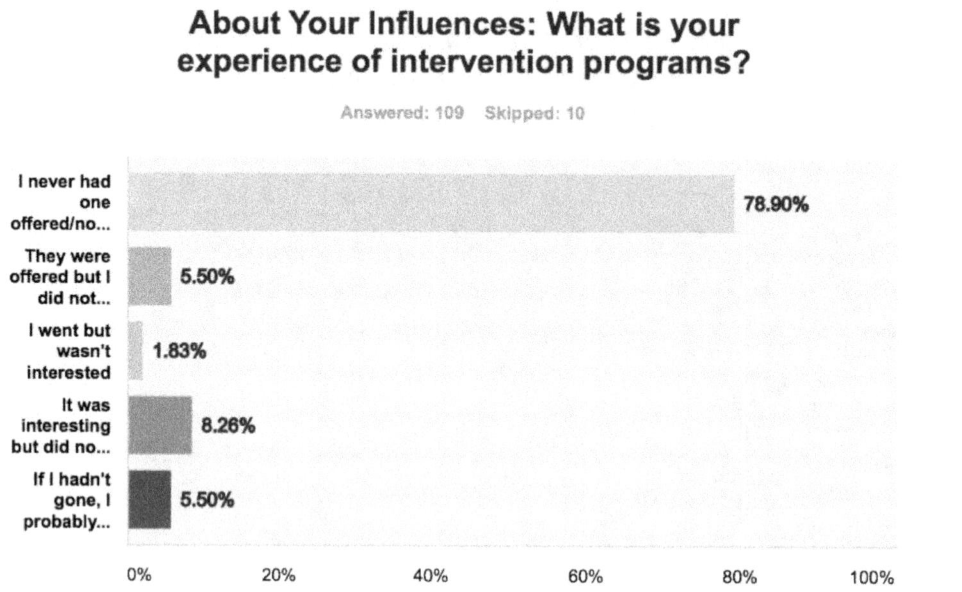

Answer Choices	Responses	
I never had one offered/no idea what this is	78.90%	86
They were offered but I did not attend	5.50%	6
I went but wasn't interested	1.83%	2
It was interesting but did not encourage me into IT	8.26%	9
If I hadn't gone, I probably would not be in IT	5.50%	6
Total		109

- I have actually participated in Technology Takes You Anywhere as a class-led instructor.
- I have only attended one of these recently, after already solidifying my IT career.
- Living in London for 12 months, turned 18, decided to leave home, college, get a job and be independent. I must have trusted my Maths lecturer. I kept his note, saying, 'you want to be a trainee computer operator', and 3 weeks later, after an aptitude test, I landed a great job with a major stock broker. I had no idea what a computer looked like. This was in the era of mainframes, being an IBM 370/135. How lucky I was to have someone believe in me.
- Scholarship for mathematically gifted women. Was only exposed to programming as part of my minor, which I changed to a major. Otherwise, I only had my first computer after I graduated – due to economic barriers.
- Have attended and participated, but didn't influence my ongoing interest in IT one way or the other
- What kind of Intervention???

Figure 4. Snapshot poll: Timing of interest in IT

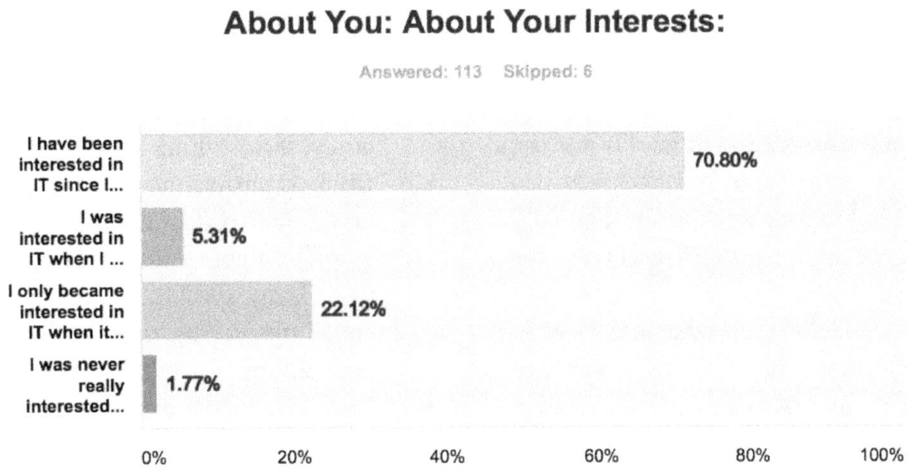

Answer Choices	Responses	
I have been interested in IT since I was young	70.80%	80
I was interested in IT when I was young but lost interest	5.31%	6
I only became interested in IT when it became part of my job	22.12%	25
I was never really interested in IT	1.77%	2
Total		113

- See above. I've experienced them in the physical sciences but have a low opinion of them.
- I went to a general women in non-traditional careers day in late high school but the focus was engineering and architecture
- I choose the IT way earlier (4th grade) and the intervention programs didn't affect me.
- There might have been some around, but I never heard about them.
- I have attended two, and THEY WERE ABSOLUTE CRAP. One was run by a bunch of young girls and transgendered individuals who sneered at me for being in social media and trying to learn to code. I've tried to teach myself to code at home using Code Academy but it was boring as hell. I want a women's "learn to code" camp. I want pathways into retraining as an adult and parent.
- I went to a computer camp (not just for girls) when I was 15. It greatly increased my interest in computers/coding and introduced me to like minded people many of whom I subsequently studied with at uni.
- I was part of the technical jobs for women program which gave women training for jobs where there were less than 30% women in those jobs. Was given 8 weeks full tilt advanced programming training and provided with a job. LOVED IT.
- My best friend's sisters were in IT and I loved to hear her stories about how her sisters made applications and thought it was really cool and awesome and that was when I decided to study IT

- Being mentored but a female IT project management guru made me realise I could do anything in IT – all skills are transferrable in Project Management.

The next question asked about IT interest (Figure 4). More than 70% responded they had been interested in IT since a young age, and 22% stated they only became interested when IT became part of their job.

When you overlay this response and those to the previous question (Figure 3) you are able to infer that those women who are in IT careers are there because: *They have always known they liked technology or they discovered (by an accident of their job) they liked IT.* Gaining interest by an accident of one's job is also noted by Liston, Peterson & Ragan (2008), who reported that within their survey "Almost 29% of respondents said they became interested in IT either when they entered the workforce or were working in another job." Again this is consistent with the extensive survey by Lyons et al. (2012), which clearly showed that "interest in the subject" was the highest-ranking "very important" and "important" response among experiences in choosing a STEM course. In fact in a graph depicting the most common reasons students gave about choosing their STEM course, personal interest scored so highly that the graph scale had to be broken so other factors could be seen clearly.

Comments posted for this question expand the interest areas further and are reflective of early interest or accidental job discovery:

- I interested in IT when I have to choose a career at University.
- Then a boss offered to pay for PHP classes so I could take on work we were giving to contractors and I got back into it.
- I'm 54 so IT for me included electronics, since the only thing generally available in the 70's was mainframe-ish.
- My interest waxed and waned a little over the course of my life. But, once I got to high school and suddenly found the IT classes easy, and found an interest in VB, our career adviser urged me to look into IT courses. Best thing ever!!!
- My Dad pushed me to get into IT but I never wanted to, feeling it wasn't something girls did. I got to university and when I had to pick my specialisation of engineering I ended up picking one I had never considered before.
- I was put off IT early by some comments from peers who saw it as not as important as hard science or engineering. Came back to it in my 30's.
- IT wasn't really a big field when I was young. Computers were still all mainframes, used by mathematicians and bankers.
- I've been seconded from time to time to help with testing of new systems (business area testing) and do a bit of level 1 tech support for various systems for colleagues and external customers.
- IT as a career was relatively new in the late eighties as a career option that was openly discussed.
- Interested since young, but never encouraged to enter the field
- I became interested in IT at university
- Loved my job in IT but moved on as 12 hour days were not sustainable with young children.
- I became interested with the first computer at home when I was about 18.

Then we asked about the primary and secondary influencers on their own choice to pursue or reject a career in IT (Figure 5). Personal interest was the highest rated as both primary (54%) and secondary (33%) influence followed by an accident of history, again both as primary (24%) and secondary (22%) influence.

Figure 5. Snapshot poll: Primary and secondary stimuli for IT careers

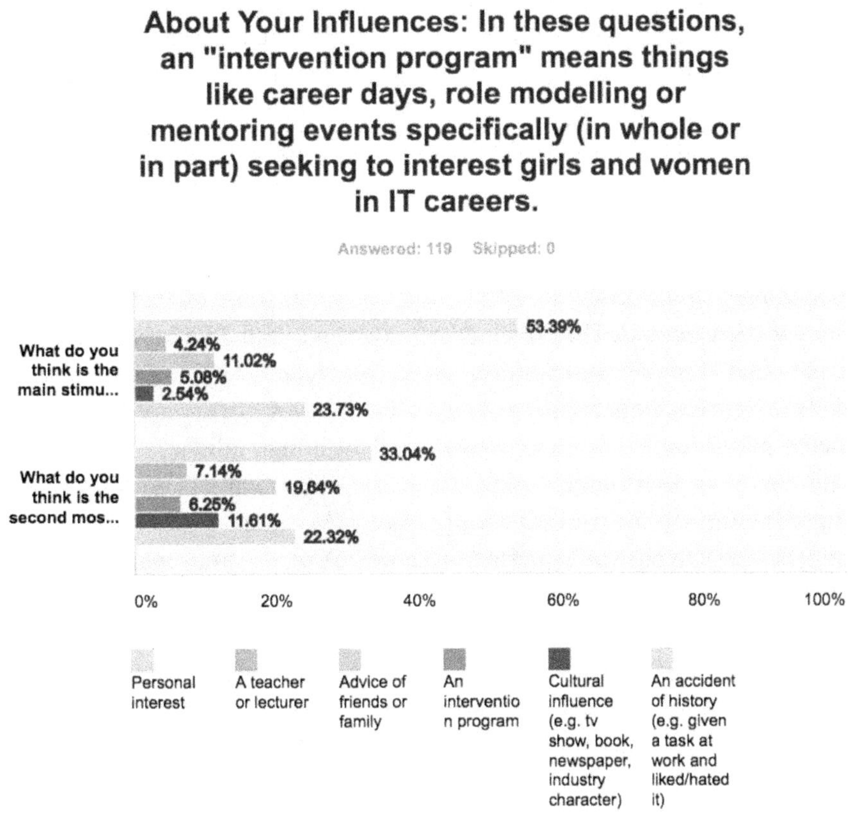

	Personal interest	A teacher or lecturer	Advice of friends or family	An intervention program	Cultural influence (e.g. tv show, book, newspaper, industry character)	An accident of history (e.g. given a task at work and liked/hated it)	Total
What do you think is the main stimulus that made you choose or reject a career in IT?	53.39% 63	4.24% 5	11.02% 13	5.08% 6	2.54% 3	23.73% 28	118
What do you think is the second most important stimulus that made you choose or reject a career in IT?	33.04% 37	7.14% 8	19.64% 22	6.25% 7	11.61% 13	22.32% 25	112

"Accident of history" may be equated to the "happenstance" defined by Hodkinson & Sparkes (1997). As such these results are consistent with results by Lang, Craig, Fisher, Bennetts, & Forgasz (2010), where it is also reported that key reasons were personal choice (always knew, influence of parents) followed by happenstance.

These results clearly support the inference made earlier that: *Most women in IT have always known they liked technology or they discovered (by an accident of their job) they liked IT.* The broader implication of this is that stopping intervention programs is unlikely to have any impact (negative or positive) beyond a minor level.

On the question of why there aren't more women in IT, former Premier of Tasmania David Bartlett (2013) suggested, "Maybe in order to find better solutions to these challenges, the industry should at least ask the people who should know: The women in ICT." It is telling that when you do ask them, their answer is that personal interest is the key and interventions just a side-show.

Comments at this question include a strong thread of individual experience and interpretation of that experience. It is interesting that these two questions resulted in the most comments:

- Took mandatory programming subject as part of soft IT degree, was surprised I enjoyed it, switched to Software Development degree.
- Influence of my Mother, who had a career in IT starting in the late 60s.
- A previous manager suggested I look into a career in IT. I was working as a Customer Service Officer.
- Two things – there will always be IT jobs (it was a fairly new field back in the early 90s) and realising that it was going to be evolving and so continue to be interesting – forcing me to keep learning.
- The first answers why I chose an IT related career, the second why I haven't chosen it earlier in my life (+my mom worked in IT and spent a lot of time on the computer so I guess I resented "it")
- We maintained a BBS in high school (my mom and I were sysops with some of my friends), but I went into journalism instead based on my personal interests. It was the accident of history that got me back.
- I have mostly worked in healthcare IT, which seems to support women in IT more than some other industries.
- We had IT classes at school and I loved them. IT came easy to me...
- I was always mechanically inclined, even though I did an Arts degree. I don't see different careers with a gendered view
- My father
- Video games were what got me interested in IT, then later the Internet. I wanted to learn all about how it worked.
- the Money! you know the rulez
- I'm a science fiction geek.
- I don't like intervention programs. I experienced a few for science and they were annoying. Focusing on gender generally annoys me.
- My father works in IT and we had computers around our house from an early age, before many other classmates. I started university in 2000 and having had at least 5 years access to the Internet and computers beforehand made a huge impact on how comfortable I was around technology.
- My Mom worked in I.T.!
- I had excelled at IT at the secondary level but found tertiary studies more difficult and less interesting.
- Wikileaks releases. I began releasing how important tech was and began a program of re-education
- There was never any other influence, which is why it took me a while to pursue that.
- It puts food on the table.

The results are also consistent with Liston et al.'s (2008) findings where it is reported that respondents were asked to indicate IT-related experiences they had during the elementary, middle school, and/or high school years. Overall, the most common experiences across age levels were access to a computer at school, playing computer games or video games, and support or encouragement from parents. The least common experiences overall were attending a job fair, having a role model and having a mentor.

Having identified their own influences, respondents were asked what they thought would most influence *other* women to enter IT careers both now and in the future (Figure 6). The responses are interesting and indicate a belief in a future trend towards social media activity becoming a key factor.

Despite a low personal involvement in intervention programs amongst the survey participants (Figure 3), 44% believe they are a top motivator for other women now and 61% believe they will be in the future. Knowing someone in the industry is the top factor identified overall at 61% for now and 56% for future. Social media, however, is considered a key influencer now by only 39% but rises to 63%, the top score, for expected future influences. Personally knowing someone in the industry is outside our control, but taking the other two top scorers at face value suggests that combining the two may be a way forward: that is, delivering "interventions" via social media. This supports the thrust of this publication and the adoption of the #SocialEra paradigm.

However it is fascinating that comparing Figures 5 and 6 reveals a starkly opposite trend from how people usually interpret their own motivations versus other people's. "The actor-observer bias is a term in social psychology that refers to a tendency to attribute one's own actions to external causes, while attributing other people's behaviours to internal causes. Essentially, people tend to make different attributions depending upon whether they are the actor or the observer in a situation" (Cherry, 2013). Yet in this survey, whilst an overwhelming majority name personal interest as their own motivator, the great majority think external influences are and will be much more important for other people. Extrapolating this a leap further might this explain why passionate people plan and run intervention programs: they themselves got into the industry due to internal factors and love it, however feel that external influences are required for others?

Comments to this question reveal that strong passions are felt, different people report wildly different experiences, and again they interpret their experiences in different ways. Where one respondent writes "I liked the 'wow, you're a girl and you can program!?' reactions," another comments on the importance of "not having gender unfriendly experiences in the field. Even when I was studying comp-sci, there were boys telling me I shouldn't be there because I'm female." The comments made were:

- It would need to be de-mystified somehow, and at the same time, made less 'brand geek'. Girls don't necessarily get enough exposure to figure out there are plenty of 'normal' people in the IT industry too. Also, the benefits are not widely understood – the flexibility of having multiple different careers and still stay in 'IT' and the flexibility of taking part time PM jobs while that is appropriate to support personal life etc – how many other careers allow for that?
- Changing discourse in society in general and in schools in particular. Teachers' approach to girls in science and IT is important, though I haven't decided what I think about girls-only classes.
- Different girls will find different influences effective.
- I hate to say it, but because of the now early (grade school) and broad influence of Internet porn on young men, it is

Figure 6. Snapshot poll: Present and future influences on others to enter IT careers

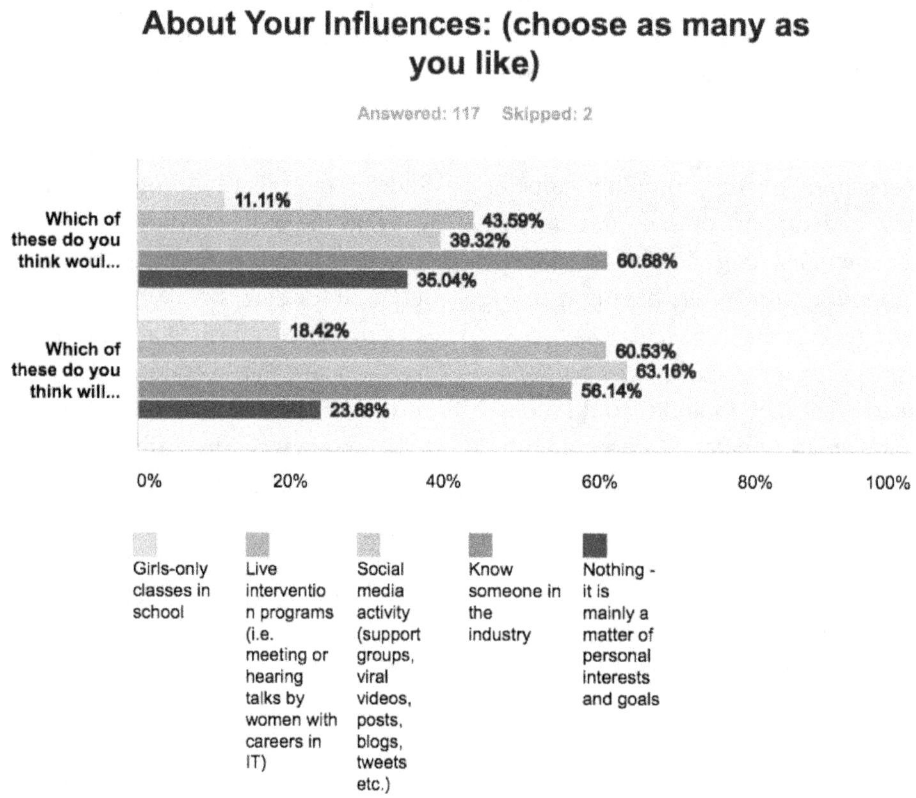

	Girls-only classes in school	Live intervention programs (i.e. meeting or hearing talks by women with careers in IT)	Social media activity (support groups, viral videos, posts, blogs, tweets etc.)	Know someone in the industry	Nothing - it is mainly a matter of personal interests and goals	Total Respondents
Which of these do you think would most influence someone like you to choose a career in IT?	11.11% 13	43.59% 51	39.32% 46	60.68% 71	35.04% 41	117
Which of these do you think will be influences for females in future generations to choose a career in IT?	18.42% 21	60.53% 69	63.16% 72	56.14% 64	23.68% 27	114

very, very difficult for boys to see girls as equals and peers. It is not the boys' fault, so much as it is a blindness to the power of high speed Internet porn (and I don't mean playboy or penthouse magazines) to derail/warp a boys natural relationship with real girls. I currently volunteer as an admin on a site that helps boys and men break up with Internet porn, and rediscover their natural relationships with women. It is www.yourbrainonporn.com. I was the only female in my high school computer/ electronics classes, and I was treated as a peer. Only once do I recall a situation that called out the fact that I was female, and that was when I beat someone at chess, and he said he couldn't believe he was beaten by a girl. Today, a girl will not generally be treated as a peer by boys, so separated classes seem to be the only option.

- I think the media helps too - IT isn't seen as something that has the 'nerd' tag attached. It's cool now and now that IT is everywhere, grads can do millions of things with the one degree. They can almost pick a secondary interest - if you want to work in fashion, you can build websites for fashion companies, you can run the online store, the possibilities are endless!!!
- My career accelerated, I enjoyed 20 years developing and managing banking software. In my case, my experience grew with the encouragement, support and respect of my colleagues, always men, I was the odd one out.
- As always the money
- I think there is a dumbing down of our school curriculum content, and lowering of expectations with respect to Science, Technology, Engineering and Mathematics (STEM). There's this idea that "I'll go into business" or ."..into PR" or whatever; and that somehow that will not require technical skills; therefore there is no importance for STEM related skills in school. This is for rich kids and poor kids alike. Compounding this dumbing down is the echo chamber effect of modern mass media: idiotic sound bites about hackers or climate change computer models get traction over complex truths, and therefore seem to win out to younger less critical ears. The industry and conservatively funded science denial programs, like the Heartland Institute are just the source, its mass media that makes such a message possible. It's perceived that someone's work in professions in which the goals products are complex, and subtle artefacts like computer programs, technical designs or experimental research do not produce anything tangible or worthwhile; at least not worthwhile compared to what is portrayed on TV as "success." It's a trend that educators & teachers, professional bodies and various other organisations are fighting. I'm a member of the NCSE for example, and there are many others in STEM working to combat this trend. Unfortunately for young women, especially in their teens these messages get more traction than they ought to. So you're combating not just "computing is for nerds"; there is also "it's for lefty subversive nerds." Many causes dear to the hearts of technology workers are at the liberal end of the political spectrum and this is scaring away young people, and especially women who are brought up to not rock the boat.
- Removing social stigma about "proper" careers/education.
- Science Fiction
- I picked intervention and social over knowing someone as these are the mechanisms to get to know someone
- I don't think talks about the industry will help, I think getting people to actually experience what being in the industry is like

by performing similar tasks and learning computer science and not how to use MS Word...

- Reducing sexism in classes at high school. I was the only girl in a group of students learning up program in grade 9. It was horrific. They boys behaved like shits. Hire more female teachers. Have after school code clubs aimed only at girls in Australia. Have women only classes teaching programming as TAFE electives. And KILL THE ADA INITIATIVE. IT DISCRIMINATES BETWEEN WOMEN, IT FORCES ITS OWN AGENDAS ON WOMEN. ADA INITIATIVE DOES NOT WELCOME WOMEN INTO TECH, IT CREATES COLLECTIVES OF GATE KEEPERS. ADA INITIATIVE WAS MY WORST EXPERIENCE EVER OF WOMEN "ENCOURAGING" WOMEN IN TECH.
- Better teaching of practical applications of IT during primary and high school years.
- Not having gender unfriendly experiences in the field. Even when I was studying comp-sci, there were boys telling me I shouldn't be there because I'm female.
- Contrary to common perception, I liked the "wow, you're a girl and you can program!?" reactions. So an opposite to the Girls-only classes but 9-1 boy-girl ratio worked for me.
- I don't think girls only classes are useful because you want to be competitive in a real world situation. Girls only classes shelter the girls from who their competitors are and they need to be prepared for that and driven to be better.

RECENT INTERVENTION PROGRAMS

As someone with a deep history in this field, I can see patterns and mistakes from the past reappearing (such as individuals cropping up and executing ideas without prior knowledge of the research and theories or other attempts). Lessons are not being learnt swiftly enough nor being applied. Despite a plethora of organisations and individuals well experienced in this field and a library of historical research, there are many, many new "splinter style" groups and individuals continuing to crop up, all with similar if not the same aims and purposes. No doubt the below examples were created out of burning passions and are well intended and seemingly impressively executed. In addition they have the advantage of being able to capitalise on aspects of #SocialEra. Yet to me and I expect others from past decades, these activities already induce feelings of *déjà vu*:

- In reporting on the IT industry's image and impact on women, Cave (2012) writes, "Belinda Parmar, founder of Lady Geek, has attempted to tackle this image crisis head on with this month's launch of Little Miss Geek. Her aim, as her website states, is: to do for the tech industry what Jamie Oliver did for school dinners; to realign attitudes from the ground up and bring about nationwide change. We want to inspire the next generation of young girls to become tech pioneers."
- Beekhuyzen (2013), through a "tech girls movement" Kickstarter project, seeks to "challenge the stereotype of the typical IT nerd" by creating "positive contemporary archetypes." Ironically the "superhero" archetypes – Sophisticate, Explorer, Creator, Tomboy and Rebel – are themselves stereotypes, albeit perceived to be more positive. This initiative follows on from Beekhuyzen's earlier release in 2008

of "The Pink Book," *Tech Girls are Chic – Not Just Geek*, that was distributed, mostly free, to 20,000 Australian schoolgirls.

- Fried (2013) reports "it's quite common to hear a room full of older techies talking about the need to get more girls interested in computers. But in Munich this week, it was a pair of 20-year-old college students who were urging older women to add coding to their repertoire. By doing so, the pair said, today's working women can serve as role models and better mentor the next generation. Ayna Agarwal and Ellora Israni, the founders of She++, made the entreaty as part of a talk they gave on Tuesday 16 July at the DLDwomen conference in Munich. The pair have been on a mission to boost the number of women coders. Their next step will come on Monday 23 July, as they make their film "She++: The Documentary" publicly available. The film has already been screened more than 100 times, translated into five languages and shown in a dozen countries."
- Girls in ICT Portal (http://girlsinict.org/) was launched in 2012 (Tandon et al., 2012). This site profiles role models, promotes International Girls in ICT Day (held on the 4th Thursday in April each year), includes tool kits on how to organise a girls in ICT day and points to a wide variety of information and resources. The site video (http://www.youtube.com/watch?v=r5rXOSDmDJU) explaining ICT Girls Day in 2012 states that 1,300 projects were held in nearly 90 countries with 30,000 girls attending: scarily repeating issues of the past in using pure attendance as a measure of success.

That could have been me, fifteen years ago. It *was* me, fifteen years ago – along with many others. But as we have seen, there hasn't been much to show for it. Sure, we made friends and we helped each other socially and in our careers, but all the thousands of hours of intense volunteer work and money spent to encourage other women into IT have left us with little to show for it in terms of our primary goal.

An interesting non-*déjà vu*, new style intervention is the *Addressing Gender Barriers in STEM through Theatre of Social Engagement* project. Run by Elieen Trauth, it involves a stage play set in New Jersey. The play *iDream* centres around three girls of different ethnic backgrounds who are approaching the end of their high school careers. In their senior year, they enrol in a course called Digital Design, in which they are encouraged and challenged by their teacher to explore careers in the IT field. As reported by Koons (2012), "Trauth decided that the best way to bring her message to the public would be to write and produce a play that communicates, in dramatic fashion, research results about barriers to women in the IT field. 'I was frustrated with the limits of the (academic publishing) medium… The play has two audiences. It was written to increase awareness among teenagers and young adults about opportunities and barriers with respect to the information technology field. But it also speaks to adults – parents, teachers and advisors – about the importance of role models and mentors who can help young people navigate the challenges presented to them as they pursue their dreams.'" A key goal of the play is to help people become aware of the subtle barriers that exist in our society, ones that are often unconsciously internalized, that hold young people back. It's about engaging students in thinking about college and careers in science and technology and awakening them to the possibility of creating their own individual dreams – and acting on them. The website describes it as "drawing from life history interviews conducted as a part of the research, the storyline of the dramatic play is used to communicate the findings from [Trauth's] work which resulted in a theory about gender and IT to explain and predict gender (under)representation in IT fields. The play dramatizes constructs of the theory, particularly the ways in which gender, ethnicity, and class affect identity and career and life decisions." Of special interest here is not only the imaginative way of publicising research findings via a dramatic medium but the role of the individuals in the play and the interplay of their individual characteristics.

My findings, supported by more extensive and formal research, reveal that such individual choice is what truly lies at the core of this issue. And it is not intervention programs that are tapping into it. In a sense this implies they are "too little, too late": but that itself implies that in terms of broad societal factors (at least in Western nations), *they aren't necessary*. Most women in IT are there because they already knew they were interested; most of the rest are there because they discovered their interest in the workplace. Very few are then netted because of intervention programs. Those facts give the lie to the idea that there is a society-wide problem causing the under-representation of women in IT, which needs addressing by forceful action. Instead they indicate that the information and opportunities already present are pervasive enough that for most women who would choose IT careers under ideal conditions: the conditions are already there.

Obviously there are other context layers (cultural, social and structural) and their associated factors (enhancers and/or inhibitors), but the core central issue is individual choice and the primary driving issues of innate interest and talent. That a small number of women have been attracted via intervention programs does show that real barriers remain. But those numbers are so small that overcoming them can be done far more effectively via the disruptive technologies, platforms and tools of #SocialIT than by continuing what we've been doing for decades without measurable success.

There is ongoing interest in the question of women in IT, with many new programs recently announced or being planned. But #SocialIT is bringing a fundamental shift. If governments, policy makers, recruiters, organisations, activity sponsors, fund sources, industry associations and women in technology still believe in interventions, at least it is time to stop repeating the same thing and expecting different results. Now is the time to accept the disruptive changes that are occurring and adjust accordingly.

Those past interventions and their recent reincarnations did not occur in a vacuum, but in the context of identifying a problem and its possible solutions. In the next chapter we examine the popular conceptual, theoretical and empirical theories that have been proposed to explain the dearth of women in IT.

REFERENCES

Anderson, N., Lankshear, C., Courtney, L., & Timms, C. (2006). Girls and ICT survey: Initial findings. *Curriculum Leadership, 4*(12).

Ashcraft, C., Eger, E., & Friend, M. (2012). Girls in IT: The facts. Boulder, CO: National Centre for Women & Information Technology (NCWIT).

Bartlett, D. (2013, September 30). ICT's masculine identity. *CIO*. Retrieved October 1, 2013, from http://www.cio.com.au/blog/comfort-zone/2013/09/30/icts-masculine-identity/

Beekhuyzen, J. (2013). *Tech girls are superheroes.* [Video]. Retrieved November 15, 2013, from http://www.kickstarter.com/projects/1891407856/tech-girls-are-superheroes

Beekhuyzen, J., Nielsen, S., & von Hellens, L. (2003). Challenging dualisms in female perceptions of IT work. *Australian Journal of Information Systems*, *10*(2), 105–114.

Beekhuyzen, J., Nielsen, S., & von Hellens, L. (2006). *Making IT fit: Research and action in Queensland.* Paper presented at the AusWIT Australian Women in IT Conference. Adelaide, Australia.

Bernhardt, S. (2001). *WIT real women unreal jobs: Post event analysis report.* Brisbane, Australia: Unpublished report.

Bernhardt, S. (2002). *ICT skills, training and role model (i-STAR) program: Final report women to stars (W2*.)* Brisbane, Australia: Unpublished Report.

Bernhardt, S. (2006). *Go girl go for IT event analysis.* Paper presented at the ACEC Conference. Cairns, Australia.

BrainyQuote. (2013). *Albert Einstein quotes.* Retrieved August 2, 2013, from http://www.brainyquote.com/quotes/authors/a/albert_einstein.html

Carbone, A., & Sheard, J. (2001). *Go girl, go for IT 2001 expo: Analysis of student and teacher surveys.* Unpublished report.

Carbone, A., & Sheard, J. (2006). *Go girl, go for IT 2006 evaluation report.* Unpublished report.

Cave, K. (2012). Women: Why doesn't IT have iPad appeal? *IDG Connect Business Management.* Retrieved May 22, 2013, from http://www.idgconnect.com/blog-abstract/654/kathryn-cave-global-women-why-doesn-t-it-have-ipad-appeal

Cherry, K. (2013). What is the actor observer bias? *About.com: Psychology.* Retrieved July 21, 2013, from http://psychology.about.com/od/aindex/g/actor-observer.htm

Craig, A. (2008). *Attracting women to computing, a framework for evaluating intervention programs.* (Unpublished doctoral dissertation). Monash University, Melbourne, Australia.

Craig, A., Fisher, J., & Dawson, L. (2011). Women In ICT: Guidelines for evaluating intervention programmes. In *Proceedings of European Conference on Information Systems* (pp. 1-13). Aalto University School of Economics.

Craig, A., Fisher, J., & Lang, C. (2007). ICT and girls: The need for a large scale intervention programme. In *Proceedings of the 18th Australasian Conference on Information Systems* (pp. 761-769). Toowoomba, Australia: University of Southern Queensland.

Craig, A., Lang, C., & Fisher, J. (2008). Twenty years of girls into computing days: Has it been worth the effort? *Journal of Information Technology Education*, *7*(1), 339–353.

DEST. (2002). *Australian selected higher education statistics, table 2: All students with user specified field of study by gender, 1989 to 2000*. Canberra, Australia: Department of Education Science and Training.

DuBow, W. M. (2011). *NCWIT scorecard: A report on the status of women in information technology*. Boulder, CO: NCWIT.

Engineer. (2011). *Decline in government support for women in engineering*. Retrieved August 26, 2013, from http://www.theengineer.co.uk/channels/skills-and-careers/news/decline-in-government-support-for-women-in-engineering/1006869.article

Fried, I. (2013). *Stanford students hope posting documentary online will get more women to code*. Retrieved July 17, 2013, from http://allthingsd.com/20130717/stanford-pair-hopes-posting-documentary-online-will-get-more-women-to-code/

Hodkinson, P., & Sparkes, A. C. (1997). Careership: A sociological theory of career decision making. *British Journal of Sociology of Education, 18*(1), 29-44.

Kaskey, V. (2012). An investigation into a career day on a student's choice of profession. *International Journal of Business and Social Science, 3*(14), 53–58.

Koons, S. (2012). *iDream play encourages young women to consider IT careers*. Retrieved August 2, 2013, from http://ist.psu.edu/news/idream-play-encourages-young-women-to-consider-it-careers

Lang, C., Craig, A., Fisher, J., Bennetts, K., & Forgasz, H. (2010). Dualisms: What women say about working in ICT. In *Proceedings of ACIS 2010*. ACIS.

Liston, C., Peterson, K., & Ragan, V. (2008). *Evaluating promising practices in informal information technology (IT) education for girls: Women in IT—Survey results*. Boulder, CO: National Centre for Women & Information Technology.

Lyons, T., Quinn, F., Rizk, N., Anderson, N., Hubber, P., Kenny, J., et al. (2012). *Starting out in STEM: A study of young men and women in first year science, technology, engineering and mathematics courses*. Armidale, Australia: University of New England. Retrieved August 13, 2013, from http://www.une.edu.au/simerr/pages/projects/132iris_report.pdf

Merchant, N. (2012). 11 rules for creating value in the #SocialEra. Boston, MA: Harvard Business School (HBR Singles).

Misa, T. J. (Ed.). (2010). *Gender codes: Why women are leaving computing*. Hoboken, NJ: John Wiley & Sons. doi:10.1002/9780470619926

Sexton, M. (2010). *Gillian Armstrong meets up with old friends*. Retrieved July 19, 2013, from http://www.abc.net.au/7.30/content/2010/s2903068.htm

Simmonds, M. (2013). *Girls in ICT: Little or no progress in 30 years*. Retrieved July 1, 2013, from http://chionwurahmp.com/2013/04/girls-in-ict-little-or-no-progress-in-30-years/

Suriya, M., & Craig, A. (2003). Gender issues in the career development of IT professionals: A global perspective. In S. Spencer (Ed.), *AusWIT 2003 - Participation, progress and potential* (pp. 97–108). Hobart, Tasmania: University of Tasmania.

Tandon, N., Pritchard, S., Savelieva, V., Smith, G., & Vogt, E. (2012). *A bright future in ICTs opportunities for a new generation of women*. Geneva, Switzerland: International Telecommunication Union.

von Hellens, L., Trauth, E., & Fisher, J. (2012). Editorial. *Information Systems Journal, 22*, 343–353. doi:10.1111/j.1365-2575.2012.00412.x

WIT. (2010). *Women in technology win with board readiness program*. Retrieved July 20, 2013 from http://www.wit.org.au/news/women-in-technology-win-with-board-readiness-program

KEY TERMS AND DEFINITIONS

ACM-W: Association of Computing Machinery – Women in Computing sub group.

AWISE: Australian Women in IT, Science and Engineering.

CC4G: Computer Clubs for Girls (A U.K. based initiative).

FITT: Females in Information Technology and Telecommunications (an Australian based group).

GIDGITS: Girls Into Doing Great IT (an Australian based group).

GKP: Global Knowledge Partnership.

ICT: Information and Communication Technology. Synonymous with IT.

IFIP: International Federation for Information Processing.

i-STAR: ICT, Skills, Training and Role Models (an Australian program).

IT: Information Technology. Synonymous with ICT.

NCWIT: National Centre for Women & Information Technology (a USA based organisation).

#SocialEra: A term (coined by Nilofer Merchant) to describe a shift in focus from traditional methods to a more social movement, which has profound implications for business and how people work and lead.

TAFE: Technical and Further Education.

UKRC: UK Resource Centre.

VET: Vocational Education and Training.

WIC: Women in Computing.

WiT: Women in Technology (a Queensland-Australian based group).

Chapter 4
Popular Theories

ABSTRACT

The issue of women in IT has attracted voluminous research with many theories framing discussions, such as Essentialist Theory, Social Construction Theory, Individual Differences Theory, Structuration Theory, Theory of Reasoned Action, and their resulting Gender Modelling, Leaky Pipeline, Life Course Approach, Critical Mass, and Dualism Models. Key theories are critically examined in this chapter, and it is concluded that not only have no real world benefits ensued, but in some cases the theories themselves may be part of the problem by negatively framing expectations. However, the years of research should not be wasted: rather, the tools of #SocialIT, such as hackfests, should be applied to gain deeper and wider understanding. The new STEMcell Model is most similar to the Life Course approach and within-gender variants of Gender Theory. However, it goes further to identify an individual's interests and talents as more drivers in themselves than something passively shaped by society. External influences and barriers do exist but need to be considered in the context of the individual, not the other way around, and those barriers will be swept away by the tools and effects of #SocialIT.

[We see that] science is eminently perfectible, and that each theory has constantly to give way to a fresh one.

– Jules Verne, A Journey to the Centre of the Earth (Goodreads, 2013)

INTRODUCTION

Without a doubt the topic of attraction, promotion and retention of females in technology has and continues to attract voluminous research over the past decades. von Hellens, Trauth & Fisher (2012) note "Accompanying the increase in volume and visibility of gender and ICT research has come a broadening of the methods used in the conduct of this research. While the 1990s introduced the use of interpretive epistemology for the conduct of gender and ICT research, the 2000s have witnessed the introduction of critical theory into gender and ICT research."

Essentialist Theory, Social Construction Theory, Individual Differences Theory, Structuration Theory, Theory of Reasoned Action and their resulting Gender Modelling, Leaky Pipeline, Life Course Approach, Critical Mass Models and Dualism Models have all been used over time to

DOI: 10.4018/978-1-4666-5860-8.ch004

frame researchers' discussions regarding the lack and decline of females in technology studies and careers. In Chapter Three: *A New Approach*, we discussed the importance in the #SocialIT era of greater engagement between researchers and the wider community. Perhaps we can express the problem in #SocialEra terms as these topics are not "trending on Twitter" and as such are almost invisible to that community.

More specifically, the frequently changing technology landscape makes it difficult for a traditionally developed and distributed research framework to keep up with the rate of change and incorporate the current influencing factors. Technology and industry game changers are introduced that impact the relevancy of a modelled theory. We are in an era where "trending" and following the latest technology craze is fast becoming not only the norm, but the main source of information for society.

There is some discussion in the literature about a disconnect between researchers, their publications and the mainstream public. Of particular interest here is the disconnect between the frameworks and models proposed in the literature and the people who design and implement intervention programs.

The following comments from personal interviews reflect this disconnect:

1. "My feeling is that there could and should be much closer relationships amongst all people involved, and engender a spirit of co-operation. Ideas should be shared and people assisted and encouraged to run/adopt programs. There are too many individual groups running programs in isolation from other groups but sharing the same aims. This leads to duplication of effort (i.e. wasted time and money), replication, and competition for funding which is in short supply. I haven't seen strong on-going relationships with researchers so their valuable information is not leveraged when new initiatives are developed." – Madeleine Sanders; co-founder of Women are IT (Victoria, South Australia, Western Australia) founding board member Australian Women in IT, Science and Engineering (AWISE) (personal communication, August 12, 2013).
2. "I have found Researchers are statistically driven which is necessary for the activists and advocates however there has often been a dis-connect because the advocates and activist are normally at the Coal Face and have a more complete picture." – Barbara Tobin; industry participant, ex President of Women in Technology (WiT) (Qld), ex Chair of Australian Women in IT, Science and Engineering (AWISE) (personal communication, August 5, 2013).

This disconnect is described as being in both directions: "the lack of research on the theoretical grounding of the interventions ... [and] design not being conducted based on being informed by the theoretical understanding of 'the problem' instead of unscientific impressions about the causes" (von Hellens, Trauth & Fisher, 2012). Trauth (2011) explains, "The problem is that there is insufficient scholarly knowledge of the factors that account for women's under representation in the IT field. Further, there is insufficient theoretical understanding of these factors. What we have, instead, is a situation in which generally well intentioned people identify and theorize factors in an ad hoc fashion. That is, since everyone experiences gender, it is commonly thought that rigorous data-driven interventions are unnecessary. This has contributed to a lack of theoretically-informed interventions to address the gender imbalance."

Trauth (2011) says when discussing the nature of research and ties to business and real world issues, "An essential challenge with research that is driven by real-world problems is that the real world doesn't fit neatly into disciplinary categories. Hence, the research is often multidisciplinary and the research literature can be found in many places.

In the case of gender and IT research, the literature can be found in the journals and conferences of disciplines such as: women's studies, psychology, education, information systems and computer science. This brings the challenge of keeping up not only with the increasing number of journals in one's own area (such as information systems) but also the relevant literature that is published in journals and conferences in the other fields. But in doing so, a researcher can encounter another, and potentially more challenging, issue: academic politics. This issue is about what journals, conferences and books are considered to be 'legitimate' in a given discipline. The problem occurs when the definition of legitimate literature is too narrow. This would be manifested by a reward system that recognizes research only when it is published in certain venues or when emerging scholars are taught to look for relevant research only when it appears in certain locations. When this occurs, there is a danger of researchers missing important research, of 'reinventing the wheel' by not sufficiently building upon the full extent of cumulative knowledge. In this digital age there is little excuse for not thoroughly searching for relevant literature; it would only be the construction of 'legitimacy' that would limit inclusion of potentially relevant research." It may be worth noting that this book has gathered research and input not only from traditional published sources, but also by tapping into digital age #SocialIT by referencing other sources such as blogs, YouTube and websites.

von Hellens et al. (2012) discuss the researcher's dilemma and notes that "It could be argued that legitimacy of a research field comes about through publishing activity, the level and quality of research conducted and the generation of models, frameworks and theories. Outcomes of research should contribute to the knowledge base and challenge current thinking." They then ask the question: "How far, therefore, have we come in our research in the women in ICT field? Adam (2002) suggested the 'Lack of citation is one reason for the failure of gender and information systems (IS) research getting anywhere near the mainstream and this may have contributed to the apparent atrophy of this paradigm of research'. She argued that there remains a paucity of reflection and critical thinking on the topic insofar as there is limited reflection on what the outcomes of research mean to the wider community and how the outcomes build on, extend or challenge earlier understandings."

I would stress the implications of that last sentence. Research should not be considered an end in itself whose success is measured by its impact on other research. The true measure of research is its effectiveness in leading to solutions to real-world problems. However the point remains that it cannot achieve that if nobody knows or cares about it. To date there is anecdotal evidence that the vast majority of intervention programs designed by industry associations have been designed without reference to the literature, and instead have been created from the experiences of the volunteers and activists. As pointed out by Trauth (2011), "The plain fact is that there is a tremendous need for theoretically-informed interventions in order to properly address real-world problems. Using the gender example, in the absence of a theoretically guided and methodologically rigorous examination of a gender issue, interventions might be developed that reflect counterproductive gender stereotypes and that end up doing more harm than good. Such an ad hoc approach to interventions does not reflect a systematic and thorough theorizing of the problem. In the absence of research rigor to understand a problem the intervention that is developed to address it runs the risk of being irrelevant."

All is not lost though. The #SocialIT era will enable a way to navigate the disconnect and extend the reach into the mainstream public. And more specifically, reach those passionate, interested groups and individual activists engaging in women and technology activities. Then the valuable past research can achieve its potential to enhance reflection and critical thinking, and become an important part of the design of activity programs in the future. How we might do this is discussed later in this chapter. But first, we will review the major models that have come out of the extensive research of the past.

STEM THE LEAK

On 25 July 2013, the UK Government Commons Select Committee posted on the parliament.uk website: "The 'leaky pipeline' is sometimes used to describe the continuous loss of women at consecutive career stages within Science, Technology, Engineering and Mathematics (STEM). These gradual losses reduce the numbers of women retained in STEM further education and work. More young people of both genders are now studying STEM subjects up to GCSE but female participation starts dropping off at A-level. Climbing up the academic career ladder, women are increasingly underrepresented in STEM."

The Science and Technology Committee has agreed to hold an inquiry into women in academic STEM careers, and the web post sought submissions on:

- "Why do numbers of women in STEM academic careers decline further up the career ladder?
- When women leave academia, what careers do they transition into? What are the consequences of scientifically trained women applying their skills in different employment sectors?
- What should universities and the higher education sector do to retain women graduates and PhD students in academic careers? Are there examples of good practice?
- What role should the Government have in encouraging the retention of women in academic STEM careers?" (Commons Select Committee, 2013)

The Zurich Office of Equal Opportunities for Women and Men website states, "The Fix the Leaky Pipeline program offers young female scientists (PhD students, PhDs and others) the opportunity to reflect on their professional situations, develop a strategy for embarking or continuing on their career paths, receive targeted further training, and extend their personal and scientific networks. The aim, actively supported by all institutions of the ETH Domain, is to support women in their scientific careers and in the process to fix the 'leaky pipeline' of women in science." This program is comprised of networking events (to meet role models), coaching and courses, and is offered from spring 2013 – fall 2014 (Falub, 2013).

In the European Commission Policy document, specific reference is made by Da Silva Reis & Schulze (2012) to "addressing the 'leaky pipeline' phenomenon by tearing down barriers preventing women from progressing in this sector and from reconciling their careers with parenthood and family responsibilities."

What's interesting about these three recent examples is the use of the leaky pipeline metaphor, as this is an earlier theory that has come under criticism and subsequently been refined/replaced. Berryman (1983) is attributed with coining the metaphor of the "Leaky Pipeline" when it was first deployed to represent the attrition of women from science. This was later picked up by Alper (1993), who summarized studies on why the pipeline is leaking women. It refers to the phenomenon in which women progressively disappear from scientific careers, so that a focus on progressive points along the pipeline will reveal fewer and fewer women. The implication of the metaphor is that to increase women's representation in science, policies must be devised to "patch" the leakage at those points where the pipeline loses more women than men (Svinth, 2006).

As already noted, the leaky pipeline metaphor has been subject to critique. Soe and Yakura (2008) flag "In IT as in other STEM occupations, the pipeline metaphor depicts the problem of under-representation in terms of barriers and the innate abilities or personal preferences of women (e.g., favouring family over work). In so doing, the burden is on the individual woman to overcome the barriers, or to opt out of a more technical IT career." They further argue that the leaky pipeline metaphor fails because it "presumes a normative linear progressive flow, with people moving from basic ICT skills to more advanced ones and from lower ICT jobs to more skilled and senior jobs. It does not provide a model where there is sideways movement into and out of occupations."

This argument was reflected by Castano & Webster (2011), who noted that the leaky pipeline analogy implies linearity, meaning people progress in an orderly fashion through pre determined stages of their technology career, e.g. education, labour market entry, career development and progression. They also note it assumes an ideal or typical timescale for progression throughout stages, it implies successful completion and positive outcomes of all stages, and there is no provision for alternative pathways or co-progression through more than one stage.

Svinth (2006) flags that "the metaphor is one sided and considers only the 'push' effect – women falling out due to leaks in the pipeline, while it more or less ignores that [a] physicist can be 'pulled' out of science in pursuit of a career in other more or less related fields." She further identifies that "Life course events such as family formation that coincide and interact with the science career trajectory are also absent from the pipeline conceptualization." Soe & Yakura (2008) warn that the pipeline metaphor encourages research questions that are defined in terms of compartmentalized segments (e.g., elementary school, college, graduate school, entry level, management), where "leakages" from the pipeline occur and cause shortages, and the logic of the pipeline implies questions of quantity and timing: "why so few?" or "why so slow?" While Svinth (2006) warns that "the metaphor oversimplifies the highly complex issue of retention and exit from science careers and thus does more damage than good."

The key argument from the literature is that the leaky pipeline metaphor leads researchers and practitioners to neglect other perspectives that may lead to enhanced understanding of multiple interplaying factors. Some researchers argue that the underlying assumptions associated with the pipeline metaphor reflect the dominant masculine culture of the IT workplace. Overall, while the leaky pipeline is easy to conceptualize and can be illustrated by easily grasped diagrams (e.g. Figure 1 in Soe & Yakura, 2008), the metaphor is too limited in scope. This limits not only how people frame their research but also may focus the design of intervention programs onto fixing specific stages of the pipeline that are not inclusive enough of the reality.

Further to that last point, it is of interest to note that the compartments or stages of the leaky pipeline do tend to map to the target areas of traditional intervention programs, which leads to speculation about the design of those interventions. Perhaps, despite the reported disconnect between researchers and practitioners, program design has been influenced by the leaky pipeline metaphor. In that case, perhaps the weakness of that underlying model has contributed to the failure of those programs (see Chapter Four: *The Old Approach*). Or could it be mere coincidence, where programs were designed without being informed by the research but arrived at a similar segmentation, possibly for similar reasons?

LET'S GET CRITICAL

Applying policies and designing programs to increase the number of girls taking up technology studies and women entering technology careers are motivated by more than the immediate effects. It is hoped that there will be positive feedback and any increased numbers themselves will result in further positive change. This is informed by critical mass theory.

Kirkup (2011) explains, "The solution often proposed relies on increasing the proportions of women in specific occupations/industries until a 'critical mass' of women is reached – after which culture change will occur automatically. The metaphor is that of a chain reaction in nuclear reactor where, once the mass of fissile material (in this case women) is large, a self-sustaining process is triggered (gendered culture change)." Malcolm Gladwell (2001) popularized this concept in his book *The Tipping Point*.

Soe & Yakura (2008) argue that instead of mentoring or recruiting strategies that target a single stage or group of women as per the leaky pipeline metaphor, "we must attack the cultural assumptions at all levels to begin to change deep-seated assumptions about women and technology work. One way to do so is to ensure that there is a critical mass of women—or men in leadership positions who fully understand the problems and issues—who can work to effectively combat assumptions that can assail 'singletons' or 'exemplars.' Only by having a group of people (and not just a 'lone voice in the wilderness') that can systematically recognize and combat unintended yet harmful assumptions as they arise, can an IT organization achieve lasting change."

In support of critical mass theory, Soe & Yakura (2008) report that "When there was a critical mass of women at senior levels, both women and men believed that women affected the organizational culture in a positive manner: by encouraging more collaboration, more participative decision-making and hence more collegial workplaces." Unfortunately, whether these "feel good" beliefs are backed up by data and statistical significance is not reported.

Like the leaky pipeline metaphor, critical mass theory has been subject to criticism, in particular by political and social theorists (Childs & Krook, 2006; Dahlerup, 2006). This in itself is interesting given that government policies on equity, gender or minority issues are often based on setting quotas. For example, the main initiative to come out of the UK Government's response to the SET Fair report (Greenfield, Peters, Lane, Rees & Samuels, 2002) was the establishment of the UK Resource Centre for Women (UKRC) in Science, Engineering and Technology (SET), targeted at meeting quotas of female participation. Launched in September 2004, the UKRC (later renamed to WISE: www.wisecampaign.org.uk) provides practical help and support to girls and women in SET, with the mission "to push the presence of female employees from 13% to 30% by 2020." Similar strategies and polices have been undertaken by the US Government (Ashcraft, Eger & Friend, 2012), the Australian Government (Beekhuyzen, Nielsen & von Hellens, 2006) and the EU (Da Silva Reis & Schulze, 2012). But while the logical response to critical mass theory is quotas – if what we need for a self-sustaining result is a certain percentage of women in IT, then all we need to do is make it so – the effectiveness of quotas themselves is questionable, except perhaps in cases of very low minority participation rates (Leonard, 1989).

However the fundamental problem with critical mass theory is not so much arguments about the effectiveness of quotas, but that it seems to be more an idea than a theory: there seems to be no agreement about how it operates to produce culture change, or how large a proportion is a "critical mass."

For example, Kramer, Konrad & Erkut (2006) argue that although critical mass theory remains popular with activists, "three women on a corporate board of governance is a critical mass, but most activists have adopted 30% as trigger for critical mass. If 30% is the critical mass figure for women in ICT professions then it is close to being reached in user support and operation technician occupations, and there should be evidence of culture change in these occupations" (Kirkup, 2011).

Another problem with critical mass theory is in the details. The Advanced Placement Computer

Science 2012 Exam national statistics show 22-25% women in the American Indian, Black, and Hispanic groups, while by far the most common group, White, had only 17% and the second most common group, Asians, 32% (Exploring Computer Science, 2013). If critical mass theory is correct, it is surprising that even poorly represented ethnicities show higher female participation.

In addition, the theory behind the original "tipping point" idea was that social science data indicates that once 13% of a population accepts a new idea, it is only a matter of time before at least 84% accept the idea (Gladwell, 2001). If we accept that basis, then we're not only there, we've been there for decades. So either the whole critical mass theory is wrong – or we are already near "saturation" compared to what we are ever going to achieve. Specifically regarding women and technology, consider the trend pointed out by Thornton (2007): "While the percentage of women in the workforce remained largely unchanged between 1996 and 2004 (at 46%), the percentage of women in IT decreased during that period, from 41% to 32%, according to the Information Technology Association of America." Which leads this author to pose the following question: if critical mass is considered the "goal," whether the original 13% or the later 30%; and the employment statistics for women in technology were well above that for a period of time; yet that not only failed to achieve self sustainability but actually began to decline: doesn't that mean that either the theory is invalid or worse, the changes that resulted from that critical mass themselves initiated the decline?

As to why, Powell, Bagilhole, & Dainty (2006) suggest that "women might be critical of other women, thus inadvertently reinforcing the negative aspects of the dominant masculine culture." And if this is the case, it may well be intensified under quota systems, where the quota may be the reason (real or perceived) that a woman has her position, rather than her own interests or skills.

However there may be more subtle reasons for encouraging a critical mass than the metaphor itself. An underlying basis for seeking quotas and critical mass to produce greater representation of women in technology, noted by Ashcraft et al. (2012), is "improving technical innovation: Right now, for the most part, we are missing out on the valuable perspectives that 50% of the population might bring to designing the technology of the future. A wealth of research in the past decade shows that diversity improves problem-solving, productivity, innovation, and ultimately, the bottom line. We need to ensure that the future technology we design is as broad and innovative as the population it serves."

Bernhardt (2006) articulated this earlier at a conference in Australia, saying: "A key reason why IT is important is because Information Technology is not just having a huge impact on the global economy; it's also affecting our social, economic, and civil institutions. We don't have hundreds of years to figure things out: innovation and obsolescence happen at light speed, and IT can literally change the world overnight. It changes who can compete in the global economy, it changes the nature of advocacy, it forces us to deal with privacy and piracy, it facilitates multi-national corporations, it allows communities to form with no proximity between members, it can reshape education and democracy … and on and on. The chief reason to work towards encouraging girls' interest in technology is to bring to the table diversity of thinking. It is well acknowledged that females bring a different perspective to issues than males do. If more females were involved in designing and creating technology we may see a world with different designs, and one that takes into account an inclusive set of perspectives. We may even see technology that is simpler to use and more attractive. The researchers and educators here today will know that technology is socially constructed. In other words, technology does not exist devoid of its creators' prejudices, biases, cultural assumptions, etc. When men design and build toys and then have other men test them, it should not be surprising that the common experiences of those men get imbibed in the technology. The trick is not to design a separate interface. The goal is to incorporate a wide variety of perspectives into the design and creation of a system, to create a system that people can repurpose to meet their needs. The goal is to encourage flexibility of expression, to not project a limited perspective into the technology. Designers must take into consideration the vast array of potential users, experiences, expectations, not simply their own. This is why we need more girls in IT: so that we get more inclusive deigns. The facts are that technology designed without female input can be critically one dimensional."

Bernhardt (2008) repeated a like theme, saying "Declining numbers of females in technology careers and studies is not just a gender issue: it is ultimately an issue about 3 key areas: (1) economics and wealth, (2) skills and (3) participation in society. The facts are that technology designed without female input can be critically one-dimensional. If more females were involved in *designing and creating* technology we may see a world with *different designs*, and one that takes into account an *inclusive set of perspectives*. We may even see technology that is *simpler to use and more attractive*."

The point for the critical mass theory is that this is a double-barrelled factor. By making technology more inclusive, more attractive, more "female" if you will: we make technology careers more interesting and attractive to girls who are choosing their education and women who are choosing their careers.

GET REAL: LIFE COURSE APPROACH

It wasn't until 2003 that consideration of individual factors and influencers was explicitly included in modelled theories in the literature. This conceptual "Life Course" framework was initially proposed by Xie & Shauman (2003) as a perspective for understanding women's pathways through science, but is also applicable to women in other technical careers including IT. The life course perspective proposes that life transitions are interdependent across education, family, and work domains and that later transitions are contingent on (but not determined by) earlier transitions.

Castano & Webster (2011) describe it as "the concept of the life course turns on the idea of a sequence of stages in individuals' lives, following different pathways. Several key concepts are used to describe and analyze differences in life courses: 'transitions' are changes in roles and statuses experienced by individual women or men; 'trajectories' are long-term patterns of stability and change that involve multiple transitions in an individual's life; 'life events' are significant occurrences involving relatively abrupt change that may produce serious long lasting events in an individual's life; and 'turning points' are a substantial change or discontinuity in direction that is not temporary, but lasting (Elder, 1999; Hutchison, 2008)." To give a short summary, this approach is about "things happen in a person's life that affect/impact what then follows."

Since Xie & Shauman's (2003) conceptual framework was proposed 10 years ago, the life course approach has gained increasing credibility and has been cited and further enhanced in the literature (Adya & Kaiser, 2005; Ashcraft et al., 2012; Castano & Webster, 2011; Ham, Junankar & Wells, 2009; Trauth, Quesenberry & Huang, 2009).

Ashcraft et al. (2012) present a model that depicts the key social and structural contexts in which influencing factors occur. They placed "Girls' Perceptions, Interests, Confidence, and Career Decisions" in the centre of this model to highlight the fact that "girls do not come by these perceptions, interests, and career decisions innately or in a vacuum. Indeed, these are shaped by the larger society and local environments in which they learn about computing and technology, and this significantly influences what appears to be their 'choices' to pursue computing and computing careers."

Castano & Webster (2011) give a similar perspective: "In advocating a 'life course approach' to the understanding of women's careers in ICT, our central contention is that life events (family relationships, educational choices and achievements, family formation, geographical mobility patterns, labour market participation patterns and decisions) separately and in combination influence women's ability to engage in this field, in ways which differ substantially from men's and which then have a decisive impact on their careers."

The STEMcell Model in this book proposes, like Ashcraft et al. (2012), that the individual is the core and is a unique cell. However it stresses that the individual's interests and talents are more a driver in themselves than something passively shaped by society. The individual's environment still determines what is possible and what is encountered, but as a modifier to what is inside the person not as its creator. From that perspective, #SocialIT is the disruptive movement which will help overcome residual negative factors society may still impose upon the individual. In that sense, this Model can be considered a modification and extension of the Life Course approach.

It is worth pointing out in that context that the forces involved in liberating the individual are wider than just #SocialEra. Rather, #SocialEra is itself a trend in those wider forces.

One example is that the technological and social trends that make #SocialIT possible lower barriers in other ways. Thus in recent years, it is reported that Australian women are now starting their own small businesses at twice the rate of men (Munro, 2011). This reflects not only women's attitudes to what is possible for them but also the greatly lowered barriers to entry, due to modern technology and the greater disposable wealth in society.

Another example is an even wider trend. Patten & Parker (2012) report "In a reversal of traditional gender roles, young women now surpass young men in the importance they place on having a high-paying career or profession… The past 15 years have also seen an increase in the share of middle-aged and older women who say being successful in a high-paying career or profession is 'one of the most important things' or 'very important' in their lives." And while we might decry the low proportion of women in IT courses, the trend in education in general is quite different: "On the education front, women have made substantial strides in recent decades and now surpass men in both college enrolment and completion. Some 44% of women ages 18 to 24 were enrolled in college or graduate programs as of October 2010, compared with just 38% of men in the same age group. In addition, 36% of women ages 25 to 29 had a bachelor's degree, compared with only 28% of men in the same age group—a record-high divergence. Women first surpassed men in these realms in the early 1990s, and the gap has been growing wider ever since" (Patten & Parker, 2012).

Cave (2013) reports similar disruptions: "Over the last decade, a new generation of women have become more ambitious and career-minded than ever before. A Marie Claire survey published in October 2012 showed that three quarters of twenty and thirty-something respondents cite work as either 'very important' or the 'single most important thing' in their lives. On top of this, Citi reported that 36% of women it polled recently didn't factor marriage into their definition of 'having it all', and 27% didn't include children."

Relevant to that, in an online survey of 4,100 business executives from medium to large organizations across 33 countries, Accenture (2013) found that 70% of both men and women say they can "have it all" and have a successful career as well as a full life outside of work. Interestingly, 80% reported that having flexibility in their work schedule is extremely or very important to work-life balance (only 2% said it wasn't important at all), and more than three-quarters agreed that technology enables them to be more flexible with their schedules.

If there is a disparity between general trends and IT in the entry of women into the marketplace, there is a similar disparity in their leaving it. We are seeing a trend of women leaving technology careers at higher rates than both women leaving other careers and men leaving technology careers. Parmar (2013) states that in the UK, 40% of women leave technology roles after 10 years, compared with 10% departures of men. Whilst in the USA, Ashcraft et al. (2012) report that 56% of women in technology companies leave their organizations at the mid-level point (10-20 years) in their careers, much higher than other industries such as law, where only 30 to 45% of women leave mid-career.

Within our own area of interest we decry these disparities. But given that they are not universal trends they lend support to Svinth's (2006) suggestion that pull into areas of greater interest rather than push out of IT could be an important factor in participation rates. Perhaps this implies that more than lowering barriers, what we need to increase the number of women in IT is simply to make it more interesting – for them. And enabling existing enthusiasts to show why they are enthusiastic is exactly what the STEMcell Model and #SocialIT is all about.

STRUCTURATION AND DUALISM

From time to time a thread in the literature resurfaces following on from Giddens' (1984) structuration theory and its central notion of dualism (Beekhuyzen, Nielsen & von Hellens, 2003; Lang, Craig, Fisher, Bennetts & Forgasz, 2010).

Whilst acknowledging that there are some issues in using Giddens' theory, Beekhuyzen et al. (2003) explore "the way that professional women working in the IT industry discuss the nature of their work and [suggest] that the way women talk about their work reinforces widely held impressions of the Information Technology industry. Structuration theory illuminated how this talk is not always consistent with the women's lived experiences." Their research was part of a project titled WinIT, which commenced in 1995 and ran over a number of years.

The WinIT project sought to understand the declining rate of female participation in technology studies and careers, and focused on the cultural and gender factors affecting female recruitment (von Hellens & Nielsen, 2001). The research took "the view that gender and IT are socially constructed. That is, IT is constructed as a domain attractive to certain types of people, primarily as a male domain, in the same way such occupations as child-care and nursing are constructed as female domains. The advantage of this view is that what can be constructed can also be deconstructed and changed. The more women enter professional-level IT education and work, especially in technical areas, the less IT will be viewed as a male domain." The WinIT research drew out the following dualisms in skills and attributes as either/or propositions, meaning for example that to be good at solving problems implies not being good at talking to people:

- Home/work
- IT industry/career certainty
- IT work/emotion
- Intuition/analysis
- Programmer/people focused
- Soft skills/technical education
- Solving problems/talking to people
- Technology/business problems
- Technical/management
- Technical/people skills
- Technology/communication skills

What is interesting here is the strong implications of common stereotypes. For example, if we believe that "women have good communication skills," under this dualism model we will also conclude they have poor technology skills.

Beekhuyzen et al. (2003) then present and discuss the specific dualisms in IT work and gender issues. Later, Lang et al. (2010) identify what we could call a "metadualism," a dualism about the dualisms: "the dualism between school students' as well as the wider society's perception of what an ICT career involves and the actual work experience of women in ICT." They discover that "An ICT career, according to the women we interviewed is quite the opposite to the narrow perceptions of students in secondary schools." That is, people outside IT careers, unfortunately including students, tend to accept dualisms like technical/communication whereas the people in those careers have learned that it is not true. This disparity between outside perception and inside reality is one factor that has driven programs such as career days that try to show the reality of life in IT. It would be ironic if the very misconceptions we have been fighting have been driven by dualism research and commentary filtering out into the wider community.

However the stereotypical dualisms have arisen, we do need to demolish them. The proposed STEMcell Model views the individual as the core. Interest in IT is not male. Ability in IT is not male. Logic is not male, emotion is not female, and any person can and should embrace both. Perhaps the most telling way to bury the dualisms is to target the "metadualism" of the previous paragraph. Bateman (2012) reports that a UK-based women in technology survey revealed that nine out of ten female technology experts would recommend the IT sector as a career choice to other females. In one sense this is hardly surprising given the results described in Chapter Four, *The Old Approach*: most women in IT are there because *they* are inherently interested in the field. But in a deeper sense it overturns all the dualisms that if accepted would exclude women from IT careers. In fact many women *love* their careers in IT. Not because they are women, and not in spite of not being men. Because they as individuals are good at it and like doing it.

GENDER MODELING

Gender theory shares aspects of the dualism model but focuses specifically on perceived gender dualisms. Historically, the issue of the small and declining participation of women in technology studies and careers, and the solutions to enhance their attraction, promotion and retention, have been wrapped around gender based assumptions and perceptions.

A statement that sums up that historical viewpoint is made by Wajcman (2010), a strong proponent of gender theory in technology, when she says "Current approaches focus on the mutual shaping of gender and technology, in which technology is conceptualized as both a source and consequence of gender relations. In avoiding both technological determinism and gender essentialism, such theories emphasise that the gender-technology relationship is fluid and situated… the distinguishing insight of feminist STS [science and technology studies] or technofeminism is that gender is integral to this sociotechnical process: that the materiality of technology affords or inhibits the doing of particular gender power relations. Women's identities, needs and priorities are configured together with digital technologies… while gender is embedded in technoscience, the relationship is not immutably fixed. While the design process is decisive, sociotechnical configurations exhibit different degrees of determination and contingency at different moments in their relationship. The capacity of women users to produce new, advantageous readings of artefacts is dependent on their broader economic and social circumstances. Such a perspective redefines the problem of the exclusion of groups of people from technological domains and activities. Technofeminism exposes how the concrete practices of design and innovation lead to the absence of specific users, such as women. While it is not always possible to specify in advance the characteristics of artefacts and information systems that would guarantee more inclusiveness, it is imperative that women are involved throughout the processes and practices of technological innovation."

Parmar (2013) states that the specific male image of IT is particularly repellent to girls: "the biggest problem why girls don't want a career in IT is … the pizza-guzzling nerds who can't get girl friends image … the image is the biggest problem." The issue is not as simple or as stark as that, as noted by Cave (2013): "not so long ago IT definitely had a geeky image, but technological changes over the last decade have seen a seismic shift in the perception of technology; however stereotypes and perceived differences do persist." Nor is the solution as stark or simple either: as noted by Wajcman above, "it is not always possible to specify the characteristics of artefacts and information systems that would guarantee more inclusiveness."

The attitude of girls to IT is summed up by Anderson, Lankshear, Timms & Courtney (2008), whose extensive research found that senior high school girls in Australia tend to perceive advanced computer subjects as boring. They have a strong aversion to such study ("I don't like computers"), and they don't see themselves as having a career in this field (irrelevancy).

The cause has frequently been framed in gender terms by statements such as "At the base of the not-enough-women-in-IT problem is a … widely held misconception of what women can and should do … Wherever we cast our attention, the assumptions surrounding gender are part of the data flow that runs perniciously under the radar screen of how we perceive the world. Like it or not, gender is an easily observable and frequently behaviour-influencing phenomenon. On various levels in the contemporary IT shop, your sex does matter… we all wish we lived in a world no longer driven by biology and instead ruled by rationality and results. But the data indicates we don't – at least not yet" (Thornton, 2007). In other words, the reason there is an imbalance between males and females in IT are the subtle yet powerful forces of gender-based perception and prejudice.

Gender-based perceptions were investigated by Cave (2013), who conducted a straw poll to assess if the IT industry could survive without women. Results showed relatively divided opinion, with 56% no and 44% yes. The reasons cited for fewer women in IT ranged from the 36% of female respondents who felt the shortage was down to a perception problem for women (as in Parmar's image statement above) to the 27% of male respondents who believed women don't generally think in the way IT requires. Cave flags that "Perhaps more concerning for the long-term, numerous studies suggest young girls simply aren't interested in IT. This is despite the growing population of 'gadget girls', the clear potential of IT as a career, and the fact that numerous studies suggest that IT is crying out for more talent."

The report concludes, "There is a strong case to be made that a gender imbalance in the IT workplace is irrelevant. The work will continue irrespective of whether there is an equal mix of men and women." The report further notes "Our findings suggest that it is widely acknowledged that women bring a different mix of skills to the workplace – the area of contention seems to be whether these differences are good or bad. But what does seem incredible is that a subject which has been discussed for decades can still inspire such passionately diametric views today."

Ironically, despite this disconnect between theory and thinking within the industry, and despite the volumes of industry surveys, academic research and theories regarding gender-held perceptions about women and technology, a thread in the literature is a belief that the field is under-theorised. This is reflected by Howcroft, Adam & Richardson (2004), who believe the issue of the decline of women in technology has been under-theorised because "much of the published work on gender and ICT has not used gender theory to inform the design of the research, to interpret the findings or to develop implications emanating from them." Similarly, Trauth (2006) states "it is ironic that coincident with a documented need for a deeper understanding of the gender imbalance in the IT field, there is insufficient attention being paid to theorizing gender and IT. Given this need, greater theorization in gender and IT research can contribute in several ways to a better understanding of women's relationships to information technology."

Harding's (1986, 1991, 1998) ideas on "Standpoint Theory" perhaps suggest ways to find new perspectives in gender theorising. As summarised by Janack (2004), "Harding argues that 'starting thought out' from the lives of the marginalized will lead to the development of new sets of research questions and priorities, since the marginalized enjoy a certain epistemic privilege that allows them to see problems differently, or to see problems where members of a dominant group do not. However, Harding emphasizes that one need not be a member of a marginalized group in order to be capable of starting one's thought from that standpoint." But other theorists have criticised the notion that "there are some experiences that all and only women have that can serve as a basis for identification with that group, arguing that the category of 'woman' is either too fractured or too regulative to do the work that feminist standpoint theorists and identity theorists need it to do." In any event, most gender theorists studying women in IT are women, so we can expect that any female-specific insights have already been revealed.

Trauth et al. (2009) took their own path, later proposing a number of constructs that enable within gender variation theorising. Major constructs presented were individual identity (personal demographics and career items), individual influences (personal characteristics and personal influences) and environmental influences (cultural, economic, policy and infrastructure).

This theme was picked up by von Hellens et al. (2012) who state, "Accompanying the need for new methods to support a deeper and more critical examination of gender relations in the IT field is the need to peer inside the 'black box' of gender. Therefore, developing a better understanding of existing gender relations also requires the use of appropriate gender theories … A promising area of new gender theorising is about within-gender variation as it relates to women and men in the ICT profession." This is an interesting change from the prior research and theories that generally focused on gender differences between males and females.

von Hellens et al. (2012) flag that "The individual differences theory of gender and IT has been developed to provide a theoretical lens that focuses explicit attention on within-gender rather than between-gender variation in the ways that individuals are exposed to, experience and respond to gender relations in the ICT profession (Trauth & Quesenberry, 2006). This theory conceptualises gender relations in the IT field at two different levels of analysis. One level – the societal level – is concerned with gender group biases that women encounter. The other level of analysis – the individual level – deals with the variation among women with respect to how they respond to gender group biases. This variation is posited as resulting from differences in demographic traits, personalities and individual and socio-cultural influences. According to this theory, these constructs account for the differences among women in the ways they relate to the ICT field and respond to gendered discourses about IT."

Shifting the gender focus from between genders to within genders may help reduce the classic issues as expressed by Spender (2011): "Is this the old stereotype argument? That it is boys who want to take things apart, while girls are directed towards cleaning up the mess afterwards? The old – 'boys are into adventure' – and 'girls are into relationships'? Or is it – Catch 22 – that because the area is dominated by males the girls think it's not for them? Do they feel locked out – and so they don't entertain IT as a possibility?" Spender (2011) further flags "There are always issues associated with non-traditional jobs (such as engineering, trades etc) where girls are put off by dirt and grease, along with ugly protective clothing and the prospect of broken finger nails: but these arguments aren't relevant when it comes to IT. It's clean, can be very creative, well paid etc – with a range of options for specialisation. So much so that in certain Asian countries, IT is considered a good job for a girl, (possibly for much the same reasons as office work and accountancy are also considered appropriate)."

Whilst to date the decades of gender related women and technology research has not discovered "the secret" to the declining rates of women taking up technology studies and careers, it may be that new directions such as individual differences within genders and adopting hard science experimental models and causal factors may shed some future light. This is reflected in von Hellens et al. (2012), who state, "In addition to qualitative, interpretive and critical research, a new level of sophistication is also being brought to positivist, quantitative studies. While there continues to be positivist/quantitative research being published that limits itself to documenting gender differences, increasing numbers of gender researchers are using these research tools – sometimes in combination with qualitative methods – to develop a deeper and more nuanced understanding of gender issues in the ICT field. For example, Armstrong, Riemenschneider, Reid & Allen (2007) used revealed causal mapping, a highly detailed qualitative method, to conduct positivist examinations of cognitive linkages that female ICT professionals make among workplace issues that influence voluntary turnover and perceived promotion opportunities."

Unfortunately, theorists focused on gender as the critical issue sometimes do so at the expense of open mindedness. As Krause (2013) notes, "Recall, for example, the oppressive and unscholarly manner in which Harvard president Lawrence Summers was vilified in 2005 for merely suggesting that, one, men and women might have distinguishable natural abilities related to math and science, and, two, that personal preference rather than discrimination might account for female 'underrepresentation' in high-end STEM careers." Such responses are more reminiscent of a religious war than a cool-headed academic search for the truth wherever that search might lead.

But if gender theory is turning to the differences between women themselves as a primary factor, then is it really still gender theory, or are the theorists finally realising that the core is in fact the individual? Is the individual a lump of clay molded by societal forces including increasingly subtle gender prejudices, or is it now the other way around? We need to remember that it is now over forty years since the publication of Germaine Greer's (1970) *The Female Eunuch*, "arguably the most galvanising, enduring and representative text of second wave feminism, [which] urged women to think beyond their social conditioning to 'discover that they have a will'" (Crabb, 2012). The *grandmothers* of high school students and young women entering IT careers today grew up in the era of that book's influence and the social trends that gave birth to it and it in turn helped shape. If, after all these years and all the efforts of activists inspired by visions of female equality, social opinions of gender are still considered a major driver, then we need to wonder why those social opinions are so immovable. It is not controversial that women bring a different mix of personalities and skills to the workplace compared to male-only ones – this is a view often raised in both the literature and by activists as a reason why we need more women in IT in the first place. Perhaps we do need to accept that women and men are different, and that extends to different *average* interests, skills – and careers.

Ultimately gender theory comparing males and females reinforces the perception of women as a "marked" category precisely because it focuses attention on women. As Wittenberg-Cox (2013) pithily put it, "Stop fixing women. And stop making them a diversity demographic." This may contribute to the UK Education minister Liz Truss's statement that they will not focus on girls, and believe that increasing the profile of computer studies will result in girls following (Onwurah,

2013). This corresponds with the findings in Chapter Four: *The Old Approach*, that women enter IT careers primarily because of who they are, not because of interventions. If IT is interesting and a satisfying career, show that and individual choice will follow.

It is interesting that theorists aside, among actual women in IT careers "from the statistics and the comments, women are overwhelmingly anti special treatment initiatives, such as gender quotas. It seems that women are keen to be promoted on their own merits and for employers to provide the facilities to help them achieve their career goals" (Berry & Kalessi, 2011). We appear to have gone beyond the era of gender and into the era of the individual. Will the theorists follow?

#SOCIALIT

If we look at the history, the criticisms and the results (or lack of them) of the traditional models, it is hard to disagree with Kirkup (2011) that "we need something more refined than those two metaphors [pipeline and critical mass] which have served us well in the past – but are now unable to explain the more complex operation of 21st century employment." But it's not just about "more complex 21st century employment"; it's also about human complexities. As summed up by Onwurah (2013), "We are all different, there isn't one thing that drives us into a particular career. What is certain is there is no single solution."

The STEMcell Model presented in this book stresses the importance of #SocialIT in driving change. How do those older models relate to the new era of #SocialIT? What can we learn from them or about them?

In the #SocialIT era the fast shifting landscape is not conducive to the staged, linear, progressed approach assumed by the leaky pipeline metaphor. #SocialIT is more of a mashup and leaky pipeline is no longer relevant (if it ever was). Meister (2012) notes "The average worker today stays at each of his or her jobs for 4.4 years, according to the most recent available data from the Bureau of Labor Statistics, but the expected tenure of the workforce's youngest employees is about half that. Ninety-one percent of Millennials (born between 1977-1997) expect to stay in a job for less than three years, according to the Future Workplace 'Multiple Generations @ Work' survey of 1,189 employees and 150 managers. That means they would have 15 – 20 jobs over the course of their working lives!" Employees are increasingly expecting to jump from job to job; employers, for their part, have to look at greater flexibility within each workplace to retain them. Individual choice has always been at the core of career paths, but now the need, desire and ability for career flexibility is making it even more central.

Critical mass theory speaks of the need to build up numbers to a self-perpetuating level. But in the #SocialIT era there are no (or no need for) "singletons," at least not in terms of the personal and career networks women can now choose at will. Nor is the "mass" of women any longer limited to single departments or companies or, beyond their own workplace, to the number of compatible people they can physically meet in their city. Its consequence, quotas, are irrelevant to social media. In #SocialIT, individuals will seek out and create their own critical mass in multiple networks that can span the globe, focus on tight interests – or both.

The main task of #SocialIT where it concerns structuration and dualism theory is not to apply it but to debunk it. It appears to have more influence on (or perhaps greater resonance with) popular stereotypes than on the literature itself. Whether it is partly to blame or not, the unrealistic and ultimately negative stereotypes its "dualisms" imply are themselves one of the obstacles we need to sweep away.

The lessons of gender theory are likewise mainly negative. #SocialIT maps closer to Liz Truss's thoughts (Onwurah, 2013) about focusing on the industry rather than on gender specifically.

Gender theory "within genders" is moving toward the idea of the individual as core, which is also a principle of the STEMcell Model. However there are still gender stereotypes and prejudices in the community. #SocialIT will play an important role in counteracting those by easing the formation of supportive networks and helping publicise both the reality of work in IT and women's potential and actual contributions to it: influencing the attitudes of both women and men.

Life Course theory is the most similar of current models to the STEMcell Model, except the latter places more emphasis on the individual as the primary driver. #SocialIT will both modify and amplify the influences on the individual: from simple information to busting stereotypes to showing what is possible to anyone with the relevant interests and talents. And it also amplifies the individual's ability to influence the world. #SocialIT both empowers individuals to influence others, and expands the influences individuals can easily seek out.

The discussion above leads to the statement that leaky pipeline, critical mass and other historical theories do not apply in the #SocialIT era, and in fact ought to be cast aside. That is not to say they have had no value. The historical theories have identified real phenomena: pipelines have leaked; isolation and being outnumbered by sometimes hostile or dismissive coworkers (or superiors) have been problems; gender prejudices and roles have contributed to that. Superseding those models does not imply denial of the existence of cultural, social and structural contexts that affect the attraction, promotion and retention of girls and women in technology studies and careers. Those contexts and their influencing factors are specifically explored in later chapters.

Rather, the STEMcell model and its #SocialIT influence is intended to take into consideration aspects of past theories in the light of the tectonic shifts occurring in technology and society in general – and a more realistic view of the individual. It is proposed as a new way both to look at the historical research and theories and to move forward: by embracing the new era and acknowledging the strength of the individual.

Hack the Research

One unique way to maximize the value of the significant volume of historical research is through engaging in a GovHack style collaborative activity. This would access the existing data sets of women in technology research and intervention programs, in order to create not merely improved access but something new through visualization techniques.

At GovHack, held 31 May – 2 June 2013 across Australia, hundreds of hackers joined together to form teams and create the best new mashups, data visualizations and apps using Australian Government data. GovHack produced results that have left everyone else 23 man-years behind: the event attracted 130 teams across 8 cities (using Hangouts to connect) and involved 900 hackers. Over 48 hours hacking, it therefore totalled 43,200 hours, equating to 5,400 eight-hour days or 1,080 weeks, or 23 years of work at 47 working weeks in a year.

Pia Waugh, who headed up GovHack (Waugh, 2013a), is one of the new generation of women who has her finger on the moving pulse of the industry. She describes GovHack as "all about supporting and encouraging hacker culture in Australia with government data. By hacker culture of course, we mean the curious, creative and clever use of tech and geek skills to solve tricky problems and do awesome" (Waugh, 2013b).

Hackathons are a trending topic. Other hackathon examples are:

- The International Open Data Hackathon organised each year. Their website (opendataday.org) describes it as "a gathering of citizens in cities around the world to write applications, liberate data, create visualizations and publish analyses using open public data to show support for and encourage the adoption of open data policies by the world's local, regional and national governments."

- AngelHack (angelhack.com) "organizes insanely large hackathons, where developers learn new tools, meet new friends, and showcase their skills to the community. To date, we've organized almost 100 hackathons in 35 cities globally. Our flagship event is the AngelHack Global Hackathon competition, which happens twice a year (Spring and Fall), bringing together 10,000+ developers each time."
- Big Data Hack Day (bigdatahack.eventbrite.com), run by AngelHack in San Francisco in 2012, was "one of the first hackathons to allow you to build upon existing code, thus allowing teams to win prizes for integrating Big Data Tools, like New Relic, into their current companies."
- MigraHack (www.chicagomigrahack.com/#!about3/cikx) in Chicago focused on participants pairing up "to discover and solve individual design challenges centered on immigration data. This session will help journalists and community members analyze and find new stories through different means of immigration data visualization. Participants will interview their partners, propose solutions, listen to feedback and work through several iterations in order to design a unique application for each other."

Can you imagine the impact of being able to visualize and easily overlay and cross-reference the data from decades of research in the field of women in IT? Imagine being able to leap ahead and gain an enhanced understanding in a matter of days instead of decades, being able to make that historical research data come alive and relevant again? Imagine regaining high quality statistical data on a disaggregated level that allows for longitudinal and comparative studies and includes research from government, educational institutions and industry? Imagine bringing global research into combined data sets and being able to see the results? Mitchell (2013) presents graphs from the United States Computer Science Enrollments that clearly show a wave style pattern of peaks and troughs of women graduating from Computer Science Studies. Over time the graph seemingly 'corrects' itself: for example there was a high for women in IT in 1985 followed by a low in 1996 and then another high in 2003. Imagine being able to hack into comparable statistics globally and overlay different perspectives, and consider the enhanced wealth of knowledge that would then be available.

A GovHack type event could even go one step further and encourage young girls themselves to form hacker teams and contribute to the outcomes. It's even possible to have age-varied hack fests, where children as young as year 4 and 5 could be given the opportunity to contribute; it would be fascinating to see what sort of use and what apps would be developed across the different age groups. Potential outcomes from this are:

- Enhanced relevance of the research via mashups and visualization techniques;
- Hands-on code development by the hacker teams;
- Participants see the value of what they, their team and the other teams create within a short timeframe, showing them that coding is relevant and not just abstract;
- Empowerment and pride of work via hackathon rewards and recognition.

Additionally, Internet and media attention would attract more mainstream interest. This would help draw out the "clever, creative and curious" (Waugh, 2013b), and go a long way towards enhancing outcomes and helping understand the frameworks for future activities.

The Hackathon concept challenges traditional views of ownership of data and clearly fits into the #SocialEra paradigm. Reluctance to free this data falls under the traditional strategies that need to be put aside (right strategy reign supreme, size matters & sustainable advantages), whereas releasing it maps to the new rules we need to undertake (power in community, collaboration control, allow all talent and consumers as co-creators) in order to move ahead (Merchant, 2012).

If governments around the world are beginning to release banks of data to allow hackathons to develop interesting and useful new apps, why not industry associations, educational institutions and research organizations? If the purpose of the industry associations is to solve problems in their industry, the purpose of educational institutions is to educate and the purpose of research is to discover the facts – then why not embrace the tools that let us do it better? What is more important to you? Owning dead data, or bringing it alive?

A NEW LOOK AT INTERESTS AND INFLUENCERS

"Things happen in a person's life that impact what follows" is certainly reflected in the snapshot poll summarized in Chapter Four: *The Old Approach*. The biggest driver attracting the poll respondents into technology was personal interest from a young age, while the second largest was an accident of history, or happenstance. A further breakdown of those results is of interest here.

Core Technology Careers: Interests and Influencers

Table 1 presents statistics of those who indicated they were in core technology career such as coders, architects and system analysts (this comprised 59% of all responses: 70 of the total 119). The country and age distribution amongst this group is similar to the overall poll results and may be considered a reasonably representative sample of those polled, as responses came from across all countries and age brackets represented.

I focus on this group in particular as ultimately it is attraction, promotion and retention of these core areas that is of primary interest for both activists and recruiters. The IT-related "soft" careers are, in contrast, more interchangeable with careers in other areas rather than being IT-specific.

Of this group, 76% were interested in technology from a young age (including then losing interest) and 23% became interested when technology became part of what they did at work or university, i.e. by happenstance rather than choice (Table 2). Both the early interest and happenstance percentages were marginally higher than in the overall results (71% and 22% respectively), but at the numbers polled the differences are not statistically significant.

As noted in Table 2, for the single responder who was never really interested in technology, her primary influence was a teacher/lecturer with the secondary influence an intervention program. For

Table 1. Country and age distributions of poll responders in "Core IT"

Country Distribution		Age Distribution	
Australia/NZ	51%	Under 25	9%
Asia	10%	25-25	44%
Europe	7%	36-45	34%
North America	21%	46-55	9%
South America	2%	Over 55	3%
UK	9%	Prefer not to answer	1%

Table 2. Interest of responders in core technology careers

Poll Response	No.	%	Comments
I have been interested in IT since I was young	50	72%	Includes one in no category (i.e. no category chosen) where comment was "I became interested with the first computer at home when I was about 18."
I was interested in IT when I was young but lost interest	3	4%	Includes one in no category where comment was "I was put off IT early by some comments from peers who saw it as not as important as hard science or engineering. Came back to it in my 30's."
I only became interested in IT when it became part of my job	16	23%	Includes two in no category where comments were "I became interested in IT at university," and "My Dad pushed me to get into IT but I never wanted to, feeling it wasn't something girls did. I got to university and when I had to pick my specialisation of engineering I ended up picking one I had never considered before."
I was never really interested in IT	1	1%	Influenced primarily by teacher/lecturer with secondary influence an intervention program
	70	100%	

those of us who have been passionately involved in intervention programs, it is frightening to extrapolate this. It would indicate only 1% of women in core technology careers got there via an intervention program changing their mind set/ career choice. While this poll is not amenable to such extrapolation, nevertheless the figures are stark and in agreement with Lyons et al. (2012).

Table 3 concentrates on the top row of Table 2, the 50 people (49 + 1 assigned from her comments) in core technology careers who were interested in technology since they were young.

The purpose of Table 3 is to identify the main triggers why those interested since an early age actually chose an IT career. By far the greatest number identified personal interest itself as the primary or secondary motive; indeed, 8% (4 people) indicated personal interest as both their primary *and* secondary influencers – reflecting very strong innate personal interest and desire in that subset.

Personal interest was followed by happenstance, closely followed by the combined advice of family, friends, teachers or lecturers. Less than 10% were influenced by cultural factors (such as TV shows, industry personalities, books etc.). And of particular interest here, only 3% were influenced by intervention programs.

Table 4 zeroes in on the 16 people (14 + 2 assigned from their comments) of core IT workers who became interested in technology when it became part of their job (happenstance) – the only other significant segment (Table 2). As in Table 3, it presents their primary and secondary influences on then choosing a technology career.

This group follows a similar pattern to the core IT workers who had always been interested, with the major influencers reversed consistently with interest group. Personal interest plus accident of history comprise the great majority, followed by advice, with culture and interventions minor factors. The comparative rankings (1=highest, 6=lowest) are shown in Table 5.

As noted above, interventions ranked low for both groups. While the numbers influenced by interventions were higher in the happenstance group, the numbers are too low for statistical significance.

We might draw two provisional conclusions from the interaction between personal interest and happenstance. First, personal interest can be fired up by exposure to technology as part of one's job, which could have implications for job design. Perhaps more importantly, it appears that a significant number of women don't find out they are interested until they are already in the

Table 3. Primary and secondary influencers: Core technology careers – Interested since young.

Influencing Factor	Primary Influence		Secondary Influence		Total
	No.	%	No.	%	
Personal interest	29	58%	19	38%	48%
Advice - teacher or lecturer	2	4%	4	8%	6%
Advice - family & friends	5	10%	8	16%	13%
Intervention program	2	4%	1	2%	3%
Cultural influence	3	6%	6	12%	9%
Accident of history (+ 1 comment: the money)	9	18%	12	24%	21%
	50		50		

Table 4. Primary and secondary influencers: Core technology careers: Happenstance

Influencing Factor		Primary Influence		Secondary Influence		Total
		No.	%	No.	%	
Personal interest		4	25%	6	38%	31%
Advice - teacher or lecturer		2	13%	1	6%	9.5%
Advice - family & friends		1	6%	2	12.5%	9.5%
Intervention program		0	0%	2	12.5%	6%
Cultural influence		0	0%	1	6%	3%
Accident of history	Secondary influence via comment "I worked with a group of terrific guys (programmers) that mentored me, taught me, encouraged me to learn and do whatever interested me." Secondary influence via comment "It puts food on the table" (classed as happenstance as considered equivalent to "just the job I ended up in").	9	56%	4	25%	41%
		16		16		

Table 5. Comparative rankings of influencers: Core technology roles: Young interest cf. happenstance

	Personal Interest	Advice: Teacher, Lecturer	Advice: Family & Friends	Intervention Program	Cultural Influence	Accident of History
Interested since young	1	5	3	6	4	2
Interest from accident of history	2	3	3	5	6	1

workforce: but interventions, culture and personal advice do little to catch them along the way. We can conclude that showing and explaining can have some effect, but *doing* and *experiencing* are far more important.

Support Technology Careers: Interests and Influencers

Looking at the 41 responses identified with a support technology career, we see a similar pattern to core technology careers. A distinct majority were interested since they were young, followed by becoming interested when technology became part of their job (Table 6).

Comparing support versus core IT careers, a lower fraction had always been interested and a higher fraction became interested via their job, respectively. However a chi-squared analysis of the difference is non-significant (P=0.53), so statistically the key interest factors are indistinguishable for the two types of career. Thus the differences in answers in this poll cannot tell us whether different strategies and actions might be required for core technology careers versus support careers, in terms of attraction, promotion or retention.

Table 6. Interest of responders in support technology careers

Poll Response	No.	%	Comments
I have been interested in IT since I was young	26	63%	
I was interested in IT when I was young but lost interest	3	7%	
I only became interested in IT when it became part of my job	11	27%	Includes one no answer but comment "interested in IT when I have to choose a career at University."
I was never really interested in IT	1	3%	
	41	100%	

Table 7. Primary and secondary influencers: support technology careers

Influencing Factor	Primary Influence		Secondary Influence		Total	Ranking
	No.	%	No.	%		
Personal interest	25	61%	11	27%	44%	1
Advice - teacher or lecturer	0	0%	3	7%	4%	6
Advice - family & friends	5	12%	10	24%	18%	3
Intervention program	3	7%	2	5%	6%	4
Cultural influence	0	0%	5	12%	6%	4
Accident of history (+ 1 comment: the money)	8	20%	10	25%	22%	2
	41		41			

Breaking the support careers information down further to analyse their primary and secondary influencers results in Table 7.

In this group we see a greater influence of intervention activities, which move from 6th and 5th place for core technology careers into equal 4th position here. Perhaps this is a hint that intervention programs may have more influence on attracting women into support IT careers, versus the very strongly personal interest driving people into core IT careers; though personal interest and accident of history remain major factors. However a chi-squared analysis comparing the primary influencers for core vs. support activities is not significant (P=0.17). So once again the differences between groups in this poll are insufficient to conclude that we need to differentiate intervention programs depending on whether the career choice is core or support technology.

Overall, the data supports the idea that the individual is the core and is a unique cell. The interests they have or acquire from an early age are the dominant factor in their entry into IT careers, whether core or support; while *personal experience* of IT is the next most important factor. Things they see or are told have only a minor influence. Nevertheless, the individual lives within a social context, and the next chapters explore the cultural, social and structural factors that comprise these contexts within the STEMcell model.

REFERENCES

Accenture. (2013). *Defining success: 2013 global research results*. Retrieved September 1, 2013, from http://www.accenture.com/SiteCollectionDocuments/PDF/Accenture-IWD-2013-Research-Deck-022013.pdf

Adam, A. (2002). Exploring the gender question in critical information systems. *Journal of Information Technology*, *17*, 59–67. doi:10.1080/02683960210145959

Adya, M., & Kaiser, K. M. (2005). Early determinants of women in the IT workforce: A models of girl's career choices. *Information Technology & People*, *18*(3), 230–259. doi:10.1108/09593840510615860

Alper, J. (1993). The pipeline is leaking women all the way along. *Science*, *260*, 409–411. doi:10.1126/science.260.5106.409 PMID:17838262

Anderson, N., Lankshear, C., Timms, C., & Courtney, L. (2008). 'Because it's boring, irrelevant and I don't like computers': Why high school girls avoid professionally-oriented ICT subjects. *Computers & Education*, *50*(4), 1304–1318. doi:10.1016/j.compedu.2006.12.003

Armstrong, D. J., Riemenschneider, C. K., Reid, M., & Allen, M. (2007). Advancement, voluntary turnover and women in IT: A cognitive study of work–family conflict. *Information & Management*, *44*, 142–153. doi:10.1016/j.im.2006.11.005

Ashcraft, C., Eger, E., & Friend, M. (2012). *Girls in IT: The facts*. Boulder, CO: National Centre for Women & Information Technology (NCWIT). Retrieved August 6, 2013, from http://www.academia.edu/2283166/Girls_in_IT_The_Facts

Bateman, K. (2012). *Men and women disagree on reasons why IT is less attractive to women.* Retrieved July 20, 2013, from http://www.computerweekly.com/news/2240159441/Men-and-women-disagree-on-reasons-why-IT-is-less-attractive-to-women

Beekhuyzen, J., Nielsen, S., & von Hellens, L. (2003). Challenging dualisms in female perceptions of IT work. *Australian Journal of Information Systems*, *10*(2), 105–114.

Beekhuyzen, J., Nielsen, S., & von Hellens, L. (2006). *Making IT fit: Research and action in Queensland*. Paper presented at the AusWIT Australian Women in IT Conference. Adelaide, Australia.

Bernhardt, S. (2006). The global failure of intervention programs. In *Proceedings of ACEDC Conference*. Cairns, Australia: ACEDC. Retrieved July 29, 2013, from http://conferences.acce.edu.au/item.asp?pid=7493

Bernhardt, S. (2008). *The global failure of intervention programs*. Paper presented at the Edge of the Web Conference. Perth, Australia.

Berry, M., & Kalessi, T. (2011). *Women's careers in the technology industry*. London, UK: Intellect and Women in Technology (Report). Retrieved August 1, 2013, from http://sciencewithart.ijs.si/pdf/Women's_Careers_in_the_Technology_Industry_2011_Report.pdf

Berryman, S. E. (1983). *Who will do science? Minority and female attainment of science and mathematics degrees: Trends and causes*. New York: Rockefeller Foundation.

Castano, C., & Webster, J. (2011). Understanding women's presence in ICT: The life course perspective. *International Journal of Gender. Science and Technology*, *3*(2), 358–363.

Cave, K. (2013). Women in IT: Does the shortage matter? *IDG Connect Infographic*. Retrieved May 22, 2013, from http://www.idgconnect.com/abstract/1251/infographic-women-it-does-shortage-matter

Childs, S., & Krook, M. L. (2006). Should feminists give up on critical mass? A contingent yes. *Politics & Gender*, *2*, 522–530. doi:10.1017/S1743923X06251146

Commons Select Committee. (2013). *Women in STEM careers*. Retrieved July 26, 2013, from http://www.parliament.uk/business/committees/committees-a-z/commons-select/science-and-technology-committee/inquiries/parliament-2010/women-in-stem-careers/

Crabb, A. (2012). Publication of Germaine Greer's the female eunuch. *ABC Personalities Tell Us Which Days Changed Their Lives*. Retrieved August 2, 2013, from http://www.abc.net.au/archives/80days/stories/2012/01/19/3411580.htm

Da Silva Reis, S., & Schulze, E. (2012). *Policy department citizens rights and constitutional affairs – Women in ICT*. Brussels: European Parliament.

Dahlerup, D. (2006). The story of the theory of critical mass. *Politics & Gender*, *2*, 511–522. doi:10.1017/S1743923X0624114X

Elder, G. H., Jr. (1999). Children of the great depression: Social change in life experience (25th anniversay Ed.). Boulder, CO: Westview Press.

Exploring Computer Science. (2013). *CS education statistics*. Retrieved September 22, 2013, from http://www.exploringcs.org/resources/cs-statistics

Falub, M. (2013). *Fix the leaky pipeline – A career building program for women in science*. Retrieved July 26, 2013, from http://www.fix-the-leaky-pipeline.ch/

Giddens, A. (1984). *The constitution of society: Outline of the theory of structuration*. Cambridge, UK: Polity Press.

Gladwell, M. (2001). *The tipping point: How little things can make a big difference*. London, UK: Abacus.

Goodreads. (2013). *Jules Verne > Quotes > Quotable quote*. Retrieved August 2, 2013, from https://www.goodreads.com/quotes/51047-we-see-that-science-is-eminently-perfectible-and-that-each

Greenfield, S., Peters, J., Lane, N., Rees, T., & Samuels, G. (2002). *SET fair – A report on women in science, engineering and technology*. London: UK Government.

Greer, G. (1970). *The female eunuch*. London, UK: Paladin.

Ham, R., Junankar, P. N., & Wells, R. (2009). *Occupational choice: Personality matters* (IZA Discussion Paper No. 4105). Bonn: IZA.

Harding, S. (1986). *The science question in feminism*. Ithaca, NY: Cornell University Press.

Harding, S. (1991). *Whose science? Whose knowledge?* Ithaca, NY: Cornell University Press.

Harding, S. (1998). *Is science multicultural? Postcolonialisms, feminisms, and epistemologies*. Bloomington, IN: Indiana University Press.

Howcroft, D., Adam, A., & Richardson, H. (2004). A decade of neglect: reflecting on the gender and IS field. *New Technology, Work and Employment*, *19*, 222–240. doi:10.1111/j.1468-005X.2004.00139.x

Hutchison, E. D. (2008). *Dimensions of human behavior: The changing life course*. Los Angeles, CA: Sage.

Janack, M. (2004). Feminist epistemology. *Internet Encyclopedia of Philosophy*. Retrieved November 17, 2013, from http://www.iep.utm.edu/fem-epis/

Kirkup, G. (2011). Preparing women for dead-end jobs? Vocational education and training (VET) for information and communication technology (ICT) jobs. *International Journal of Gender Science and Technology*, *3*(2), 460–482.

Kramer, V. W., Konrad, A. M., & Erkut, S. (2006). *Critical mass on corporate boards: Why three or more women enhance governance*. Wellesley, MA: Wellesley Centers for Women's Publications Office.

Krause, K. W. (2013, March 13). The progressive war on science. *eSkeptic*. Retrieved August 2, 2013, from http://www.skeptic.com/eskeptic/13-03-13/

Lang, C., Craig, A., Fisher, J., Bennetts, K., & Forgasz, H. (2010). Dualisms: What women say about working in ICT. In *Proceedings of ACIS 2010*. ACIS.

Leonard, J. S. (1989). Women and affirmative action. *The Journal of Economic Perspectives*, *3*(1), 61–75. doi:10.1257/jep.3.1.61

Lyons, T., Quinn, F., Rizk, N., Anderson, N., Hubber, P., Kenny, J., et al. (2012). *Starting out in STEM: A study of young men and women in first year science, technology, engineering and mathematics courses*. Armidale, Australia: University of New England. Retrieved August 13, 2013, from http://www.une.edu.au/simerr/pages/projects/132iris_report.pdf

Meister, J. (2012). Job hopping is the 'new normal' for millennials: Three ways to prevent a human resource nightmare. *Forbes*. Retrieved July 28, 2013, from http://www.forbes.com/sites/jeannemeister/2012/08/14/job-hopping-is-the-new-normal-for-millennials-three-ways-to-prevent-a-human-resource-nightmare/

Merchant, N. (2012). 11 rules for creating value in the #SocialEra. Boston, MA: Harvard Business School (HBR Singles).

Mitchell, R. L. (2013). *Women computer science grads: The bump before the decline*. Retrieved August 28, 2013, from http://blogs.computerworld.com/it-careers/21993/women-computer-science-visual-trendline

Munro, K. (2011, June 13). More women than men taking the plunge into small business. *The Sydney Morning Herald*. Retrieved July 28, 2013, from http://www.smh.com.au/business/more-women-than-men-taking-the-plunge-into-small-business-20110612-1fzbj.html

Onwurah, C. (2013). *Women in IT: Reclaim the byte*. [Video]. Retrieved July 28, 2013, from http://www.computerweekly.com/video/Women-in-IT-Chi-Onwurah-Labour-Shadow-Cabinet-Office-Minister?videoId=2b0b3dc9692ef310VgnVCM1000000d01c80aRCRD

Parmar, B. (2013). *Women in IT*. [Video]. Retrieved July 28, 2013, from http://www.computerweekly.com/video/Women-in-IT-Belinda-Parmar-Little-Miss-Geek?videoId=eeff68e093fef310VgnVCM1000000d01c80aRCRD

Patten, E., & Parker, K. (2012). *A gender reversal on career aspirations: Young women now top young men in valuing a high-paying career*. Pew Research. Retrieved July 28, 2013, from http://www.pewsocialtrends.org/2012/04/19/a-gender-reversal-on-career-aspirations/

Powell, A., Bagilhole, A., & Dainty, A. (2006). The problem of women's assimilation into UK engineering cultures: Can critical mass work? *Equal Opportunities International*, *25*, 688–699. doi:10.1108/02610150610719146

Soe, L., & Yakura, E. K. (2008). What's wrong with the pipeline? Assumptions about gender and culture in IT work. *Women's Studies. An Inter-Disciplinary Journal*, *37*(3), 176–201.

Spender, D. (2011). *Girls and IT – What's changed?* Retrieved July 27, 2013, from http://dalespender.com.au/~dalespen/wp-content/uploads/2011/05/GIRLS-AND-IT.pdf

Svinth, L. (2006). *Leaky pipeline – To be or not to be a useful metaphor in understanding why women to a disproportional degree exit from scientific careers.* Paper presented at the 6th European Gender Research Conference – UPGEM. Retrieved July 27, 2013, from http://www.dpu.dk/upgem/conferencesandseminars/europeangender-researchconference/

Thornton, M. (2007). *Who's minding the gender gap in IT?* Retrieved June 10, 2013, from http://searchcio-midmarket.techtarget.com/magazine-Content/Whos-Minding-the-Gender-Gap-in-IT

Trauth, E. M. (2006). Theorizing gender and information technology research using the individual differences theory of gender and IT. In E. M. Trauth (Ed.), *Encyclopedia of gender and information technology* (Vol. 2, pp. 1154–1159). Hershey, PA: Idea Group Reference. doi:10.4018/978-1-59140-815-4.ch182

Trauth, E. M. (2011). What can we learn from gender research? Seven lessons for business research methods. *The Electronic Journal of Business Research Methods*, *9*(1), 1–9.

Trauth, E. M., & Quesenberry, J. (2006). Are women an underserved community in the information technology profession? In *Proceedings of the International Conference on Information Systems* (pp. 1757-1770). Milwaukee, WI: University of Wisconsin.

Trauth, E. M., Quesenberry, L. L., & Huang, H. (2009). Retaining women in the U.S. I.T workforce: Theorizing the influence of organizational factors. *European Journal of Information Systems*, *18*(5), 476–497. doi:10.1057/ejis.2009.31

von Hellens, L., Trauth, E., & Fisher, J. (2012). Editorial. *Information Systems Journal*, *22*, 343–353. doi:10.1111/j.1365-2575.2012.00412.x

von Hellens, L. A., & Nielsen, S. N. (2001). Australian women in IT. *Communications of the ACM*, *44*(7), 46–52. doi:10.1145/379300.379310

Wajcman, J. (2010). Feminist theories of technology. *Cambridge Journal of Economics*, *34*, 143–152. doi:10.1093/cje/ben057

Waugh, P. (2013a). *Pia Waugh: Director of coordination and gov 2.0 for technology & procurement division, department of finance and deregulation.* Retrieved July 22, 2013, from http://www.linkedin.com/pub/pia-waugh/0/a7b/990

Waugh, P. (2013b). *GovHack 2013 report – How the beast went national.* Retrieved July 22, 2013, from http://www.govhack.org/govhack-2013-report-how-the-beast-went-national/

Wittenberg-Cox, A. (2013). *What Cisco CEO John Chambers needs to know about gender balance.* Retrieved June 4, 2013 from http://blogs.hbr.org/cs/2013/03/what_cisco_ceo_john_chambers_n.html

Xie, Y., & Shauman, K. (2003). *Women in science: Career processes and outcomes.* Boston, MA: Harvard University Press.

KEY TERMS AND DEFINITIONS

Critical Mass Model: A model to aid understanding aspects of human behaviour in larger social settings, where critical mass is a sufficient number of adopters so that the rate of adoption becomes self-sustaining and creates further growth.

Dualism Model: A model that outlines binary opposition in which qualities such as intuitive/analytical are regarded as mutually exclusive.

Essentialist Theory: invokes relatively fixed and unified biological differences between men and women to explain differences in their relationship to technology.

GovHack: Hacker teams meet across Australia to work together to create new mashups, data visualizations and applications with Government data.

ICT: Information and Communication Technology. Synonymous with IT.

Individual Difference Theory: takes elements from essentialist and social construction theories to posit a variety of relationships within gender and IT based on the reaction of personal characteristics to environmental influences.

Leaky Pipeline: An analogy used in association with STEM careers to explain the loss of women at different career stages.

Life Course Approach: A multidisciplinary paradigm for the study of people's lives within structural, social and cultural contexts, treating life decisions across all domains of a person's life as interdependent.

Social Construction Theory: argues that the influences of various socio-cultural factors are the primary constructs shaping individuals and their relationship to IT. Hence, IT has been socially shaped as "men's work", which places IT careers outside the female domain.

#SocialEra: a term (coined by Nilofer Merchant) to describe a shift in focus from traditional methods to a more social movement, which has profound implications for business and how people work and lead.

#SocialIT: a term coined for the layer of the STEMcell Model derived from #SocialEra concepts. It is a disruptive, penetrating force that can enhance the positive and reduce the negative aspects of the Cultural, Social, Structural and Individual contexts affecting women in IT.

STEM: Science, Technology, Engineering and Mathematics, conceptually related fields that share issues of under-representation of women. An extension of SET to include maths.

Structuration Theory: a social theory of the creation and reproduction of social systems that is based in the analysis of both structure and agents.

Theory of Reasoned Action: a model for the prediction of behavioural intention, spanning predictions of attitudes and predictions of behaviour.

Chapter 5
Cultural and Social Contexts and Influencing Factors

ABSTRACT

The first two layers of the STEMcell Model are detailed in this chapter: the cultural and social contexts and their influencing factors. These are largely identified in the voluminous preceding research. Key cultural influencing factors are popular culture, cultural norms, parental expectations, and occupational culture. Key social influencing factors are stereotypes, role modelling, mentoring, clubs, networks, media, peers, family, hygiene factors, and social norms. These factors and the degree of their actual influence are discussed critically, highlighting potential warning signs and issues. The overall conclusion is that, with the exception of cultures that strictly limit female participation, both the contexts themselves and interventions targeted at them have much less influence than is commonly assumed.

Marilyn once sang diamonds are a girl's best friend. These days that's not true. ICT skills are a girl's best friend. Have them, and the diamonds will follow.

– Neelie Kroes, VP of the European Commission responsible for the digital agenda (25 April 2013) (Kroes, 2013)

INTRODUCTION

Cultural and Social contexts feature strongly throughout the literature on women in technology. Given that the majority of research on this topic is in the social science field, it is not surprising that the key factors identified as influencing female participation in computing, often deterring them from choosing future technology education or careers in IT, have tended to have social science roots.

This chapter explores both the cultural and social factors raised in the past research, with each context represented sequentially.

CULTURAL CONTEXT AND INFLUENCING FACTORS

In the STEMcell Model, cultural context is represented by an earth-like crust that expands or shrinks according to its own strength and the impact of the

DOI: 10.4018/978-1-4666-5860-8.ch005

Figure 1. Cultural breakdown: Cultural factors influencing female participation in IT

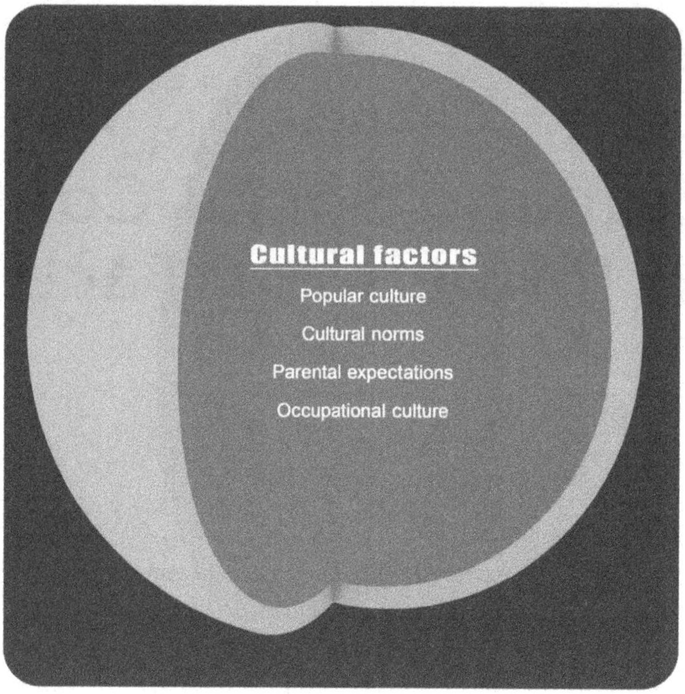

other contexts (social, structural, individual and #SocialIT). For example, in cultures that strictly limit or ban female participation or technology the cultural crust will be the dominant pervasive context. A visualization of the cultural "crust" listing specific influencing issues is diagrammed in Figure 1.

Several studies (Ahuja, 2002; Gras-Velazquez, Joyce & Debry, 2009; Castano & Webster, 2011; Ashcraft, Eger & Friend, 2012) have addressed the topic of varied cultural influences in analyses of gender and IT. Table 1 summarises a review of the literature on noted cultural influencing factors.

Popular Culture

Popular culture is defined on Wikipedia as "the entirety of ideas, perspectives, attitudes, memes, images and other phenomena that are within the mainstream of a given culture." It is identified as having a "pervasive and increasingly interconnected nature." Examples of historical elements that have had a role in defining popular culture have been rock music, *Star Wars* and *The Simpsons*.

If the main cause of women entering IT is their personal interest from a young age (Chapter Four: *The Old Approach*), then we can see the importance of popular culture as experienced by children. Historical examples of "young children" popular culture are *The Wiggles* and *Dora the Explorer*. Today a computer game called *Minecraft* is shaping popular culture among children. It and games like it have an immense potential to be drivers of tectonic change encouraging the organic rise of girls' and women's interest and participation in technology.

The Game Changer

Since its initial release in 2009, Minecraft has sold over 20 million copies across various platforms (smartphones, computers and tablets) worldwide and has attracted millions of global players. The

Table 1. Cultural context and influencing factors

Influencing Factor	Reference
Popular culture	Ashcraft et al. (2012); Hayes (2005, 2008)
Cultural norms	Castano & Webster (2011); Gras-Velazquez et al. (2009); UNESCO (2012)
Parental expectations	Ashcraft et al. (2012)
Occupational culture	Ahuja (2002); Guzman, Stanton, & Eischen (2006); Guzman & Stanton (2009); Modi, Schoenberg & Salmond (2012)

game is about activating minds: to build, be challenged, have fun and interact socially with other gamers (collaboratively or competitively). However the underlying skills developed are IT. Groom (2012) comments, "Minecraft is a visual programming language. Yes mum, your six year old is engaged in computational thinking and is writing code with those blocks. Minecraft is perhaps the start of a kid's interest in their future job – the fact it looks like cubes ignores the cognitive development that is happening with that technology." Garratt (2012) describes the experience, when playing Minecraft with his young children, as "You can build anything, go anywhere. We explored together, put up a large house on a hill with a glass roof, visited snowscapes and deserts. We dug tunnels, had little tantrums over whether to dig for coal or go look at the lava pool for the fiftieth time, and we've planted special trees in our garden. We even learnt about smelting and metal ore. Minecraft truly is an amazing feat."

Ashcraft et al. (2012) recognize that "The rise of gaming and its influence on girls' participation in computing merits further research. In addition to more traditional media texts, games have become a significant aspect of popular culture and are often children's first introduction to computing kinds of activities." The increasing trend of girls participating in games (Denner, 2011; Hayes, 2008) and specifically Minecraft is starting to be noticed. As discussed by Frankincense (2012), "At the server I'm playing at right now we got quite a surprise when we discovered that about 65-70% of the members were actually girls. None of us presumed the players were girls, we just naturally presumed they were boys. It's something a lot of us do, to be fair, and it's pretty funny when you think about it. Because when I've been looking around on the internet – I realize that the amount of girls who play Minecraft is actually very, very large indeed." Frankincense (herself a female often referred to as "Sir" in forums) further states "the fact is: Lots of girls do play Minecraft. However, most girls don't have very girly nicknames, and they won't say: 'Hello! I am a girl!' once they meet you. They just play the game in the same way you do, and just like you don't say: 'Hello, I am male!' when you meet someone, they won't declare what sex they are when they're just playing a game."

This is exactly the influence we hope and expect from #SocialIT and people thinking of themselves primarily as individuals. They do not identify themselves by their gender or any other group, just as themselves. And nobody notices or cares.

What is particularly interesting about Minecraft is it has not been specifically tailored to appeal to girls. It has not been pink rebadged or designed to fit some designer's preconceptions of what girls want. As Kroes (2013) noted, "We've all seen industry attempts to create 'special' women's ICT products. Often, regrettably, they're designed by men, following the tired philosophy of 'shrink it and pink it'. And sometimes the result is excruciating. But women don't need 'woman-friendly' smartphones or apps, any more than they need woman-friendly pens or cars. That's not the problem." Minecraft is mine craft: it's about meaningful building. Smith (2011) describes it as "There is no bloodshed, unless you count a pig being turned into a pork chop… you don't see slaughter etc… there are no guns YAY and only minor sword, bow and arrow combat, most of the time people playing Minecraft are just building things and playing in them. You will hear things like 'Hey I chucked you some mushroom soup', 'I have wheat now'… 'Oh look some lead or something'… 'I'm mining some gold!'… much better than hearing kill that guy! KILL KILL, well except for a few creepers, and spiders and you will want to avoid them or kill those…Yes you can kill each other but it's not blood thirsty, and friends don't do that 'cause it takes a long time to build your health back up again…(re-spawn). There are griefers… people who go around trying to destroy your stuff, but if you have a private map that's not going to happen. And the game moderators are pretty much on top of any bad behaviour. This game is great for creativity, for fun, for teamwork, for challenges and collaboration. My kids only play with people they know, and only sometimes go out onto the public grids. They love it! The things they can make are anything from houses, to castles, to huge statues, roads, anything that can be made of blocks basically with lots of ways to make their constructions unique."

While in the past boys spent more time gaming than girls, the Minecraft phenomena, *The Sims* to some extent and Hayes' (2008) findings suggest that the divide is narrowing. Thus games are showing promise of being game *changers*, to make IT more relevant and involve children early in actual computing activities (Hayes, 2008; Kafai, Heeter, Denner & Sun, 2008). It is even spreading into more formal education. One comment on a blog post by Groom (2012) noted: "Never fear there are a group of educators leading the way using Minecraft in education! I'm a teacher in an international school in Singapore and we are using Minecraft in Creative mode in a unit of work called 'How We Organize Ourselves'. Grade 3 students plan for two weeks on pencil and paper the layout of a functioning community and the systems in place to make it run smoothly. They create teams who are in charge of certain aspects and then they get to create their community in Minecraft… I can't even fathom how much we have transformed the student's learning by doing this."

As noted by Ashcraft et al. (2012), "This potential is complicated, however, by the fact that historically games have been primarily made by men and for male audiences… Research has shown that it is important to move beyond stereotypes about what kinds of games interest girls versus boys and take a more complex look at how women actually interact with a variety of games and the nuanced reasons that they like or dislike certain aspects of games (e.g., rather than for example, assuming all girls or women do not like violent games) (e.g., Hayes, 2005; Kafai, 2008)." Yet Minecraft lets us see more deeply into that issue, and has shown three things. First, beneath gender differences are more significant human commonalities: boys and girls both enjoy Minecraft, often for similar reasons of creativity, design and problem solving. Second, "open" games like Minecraft, where you choose your own goals and methods, appeal not only to any "gender stereotypes" (I was amused one day listening to boys and girls talking to each other about Minecraft: the girls were all cooperating and the boys were all fighting in the game!), but more importantly to any *individual* preferences. Third, despite worries about games designed by and for males, Minecraft was originally designed by men – yet may attract more girls than boys.

The current and future impact of Minecraft and games it will spawn is likely to be felt strongly. Groom (2012) notes, "no one can deny this one game changed the course of games to come. Go onto Youtube and just type in the name. Thousands of videos pop up on the screen from silly moments to grand monuments of engineering. Someone even built a working computer in the game. Music videos, sketches, and life-size replicas of the Enterprise; the very thing that made *Minecraft* fun to play also made it easy for someone watching from the outside to understand. And from this one game a single thought rose from gamers' minds, 'There must be more great games like *Minecraft* out there.'"

Or better yet, lead girls' thoughts to turn to "There must be more great games like Minecraft *in here. I* can design a great game too!"

Forensic Analysis

Cave (2013) proposed "Maybe HBO should commission a glamorous IT drama with Megan Fox cast as the head geek?" and indeed I proposed a like "solution" in a Government report circa 2000. This style of solution attempts to exploit how popular culture influences perceptions and drives outcomes.

There is no denying the effect that a popular glamorisation can have on career interest in a field. The TV series "CSI: Crime Scene Investigation" is a classic case. In the USA, "180 people applied for 20 spots in the forensic-science master's program at Michigan State University in East Lansing" (Lovgren, 2004), while "In Australia, the number of education institutes offering forensic science qualifications has boomed from one university in 1994 to nearly 20 in 2005. In the UK, the number of students enrolled in forensic science majors have increased from 2,191 in 2002-03 to 5,664 in 2007-08" (Samarji, 2013). Ashcraft et al. (2012) report "One survey of 508 U.K. students aged 14-18 found that forensic scientist — an occupation only recently popularized in recent crime dramas such as CSI — was girls' 6th most popular job choice and boys' 8th most popular job choice (Miller & Hayward, 2006)." In addition there has been an overall increase in the use of the word forensic in titles of science courses worldwide (Samarji, 2013), as well as in job descriptions in science and other areas such as forensic accounting.

The effect of popular culture on career interest is not a recent phenomenon. For example in Australia the TV series "A Country Practice" aired from 1981 – 1993, and whilst it was primarily about a country medical practice and hospital, the show included a very popular veterinary practice and anecdotal reports of increased enrolments in vet studies followed. Given those trends and the popularity of the TV series *The Big Bang Theory*, we may be about to see a similar spike in astrophysics-flavoured courses.

These examples hint at the power of popular culture to raise awareness and influence perceptions about occupations. A word of caution though is flagged by Rincon (2005): "People have unrealistic expectations of forensic science thanks to the success of the CSI TV shows." Consequently Samarji (2013) writes, "Some Year-12 students, I would contend, are taken in by TV shows to the extent they start enquiring about forensic science courses before even considering whether they truly enjoy science or whether there are job opportunities for them when they graduate. Some students, in my experience, want to become forensic experts without considering whether or not they are prepared to work at 2am picking blowfly larvae from a corpse with a pair of tweezers. The fact forensic science is very specialised and forensic investigations can be challenging, time-consuming and complicated is often overlooked by movie and TV show makers – and consequently students and the public at large."

A further downside can be a flood of qualified applicants into a market that hasn't enough jobs for them – or has no jobs of the flavour sought. For example, "In Australia there are just over a thousand forensic scientists in a very stable environment. Consequently, there are very few vacant positions per year" (National Institute of Forensic Science [NIFS], 2001). The Victorian Police Force in Australia were prompted to publish a statement titled "Is Forensic Science really like the television show CSI?," which compares reality to the show and concludes "there are no jobs in Australia like those depicted on CSI" (Victoria Police, 2013). And while demand for IT workers greatly exceeds that for forensic scientists, if our aim is to encourage girls into IT the last thing we need is a horde of women being disillusioned by such careers. Much as I like the female geek character Felicity in the TV series *Arrow*, the chance of a real woman finding herself aiding a romantic masked vigilante by hacking into government systems in order to bring justice to a corrupt city is rather remote!

Such glamorised popular stories can have yet further unexpected and negative roll on effects in society at large. For example, the "CSI Effect" has given the general public and even police officers exaggerated impressions of the power and speed of forensic science, leading to all kinds of unrealistic expectations from jurors expecting extensive forensic evidence even where it isn't necessary, to police and families expecting answers in hours rather than months (Rincon, 2005; Samarji, 2013).

These are important warning signs regarding injecting an artificial solution through glamorised, exaggerated portrayals spread via popular culture. To put it in terms of the "leaky pipeline" metaphor (Chapter Four: *The Old Approach*), there is no point doubling the number of girls entering IT courses if half of them quit because what attracted them does not actually exist. Or worse, they enter IT careers and end up as negative role models complaining about how disillusioned they are.

Cultural Norms

Cultural norms are defined as cultural regulations, morals or guidelines, which designate approved and proper actions within the framework of a particular society.

These norms can affect how women access and view IT. As Shen, Zhang & Tarmizi (2009) state, "The gaps between men and women interactions with ICT can be dependent on the specific national or ethnic culture. The gap is wider in some of the cultures such as Arabic culture where women tend to be subject to strong social norms and restricted from social interaction with people outside their family members. Yet in other cultures, the gap can be either minimum or not noticeable."

To date most research has been on "the Anglo-Saxon countries (particularly the USA and the UK)" (Castano & Webster, 2011). Thus, Shen et al. (2009) note that "we still lack understanding of how such differences vary for different cultures since the role perceptions of women are largely shaped and embedded in their respective culture. Most prior research is dominant with the Western culture. Then to what extent such conclusions can be applied to the other cultural contexts, e.g., Chinese culture, Arabic culture, and etc.? Is there any unique pattern of ICT usage, motivational factor for different cultural contexts?" Castano & Webster (2011) comment along similar lines: "In different countries, there are contrasting education systems, gender regimes and family structures, and employment cultures," and these naturally bring with them influencing factors.

Thus, much of the research referenced in this book could be considered to be about our own cultural norms, which raises some interesting questions. Chapter Ten: *Differences – Industries and Ethnicities* specifically addresses differences in other ethnicities such as Hispanic or Asian. Issues experienced in Western societies regarding the "problem" of women in technology do not exist in some cultures throughout Asia – or at least not in the same form.

Studies over the past decade are beginning to add to this body of knowledge, e.g. Italy, Poland, UK, Netherlands and France (Gras-Velazquez, Joyce & Debry, 2009); non-Anglophone Western Europe (Valenduc et al., 2005; Castaño, Müller, Gonzalez & Palmén, 2010); southern and eastern Europe (Turner, 2005), Africa (Rathgeber & Ofwona Adera, 2000); and South East Asia and India (Ng & Mitter, 2005; D'Mello, 2006).

These more recent studies provide a nuanced picture, and "suggest that some of the explanation for variation lies in the different social contexts and social arrangements within which ICT education and employment takes place: the educational culture and curriculum structure; the gender culture of the society; women's labour market situation;

and the provision of support systems by the state, the family, and other institutions" (Castano & Webster, 2011).

The following example is for science but eerily maps to our experience in IT. Akst (2013) reports "Globally, 15-year-old girls outscored boys in 43 of the 65 countries tested. In Asian, eastern and southern European, and Middle Eastern countries, teenage girls perform better, on average, than teenage boys on a test for science comprehension. But in the United States and a handful of other countries, particularly those in western and northern Europe and the Americas, the reverse was true, *The New York Times* reported. The test, administered by the Organization for Economic Cooperation and Development and given in 65 developed countries, points to culture differences in the incentives offered for learning math and science, project lead Andreas Schleicher told *The Times*. In the U.S., he said, boys are more likely than girls to 'see science as something that affects their life.' Christianne Corbett, a senior researcher at the American Association of University Women, agreed, saying, 'we see that very early in childhood—around age 4—gender roles in occupations appear to be formed. Women are less likely to go into science careers, although they are clearly capable of succeeding.' In contrast, Schleicher said, 'for girls in some Arab countries—such as Jordan, where girls outscored boys by an impressive 8 percent—education is the only way to move up the social structure. It is one way to earn social mobility'."

The Middle East and North Africa are putting a spotlight on women and technology as described by Satterfield (2013): "Last week in Jordan 50 women from Algeria, Egypt, Jordan, Lebanon, the Palestinian Territories, Tunisia, Yemen and the United States came together to map out ways in which they could use the TechWomen network to encourage more women and girls to pursue professions in science, technology, engineering, and mathematic (STEM). TechWomen is a program… that pairs emerging women leaders in technology from the Middle East and North Africa with leading American women from the Silicon Valley area, using technology as a means to empower women and girls. While in Jordan, these TechWomen participated in workshops and even pitched project ideas to organizations that provide support services to individual entrepreneurs hoping to start their own businesses… which allowed students and professional women to discuss the latest innovations in the field, share best practices, and build a global network."

That example highlights the increasing globalization of information and human networks in the modern era. Such globalization can only help overcome barriers from cultural norms. While such norms will obviously continue to affect the women living in them, greater communication between cultures will help show, to women of all cultures, what other things might be possible to them. An example is the Arab world, where "The young generation in the Arab world are influenced by both Islamic and modern cultures (Solberg, 2002), which may not stay in harmony. The conflict brought by the usage of Internet and exposure to western culture, fundamentally shapes the self-perception of young generation and affects their identity development. Particularly, compared to their counterparts, women in the Arab world may experience more conflicts and transformation in their self-identity: 'The Internet, blogs, and social networking sites now give voices to those most marginalized in the Middle East today – young people and women' (Eltahawy, 2008)" (Shen et al., 2009).

Parental Expectations

Parental expectations and how much influence they have are obviously themselves affected by cultural norms. Presumably they are both less rigid and less influential the freer and more cosmopolitan the society is. In any culture parents clearly have an influence on girls' choices, but how much is less clear.

Ashcraft et al. (2012) flag "Parental or familial expertise or career in computing can play an important role, but the exact role is unclear or varies. In one survey of 937 women currently working in computing occupations (Liston, Peterson & Ragan, 2008), 38% of the women had fathers who worked in a STEM field and 10% had mothers who did. Barron (2004) found that 75% of girls reported having a parent or family member in the computing field as a reason for choosing to take a programming course; only 29% of the boys chose this as a reason for taking the course. In contrast, however, Gal-Ezer, Shahak & Zur (2009) surveyed 229 high school students to better understand why CS continues to be male-dominated throughout the western world. The authors found that parents encouraged their sons to pursue CS courses in high school more than their daughters but that parents' careers were not a significant factor in students' decisions to take CS for either boys or girls. Cultural differences may be at play here as this study was conducted in Israel. Regardless, the question remains open since we do not really know how many girls (or boys) who do not choose computing careers might also have a parent in the field and cite this as a reason for not selecting this career."

A study by Gras-Velazquez et al. (2009) "of 348 students in the UK shows that parents' expectations have a strong influence on career decisions: boys being more directly influenced by their fathers, girls by their mothers (Kniveton, 2004). This is important when we consider that 'computer-savvy' parents are three times more likely to be male than female (Carrington, Tymms & Merrell, 2008)." Furthermore, they found "a direct correlation between the enthusiasm of mothers for ICT and that evidenced by their daughters. Pleasingly, most mothers surveyed as part of the European Schoolnet-CISCO project were positive about ICT studies."

It is interesting that the ratio of "computer-savvy" fathers to mothers cited by Gras-Velazquez et al. (2009) is similar to the ratio of fathers to mothers in STEM fields cited by Ashcraft et al. (2012) above, despite the former's finding that girls are more influenced by their mothers. This illustrates the complexities of trying to untangle the effects of parental influence and personal interest.

With technology and society changing rapidly and the time lag between those changes and academic survey results, it will be interesting to see what the future holds. We can expect parents to continue to have an influence, but negative influences of prejudice and lack of parental IT familiarity to reduce rapidly. Today's parents are themselves becoming increasingly technologically savvy, and tomorrow's parents are today's highly e-connected teenagers. And today's toddlers, the parents in 20 to 30 years time, are already using their own iPads.

Occupational Culture

Occupational culture is defined as the "distinctive norms and practices, formal and informal, associated with particular occupational groups" (Guzman, Stanton & Eischen, 2006). Guzman et al. (2006) further explained that "Occupational cultures have the same characteristics as any culture with a different degree of distinctiveness based on the occupation," and that "Occupational socialization is the process by which individuals acquire, learn, and adopt the ideologies, beliefs, cultural forms, and practices of an occupational culture."

The first documented empirical study of IT occupational culture was conducted by Duliba & Barouid (1991). They concluded that there was a distinct IT occupational culture, though a weak influence at the time. IT occupational culture in educational institutions is outlined by Ahuja (2002) as almost an encapsulation of the geek stereotype: "This 'occupational-culture' prevalent in the world of IT in universities and colleges incorporates exceptionally long hours, late nights and highly focused, almost obsessive behaviour."

The issue from our perspective is that women entering IT careers may find the culture waiting for them incompatible with their own values. As Guzman et al. (2006) explain, "Individuals who are part of the occupation first come into it with values derived from family, school, and community. As they evolve in their occupational communities, individuals go through a process of adaptation where they manifest positive and negative reactions of adjustment to the culture." As a consequence, "The results suggest that women, ethnic minorities and those with less work experience encountered greater difficulty fitting into different dimensions of ITOC [IT Occupational Culture]. The results also showed that cultural fit is a good predictor of occupational commitment and affective commitment in particular" (Guzman & Stanton, 2009). Similarly, Ahuja (2002) notes, "For many women, [the long hours and highly focused] work ethic may conflict with their safety concerns and family responsibilities. The hackers who are predominantly male are seen as being 'bright and creative'. Women remain on the periphery of this dominant culture… The occupational culture interacts with social expectations to keep women outside the inner circles of IT." Thus Ahuja (2002) proposes that "The perception of occupational culture will negatively influence women's' choice of… and persistence in IT careers."

However IT occupational culture is not something that is set and we should not assume that historical studies still apply. And not only is IT evolving and subject to rapid change, individual motivators can override occupational culture. The power of the individual is demonstrated by Advincula (2012) in a post that advises, "If you are a young girl in tech, realize that you will be different, accept that, but don't expect others to change for you….hard work and coding skills will earn their respect …embrace that fact and instead of losing confidence over it, use it to your advantage." Indeed, girls are already embracing that fact: "All [STEM] girls think that obstacles make them stronger … and feel motivated to prove people wrong who question their capabilities" (Modi et al., 2012).

SOCIAL CONTEXT AND INFLUENCING FACTORS

In the STEMcell Model, social context is represented by an earth-like mantle that operates within the crust of cultural context and wraps around the individual at the core. A visualization of the social "mantle" and its specific influencing factors are shown in Figure 2.

Noted social influencing factors identified in the literature are listed in Table 2.

Stereotypes: Gender and ICT

It is frequently proposed that widespread stereotyping of ICT workers is a major inhibitor to increasing women's uptake of ICT in education and as an occupation. As such, debunking gender and ICT stereotypes has been a major focus of intervention programs. As Berry & Kalessi (2011) comment, "The nerdy image of the industry is still seen as a major concern for most women. 41% of respondents believe that young girls are put off pursuing a career in the technology industry by the sector's 'nerdy' image." Cheryan, Plaut, Handron & Hudson (2013) describe research that specifically tested IT stereotypes and whether changing these stereotypes using the media can influence women's interest in computer science, and reported that "Women who read that computer scientists no longer fit the stereotypes expressed more interest in computer science than those who read that computer scientists fit the stereotypes."

Research by Gras-Velazquez et al. (2009) revealed some highly relevant results: "An important conclusion emerged from the study in terms of attitudes towards the sector in general. The older generation continue to see the sector as better

Figure 2. Social breakdown: social factors influencing female participation in IT

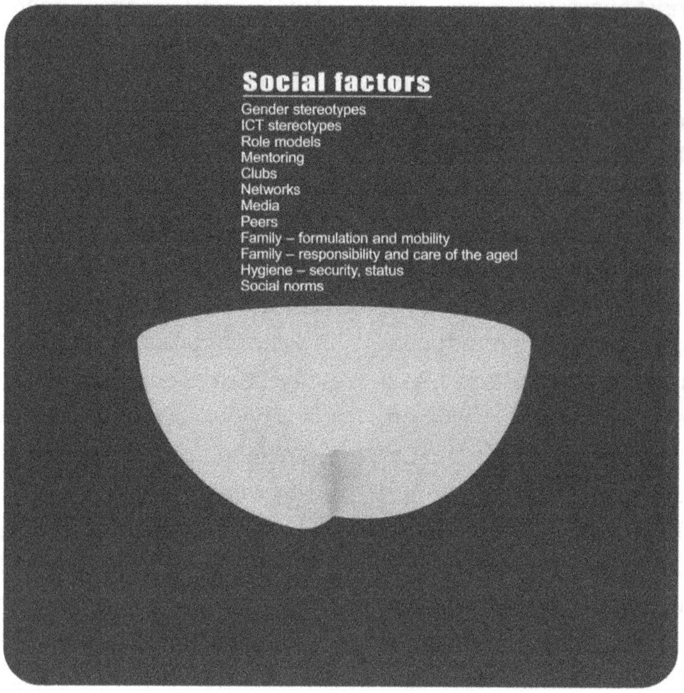

Table 2. Social context and influencing factors

Influencing Factor	Reference
Gender stereotypes	Denner (2011); Gras-Velazquez et al. (2009); UNESCO (2012)
ICT stereotypes	Clayton, Beekhuyzen & Nielsen (2012); Denner (2011); UNESCO (2012)
Role models	Ahuja (2002); Ashcraft et al. (2012); Barker & Aspray (2006); Clayton et al. (2012); Cozza (2011); Gras-Velazquez et al. (2009); Miliszewska & Moore (2011)
Mentoring	Craig, Fisher & Lang (2007); Trauth, Quesenberry & Huang (2009)
Clubs	Lang, Fisher & Craig (2007); Miliszewska & Moore (2011)
Networks	Margolis & Fisher (2002); UNESCO (2012)
Media	Adya & Kaiser (2005); Ashcraft et al. (2012); Barker & Aspray (2006); Clayton et al. (2012); Cozza (2011); Lyons et al. (2012)
Peers	Adya & Kaiser (2005); Barker & Aspray (2006); Clayton et al. (2012); Cozza (2011); Denner (2011); Margolis & Fisher (2002)
Family – formulation and mobility	Adya & Kaiser (2005); Barker & Aspray (2006); Castano & Webster (2011); Clayton et al. (2012); Griffiths & Moore (2010); Margolis & Fisher (2002)
Family – responsibility and care of the aged	Adya & Kaiser (2005); Castano & Webster (2011); Clayton et al. (2012); Lang & McKay (2006); Trauth et al. (2009)
Hygiene – security, status	Beekhuyzen, Nielsen, & von Hellens (2006); Nielsen, von Hellens, Pringle & Greenhill (1999)
Social norms	UNESCO (2012)

suited to men… Interestingly, the younger male generation is more positive than any other group about girls' aptitudes and potential. This may indicate that attitudes are evolving." Continuing this trend, Denner (2011) found that "girls endorse less traditional gender stereotypes than a generation ago." Similarly, Gratton (2012) writes, "Generation Z will begin to enter the workforce within the next 10 years… Both men and women will have lifelong experience of using communications and media technologies that are at once sophisticated and simple to use. We can expect many jobs to be done anywhere anytime… Generation Z are growing up in a world with increasing equality between men and women… We can imagine that this generation will be more accepting of gender equality… I believe that gender equality and communication technologies will be key aspects of the information age. There are currently few women leading companies – and very few leading technology companies. But the experiences of our youngsters suggest that this will change. The next Steve Jobs could indeed be a woman."

I too believe that attitudes are indeed evolving, so rapidly that if today's youth were surveyed in the absence of preconceptions from the industry's history the results would already be markedly different. In that light we also need to consider whether loudly decrying the problems of stereotypes is part of what keeps the stereotypes alive. Perhaps older generations passing down their perceptions, over-discussing them, and running campaigns to fight them, are themselves raising this awareness. It's almost like the CSI effect, where continual presentations and reminders are helping it prevail in popular culture.

Stereotypes affecting women are not limited to IT itself. Cohoon (2012) writes, "if Steve Jobs had been a woman, he would have lived in a different world than the world he knew as a man. Steve Jobs, the man, lived in a world where technical interests, technical education, and aggressive business behaviour were appropriate. Investors saw potential for his success, because Jobs fit their expectations for technical business genius. Employees tolerated his eccentricities because they saw him as a successful leader. Had Jobs been a woman, his behaviour may not have been interpreted in such a positive light." No doubt there is some truth in those stereotypes, but they are just stereotypes: of businessmen, of investors, of co-workers. And all these things are changing. If we want to encourage women into IT, it will not help to tell them they are doomed to be discounted or despised by everyone from the investors to their bosses to their peers.

Replacing one stereotype with another may not be the best way to go either. Randi Zuckerberg "is propelled by a feminist mission to make tech entrepreneurship more accessible and exciting to women. Others have tried to do the same, by encouraging girls to pursue math and science, creating women's networking groups, and calling out the frat boy culture of many tech companies (Facebook in its early days was a notorious culprit)… Zuckerberg's approach is to make Silicon Valley's public image 'a little more glamorous,' and let women know that they don't need math or science skills to be part of the fun." Her first attempt, a reality TV show *Start-Ups: Silicon Valley* failed in the public eye and left some "offended that Zuckerberg tried to inspire women to go into tech through a dumbed-down, sexed-up reality show, which skips out most of the boring 'making something' part" (Gordon, 2012).

During my lifetime I have been actively involved in a variety of projects and activities aimed at debunking the perceived stereotypes. These have targeted school children, university students, the general public and industry participants. One of particular note-worthiness was a project undertaken in North Queensland, *Rural and Remote IT Stars*. This project was for attracting Indigenous Australian females to IT, and placed particular emphasis on debunking popular misconceptions of IT careers. It was a residential camp where participants worked in groups on self-selected areas of interest to explore and use various IT programs.

In addition, information was readily available on pathways for technology careers. The overall experience was un-school-like, with evening events and industry role model discussions, as well as assistance to establish links between students and industry to assist with future work opportunities (Anderson, 2003). This project seemed to have all the elements of success – however student responses to the post-camp question "Are you more likely now to choose a job involving computers?" recorded the lowest score of all post-camp survey questions. This illustrates the problems of applying interventions to artificially interfere with choices that occur organically over time according to the individuals' interests. It appears that a majority of participants, whilst they enjoyed the experience, really were just not interested in careers in technology. And this is with the kind of group – remotely situated with relatively poor access to IT – in which we might expect interventions to have the greatest benefit.

It is always worth challenging stereotypes – so perhaps we should challenge the stereotypes *about* stereotypes. Given my main premise that most women who would be in IT are in IT, and they came there due to their own interests whether discovered early or through an accident of history; and given the self-powered strength of "STEM women": I propose that the stereotypes actually have little impact on the individual's decision to pursue IT studies or career. I am not saying there is no geekiness in IT – but that it isn't a deterrent to those genuinely interested in IT careers.

To go even further, perhaps there is a case for the opposite: that the quirky geekiness of many who inhabit IT is *attractive* to others interested in the area. It seems OK to speak of stereotypes in other careers: that people who pursue early education careers are kind and like children; that people who own and run bookshops like to read and get lost in a book. In fact such stereotypes have an obvious basis in reality: any specialised job has aspects which will attract some people and repel others, whether the job involves "picking maggots off corpses," teaching, accounting – or IT. Some percentage of people in technology may be geeky and may indeed have awkwardness in social situations. But attempting to blame, deny or wipe out those aspects of the people inhabiting IT is what is not realistic.

Gender stereotypes can also have an effect in the other direction, in hiring decisions rather than career choice. For example, Moss-Racusin, Dovidio, Brescoll, Graham & Handelsman (2012) found a significant bias against female applicants in perceived competence, hireability, salary and mentoring by both male and female academics in biology, chemistry, and physics, from a cross-section of research-intensive universities in the USA. However the significance of this result in the real world is unclear, given that a survey of 1,800 faculty members at 89 top-tier institutions concluded "that 'gender does not appear to have been a factor in a number of important career transitions'. Indeed, women were more likely to have been interviewed for tenure-track positions (2% more than their application rate), to obtain an offer (10% higher than application rate) and as likely to achieve tenure" (Nature Cell Biology, 2009).

Role Models

Jasna Matic, the State Secretary for Digital Agenda (Republic of Serbia), said in her *Women and Girls ICT Information Session* on 24 January 2012: "the key obstacle for girls to pursue education and careers in information and communication technology is lack of role models" (Matic, 2012).

Similarly, Ashcraft et al. (2012) flag that "A wealth of research in science education in general, and in computing education in particular, finds that role models are important factors influencing girls' decisions to pursue computing (Barker & Aspray, 2006; Clark Blickenstaff, 2005; Cozza, 2011)." In the light of the recognised importance of female role models, the cries in IT research and industry are that there is an absence, or more accurately a lack of visibility, of such women. This is reflected in a survey by Berry & Kalessi (2011), which found "Many respondents think that the industry needs to set up more initiatives to inspire and educate young girls about technology. Also, more positive role models could help to dispel the myth that the industry is 'geeky'."

A women and IT survey conducted in Italy, Poland, UK, Netherlands, and France found that with the exception of the Netherlands, more than 50% of students are influenced by role models (Gras-Velazquez et al., 2009). Parents, female teachers and female relatives figure prominently amongst those nominated as role models, however so too did celebrities (Miliszewska & Moore, 2011). This result and the fact that celebrities often form a key part of popular culture is sometimes picked up by intervention programs. For example, Miliszewska & Moore (2011) discuss a program called ITBeat, conceived in 2002 as part of a three year Image Impact Program to improve IT's poor image in the UK. ITBeat, in partnership with teenage magazine J-17 and the pop music industry, had at its core a competition for teenage girls in which they designed a website for their favourite pop star. Finalists were then invited to a celebrity event with an opportunity to meet their celebrity. You would think that this overlay of glamour and popular culture would be an ongoing success that would be repeated, but the program now appears defunct.

Not only are female role models a benefit, but their absence has been identified as an important deterrent for women considering a role in sectors not traditionally viewed as 'female friendly' (Mason & Mason, 2007). Furthermore, Ahuja (2002) made an interesting observation that "Without positive female role models in non-traditional fields, girls may 'self-select' themselves towards careers in which they observe other women, thus further intensifying the gender-based stereotyping of professionals."

This vicious circle idea is echoed by Karen Gill, co-founder of Everywoman, who made the point that "the fewer role models we have in the industry, the fewer we'll have at the top," and highlighted a lack of role models at all levels of the technology sector (Batemen, 2013). By stressing not just the top but all levels, Gill means "Some young women will see such a big leap between themselves and their female role model at the top that they can't envision themselves that far ahead… Gill believes this indicates the need to rethink, reshape and put much more emphasis around a framework for female role models to be accessible on all levels. However, Parry-Jones [David Parry-Jones, regional director for UK & Ireland at VMware], said the role model does not always have to be female. 'It may be a man, but as long as the values are communicated well, it works,' he added. Berry agreed that it is important to have different role models at different points in your career – to give women something to aspire to at all levels, and to be able to clearly identify what their next step would be or which promotion to chase" (Bateman, 2013).

An interesting additional perspective is the importance of the mix of presenters at conferences. Donald (2013) asks, "Do role models matter? And if so, in what kind of situation are they most important?" She then outlines how the Royal Society specifically identifies speakers in conference submissions, allowing the approval committee to ensure they are "appropriately diverse." She also reports on a pledge for "participation in conferences – whether as an organizer, sponsor, or invited speaker – conditional on the invitation of women and men speakers in a fair and balanced manner." In similar vein, Rosen (2013) presents a simple solution: "Men: You can help fix this. Refuse to participate unless there are women on stage with you." Interestingly, this is not all due to bias by organisers. Cohen (2013) discusses the frustration TED and TEDx have in sourcing female presenters. She points out that the 3 key reasons for non-acceptance given by women are: "I'm not ready" (parenthetically Cohen notes here that she has never had a male say that!), "The family needs me" and "The team needs me." She also flags that in her 8 years of experience with TED, women generally do not appear motivated by the prestige and self gratification of presentation so instead TED frame their requests to reflect the social impact of the presentation.

Profiling women and making those profiles accessible is an obvious part of role model visibility and no doubt #SocialIT can greatly assist both. In addition, in the #SocialIT era the community itself is just doing it, showcasing role models of all kinds as part of the process. Thus Chang (2013) reports that at a developer conference in March 2013 for the Python (open-source programming language) community, there were free workshops for children from age 7 to learn Python, a female hacker lounge hosted by the Ada Initiative, many booths in the expo area for groups like PyLadies and CodeChix, and a record number of female presenters at the conference.

Yet we have to acknowledge that in fact there is no shortage of role models. We have the last 20 years of role model events and building up of profiles. There are recent initiatives such as TechWomen's *Emerging Leaders* that profiles 57 women in technology from countries such as Tunisia, Zimbabwe, Lebanon, Jordon, Morocco, Palestinian Territories, Kenya, Nigeria, Libya, Egypt, South Africa, Yemen, Cameroon, Algeria and Rwanda (TechWomen, 2013a). Some role models are as high profile as actress Geena Davis, now special envoy for women in ICT (McCaskill, 2012). In July 2013, the White House honoured eleven people as *Champions of Change for Tech Inclusion*. All of them are doing interesting things to improve the educational opportunities for women and underrepresented minorities in computing and related disciplines, most focusing on K-12 education (Whitney, 2013).

But that itself raises a further question. Despite all the role models publicised, including high profile, multi-year programs like ITBeat above, no significant improvement in girls' participation in IT studies has occurred. So again we have to ask ourselves if our perception of needing more role models is real. Or is it another case where we all think more role models are vital – for everyone else, just not in our own case? In other words, do role models actually help the "bottom line" of more women in IT?

Mentoring

There are many definitions of mentoring from as simple as the dictionary's "to advise or train someone" to "Mentoring is an offline, confidential activity with a self-directed focus, where the gap between the two individuals (or group of individuals) enables a learning and development outcome" (Australian Mentor Centre, 2008) and "Mentoring is to support and encourage people to manage their own learning in order that they may maximise their potential, develop their skills, improve their performance and become the person they want to be" (MentorSET, 2008).

Craig, Fisher & Lang (2007) identified lack of mentoring as contributing to girls not selecting IT subjects. Allen, Armstrong, Riemenschneider & Reid (2006) showed that mentoring can serve as an important intervention to enhance the retention of women in the ICT workforce because of its correlation with professional advancement, evidenced by standpoint theory and causal mapping (von Hellens, Trauth & Fisher, 2012).

Yet along with profiling role models, industry associations have been designing and running mentoring programs for years. For example the *Grace Hopper Celebration Of Women In Computing* has been running since 1994 (whilst this is a conference it is significantly about mentoring and role models), the WiT (Queensland, Australia) mentoring program commenced 15 years ago, and similar industry associations around the globe have been involved similarly. The programs are targeted at mentoring or coaching either girls studying or women already in the industry, and are varied in their design and processes. Top down, bottom up, sideways, inside companies and outside companies have all been tried. And in addition to specific programs for women in IT, there are general business and women networks mentoring programs.

If anything this is increasing. Throughout the course of a year the media highlights the launch of new mentoring programs. Two recent examples are The US Department of State Bureau of Educational and Cultural Affairs' *TechWomen* initiative (TechWomen, 2013b) and NetHope's *TechConnect* program (NetHope, 2013), both of which reach into the Middle East and African nations. Another, from actress Natalie Portman and Marvel Comics, is *Marvel's Thor: The Dark World Ultimate Mentor Adventure* (Haskins, 2013), which targets girls in grades 9 through 12, pairing them up with female mentors across the STEM spectrum to learn about STEM careers.

In short there is no lack of existing mentoring programs, both face to face and e-mentoring, designed and led by associations, industry, educational institutions and governments. Websites and tool kits exist too. Mentoring is not a missing component. Therefore, whatever its importance for individual professional development, more is not the solution.

Clubs

Clubs bring girls or women together to learn about IT. An example is CC4G (Computer Clubs for Girls), a nationally coordinated initiative launched in 2005 as part of the e-skills strategy, which reached into more than 3,600 schools across the UK. Based on the CC4G 2007/2008 evaluation report (no longer available), Miliszewska & Moore (2011) relate "62% of members surveyed said that CC4G had made them more likely to want to work in a career involving technology. In the same report, 98% of surveyed club facilitators agreed that membership of CC4G would have 'a positive impact on members' achievements at KS2/3 in IT. Moreover, of those schools who participated in surveys for the July 2008 report, 98% said they would continue to run CC4G for the next school year." Typical comments captured were the head of IT at one English school saying "the number of girls studying IT GCSE at her college had trebled in five years" and "I think CC4G does make more girls consider IT as a career because it makes it seem more fun. And because it is so fun for them, they are learning and thinking about IT without realizing it" (Miliszewska & Moore, 2011).

However an attempt to translate the perceived CC4G success into Australia failed. Lang, Fisher & Craig (2007) established a weekly lunchtime club for girls at Brentwood Secondary College in Melbourne, initially enrolling 27 Year 7 students. By week four there were only 5 remaining students and they were all from the one class. This may be due to Australia not having a culture of lunchtime classes, despite support from the school principal, the participating IT teacher, and students who reported liking the materials and experiences.

Another example provides clues on how clubs should be implemented. As described by Miliszewska & Moore (2011), "Whilst the Amsterdam Westerpark project, and possibly many more of the 234 local initiatives begun under the Dutch *digitale trapvelden* plan, proved successful in attracting significantly greater numbers of women than men, Rommes (2003) suggested, it was not quite so successful in raising their ICT participation rates or their use of the Internet. Nor, it would appear, was the program as successful as had been hoped in its community building endeavours. The explanation for this, she argues, lay in the program organisers' decision to prioritise the technology rather than the people using it. That is, program organisers opted for courses in which attempts were made to give participants 'an overview of everything that is possible with a computer', rather than designing courses that were less complicated but given to building networks of learners capable of learning from each other (Rommes, 2003, p. 14)."

Miliszewska & Moore (2011) continue to comment "This suggestion that efforts to raise female participation rates in ICT studies (and, consequently in careers) should be person-centred rather than technology-focused echoes in the recent Victorian (Australia) Government report on Attitudes to ICT careers and study among 14 to 19 year old Victorians, wherein students presented with a range of options to promote ICT careers to young people ... nominated work placements or job experience with ICT companies as the most effective methods, followed by scholarships, the opportunity to explore emerging technologies through expos and opportunities to speak with already engaged in ICT careers."

Or perhaps the reason is that most girls who are interested in technology have already been exposed to it and already discovered their interest, and attempts to widen the net mostly draw in girls who simply aren't deeply interested, and whatever their casual interests they are unlikely to choose it as their career. CC4G itself, seemingly a poster child for these interventions, may actually be the most sobering lesson. It is an ongoing national program launched eight years ago, with glowing reports of efficacy. Yet while women now outnumber men in UK universities, the number of women in IT courses is still less than 20% (Ratcliffe, 2013) - whilst statistics from 2005 show female participation in computer science was over 23% when the program began (Higher Education Statistics Agency, 2013).

Despite that there is an interesting new wave trend for Internet-based bootcamps, learn-to-code clubs and other online clubs. O'Dell (2013) notes "In the learn to code craze, online schools like Codecademy and in-person courses like Dev Bootcamp are springing up to meet a huge need for more developers across a wide range of industries. But while this option is a quick fix for tech's gender imbalance, some worry it's not enough to fix the industry's brogramming culture." The craze is also mapping back into face to face, intensive immersion coding bootcamps, such as Stirland's (2013) *Black Girls Code* summer camps. There are even some that guarantee a job at the end of the bootcamp (Newman, 2013). Perhaps these new style clubs and camps will replace the traditional clubs. It's interesting to note that the experience for Brentwood Secondary College and CC4G style clubs noted above did not dampen their IT spirit, as in August 2013 they joined up as a pilot site to a new style learn to code club 'Learnable' for it's students (Powell, 2013).

Networks

Networking is about connecting, remotely or face to face. It may form powerful connections between people. As reported by UNESCO (2012), "Networking is perhaps the most common ICT usage among women in developing countries. They use ICTs to address women's rights, communicate, spread information, mobilize action in times of crisis, debate policies, voice their opinions, and discover allies or peers across the Internet."

As well as providing support, advice and enabling joint action, networking can assist in finding or obtaining jobs. Yet Goodwin (2006) reports "Research by E-Skills UK suggests that only 10% of women obtain their jobs by networking with other IT professionals, compared to 22% of men. This may explain the declining proportion of women in the IT profession... 'Networking is a good way to build relationships and knowledge in business and may be a route to securing a new job,' said E-Skills...This data appears to suggest that women in the IT sector could be missing out on roles secured through networking alone, but that should be considered in the context that many organisations have excellent programmes in place to encourage and support diversity - including structured recruitment programmes."

Returning to an IT career in an environment of constant change has its own difficulties: "flexibility is required of both businesses and adult returners. You can't expect to ramp off and come back 12 months later to the same seat, same desk, and there's your same plant. People have trouble re-entering the industry, as things have moved on so quickly" (Blair, Gill & Benson, 2013). Here too networking can help. Bateman (2013) flags that "Personal relationships and networking can be a great strength for 'adult returners'... Returning to the workplace after long periods of absence can be a difficult challenge for both men and women – one which is believed to be a culture issue... Maxine Benson, co-founder of everywoman, said: 'It is preconceived that if you're 50, then you're not even on the starting blocks to get a job. You have to be young and willing to work 24/7'."

A traditional response to the needs of women in IT has been women-only networks. However recent research leads to questioning their effectiveness. A UK-based women in technology survey found a staggering 76% chose not to be involved in women's networks, stating they should not be gender specific as they did not want to be treated differently from their male colleagues (Berry & Kalessi, 2011). Of the survey population, 36% were under 35 years of age and 37% between 36 and 45 years of age: so this may reflect the beginning of a new trend, as the old guard of traditional gender-based industry associations and networking groups fades.

An interesting attraction/recruitment tactic using networks is suggested by Goode, Estrella & Margolis (2006). They highlight the importance of building supportive networks for girls interested in computing but rather than targeting individual girls, targeting groups of girls who already know and support one another. Thus instead of getting one and making her feel separated from her friends, using that one to reach all those others as well. Perhaps this could be extended to recruitment in companies by tapping into the existing networks of those already employed.

Media

By its very nature, image portrayal in the media is a shifting target. Popular forms of media are changing, as are popular culture and industry trends. Research literature prior to the past one or two years may already be irrelevant and certainly will be in the near future, e.g. Klawe's (2002) discussion on stereotypical media images of solitary, boring jobs, etc.; Adya & Kaiser's (2005) comments on teen magazines and trade journals; and Barker & Aspray's (2006) discussion of geek negative imagery and implicit but significant messages about gender roles.

However Ashcraft et al. (2012) report "media representations still largely portray stereotypes but progress has been made in portrayals of other occupations, showcasing the power of media to alter these perceptions. More recent research finds that women are still represented stereotypically in popular culture, such as holding little power or understanding ... occupying marginal roles in organizations, and being passive individuals (Cozza, 2011)."

This is changing. Ashcraft et al. (2012) point out "when it comes to computing careers, interesting but complicated developments are on the horizon and worth paying close attention to. Few movies or prime time television shows take place in a technology setting and even fewer have a powerful female lead character (Clayton, et al., 2009). Clayton et al. do highlight one recent positive example of a female in a computing role, Penelope Garcia, from the crime drama *Criminal Minds*. However, while her character is positively portrayed in many ways, her character also tends to reinforce many stereotypes as she is portrayed to be a somewhat 'quirky' person, is obsessed with online gaming, wears glasses, dresses in what might be considered somewhat funky or 'geeky' attire, and is often referred to as the 'tech with glasses.' When she is shown actually working with computers, she also is usually shown working alone in a darkened room. An eerily similar pattern emerges in the character of Abby Sciuto, the female character in a computing role in another crime drama, *NCIS*. In some ways, of course, these characters are very positive developments because they are very likable female characters and some girls are likely to identify with them, see themselves represented, and have these aspects of their identities validated. At the same time, it is curious that the two leading female technical characters on prime time television would be portrayed in such similar ways. These patterns are worth watching because if all of the female characters in technical roles end up having these kinds of similar characteristics, this can reinforce certain stereotypes and limit the number and kinds of girls who see themselves in these representations."

Along those lines, the Geena Davis Institute on Gender in Media has extensively studied female portrayal in the media and is targeting Hollywood for improved female role placement (Barry, 2012). Hopefully that, combined with her 3-year appointment as ITU "Special Envoy For Women and Girls In ICT" (McCaskill, 2012), will promote effective female technology characters in movies.

An alternative to fighting the "geek" label is to reclaim it as a cool image, e.g. TV shows like *Numb3rs* and *Chuck*, and girl geek coffee gatherings. However Cheryan, Meltzoff & Kim (2011) warn that any geek labelling can negatively impact many girls' perceptions of the study of IT and computing.

A recent addition to the TV female geek role is Felicity Smoak on *Arrow*. In my own opinion, Felicity is portrayed as a clever person who enjoys solving puzzles and is utilised in that way. That is a nice extension of "at keyboard" work and is a realistic reflection of the curious and creative minds of many in the IT industry. On the down side she is portrayed with glasses and clumsy social awkwardness, though this is done in a charming and humorous way and not as a main focus.

I conducted a quick web based opt-in poll to gather current thoughts on TV technology role models. The poll basically presented a limited list of current geek TV roles and asked participants to indicate which ones they liked, did not like, were neutral towards or did not know. The quick poll was open to males (33%) and females (67%) and not limited to the IT industry (approx. 32% core IT, 32% support IT, 32% non-IT and 6% no career). It was not mandatory to respond to all 13 characters presented, but most did. The results are shown in Figure 3.

Possibly unsurprisingly given its current popularity, *The Big Bang Theory* characters rated highly – with Amy Farrah Fowler scoring the highest number of likes followed by Bernadette Rostenkowski Wolowitz; however it is also interesting that Leslie Winkle scored by far the most dislikes both in raw numbers and compared to her "likes."

There is insufficient data or variation in the statistics to really draw any conclusions apart

Figure 3. Snap poll: Attitudes to TV geek characters

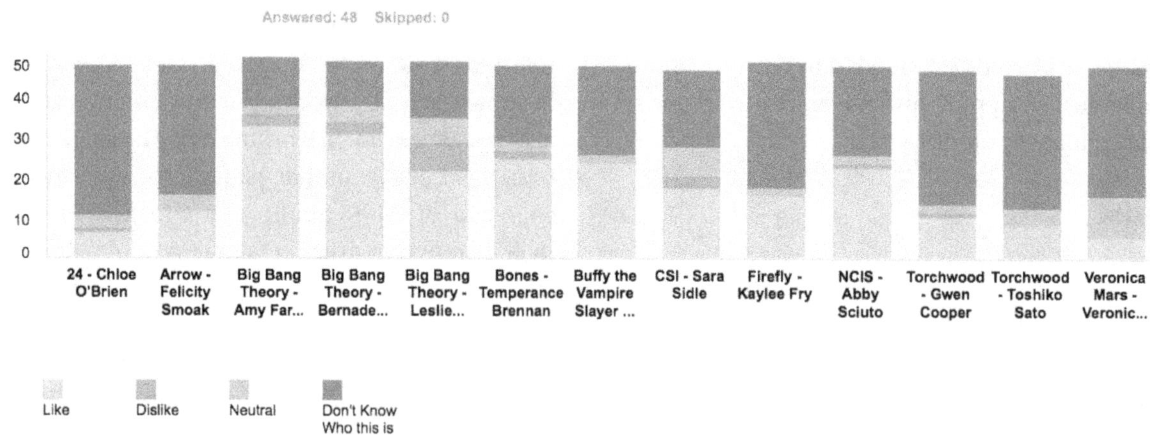

from there being no major outpouring of dislike for any specific character. The comments (17) provide further insights and characters:

- Criminal Minds - Penelope Garcia.
- Other icons: Two female doctors in Star Trek NG - clever characters. Two other geeky women in Bones - very capable. Female pathologists in Silent Witness - good characters generally.
- Don't like Abby's goth style it's overdone; love Felicity's smart at everything loves a challenge and puzzle approach.
- Samantha Carter – Stargate.
- Dislike Temp Brennan because she's not likeable, seems too false and arrogant about her intelligence. Abby, Willow, Amy, Bernadette etc seem to acknowledge the struggle they had to gain/maintain their intelligence, and their enthusiasm for using their intelligence.
- What I don't like of any geeks in TV is how they are portrayed as (gender aside) people who have immediate access to any and all systems everywhere (including government, banks etc) and are immediately able to - by a click of a few buttons - to access vast databases and/or information systems and then absorb, understand structure, link and query whatever they are looking for. And almost invariably they find whatever it is they are looking for, on the first query. Firstly I object to the unrealistic way this is portrayed and secondly (and even more strongly) I object to the notion that every detail of everyone's life is supposedly so easily accessible to anyone with a bit of geek in them. (I think this sets the expectation of no-privacy in the popular culture and leads the way to us all losing all rights to privacy, which to me is absolutely abhorrent.)
- Star Trek Series - Uhura; Captain Janeway, others.
- Zelda Gilroy - Dobie Gillis - one of the first geeky female on TV.
- Love Willow Rosenberg her transformation from shy nobody to powerful Technowitch powerful and held her own with all characters (eventually). Temperance Brennan was enjoyable to watch and made you want to see what she would say or do next. Abby Sciuto she is the classic don't judge a book by its cover look.
- Criminal Minds - Penelope Garcia. The Newsroom - Sloan Sabbith. Gwen Cooper is a strong female character but I would not necessarily regard her as a female geek. She is a female character the excellence in a male dominated career. In my opinion if Gwen Cooper is on this list Peggy Olson from Mad Men should be too.
- Clara Oswin Oswald - Dr Who! She's awesome:)
- Sorry. I obviously don't watch enough TV. I would like to help you more but don't know any of the characters.
- Out of them all NCIS - Abby Sciuto is my favourite by far!
- The characters that I like tend to be more well developed characters, that have other facets to their personality besides being the female geek.
- All 3 Big Bang characters appeal for their sarcastic wit, Temperance Brennan and Sara Sidle for their intelligence. Abby Sciuto would be my favourite because for her Geeky does not equal Nerdy/Dorky. She has plenty of individuality.
- Gillian Anderson – X-Files. Does Lisa Simpson count?
- Clara Oswald from Dr Who. Most attractive Dr Who assistant ever (well maybe except for Jo Grant).

The next key question concerned the portrayal of female geeks on TV. Not surprisingly, the over-

Figure 4. TV Portrayal of female geeks – realistic or not

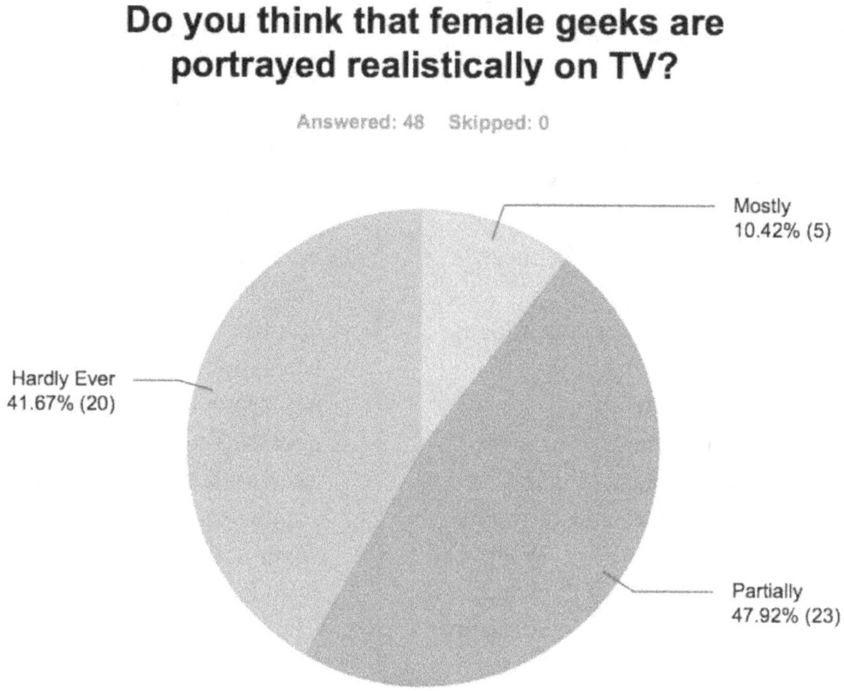

whelming majority voted the portrayal of female TV geeks as not realistic (Figure 4).

Comments (15) were:

- Their characteristics are a bit exaggerated. Sometimes displayed as more fragile than their male counterparts. I don't like this.
- Sometime they get it right. Female geeks are usually very strong women however they sometimes get that silly girly image like in Big Bang.
- With the exception of criminal minds (you haven't included her for some reason) the characters are all way too beautiful, while male geeks are depicted as "geeky."
- See above comment. I know enough about data structures to understand that viewing someone else's data system requires quite a bit of work to understand the data structures and how things are linked. You just cannot immediately find the right information on first attempt.
- Neither are male geeks.
- Your list: it's TV... hardly anyone is real. Like this clip, anything in TV is... just fiction. http://www.youtube.com/watch?v=hkDD03yeLnU
- Some but need a movie/TV show like the Facebook movie but with a cast of women that create, plan, program, code, execute (everything) that would be great.
- The portrayal is improving, but on many shows female geeks are still overly sexualized. I believe Sloan Sabbith in The Newsroom is one of the best portrayals so far. She is a brilliant economist and is very socially awkward. Whilst she also happens to be a pretty female, it is mainly her intellect and social quirks that the show focuses on.
- Somewhat glamorised.

- Female geeks are just like any other group of people - wildly varied. The crazy-woman or has-to-be-emotionally-stunted tropes irritate me profoundly.
- I sometimes wonder if there are really women of the nature portrayed in characters such as those on The Big Bang Theory but love the characters themselves & hope they really exist.
- I would really prefer to answer in the neutral as I can't think of characters I am familiar with.
- As with all TV characters, they are purely a caricature of the stereotype, but usually with about 10 times the looks that you generally find...
- Female geeks are never "hot" like they are on TV (apologies for being a shallow male).
- In most cases an exaggerated version of the real thing.

However, despite the interest in TV representations as positive or negative role models, it may be less important than we assume. Lyons et al. (2012) asked respondents about the importance of STEM-related media and outreach in their decisions about university courses. Overall, media-related importance was lower than school-based importance. Within media, popular science television or radio programs were considered the most important, with around 44% of respondents regarding them as either important (29%) or very important (15%) to their decisions and only 21% considering them unimportant. In contrast, films or drama on television (e.g. *CSI*, *Stargate*, etc.) had very low ratings of importance (with no significant difference between males and females in responses to either factor).

Peers

Research has identified that peers may exert a powerful influence on beliefs and behaviours about the value of education, gender roles and academic subject choices. Additionally it has been reported that throughout their teenage years girls experience an increased need to conform to the qualities that their peers feel are acceptable (Margolis & Fisher, 2002; Barker & Aspray, 2006). Cozza (2011) also flags that "if there is a lack of adult mentors or role models then youth consider peers as guides."

The issue here is if peers can play such a powerful role, they can undermine girls' interest in computing careers by sending negative messages (Meszaros, Lee & Laughlin, 2007). Or as described by Lanzer (2009), we need to reach them "before they reach a critical time of their lives, when peer pressure drives so many to lose self-confidence and 'swallow their voices'."

However peer pressure might not really be such a big barrier. Adya & Kaiser (2005) found that "in teenage years peers have more impact on social responsiveness, behaviours, fashion styles, and attitudes but little on career choices." And Lanzer's (2009) suggestion, just quoted, itself implies that pre-existing interest can negate later peer pressure. That interest overrides outside pressures is also indicated by Denner (2011), who found that "frequency of computer use predicted perceived support from both parents ... [and] school peers/teachers and perceived support from peers at school to pursue computing is associated with girls' interest in computing." This was also found by Clayton et al. (2012), who reported results from a robotics hands on workshop as "the TTYA intervention shows that girls are able to resist peer pressure… For example, in the TTYA sessions that focused on robotics, programming and computer hardware, the girls showed a strong level of competitiveness."

Perhaps part of this is that peers are not entirely imposed from outside. Neither schools nor society at large are homogeneous: to whatever extent they can, children will choose their friends and consequently their peer group according to their own personalities and interests. Don't you?

Family: Formulation, Mobility and Responsibility

Children are keen observers and notice the role that their parents take in everyday life (Margolis & Fisher, 2002). Family influence and expectations contribute towards girls' decisions to enter IT study or career pathways (Lang & McKay, 2006; Barker & Aspray, 2006). However this section is not primarily about family influence in that way. Rather it focuses on the impacts on women when they have a family, e.g. having children, mobility issues with children, and carer responsibilities for children as well as ill or ageing parents and other relatives.

The social sciences view of family is captured by Trauth & Quesenberry (2006), who structure their research into the categories of Domestic Responsibility, Independence and Equality, and Childrearing. They argue that women's family choices are largely absorbed from society: "The women articulated messages they have received throughout their lives, which suggest that they should sacrifice their careers for domestic responsibilities."

Castano & Webster (2011) comment "women's engagement with the labour market generally, and with science and technology careers specifically, is often sporadic, and cannot be understood without reference to other life events, such as family formation, geographical mobility, and elderly care activities, all shaped by women's role in the domestic sphere. Clearly, the organisation of family and household labour influence the ability of women to pursue their employment and careers, and these gender divisions of labour vary across societies. Women's engagement with ICT careers has to be assessed within these contexts… At and after family formation, some women can appear less committed to their work, and on top of this they begin to experience discrimination in promotion opportunities… Life course events such as growing responsibility for care of elderly relatives in combination with continuing responsibility for children create difficulties for women in senior roles." Though in contrast, Accenture (2013) found that 70% of both male and female business executives say they can "have it all" and have a successful career as well as a full life outside of work, though not necessarily at the same time.

Griffiths & Moore's (2010) very interesting study of women who left ICT careers provides some consistent reasons for departure: "All the women in our sample reported a lack of job satisfaction, a continuous struggle to maintain a family/work/life balance due to long periods at work and a burgeoning workload." A common reaction to reports of such issues is voluntary or legislated family-friendly practices. Yet a survey revealed "Creches, childcare assistance ... are only offered by a quarter of employers, reflected by the fact that the majority of women who are offered these facilities don't use them" (Berry & Kalessi, 2011).

I propose that whilst family formation (or not), mobility (or not) and responsibilities (or not) are certainly part of a person's life, the research hints that each person manages these circumstances in their own unique way, and perhaps more importantly from our viewpoint there is no specific issue relating to careers in IT. This is reflected in the Berry & Kalessi (2011) survey, which found "In general, respondents think that the technology industry does not impact family life any more than other sectors."

In addition we have to recognise the possibility that (statistically) women are more interested in family life than in technology careers. Such questions are debated even within feminism (Satz, 2011), and whilst there is no definitive scientific evidence either way, I believe the evidence overall supports the idea that there are real statistical differences between male and female preferences (Sommers, 2008). That is not to say we should not do all we can to empower individual choice. But it implies that when we *leave* things to individual choice the outcomes might not be what our ideology would prefer.

Hygiene: Security and Status

Herzberg's motivation-hygiene theory and dual-factor theory states "there are certain factors in the workplace that cause job satisfaction, while a separate set of factors cause dissatisfaction." Factors influencing decisions to enter the IT field include high salaries and flexible working conditions (Nielsen, von Hellens, Pringle, & Greenhill, 1999; Beekhuyzen, Nielsen, & von Hellens, 2006), while reasons for leaving the field include lack of clear career paths, uncertainty about long term employment, family unfriendly work practices and the perception that IT work lacks a social dimension.

Continuing their work on structuration and dualism theories and applying Herzberg's theory, Neilson & von Hellens (2006) identified security and status as two key hygiene factors in their model of "Changing environment of IT professionals." That is, beliefs about job security and status contribute to students' perceptions of the long term prospects of IT careers and may operate as dissatisfaction factors.

Thus high profile job cutting, as in media reports of massive layoffs in brand-name technology companies, may bring these factors into play despite talk about an IT skills crisis. On the whole students and those entering the workforce do not like to see "trouble employment cycles" in industries – they want to be able to get a job and keep it or be able to find new ones. Perhaps the dynamic nature of IT exacerbates this. However whether such factors affect women more than men depends on whether they differ in their perceptions of or attitudes to such risks.

Social Norms

Social norms are the accepted and expected standards of behaviour of social groups, unwritten rules about how to behave. They have been extensively studied in the social sciences, in particular their differences across diverse cultures.

UNESCO (2012) reports that cultural and social norms cause a digital divide. An example of an IT industry social norm is reported by Berry & Kalessi (2011): "Women in the technology sector appear to be split on whether or not it's necessary to act like a man in order to get ahead. 52% disagree with the statement, while 47% think that it's necessary to level the playing field by behaving in a masculine way. This could be another load bearer of the infamous glass ceiling, as there is no general consensus on what kind of behaviour results in career success."

Karen Bard (CIO – retired, and industry advocate; personal communication, October 3, 2012) notes "Contradiction abounds in our messages to girls and women regarding their careers. We tell them that they can have it all and be whatever they want to be… But the other side of the coin is filled with messages as to how difficult things are for women in these sectors to succeed, get ahead or just to be paid equitably."

The issues of social norms substantially overlap those of Cultural Norms and Occupational Culture, which are discussed above in Cultural Context so do not need repeating here.

In the next chapter we move to another traditionally recognized factor: structural context and influences.

REFERENCES

Accenture. (2013). *Defining success: 2013 global research results*. Retrieved September 1, 2013, from http://www.accenture.com/SiteCollectionDocuments/PDF/Accenture-IWD-2013-Research-Deck-022013.pdf

Advincula, F. (2012). *A letter for new engineers: You will be different and that's OK*. Retrieved July 10, 2013, from http://women2.com/a-letter-for-new-engineers-you-will-be-different-and-thats-ok/

Adya, M., & Kaiser, K. M. (2005). Early determinants of women in the IT workforce: A models of girls' career choices. *Information Technology & People*, *18*(3), 230–259. doi:10.1108/09593840510615860

Ahuja, M. K. (2002). Women in the information technology profession: A literature review, synthesis, and research agenda. *European Journal of Information Systems*, *11*(1), 20–34. doi:10.1057/palgrave.ejis.3000417

Akst, J. (2013). *Some girls better at science*. Retrieved July 2, 2013, from http://www.the-scientist.com/?articles.view/articleNo/34284/title/Some-Girls-Better-at-Science/

Allen, M. W., Armstrong, D. J., Riemenschneider, C. K., & Reid, M. F. (2006). Making sense of the barriers women face in the information technology workforce: Standpoint theory, self-disclosure, and causal maps. *Sex Roles*, *54*, 831–844. doi:10.1007/s11199-006-9049-4

Anderson, N. (2003). *Making the link: Three successful university, industry and community collaborations around ICT development*. Paper presented at Higher Education without Borders – Sustainable Development in Education. Khon Kaen, Thailand. Retrieved August 3, 2013, from http://eprints.jcu.edu.au/834/

Ashcraft, C., Eger, E., & Friend, M. (2012). *Girls in IT: The facts*. Boulder, CO: National Centre for Women & Information Technology (NCWIT). Retrieved August 6, 2013, from http://www.academia.edu/2283166/Girls_in_IT_The_Facts

Australian Mentor Centre. (2008). *What is mentoring?* Retrieved August 10, 2013, from http://www.australianmentorcentre.com.au/what+is+mentoring

Barker, L. J., & Aspray, W. (2006). The state of research on girls and IT. In J. M. Cohoon, & W. Aspray (Eds.), *Women and information technology: Research on underrepresentation* (pp. 3–54). Cambridge, MA: MIT Press. doi:10.7551/mitpress/9780262033459.003.0001

Barron, B. (2004). Learning ecologies for technological fluency: Gender and experience differences. *Journal of Educational Computing Research*, *31*(1), 1–36. doi:10.2190/1N20-VV12-4RB5-33VA

Barry, D. (2012). *Geena Davis wants to give Hollywood a heads up that female characters need way more speaking roles*. Retrieved August 4, 2013, from http://jezebel.com/5963090/geena-davis-wants-to-give-hollywood-a-heads-up-that-female-characters-need-way-more-speaking-roles

Bateman, K. (2013). *Is outdated terminology deterring females from roles in IT?* Retrieved July 2, 2013, from http://www.computerweekly.com/feature/Is-outdated-terminology-deterring-females-from-roles-in-IT

Beekhuyzen, J., Nielsen, S., & von Hellens, L. (2006). *Making IT fit: Research and action in Queensland*. Paper presented at the AusWIT Australian Women in IT Conference. Adelaide, Australia.

Berry, M., & Kalessi, T. (2011). *Women's careers in the technology industry*. London, UK: Intellect and Women in Technology (Report). Retrieved August 1, 2013, from http://sciencewithart.ijs.si/pdf/Women's_Careers_in_the_Technology_Industry_2011_Report.pdf

Biology, N. C. (2009). Attracting women (editorial). *Nature Cell Biology, 11*, 915. Retrieved October 9, 2013, from http://www.nature.com/ncb/journal/v11/n8/full/ncb0809-915.html

Blair, R., Gill, K., & Benson, M. (2013). *Focus on the pipeline*. Alexander Mann Solutions and Everywoman.

Carrington, B., Tymms, P., & Merrell, C. (2008). Role models, school improvement and the gender gap – Do men bring out the best in boys and women bring out the best in girls? *British Educational Research Journal, 34*(3), 1–13. doi:10.1080/01411920701532202

Castaño, C., Müller, J., Gonzalez, A., & Palmén, R. (2010). *Meta-analysis of policy towards gender equity in science and research* (Topic Report, RTD-PP-L4-2007-1). Meta-Analysis of Gender and Science Research. Retrieved from genderedinnovations.stanford.edu/images/TR7_Policies.pdf

Castano, C., & Webster, J. (2011). Understanding women's presence in ICT: The life course perspective. *International Journal of Gender. Science and Technology, 3*(2), 358–363.

Cave, K. (2013). Women in IT: Does the shortage matter? *IDG Connect Infographic*. Retrieved May 22, 2013, from http://www.idgconnect.com/abstract/1251/infographic-women-it-does-shortage-matter

Chang, A. (2013). *Record number of women give tech talks at PYCON 2013*. Retrieved August 8, 2013, from http://women2.com/5-great-talks-by-women-software-engineers-at-pycon-2013/

Cheryan, S., Meltzoff, A. N., & Kim, S. (2011). Classrooms matter: The design of virtual classrooms influences gender disparities in computer science classes. *Computers & Education, 57*(2), 1825–1835. doi:10.1016/j.compedu.2011.02.004

Cheryan, S., Plaut, V. C., Handron, C., & Hudson, L. (2013). The stereotypical computer scientist: Gendered media representations as a barrier to inclusion for women. *Sex Roles, 69*(1), 58–71. doi:10.1007/s11199-013-0296-x

Clark Blickenstaff, J. (2005). Women and science careers: Leaky pipeline or gender filter? *Gender and Education, 17*(4), 369–386. doi:10.1080/09540250500145072

Clayton, K., Beekhuyzen, J., & Nielsen, S. (2012). Now I know what ICT can do for me? *Information Systems Journal, 22*(5), 1–16. doi:10.1111/j.1365-2575.2012.00414.x

Clayton, K. L., von Hellens, L. A., & Nielsen, S. H. (2009). Gender stereotypes prevail in ICT: A research review. In *Proceedings of the Special Interest Group on Management Information System's 47th Annual Conference on Computer Personnel Research* (SIGMIS CPR) (pp. 153-158). ACM.

Cohen, J. (2013). *We're frustrated too! The challenge of finding women presenters*. Retrieved September 15, 2013, from http://tedxcanberra.org/2013/08/were-frustrated-too-the-challenge-of-finding-women-presenters/

Cohoon, J. M. (2012). *Different genders, different worlds*. Open Thoughts 2012: Universitat Oberta de Catalunya. Retrieved August 17, 2013, from http://openthoughts.blogs.uoc.edu/2012/11/different-genders-different-worlds.html

Cozza, M. (2011). Bridging gender gaps, networking in computer science. *Gender, Technology and Development, 15*(2), 319–337. doi:10.1177/097185241101500207

Craig, A., Fisher, J., & Lang, C. (2007). *ICT and girls: The need for a large scale intervention programme.* Paper presented at the Association for Information Systems ACIS 2007. Toowoomba, Australia.

D'Mello, M. (2006). Gendered selves and identities of information technology professionals in global software organizations in India. *Information Technology for Development*, *12*(2), 131–158. doi:10.1002/itdj.20031

Denner, J. (2011). What predicts middle school girls' interest in computing? *International Journal of Gender. Science and Technology*, *3*(1), 53–69.

Donald, A. (2013). *Invited speakers, role models and women.* Retrieved August 2, 2013, from http://blogs.royalsociety.org/inside-science/2013/06/24/invited-speakers-role-models-and-women

Duliba, K. A., & Barouid, J. (1991). *IS personnel: Do they form an occupational community?* New York: Stern School of Business, New York University. doi:10.1145/111084.372748

Eltahawy, M. (2008). *Arab bloggers keep watch over government – and each other.* Retrieved August 1, 2013, from http://newsweek.washingtonpost.com/postglobal/mona_eltahawy/2008/05/arab_bloggers_keep_watch_over.html

Frankincense. (2012). *Really, no girls play Minecraft? What do you think?* Retrieved August 3, 2013, from http://www.minecraftforum.net/topic/1262129-really-no-girls-play-minecraft-what-do-you-think/

Gal-Ezer, J., Shahak, D., & Zur, E. (2009). Computer science issues in high school: Gender and more.... *Inroads SIGCSE Bulletin*, *41*(3), 278–282. doi:10.1145/1595496.1562963

Garratt, P. (2012). *Minecraft - Why I stopped playing it with my kids.* Retrieved August 3, 2013, from http://www.vg247.com/2012/08/07/minecraft-why-i-stopped-playing-it-with-my-kids/

Goode, J., Estrella, R., & Margolis, J. (2006). Lost in translation: Gender in high school computer science. In J. Cohoon, & W. Aspray (Eds.), *Women and information technology: Research on underrepresentation* (pp. 89–114). Cambridge, MA: MIT Press. doi:10.7551/mitpress/9780262033459.003.0003

Goodwin, B. (2006). *Better networking keeps me in the top IT jobs, research suggests.* Retrieved June 2, 2013, from http://www.computerweekly.com/news/2240076516/Better-networking-keeps-men-in-the-top-IT-jobs-research-suggests

Gordon, C. (2012). *Randi Zuckerberg: The controversial ambassador for women in tech.* Retrieved July 4, 2013, from http://jobs.aol.com/articles/2012/11/02/randi-zuckerberg-the-controversial-ambassador-for-women-in-tech/

Gras-Velazquez, A., Joyce, A., & Debry, M. (2009). *Women and ICT: Why are girls still not attracted to ICT studies and careers?* (White Paper). Brussels: European Schoolnet (EUN Partnership AISBL).

Gratton, L. (2012). *Could Steve Jobs have been a woman?* Open Thoughts 2012: Universitat Oberta de Catalunya. Retrieved August 17, 2013, from http://openthoughts.blogs.uoc.edu/2012/05/could-steve-jobs-have-been-woman.html

Griffiths, M., & Moore, K. (2010). 'Disappearing women': A study of women who left the UK ICT sector. *Journal of Technology Management and Innovation*, *5*(1), 95–107. doi:10.4067/S0718-27242010000100008

Groom, D. (2012). *Why won't she get off Minecraft?* Retrieved August 3, 2013, from http://deangroom.wordpress.com/2012/11/28/why-wont-she-get-off-minecraft/

Guzman, I., & Stanton, J. (2009). IT occupational culture: The cultural fit and commitment of new information technologists. *Information Technology & People*, *22*(2), 157–187. doi:10.1108/09593840910962212

Guzman, I., Stanton, J., & Eischen, D. (2006). Female perceptions of the information technology culture. In E. M. Trauth (Ed.), *Encyclopaedia of gender and Information technology* (Vol. 1, pp. 304–309). Hershey, PA: Idea Group Reference. doi:10.4018/978-1-59140-815-4.ch047

Haskins, J. (2013). *Natalie Portman and Marvel team up to get girls into science*. Retrieved October 7, 2013, from http://www.healthline.com/health-news/women-natalie-portman-and-marvel-host-girls-contest-100613

Hayes, E. (2005). Women, video gaming, and learning: Beyond stereotypes. *TechTrends*, *49*(5), 23–28. doi:10.1007/BF02763686

Hayes, E. (2008). Girls, gaming and trajectories of IT expertise. In Y. B. Kafai, C. Heeter, J. Denner, & J. Y. Sun (Eds.), *Beyond Barbie and Mortal Kombat: New perspectives on gender and gaming* (pp. 217–230). Cambridge, MA: MIT Press.

Higher Education Statistics Agency. (2013). *Students and qualifiers data tables*. Retrieved September 21, 2013, from http://www.hesa.ac.uk/index.php/content/view/1973/239/

Kafai, Y. B. (2008). Considering gender in digital games: Implications for serious game designs in the learning sciences. In *Proceedings of the 8th International Conference on Learning Sciences* (vol. 1, pp. 422-429). ICLS.

Kafai, Y. B., Heeter, C., Denner, J., & Sun, J. Y. (Eds.). (2008). *Beyond Barbie and Mortal Kombat: New perspectives on gender and gaming*. Cambridge, MA: MIT Press.

Klawe, M. (2002). Girls, boys and computers. *SIGCSE Bulletin*, *34*(2), 16–17. doi:10.1145/543812.543818

Kniveton, B. (2004). The influences and motivations on which students base their choice of career. *Research in Education*, *72*, 47–59. doi:10.7227/RIE.72.4

Kroes, N. (2013). *ICT and women speech*. European Commission. Retrieved July 21, 2013, from http://europa.eu/rapid/press-release_SPEECH-13-366_en.htm

Lang, C., Fisher, J., & Craig, A. (2007). *Digital divas: Computer clubs for girls trial*. Brentwood Secondary College, Swinburne University of Technology Women in ICT Group and Victorian ICT for Women Network. Retrieved August 1, 2013, from http://www.swinburne.edu.au/ict/wict/documents/Report%20on%20Brentwood%20Computer%20Club%20Trial.pdf

Lang, C., & McKay, J. (2006). Australian IT enrolment trends and model of contributing factors. In E. M. Trauth (Ed.), *Encyclopaedia of gender and information technology* (Vol. 1, pp. 50–56). Hershey, PA: Idea Group Reference. doi:10.4018/978-1-59140-815-4.ch009

Lanzer, F. (2009). Attracting girls to engineering & technology: Reach them before they're turned off. In *Proceedings of the 2009 Mid-Atlantic Section Conference of the American Society for Engineering Education*. Baltimore, MD: AACC. Retrieved August 5, 2013, from http://ola3.aacc.edu/fplanzer/documents/Attracting%20Girls%20to%20Technology%20Reach%20Them%20Before%20Turnoff.doc

Liston, C., Peterson, K., & Ragan, V. (2008). *Evaluating promising practices in informal information technology (IT) education for girls: Women in IT—Survey results*. Boulder, CO: National Center for Women & Information Technology.

Lovgren, S. (2004). *CSI effect is mixed blessing for real crime labs.* Retrieved August 4, 2013, from http://news.nationalgeographic.com/news/2004/09/0923_040923_csi.html

Lyons, T., Quinn, F., Rizk, N., Anderson, N., Hubber, P., Kenny, J., et al. (2012). *Starting out in STEM: A study of young men and women in first year science, technology, engineering and mathematics courses*. Armidale, Australia: University of New England. Retrieved August 13, 2013, from http://www.une.edu.au/simerr/pages/projects/132iris_report.pdf

Margolis, J., & Fisher, A. (2002). *Unlocking the clubhouse: Women in computing*. Cambridge, MA: MIT Press.

Mason, M. A., & Mason Ekman, E. (2007). *Mothers on the fast track: How a new generation can balance family and careers*. New York: Oxford University Press. doi:10.1093/acprof:oso/9780195182675.001.0001

Matic, J. (2012). *Women and girls in ICT information session - Side event @ WRC-12*. Retrieved August 4, 2013, from http://www.youtube.com/watch?v=RIWB0jF9kxE

McCaskill, S. (2012). *Geena Davis named ITU special envoy for women in ICT.* Retrieved August 4, 2013, from http://www.techweekeurope.co.uk/news/itu-geena-davis-women-i-82154

MentorSET. (2008). *What is mentoring?* Retrieved August 10, 2013, from http://www.mentorset.org.uk/pages/mentoring.htm

Meszaros, P. S., Lee, S., & Laughlin, A. (2007). Information processing and information technology career interest and choice among high school students. In C. J. Burger, E. G. Creamer, & P. S. Meszaros (Eds.), *Reconfiguring the firewall: Recruiting women to information technology across cultures and continents* (pp. 77–95). Wellesley, MA: AK Peters, Ltd. doi:10.1201/b10634

Miliszewska, I., & Moore, A. (2011). Attracting girls to ICT studies & careers – A snapshot of strategies. *Redress*, *20*(3), 10–14.

Miller, L., & Hayward, R. (2006). New jobs, old occupational stereotypes: Gender and jobs in the new economy. *Journal of Education and Work*, *19*(1), 67–93. doi:10.1080/13639080500523000

Modi, K., Schoenberg, J., & Salmond, K. (2012). *Generation STEM: What girls say about science, technology, engineering, and math.* Girl Scouts of the USA. Retrieved August 10, 2013, from http://www.girlscouts.org/research/pdf/generation_stem_full_report.pdf

Moss-Racusin, C. A., Dovidio, J. F., Brescoll, V. L., Graham, M. J., & Handelsman, J. (2012). Science faculty's subtle gender biases favour male students. *Proceedings of the National Academy of Sciences of the United States of America*, *109*(41), 16474–16479. doi:10.1073/pnas.1211286109 PMID:22988126

National Institute of Forensic Science. (2001). *Career information.* Retrieved August 16, 2013, from http://www.nifs.com.au/F_S_A/FSA_frame.html?Careers.asp&1

NetHope. (2013). *Women's TechConnect*. Retrieved August 17, 2013, from http://nethope-academy.org/womens-techconnect/

Newman, K. M. (2013). *Code fellows to hold Ruby on Rails bootcamp for women only.* Retrieved August 4, 2013, from http://tech.co/code-fellows-ruby-on-rails-bootcamp-for-women-only-2013-05

Ng, C., & Mitter, S. (2005). *Gender and the digital economy: Perspectives from the developing world*. Thousand Oaks, CA: Sage. doi:10.4135/9788132103622

Nielsen, S., & von Hellens, L. (2006). The social construction of Australian women in IT. In E. M. Trauth (Ed.), *Encyclopedia of gender and information technology* (Vol. 2, pp. 1105–1111). Hershey, PA: Idea Group Reference. doi:10.4018/978-1-59140-815-4.ch174

Nielsen, S., von Hellens, L., Pringle, R., & Greenhill, A. (1999). Students' perceptions of information technology careers: Conceptualising the influence of cultural and gender factors for IT education. *GATES Journal*, *5*(1), 30–38.

O'Dell, J. (2013). *Tackling tech's gender problem the right way: Teaching women to code*. Retrieved June 2, 2013, from http://venturebeat.com/2013/01/10/hackbright/#gO5dqOMhKArT117p.99

Powell, R. (2013). *Learnable opens $10 million in online coding education for young people as fears mount Australia is falling behind.* Retrieved August 19, 2013, from http://www.startupsmart.com.au/growth/business-advice-and-education/learnable-donates-10-million-worth-of-coding-training-to-school-students/2013081910498.html

Ratcliffe, R. (2013, January 30). The gender gap at universities: Where are all the men? *The Guardian.* Retrieved September 21, 2013, from http://www.theguardian.com/education/datablog/2013/jan/29/how-many-men-and-women-are-studying-at-my-university

Rathgeber, E.-M., & Ofwona Adera, E. (2000). *Gender and the information revolution in Africa.* Ottawa, Canada: International Development Research Centre.

Rincon, P. (2005). *CSI shows give 'unrealistic view'.* Retrieved August 4, 2013, from http://news.bbc.co.uk/2/hi/science/nature/4284335.stm

Rommes, E. (2003). *I don't know how to fit it into my life: Courses computers and the internet for everybody in Amsterdam* (Deliverable D03/Appendix 2.4 of IST-2000-26329 SIGIS Project).

Rosen, R. (2013). *A simple suggestion to help phase out all-male panels at tech conferences.* Retrieved August 2, 2013, from http://www.theatlantic.com/technology/archive/2013/01/a-simple-suggestion-to-help-phase-out-all-male-panels-at-tech-conferences/266837/

Samarji, A. (2013). *Get real, forensic scientists: The CSI effect is waning.* Retrieved August 4, 2013, from http://theconversation.com/get-real-forensic-scientists-the-csi-effect-is-waning-13260

Satterfield, L. (2013). *TechWomen collaborate, code and connect in Jordan.* Retrieved June 2, 2013, from http://blogs.state.gov/stories/2013/02/14/techwomen-collaborate-code-and-connect-jordan

Satz, D. (2011). Feminist perspectives on reproduction and the family. In E. N. Zalta (Ed.), *The Stanford encyclopedia of philosophy* (Summer 2011 Ed.). Retrieved August 18, 2013, from http://plato.stanford.edu/archives/sum2011/entries/feminism-family/

Shen, K. N., Zhang, P., & Tarmizi, H. (2009). The role of culture in women interacting with ICT. *University of Wollongong Research Online.* Retrieved August 16, 2013, from http://ro.uow.edu.au/cgi/viewcontent.cgi?article=1049&context=dubaipapers

Smith, L. (2011). *Should kids play Minecraft?* Retrieved August 3, 2013, from http://thecybersafetylady.com.au/2011/05/should-kids-be-playing-minecraft/

Solberg, C. A. (2002). *Culture and industrial buyer behavior: The Arab experience.* Paper presented at the 18th IMP Conference. Retrieved August 16, 2013, from http://impgroup.org/uploads/papers/522.pdf

Sommers, C. H. (2008, March/April). Why can't a woman be more like a man? *The American*. Retrieved August 18, 2013, from http://www.american.com/archive/2008/march-april-magazine-contents/why-can2019t-a-woman-be-more-like-a-man

Stirland, S. L. (2013). *Kimberly Bryant wants black girls code to be girl scouts of technology*. Retrieved July 24, 2013, from http://techpresident.com/news/23974/kimberly-bryant-wants-black-girls-code-be-girl-scouts-technology

TechWomen. (2013a). *Meet the 2013 emerging leaders*. Retrieved August 10, 2013, from https://www.techwomen.org/participants/2013-techwomen

TechWomen. (2013b). *What is TechWomen?* Retrieved August 17, 2013, from https://www.techwomen.org

Trauth, E. M., & Quesenberry, J. (2006). Are women an underserved community in the information technology profession? In *Proceedings of the International Conference on Information Systems* (pp. 1757-1770). Milwaukee, WI: University of Wisconsin.

Trauth, E. M., Quesenberry, L. L., & Huang, H. (2009). Retaining women in the U.S. I.T. workforce: Theorizing the influence of organizational factors. *European Journal of Information Systems*, *18*(5), 476–497. doi:10.1057/ejis.2009.31

Turner, E. (2005). New Europe – New attitudes? Some initial findings on women and computing in the Czech Republic. In J. Archibald, J. Emms, F. Grundy, J. Payne, & E. Turner (Eds.), *The gender politics of ICT* (pp. 133–148). London: Middlesex University Press.

UNESCO. (2012). *Girls in STEM and ICT careers: The path toward gender equality*. New York: UNESCO.

Valenduc, G., Vendramin, P., Guffens, C., Wagner, I., Birbaumer, A., & Tolar, M. et al. (2005). *Widening women's work in information and communication technology: Synthesis report of European project*. Namur: Fondation-Travail Université.

Victoria Police. (2013). *Is forensic science really like the television show CSI?* Retrieved August 10, 2013, from http://www.police.vic.gov.au/content.asp?Document_ID=699

von Hellens, L., Trauth, E., & Fisher, J. (2012). Editorial. *Information Systems Journal*, *22*, 343–353. doi:10.1111/j.1365-2575.2012.00412.x

Whitney, T. (2013). *The White House tech inclusions champions of change!* Retrieved August 16, 2013, from http://anitaborginstitute.tumblr.com/post/56988102023/the-white-house-tech-inclusion-champions-of-change?utm_source=15+August+2013+Newsletter+ABI&utm_campaign=2013+Aug+15+Newsletter&utm_medium=email

KEY TERMS AND DEFINITIONS

CSI: Crime Scene Investigation (TV series).

ICT: Information and Communication Technology. Synonymous with IT.

IT: Information Technology. Synonymous with ICT.

NIFS: National Institute of Forensic Science (an Australian organisation).

#SocialIT: a term coined for a layer of the STEMcell Model. It is a disruptive, penetrating force that can enhance the positive and reduce the negative aspects of the Cultural, Social, Structural and Individual contexts affecting women in IT.

STEMcell Model: A model designed by Sonja Bernhardt that provides a conceptual framework for viewing contexts and layers impacting STEM fields.

Chapter 6
Structural Context and Influencing Factors

ABSTRACT

Structural context and influencing factors form another layer of the STEMcell Model, interacting with the cultural and social contexts and the individual core. Key structural factors identified in the literature are industry branding, information, access, education, support mechanism, and government policies. These traditionally identified factors are explored critically in relation to the STEMcell Model. A key conclusion drawn in this chapter is that the structural factors are not significant today and, consequently, interventions to address them have had minimal effects. It is argued that individual interest is the greatest driver; however, interest in STEM fields does not necessarily translate into choosing STEM as a career, as individuals have competing interests and motives. In addition, some warnings are issued against using attraction methods that lead to false or misleading expectations. An overall conclusion is that in a rapidly changing world perhaps what we need are less solutions imposed from above and more solutions grown from below.

You study Medicine to become a doctor to help people when they are ill. You study Law to become a barrister to help people navigate the law. You study IT to ??? to ??? That is the crux of the issue.

– Sonja Bernhardt (2005)

INTRODUCTION

The body of women in technology research has recurring themes of several structural factors that influence female participation in computing, often deterring them from choosing future technology education or careers in IT (Adya & Kaiser, 2005, 2006; Castano & Webster, 2011; Ashcraft, Eger & Friend, 2012).

These issues are reinforced by comments made by Telle Whitney, CEO of the Anita Borg Institute for Women and Technology, in her introduction to the *ABI Solutions To Recruit Technical Women* report (Simard & Gammal, 2012): "The barriers facing women as they strive to enter the computing field often persist throughout their careers and affect their advancement… This resource is Part 1 in a series of reports focused on solutions

DOI: 10.4018/978-1-4666-5860-8.ch006

companies can employ to improve the recruitment, retention, and advancement of technical women... These solutions are not intended as one-offs for companies to pick and choose from, but an 'arsenal' that companies should bundle together and deploy broadly to achieve maximum impact. Companies wishing to benefit from gender diversity need integrated strategies on the recruitment, retention, and advancement of technical women through the highest levels of the organization. We do not prescribe a particular path to success but instead suggest that each company start by looking at the numbers, taking stock of where its challenges are most acute and then developing a coherent strategy that best addresses its particular culture given available resources. Rather than relying on ad hoc efforts, success depends largely on the development of an integrated array of programs and tactics to address each company's particular challenges as it seeks to recruit, retain and advance women."

This chapter explores the structural factors raised in past research such as that report. The issues are summarized in visual form in Figure 1, as the Structural component of the STEMcell Model.

The structural influencing factors shown in Figure 1 were identified from the literature sources shown in Table 1. These factors are dissected below and provide input to the recommendations presented in Chapter Eleven.

IT INDUSTRY FACTORS

Key industry factors that may have an influencing impact on an individual's perception of the IT industry and thereby affect their study or career decisions are a lack of industry branding and attractive jobs packaging, pay inequities and lack of a clearly defined, achievable promotional pathway.

Figure 1. Structural breakdown: structural factors influencing female participation in IT

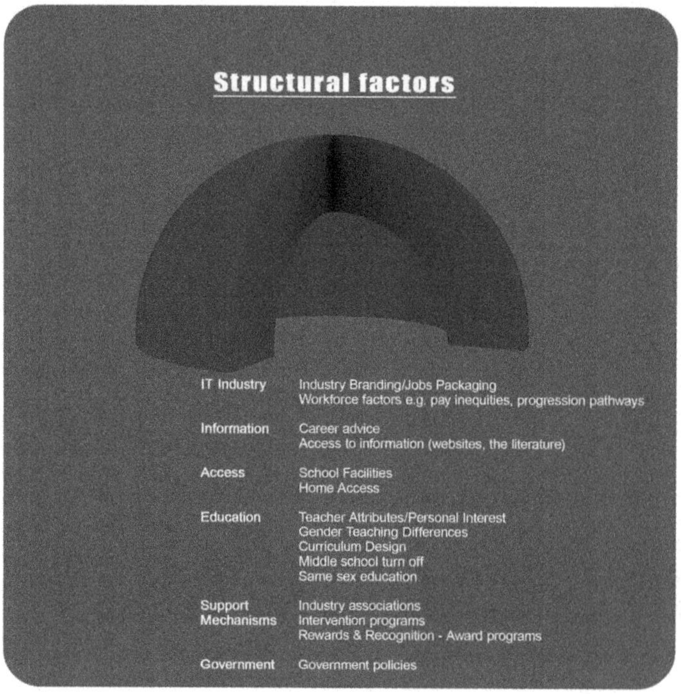

Table 1. Structural context and influencing factors

Structural Context		
Area	**Influencing Factor**	**Reference**
IT Industry	Industry Branding/Jobs Packaging	Bateman (2013); UNESCO (2012)
	Workforce factors, e.g. pay inequities, progression pathways	Bateman (2012); Blair, Gill & Benson (2013); Kirkup (2011); Tandon, Pritchard, Savelieva, Smith & Vogt (2012)
Information	Career advice	Gras-Velazquez, Joyce & Debry (2009)
	Access to information (websites, the literature)	Ashcraft, Eger & Friend (2012); Baker (2012); Clayton, Beekhuyzen & Neilson (2012); Gras-Velazquez et al. (2009); Miliszewska & Moore (2011)
Access	School Facilities	Cheeseman Day, Janus & Davis (2005); Clayton (2007); Clayton et al. (2012); Gras-Velazquez et al. (2009); Heemskerk, Brink, Volman & ten Dam (2005); Lang & McKay (2006); Miliszewska & Moore (2011)
	Home Access	Clayton (2007); Clayton et al. (2012); Gras-Velazquez et al. (2009)
Education	Teacher Attributes/Personal Interest	Adya & Kaiser (2005); Baker (2012); Clayton (2007); Clayton et al. (2012); Goode, Estrella & Margolis (2006); Gras-Velazquez et al. (2009)
	Gender Teaching Differences	Ashcraft et al., (2012); Barker & Aspray (2006); Castano & Webster (2011)
	Curriculum Design	Ashcraft et al. (2012); Bateman (2012); Barker & Aspray (2006); Clayton, von Hellens & Nielsen (2009); Clayton et al. (2012); Gras-Velazquez et al. (2009); Liston, Peterson & Ragan (2009); Margolis & Fisher (2003); Newmarch, Taylor-Steele & Cumpston (2000); Palmen (2011); Timms, Courtney & Anderson (2006)
	Middle school turn off	Anderson, Lankshear & Courtney (2008a); Gras-Velazquez et al. (2009); Modi, Schoenberg & Salmond (2012)
	Same sex education	Adya & Kaiser (2005); Ashcraft et al. (2012); Goode et al. (2006)
Support Mechanisms	Industry associations	Berry & Kalessi, (2011); Personal observation of the establishment and growth of niche associations (globally)
	Intervention programs	Lyons et al. (2012); Miliszewska & Moore (2011)
	Rewards & Recognition - Award programs	Kroes (2013); Modi et al. (2012); Tandon et al. (2012)
Government	Government policies	Barker & Aspray (2006); Gras-Velazquez et al. (2009); Miliszewska & Moore (2011); Palmen (2011); Personal observation of government established taskforces and resulting papers

Branding/Packaging

There have been cries in the IT industry that there is no branding, no elevator pitch or indeed no catchy jingle. In Australia both Women in Technology and the Australian Computer Society flagged from as early as 2003/2004 that the terms IT and later ICT lack clarity of definition, and equally it is not easy to draw boundaries around what are technology occupations. The resulting grey areas and broad-brush definitions seemed to sweep everyone from coders and architects to marketers in technology companies into "ICT roles," adding confusion to the issue.

Those cries have recently been re-raised as described by Bateman (2013) in March 2013, who relates "an online support network for women who want to advance their careers and develop themselves, everywoman, invited senior leaders and influencers of global technology organizations to a roundtable discussion... The senior executives who attended the event came to the conclusion that the terminology, branding and way in which IT jobs are packaged could be deterring females from applying for those roles."

Comments quoted by Bateman (2013) highlight "Tim Skinner, director of UK enterprise at Cisco UK & Ireland, believes the issue stems from the outdated branding and terminology used to advertise job roles." Supporting the lack of branding approach, "Rebecca George, chair, BCS, the Chartered Institute for IT, Policy & Public Affairs Board, and partner at Deloitte, noted that the way roles are packaged and the terminology used is also an age thing. Many 17-24-year-olds are coming into social media and gaming roles, not traditional IT roles."

Bateman (2013) further points out, "Research from Intellect and Women in Technology – *Women's Careers in the Technology Industry, 2011 Report* – found that job advertisements with long lists of requirements can be a turn-off for females when considering which roles to apply for. Of the females questioned, only one in 10 said they would apply for a job role if they only met up to half of the criteria. Over 80% of respondents said they would have to fill over three-quarters of the criteria for a new role before they even considered sending an application. In agreement with this statistic, David Parry-Jones, regional director for UK & Ireland at VMware, drew attention to how men and women interpret job applications very differently. 'If a job description says 15 years' experience and a female candidate has 14, she won't even apply for it. Women feel they have to ask for permission, whereas men ask for forgiveness,' he said."

The age-old adage "A rose by any other name would smell as sweet" may not apply to our IT industry. In fact we may be looking at a dramatic difference, where ICT by any other name will smell sweeter. By way of three examples:

1. In the early 2000's, in response to a rapid decline in female enrolment in their core IT course, one Australian university chose to rename the course to "Creative Industries." Anecdotal and now statistical evidence is that since that simple rebadging the university has been consistently oversubscribed with female enrolments and has waiting lists (Dale Spender, personal communication, July, 2002). Key to note here is that the underlying structure of the course did not change. It still included "hard technology" subjects such as programming and design – yet the course attraction factor for women was dramatically enhanced with the name change.
2. Similarly reported by UNESCO (2012), "university courses renamed to appeal to non-geeky students have seen a rise in popularity among young women."
3. This reflects a more general trend. Lewis (2013) reports that games writer Leigh Alexander flagged that "some games are also given subtle tweaks to appeal to women: after Skunk Studios renamed its macho *King of Thieves* game *Raven's Flight*, its sales rose."
4. Harvey Mudd College in the USA increased its proportion of female computer science graduates from 10% to 45% in six years by making several changes. These included making introductory classes more interesting for freshmen with non-technical backgrounds, by shifting course content from "the inner details of computers and software" to "practical applications, such as solving games and puzzles"; encouraging women to "see working hard as normal and expected"; and classes grouped according to previous experience (Shellenbarger, 2013).

These examples raise a telling point. For our problem is not lack of *people* in IT, it is lack of *women* in IT. The industry branding, packaging, course names and job descriptions do not inhibit *men* from these careers, only *women*. The solutions proposed are an implicit acceptance of that, and it is time we gave it our explicit acceptance. Statistically, compared to men women do have different interests and are attracted to different things. And the evidence so far is that this is not something that is going to change with a bit of social engineering. Perhaps it is time to embrace our collective differences and our individual uniqueness – and move on.

So we can accept that different "branding" might attract more women. But we have to be careful. There is no point attracting women into courses with flashy names only to see the pipeline leak rivers because once there they find the material uninteresting or irrelevant to the motives that attracted them. But if we can come up with a rebranding that accurately reflects the reality in an attractive way, then that is worth doing. The example of Harvey Mudd College is interesting in that respect but raises its own warning flag. The one individual example given was of a girl who wanted to do engineering and finally chose the college because she preferred to go where women were not a tiny minority (Shellenbarger, 2013). In other words, she represents less an increase in female participation than poaching from another college. So whether the experience of that small college (less than 800 students) can be translated to societally significant levels is an open question.

My preferred new branding of ICT (Information, Communications and Technology) is "Innovation, Creation, Transformation." While we still need the original words to define what it *is*, I feel this rebranding better describes who we *are* and what we *do*. I believe that Innovation, Creation, Transformation is:

- More descriptive;
- More accurate about what the industry really is about; and
- Lends itself towards being able to say who you are and what you do. With this rebadging we could easily answer that question along the lines of "I'm a transformationist – I use technology in innovative and creative ways to transform your business and life."

In the era of #SocialIT, the Issue – lack of branding – has the Solution – a crowdsourcing project to rename, rebadge and develop catchy promotional materials such as jingles and videos.

Workforce Factors

Jenny Barbour (Director of Jenny Barbour IT & Project Recruitment Pty Ltd, and co founder of Women are IT [Victoria, South Australia and Western Australia]), said "There are numerous elements taken into consideration by females when selecting a career path. Flexibility of the work place environment and global opportunity being two key decision making considerations" (J. Barbour, personal communication, July 21, 2013). In fact workforce factors affecting IT careers and career choice for women make up a complex mix. Pennington (2013) notes, "Despite comprising 52 per cent of the population, women make up just 18 per cent of the information communication technology (ICT) industry, according to the Australian Bureau of Statistics. Evening up the numbers remains on the to-do list for universities, industry associations and employers, with some employers like Westpac, VMWare and Microsoft running programs to attract more women to their tech ranks and the industry in general. Despite complaints of sexism, discrimination and inequality, and under reporting of their contribution, some women continue to carve a place and thrive in tech."

Intersecting with those negative elements and positive inducements are women's own desires. Pennington (2013) tagged five reasons why women do choose to work in technology: A Ticket to Ride (travel opportunities), Chasing a Dream (being their own boss), Something Different (never getting bored, lots of variety) and A Balancing Act (troubleshooting).

Another factor inherent in IT careers is constant change. The emerging IT paradigm "requires much more of ICT professionals than the constant upgrading of technical skills. Today's ICT professionals must have a sound understanding of technology and develop high-level business, management, and communication skills. Therefore, in order to make successful employment inroads, ICT professionals will need the know-how and the psychological make-up to function in a turbulent job market in which the boundaries and requirements will constantly change. The only constant in the sector is perpetual change" (Tandon, Pritchard, Savelieva, Smith & Vogt, 2012). This indicates that a certain psychology is an asset in an IT career. Whether that has any implications for the representation of women in IT is another question that would require research. However we do know that while common popular stereotypes about large differences between the sexes are simplistic and there is a large overlap in psychological measures between men and women, there are indeed average differences (Nauert, 2013).

On top of any general *de facto* negative discrimination, deliberate positive discrimination and personal goals, the literature notes two important specific negative factors: pay inequities and lack of promotional pathways. Not surprisingly, an industry survey ranked salary, benefits, career opportunities and flexible working conditions as the top four reasons that women apply to certain businesses (Berry & Kalessi, 2011). This implies that companies should take note of those factors if they wish to remain competitive and attract female talent. It must be noted however that these factors do not only apply to IT and need to be compared to other careers.

Pay Equity

Inequality in pay is not restricted to IT careers either. Flynn, Heath & Holt (2013) describe the "Pay Paradox" as "According to the latest figures, women are better educated than ever, earning almost 60 percent of all college degrees. Yet, we are paid 23% less than men on average. Some of the gap can be attributed to career choice: more women than men choose to go into teaching and social work, for example, which pay less relative to 'male' professions such as finance and technology. But career choice does not fully explain The Pay Paradox. An analysis of full-time workers 10 years out of college, for instance, found a 12 percent difference in earnings that was entirely unexplained by choice of profession. The bottom line is that progress in wage equity has hit a wall."

However it must be noted that some analysts conclude there is no real pay gap. That is, we need to look not only at choice of profession but also choices within professions. CONSAD's (2009) analysis of the reasons for the disparity in wages concluded that "the differences in the compensation of men and women are the result of a multitude of factors and that the raw wage gap should not be used as the basis to justify corrective action. Indeed, there may be nothing to correct. The differences in raw wages may be almost entirely the result of the individual choices being made by both male and female workers." Those choices include not only factors like relative preferences for part time versus full time work and family activities, but also the value placed on non-wage benefits such as health insurance and fringe benefits.

No doubt that conclusion is controversial, and the CONSAD report itself notes that the available data is insufficient to consider all the factors simultaneously or longitudinally, so additional research would be needed to be sure. However Dougherty (2010) reports that Census Bureau data showed that in 2008, single, childless women aged 22 to 30 in U.S. cities were paid an average 8% more than their male peers, consistent with their average higher education. Also interesting is a report by Tobak (2011), quoting author Marty Nemko, that "Women business owners make less than half of what male business owners make, which, since they have no boss, means it's independent of discrimination. The reason for the disparity, according to a Rochester Institute of Technology study, is that money is the primary motivator for 76% of men versus only 29% of women. Women place a higher premium on shorter work weeks, proximity to home, fulfillment, autonomy, and safety, according to Nemko."

Arguments about the cause and significance of the wage gap aside, the good news is that according to Tandon et al. (2012), the gender pay gap for women in technology careers is less pronounced than that within the workforce as a whole. Pay is more closely aligned immediately after career commencement, after which the pay gap widens (Merrett, 2012), but this also is consistent with the workforce as a whole (Dougherty, 2010).

However, if the gender pay gap for women in IT is less than average, then this structural element moves from negative to positive. It means women are better off in IT than in many other industries. As noted when discussing dualisms (Chapter Five: *Popular Theories*), discussions of why there are too few women in IT can be one of the causes. If we talk about gender pay gaps as a barrier to women in IT then we imply it is a problem *specifically in IT careers.* If our aim is to attract more women into IT, we are better off trumpeting the fact that pay is *more equal*, rather than focusing on the remaining inequality.

Promotional Pathways

According to the Blair, Gill & Benson (2013) *Focus on the Pipeline Report*, 25% of female middle managers in the STEM sector surveyed said a lack of senior management sponsorship was holding back their progression in the sector. Berry & Kalessi's (2011) survey identified that "Many feel that they are being passed over for promotion in favor of male colleagues… There were also concerns raised that flexible working hours were offered in theory but rarely implemented in reality which could be one of the factors holding women back from career progression, particularly where they have caring responsibilities for children or dependents."

However the issue is not as simple as single factors. Flynn et al. (2013) describe the Promotion Paradox: "It is as plain as day that women are equally qualified to lead in terms of skill and talent, yet we capture far fewer job slots at the top. Only four percent of the CEOs in Fortune's top 1,000 companies are female and less than 20 percent of Congress is female. Even worse, progress has been relatively flat over the past several years. This is a sticky wicket because there are a dozen different ways to explain this sad situation and each one rings true to some extent: Women are less aggressive than men in stepping up to ask for the big jobs they want. Men at the top are more likely to pull other men up by their collars into the C-suite to join them. Women have fewer leadership role models and they arguably have greater demands outside of work competing for their attention. Regardless of whether the mitigating factor is discrimination, the leadership pipeline, society, or something altogether different, the extreme disparity of women versus men at the highest levels provides fuel for many of us to push harder. Unfortunately, it also leads many of us wonder if the struggle for career parity is truly worth it. The effect is that the pool of qualified female candidates for top jobs gets smaller when the best women leave to raise families or pursue part-time work or other endeavors."

One possible factor is the different approach women take. Bateman (2013) reports "Research suggests that many promotions are based on personal relationships, leading to a higher proportion of men having access to these opportunities. Julie Stone, CFO and chief operating officer at Alcatel-Lucent UK & Ireland, said 'women network in a very different manner to men. Men network to get on in the workplace, whereas women tend to network with each other to enable them to do their jobs better… Women want to be appointed into senior positions through their own merits, rather than feeling like they had a leg up.'"

Unfortunately although the field has gathered a lot of anecdotal evidence and some empirical studies, the issue is neither pinpointed nor resolved.

Whatever the issue, there seems to be a disconnect between recruitment and promotion opportunities. Cave (2013) reports that Martha Heller, President of a CIO recruitment company and author of *The CIO Paradox* explained, "I'm going to say 80% of the searches that we do whether they're at the CIO level or at the VP or director level, will say to us, 'If you could get us a woman that'd be really great.' But the women I talk to are asking but not getting those opportunities internally. So somewhere there's a serious disconnect – where on one hand you've got women saying we're not being considered and on the other, companies saying we want women."

Simard, Davies Henderson, Gilmartin, Schiebinger & Whitney (2008) present an extensive empirical research report that proposes data driven solutions for the retention and promotion of technical women. The report was commissioned to "learn why the mid level is a 'glass ceiling' for women on the technical ladder … [by undertaking] an empirical study of female scientists and engineers at seven mid to large, publicly traded Silicon Valley high-tech firms." Some of the many findings are:

- The popular image of the successful technical worker as an isolated "hacker" does not reflect today's mid-level technical employees. Survey results show that the core values and perceptions of success of both women and men at that level involve teamwork and collaboration.
- Both technical men and women identify more strongly with their technical profession than with their current company. Company retention efforts hinge on this issue.
- Technical women value professional development above all else. Career development policies and practices should include training to enhance technical, leadership, and managerial skills, coupled with career planning and coaching, mentoring, and networking opportunities.

There are a number of aspects of this topic that need open discussion.

It is clear that there are fewer women in higher positions and the discrepancy increases as the level rises. But the cause is less clear. The gap, and the way it increases, reflects the situation with pay, and it is not a big stretch to think they are related. No doubt there is bias and discrimination in the workplace, especially among a certain type of man – many of us have encountered *them!* But is it the reason, in more than a minority of cases? Many of us also know men in high positions who are sensible and would not discriminate against women and would even discriminate in their favor.

The problem with anecdotal evidence is that correctly identifying trends, let alone causes, requires proper statistics. Consider the statement earlier by Blair et al. (2013) that 25% or women said a lack of senior management sponsorship was holding them back. This is not unique to women, in fact the trend is pervasive. Fisher (2006) quotes one male worker saying, "The people above me were all ages 45 to 65 and weren't about to leave. It was clear to me I wouldn't get promoted no matter how good I was." Another complained that "In advertising – and I saw this at more than one agency – youthfulness is valued because it's seen as with-it and relevant, but it's a paradox… The senior managers in their 40s and 50s are paranoid about keeping their own jobs, so they do everything they can to keep you down." Fisher goes on to note "increasingly, younger workers are finding that no matter how many hours they put in or how much their bosses rave about their work, they're just plain stuck. An entire generation is bumping against something no amount of youthful vigor can match. Call it the Gray Ceiling… A generation of workers can't get ahead – because aging boomers above them won't budge." She also quotes Janelle Shubert, a professor of management and associate director, who said, "The glass ceiling is being replaced by a Gray Ceiling of baby-boomers. Those of us who've spent decades paying our dues are finally reaping the rewards, both psychological and financial, and we don't see any reason to step aside now. We're now the ceiling that our young colleagues are going to have to break through." Six years after that, Fisher (2012) writes that "Getting promoted is tougher than it used to be... there are fewer management jobs to move into... Even before [the global recession] ... companies had been running leaner and cutting out layers of management jobs... Then there's the notoriously lofty failure rate of people promoted into bigger jobs, which according to some studies runs as high as 40%. 'Companies are being extremely cautious about moving people from one level to the next higher one,' Crandell observes, and no wonder: 'We've heard plenty of horror stories about managers who got promoted and then flamed out – and executives themselves often tell us how much harder it is to adjust to a bigger job than they thought it would be.'"

In other words, women at middle levels might find little help from above because the higher levels aren't helping anyone.

Second, numerous of the references quoted refer to the different aspirations and styles of women. As with the gender pay gap, we must ask the question of how much of the promotion gap is also due to women's personal choices. If women are being held back consciously or unconsciously, that is something we need to fight (and #SocialIT provides one of our weapons). But it is not up to us to impose our choices.

Third is that moves to push women up the corporate ladder can have unintended, negative consequences. Glenn Wightwick of IBM Australia is quoted as saying "there are plenty of challenges, including the habit of some companies to rapidly promote female employees rather than letting them gain further valuable experience in the trenches: 'One of the things I've noticed over the years in IT is when you see high potential in male and females, you see women directed to management roles and it can have an impact on their work or research careers'" (Research Career, 2013). So rather than women building up breadth and depth of experience "in the trenches," there is a trend to promote them quickly just to increase their representation: with negative effects on their ability to do their new jobs most effectively. This has further knock-on effects on both their future promotion prospects and the reinforcement of negative stereotypes.

Fourth, while we would justly decry a promotion gap in business in general caused by prejudice, that has nothing to do with attracting women into IT unless things are *worse* in IT. And again as with the pay gap, if things are no worse in IT – let alone if they are better! – we run the risk of our own arguments turning women off IT careers.

That leads to the final point. As Flynn et al. (2013) put it, the large disparity between women and men in top positions "also leads many of us wonder if the struggle for career parity is truly worth it." That is one of the reasons that we need to know why the disparity exists, not just assume it is due to prejudice and structural factors too large to fight. If we know what it is, we know what to fight. But to the extent that it is due to women's own choices, then that doesn't affect the chances of the many women who do choose to seek high positions.

INFORMATION

Obviously nobody will pursue a particular career if they don't know it exists. Even knowing it exists, few will be interested if the information is too hard to find or inaccurate. At the other end of the pipeline, if the information attracts people but is misleading then there will be a high dropout rate.

Traditionally, key factors here have been career advice and information about the industry from promotional material, advertising and more recently, websites. Parents are another traditional source of information and advice on suitable careers, and in a relatively new and certainly dynamic industry like IT that raises the additional obstacle of parental ignorance. Thus Clayton, Beekhuyzen & Nielsen (2012) flag that "Parents whose daughters attend TTYA [Technology Takes You Anywhere, an IT Careers intervention program] sometimes recognize their own ignorance of ICT careers and the need for access to better information. As one parent commented, parents do not realize 'where and how girls can go to achieve a great career in IT.'"

Today there is an abundance of information available at people's finger clicks, something that can only increase in the #SocialEra. This runs the gamut from general STEM information on association, industry and government portals to specific topics such as an ebook by Baker (2012) described as "addressing the question 'How does GIS [Geographic Information Systems] enhance STEM learning?' The ebook is filled with rich case studies of STEM in formal and informal environments. The power of STEM collaborations and partnerships and ties to career and workforce development is also a central theme of the volume. The ebook outlines three beneficial tracks for student learning in STEM by integrating GIS technology."

There are educators to assist recruiters and educators, for example Donna Milgram – Executive Director from National Institution for Women in Trades, Technology and Science (IWITTS: www.iwitts.org). IWITTS provides online training in best practice ways to increase female participation in STEM classes, as well as other resources and case studies. Additionally many information toolkits exist, e.g. Eva Fabry – Director of the European Centre for Women and Technology (ECWT) points to rich information and many resources provided by the ECWT website http://www.womenandtechnology.eu, and NCWIT (National Centre for Women and Information Technology) provides well designed and freely available tools (Ashcraft et al., 2012):

- **The Scorecard:** The NCWIT Scorecard shows trends in girls' and women's participation in computing in the U.S. over time, providing a benchmark for measuring progress and identifying areas. Available at www.ncwit.org/scorecard
- **Computing Education and Future Jobs Interactive Map:** An interactive map that presents education and workforce data at the national, state and congressional district level. Available at www.ncwit.org/edjobsmap
- **Counselors for Computing Campaign (C4C):** A four-year campaign that equips counselors with up-to-date information and resources they can use to advise students — especially girls — regarding education and careers in IT. See www.ncwit.org/c4c
- **Why Should Young Girls Consider a Career in Information Technology?** This is a "talking points" card giving adults talking points and additional resources for a conversation with their daughters and/or other young people. Available at www.ncwit.org/youngwomen
- **Moving Beyond Computer Literacy:** Why Schools Should Teach Computer Science? This "talking points" card provides information about the value of computer science curricula for students, educators, local and national economies as well as global society. Available at www.ncwit.org/schools

- **K–12 Promising Practices and Programs-in-a-Box:** Offers a number of short case studies describing promising programs and practices for improving K–12 curricula and increasing girls' participation in computing. Other "in-a-box" items are Outreach-in-a-Box: Discovering IT (www.ncwit.org/outreach), a toolkit for industry professionals who would like to be guest speakers in K–12 classrooms; and Computer Science-in-a-Box: Unplug Your Curriculum (www.ncwit.org/unplugged), a toolkit for introducing computing in engaging, "non-wired" ways. All of these resources are available at www.ncwit.org/resources

There is more than enough information out there. The problem is finding accurate information.

On the negative side, the most visible information is not necessarily the most accurate. In my opinion our general admiration for companies like Google has a lot to answer for. I'm not denying the amazing innovations the whole world enjoys from companies like Google or Apple. My issue is more to do with the perception it engenders: that life in the IT industry is about some great sexy giant that does all these amazing interesting things, and your goal is to be employed by that giant. Yet the reality of employment is very different. More than 90% of all IT companies not just in Australia but around the world are in the small to medium range, and more than 80% of those are "Micro" firms with less than five full-time staff members. If we're thinking about obstacles to continuing in IT careers, think about the young person dreaming of working in a Google office surrounded by a host of dynamic people at least as smart as they are, overflowing with free breakfasts and massages (Albom, 2013): and then finding themselves in a cubicle in a small-to-medium enterprise where they bring their own coffee.

However there is truth to the perception. In the USA, "Census Bureau data show that 78 percent of businesses have no employees. Among those with employees, three-fifths have one to four employees, and 98 percent have fewer than 100. However, half of all workers are employed by large companies (those with more than 500 employees), and a third work for very large companies (those with more than 5,000 employees)" (Bartlett, 2012). Also, "jobs offered at large businesses were better than those at small businesses," with both hourly wages and benefits considerably better (Kenny, 2011). But despite that, and for all the romance of Google's highly publicized work conditions, life in the average medium to large enterprise can be more like the "cubicle-land" world of *Dilbert* cartoons: so much so that "Many employees are highly cynical about the effectiveness of management and view large, bureaucratic organizations with disdain and contempt" (Feldman, 2000).

The high profile of the largest firms is also a double-edged sword. They hire so many people that when they lay off workers, the numbers can be large (attracting more media attention), giving the perception of job instability. Yet this is an illusion of numbers. In fact, in the USA "each year, 22 percent of staff in companies with fewer than 100 employees quit or are fired, compared with only 8 percent for companies with 2,000 or more workers" (Kenny, 2011).

To make the point again, while we want to make sure that the advantages of a career in IT are known, we need to beware of boosting people's expectations so much that what we gain in recruitment we lose in the face of the reality of the job. "Selling" IT careers by excitedly telling students "they can have a job at a place like Google" is basically a lie. The reality is they are far more likely to work in a smaller, relatively unknown business with lesser benefits.

Think for a minute how much in your courses your students get engaged with smaller, non-brand-name businesses versus the Microsofts, IBMs and Googles. And there is much more to IT than a career path as hired staff from entry level to management. It is the start-ups of today, made by innovators, creators and risk takers, who will be the Apples and Googles of tomorrow; and innovators, the creators of new jobs, are especially important in a declining economic environment. How much encouragement is given to students to be the key innovators or entrepreneurs to create the technologies themselves, rather than have the goal of being an employee of a major firm?

Whatever the limitations of the information out there and as presented, if the results of the poll in Chapter Four: *The Old Approach* are even approximately representative, then we can say that it has not stopped those interested in IT. Nor have intervention programs specifically aimed at providing more or better information netted many more.

Nevertheless, intervention projects have some effect, and improving access to quality information can only be good. Perhaps a #SocialIT solution is a Hackathon or similar activity aimed at creating an exciting, user friendly portal. This could provide a good conceptual framing of IT careers and allow people to drill down to whatever detail they want to pursue, in whatever aspect that grabs their interest.

ACCESS FACTORS

A reported key factor that has a direct influence on early stage and ongoing interest in technology is access to technology, both at home and at school.

Turner, Brent & Pecora (2002) report that women IT professionals cite school access to computers as the most prominent reason for their interest in an IT career. The amount and quality of school ICT resources and Internet access that are available are important if the student does not have home access (Cleary Pierce & Trauth, 2006). If physical access to computer resources is limited a usual strategy that has been adopted is the creation of school based computer clubs, where access is provided during break periods or after school (Gras-Velazquez et al. 2009; Lang & McKay 2006; Miliszewska & Moore 2011).

Clayton et al. (2012) note "the quality, availability and maintenance of ICT related resources (including computers and other ICT devices, internet access and equipment and environment to use the computers and devices) can have a powerful influence on how ICT is perceived by students and people who influence them. This influence can range on the spectrum from being extremely positive to strongly negative."

This may have had an influence on girls' interest in IT. Palmen (2011) reports "There seems to be few significant differences to girls' access and use of technology within schools (Haywood, Alty, Pearson & Martin 2003; Selwyn & Bullon, 2000). At home boys tend to have greater access to ICT and use it more … girls were more likely to have no access to a computer, or to have access to only one computer/ laptop at home where as boys were more likely to have access to two or more computers/laptops."

However access as an issue is rapidly diminishing in importance. Just a generation ago, in 1984, only 8.2% of US households had a personal computer, but by 2003 this rose to 62% with a computer and 55% with Internet access (Cheeseman Day, Janus & Davis, 2005). Interestingly, families with children showed higher uptake (Cheeseman Day et al., 2005), so that by 2003, 80% of children in the USA had access to a home computer and 95% of them used it (Beltran, Das & Fairly, 2008). By 2011, three quarters of US households had a personal computer, with no significant difference between males and females in how many used them (File, 2013).

That is just computers at home. A Pew Research survey in 2013 found that 95% of teens are online, 37% of them have their own smartphone, and nearly one in four have a tablet (Madden, Lenhart, Duggan, Cortesi & Gasser, 2013). Interestingly, while somewhat more boys access the Internet than girls, more girls than boys access it via mobile devices (Madden et al., 2013). The main drivers of Internet access are not gender but the education and income of their parents: fully 99% of all teens with parents with at least some college education or income over $50,000 have Internet access (though even in households with income less than $30,000, three quarters of teens owned a computer and 15% owned a tablet). Highly relevant from our point of view is that more girls than boys now own computers or tablets, in both the 12-13 and 14-17 year brackets (Madden et al., 2013).

Even in 2005, Oblinger & Oblinger (2005) referred to the current generation of school children as the "Net Generation." More broadly grouped they are known as Generation Z, where Gen Z kids are growing up in highly sophisticated media and computer environments and will be more Internet savvy and expert than their Gen Y forerunners. Even as babies and toddlers and through early childhood they are exposed to a range of technology, and have been familiar with computers and the Internet from an early age. Consequently, they are confident and competent users of tablets, computers, mobile phones, the Internet, computer games and a variety of instant messaging tools. One classic YouTube video (that we can call a two year old YouTube video "classic" emphasizes how rapidly things are changing!) shows a toddler given traditional magazines: she tries to swipe, click and flip the magazines in iPad style, and when it doesn't work looks puzzled, checks whether her finger is working and finally gives up, saying it's broken and doesn't work: then when she is given an iPad she merrily accesses a myriad of information (Userexperienceworks, 2011).

EDUCATION FACTORS

A number of key education factors that influence perceptions and reactions toward technology have been identified. While all are interrelated, particular focus is on teacher attributes and their personal interest, teaching style differences due to gender interpretations, curriculum design, middle school turn off and same sex education.

In terms of barriers, Castano & Webster (2001) comment "At school, the sex of ICT teachers, their competence in the subject, and the coverage of the curriculum all play a role in encouraging or discouraging girls and boys from engaging with ICT (Goode, Estrella & Margolis, 2006; Palmen, 2011)." In addition to the specific factors, the interplay between institutional and psychological factors can also contribute to turning potential students away from IT studies (Goode et al., 2006; Margolis & et al., 2003).

On the positive side, Baker (2012) notes "High-quality STEM education directly supports STEM-based careers and, collectively, a work force that is more globally competitive. STEM education requires effective curriculum standards, high-quality teacher preparation, and support for national policies and frameworks... STEM education is about robust and coherent STEM curriculum and experiences that are multidisciplinary, integrative problem solving inquiries that foster critical and computationally driven thinking. It is about engaging students with real data in real problems that are approached creatively and collaboratively, the way professionals need to work."

The Teacher and Gender Styles

A teacher's beliefs about gender plus their own attributes and attitudes toward technology readiness may have an influence on their students. If they hold negative values they can subtly influence girls not to study IT (Barker & Aspray, 2006). More positively, Adya & Kaiser (2005) suggest

"K-12 systems need to provide an environment where teachers can become comfortable with their technology preparedness and convey enthusiasm about it to students." Similarly, Goode (2008) states "powerful teachers serve a vital role in drawing in traditionally underrepresented students into CS [Computer Science]… almost all the strategies for supporting underrepresented students in CS education rely on the active role of the teacher. Teachers drive the recruitment, instruction, college-going information, and other important conditions needed to engages students in CS." Goode (2008) further identifies three key strands for individual teachers:

- Content: knowledge of the area, e.g. having an interest and extensive amount of subject knowledge, while being able to rapidly adjust as new innovations appear and dramatically reshape the discipline;
- Pedagogical awareness, e.g. being able to draw from a range of teaching strategies;
- Cultural diversity knowledge, e.g. being aware of issues that prevent females and minorities from entering CS studies.

Volman, van Eck, Heemskerk & Kuiper (2005) note an interesting further problem regarding teachers' own IT skills level: if they believe their students' skills are greater than their own, teachers tend to undervalue what they are able to contribute to IT education. This is made worse by a lack of uniformity, with Heemskerk, Brink, Volman and ten Dam (2005) suggesting that teacher engagement issues may be exacerbated by "the different ways in which computers are used within and between schools." However IT is such a rapidly evolving field that any solution must involve coping with that rather than resisting it.

The role and influence of the gender of the teacher noted above by Castano & Webster (2011) is also reflected by Ashcraft et al. (2012), who comment "many teachers of primary and secondary education are women who, to date, have low levels of CS and IT training (Barker & Aspray, 2006). Teachers also are influenced by cultural biases about who does (and does not do) CS work and are significantly affected by the infrastructure and lack of resources for CS education available in their schools (Barker & Aspray, 2006; Margolis et al., 2008)."

Following Baker's (2012) quote above, perhaps the most positive thing teachers can do is use high quality preparation to engage students in creative problem solving with real world data and issues.

The Curriculum

Considerable evidence over time points to the importance of the content and delivery of secondary school ICT curricula for interesting students, especially girls, to continue along ICT pathways (Newmarch, Taylor-Steele & Cumpston, 2000; Barker & Aspray, 2006; Ashcraft et al., 2012; Clayton et al. 2012).

Unfortunately other research indicates that to girls IT is "boring." Rich qualitative responses reported by Timms, Courtney & Anderson (2006) indicated that high school information technology subjects were generally perceived by girls as boring, dull and uninteresting. Subsequent research found similar results (Anderson, Lankshear & Courtney, 2008a; Anderson, Lankshear, Timms & Courtney, 2008b). These results resonate with Margolis and Fisher's (2003) comment that "girls are rarely inspired by computers and when they are it is only to have the interest extinguished during the school experience."

Ashcraft et al. (2012) report that "computer science courses still routinely fail to make computing curriculum relevant for students…Computing is often taught in the abstract, preventing students from recognizing how technology can help address relevant social problems... This lack of relevancy is troubling because making relevant connections is particularly important for increasing girls' interest in computing courses and careers." The key issue here is that an outdated, boring curriculum reinforces IT stereotypes as a lonely, isolated, machine-focused set of tasks (Clayton et al., 2009; Margolis, Estrella, Goode, Holme & Nao, 2008).

Another factor that appears almost designed to make IT boring is focusing on the most basic skills. As Goode, Estrella & Margolis (2006) comment, "even at schools that are 'heavily wired,' computer science is too often interpreted as 'computer literacy' and only low-level user skills are taught." The students are obtaining a skewed view of the ICT field because of the focus on mastering software packages and the perception of ICT being simply word processing (Newmarch et al., 2000; Downes, 2004). This attitude is reflected in a story related by Parmar (2013) about a student who, when discussing tedious and boring IT classes, jokingly said that ICT ought to be renamed "I Can Type."

In contrast to that, Ashcraft et al. (2012) identify that "a wealth of broader educational research rooted in constructivist, constructionist, and culturally relevant learning theories has long emphasized the importance of connecting instruction to students' interest and prior knowledge and of using active and collaborative learning pedagogies." Their research highlights "how these approaches are important not only for improving learning for girls and other underrepresented students, but for all students… research has focused specifically on how curriculum and teaching practices in science-related fields do not employ these pedagogies and, therefore, contribute to girls' lack of interest in these areas... In sum, these factors include: 1) curriculum that is irrelevant, 2) pedagogies that discourage collaboration, 3) lack of opportunities to take risks and make mistakes, and 4) heavy reliance on lecturing instead of active, hands-on, project-based learning."

In support of those latter points, research by Liston, Peterson & Ragan (2009) provides some practical clues to what aspects of education are most critical: "Hands-on and project-based activities and real-world, relevant content were considered to strongly contribute to program success… Further, the women who participated in an IT-related education program were significantly more likely to have positive attitudes toward the field during middle school and high school, including feeling more competent in IT skills and more comfortable in IT environments. The six most highly rated practices from the survey were hands-on experiences, opportunities to work together with other people, opportunities to use technology to be creative and explore, and project-based learning opportunities."

Whilst the Liston et al. (2009) research involved adult women in the USA and their perceptions of what worked when they were girls, their findings are similar to those of Anderson et al. (2008b). The latter looked at 1,453 Australian female secondary students, of whom 131 were "Takers" of advanced IT classes and 1,322 were "Non-Takers." The Non-Takers identified two primary reasons for not taking IT classes: "the subjects are boring" and "the subjects would not be helpful to me in my chosen career path." It is interesting to note that the girls perceived the courses to be almost exclusively about programming even though they were not, and that both Non-Takers and Takers expressed an aversion to programming. However the Takers had more awareness about the creative aspects of the courses, and the creative aspect was the attraction.

In a familiar scenario for efforts to increase representation of women in IT, despite considerable research and focus on the ICT curriculum it is still identified as a key factor that may negatively impact on girls' uptake of technology. For example in Bateman's (2012) article, Sheila Flavell, COO of FDM group, said "more needs to be done to encourage this… The lack of women stems from the ICT school curriculum, as it doesn't prepare students with relevant knowledge of commercial IT programs. This, in turn, filters up through the education system to university education and into the workplace."

It may be worse than that. The theory is that attracting girls into IT courses is the first step to attracting them into IT careers. But Ashcraft et al. (2012) found "that while relevant computing curriculum increases girls' interests in computing, it doesn't always increase their belief that computing is of value for their future plans or goals." The implication of this is that even improving the overall technology curriculum may not have a positive influence on the number of girls taking on further technology studies or careers.

A key issue we need to face is: why? These points might all be valid, but they do not explain why *boys* are comparatively immune to them. The problem is not nobody becoming interested in IT because of defective curricula: it is that *girls* are not.

Cohoon (2003) suggests that girls' interest in computers tend to develop later than that of boys and consequently boys enjoy a head start in computer awareness, which then becomes assumed knowledge within high school curricula. But then we have to ask why is that so, especially given the trends in computer access and experience described above.

One clue comes from the Anderson et al. (2008b) quote above, which identifies an aversion to programming versus the attraction for girls of the "creative aspects" of IT. But in contrast to that is feedback provided after an Australian school based IT career event, TTYA (Technology Takes You Anywhere): "One teacher commented during TTYA, 'don't downplay the role of PROGRAMMING and MATHS too much! – some of us women get a buzz from this! What is required is the early exposure of girls to these ICT domains to inform them about what is available'" (Clayton et al. 2012). This comment supporting a clear focus on the core IT streams relates back to the findings in my snap poll (Chapter Four: *The Old Approach*), which identified interest from an early age as the chief driver of women who enter IT careers. Ironically, if we try too hard to "interest" girls in IT by focusing on "creative aspects" to the detriment of its more mathematical and technical aspects, we might risk losing the interest of the kinds of girls that would make a huge difference and who are, at least to some extent, the girls we are really trying to encourage.

Nevertheless, whether the truth is that poor curricula are turning off girls who would otherwise be interested, or that the girls who are interested will be no more turned off than the boys, educators owe it to all schoolchildren to produce engaging curricula. The school curriculum should not be just about learning how to enter data or use a piece of software that will probably be gone or unrecognizable by the time they hit the workforce (well I remember my son learning MS-DOS in High School less than 15 years ago. iChat one of today's teenagers on their iPhone and ask what MS-DOS is). It ought to be about engendering a spirit of innovation and curiosity about how to create and design technologies: how to *do* things and *why* to do them. IT (and STEM more generally) have a severe inherent problem in the pace of change in the ever-evolving technology landscape compared to the time it takes to develop, approve and implement curriculum changes. Perhaps its only hope is to leave the core curriculum at the level of universal principles and concepts, and set up a more agile service to provide fast-response tools for learning the application of those principles. We cannot properly teach modern IT without embracing it ourselves.

The School

The overall school environment influences ICT access. The school's budget and level of technical expertise affect technology uptake by the school.

Once they have it, they do not always know how to use it most effectively. Margolis et al. (2003) report that "teachers and school administrators become fixated on the number and types of computer equipment they have at their disposal, whether the equipment works, whether their school has Internet access, and whether their students are learning the basic computing skills and becoming technologically proficient." Thus while some schools might actually teach computer science, others might regard IT education as simply basic computing skills or computer literacy.

One criticism has been schools using avoidance tactics. Quoting a 2003 study, Miliszewska & Moore (2011) write "schools may claim that not only do students have better access to and better computers at home, but that they also already have superior ICT skills to their teachers. In addition, it has been argued, schools can operate under perceptions that 'digital and gender divides will diminish in due course because of the constant diffusion of the technology in society.'" However we must admit that those schools had a point: the diffusion happened (Madden et al., 2013). But what that means is that schools should approach IT education more intelligently along the lines described above (*The Curriculum*).

Middle School Turn Off

Gras-Velazquez et al. (2009) report that in Europe "Most girls drop out of ICT studies after secondary education. This can be attributed partly to lack of support from role models, persistent stereotyped views that the sector is better suited to men, a lack of understanding about what ICT jobs entail, and in some cases, how easy or difficult they find the subject."

In 2010 my company ThoughtWare was a partner in an ARC grant exploring the upper middle school "turn off" among girls in IT. Previous research had identified the school years as an especially promising intervention point for tackling the gross under-representation of women in the ICT industry (Anderson, Lankshear & Courtney, 2008a). The resulting report presented evidence-based strategic responses to factors associated with girls forming negative perceptions of ICT during their upper middle school years; perceptions so negative that they overwhelmingly reject ICT as an option for advanced study and future careers (Anderson et al., 2008a).

There already exist a variety of activities targeting middle school. For example Koch (2009) explains the *Build IT* program, where the focus is to assist girls in middle school not only by hands on experience with technology but also to conceptualize and understand, with the ultimate aim of encouraging girls to take up technology careers.

However despite the programs and the explanations, the data might tell a different story. Modi, Schoenberg & Salmond (2012) found that "Girls are overwhelmingly interested in STEM. Our findings show that a total of 74% of teen girls are interested in STEM." Not surprisingly, "Nearly all girls (98%) wish to be in a career that they love," but perhaps more surprisingly (for stereotypes at least), "more STEM girls have philanthropic motivations such as helping people (94% vs. 83% non-STEM) and making a difference in the world (92% vs. 82%), compared to non-STEM girls."

The critical result from Modi et al. (2012) is this: "Interest in STEM fields doesn't necessarily translate into choosing one of these fields for a career. Although interest in STEM is high, few girls consider it their number one career choice, given competing opportunities and interests. A high 81% of STEM girls express interest in pursuing a career in a STEM field—specifically, in engineering, physical/life science, math, computer science/information technology, or software development. However, only 13% say that it is their first choice. Two-thirds of STEM girls are interested in medicine/healthcare (careers such as a doctor, veterinarian, nurse, pharmacist, dentist) as a career choice and STEM girls choose this field as their number one choice over any other career (30%)... STEM girls are interested in a wide variety of STEM and non-STEM subjects. The top four ranked careers of interest are medicine/healthcare (65%), arts/design (64%), social science (60%), and entertainment (59%). STEM careers are not as highly ranked, when compared to other career categories. Additionally, one-third of girls (30% STEM, 34% non-STEM) are interested in being stay-at-home moms."

Whilst Modi et al. (2012) attribute at least some of this disparity in school interest vs. career choice to barriers, as with my snap poll the girls' opinion of those barriers applies more to other people ("I think some girls don't want to do [STEM] because they don't think it's something girls should do. It's a boy subject; they should stay far away from it.") than to themselves ("All girls think that obstacles make them stronger … and feel motivated to prove people wrong who questions their capabilities … 'You can do whatever you want if you work hard and persist—but you have to have the skills. You have to prove them wrong. Don't give up. If they keep saying yes to everything, it's not good. It's good to have a certain amount of resistance; good for someone to tell you 'no,' because that will happen in your life.'")

Same Sex Schools

Ashcraft et al. (2012) report "Research on single-sex education, in general, has often found many benefits for girls, including increased confidence and interest in traditionally male-dominated subjects (Barker & Aspray, 2006). Adya & Kaiser (2005) found that same sex classes serve to reduce career bias against IT, a general hypothesis for that was the expectation that students of same sex schools would be less likely to embrace gender-specific career choices."

Reviewing the literature, Herrick (2009) also reports benefits for both girls and boys, and notes that boys and girls have different learning styles and boys are more assertive in the classroom.

That difference is also noted by Buser, Niederle & Oosterbeek (2012): "While boys and girls have very similar levels of academic ability, boys are substantially more likely than girls to choose more prestigious profiles. We find that competitiveness is as important a predictor of profile choice as gender. More importantly, up to 23 percent of the gender difference in profile choice can be attributed to gender differences in competitiveness."

Others point to more mixed results from segregation. An Austin Independent School District (2011) White Paper notes "Previous studies – which have analyzed the academic achievement at single-gender private schools in the United States and both public and private schools in other countries – are hotly debated by both proponents and critics. The result of such debate has been varying policy recommendations based on the same evidence." Furthermore, "Of existing studies of single-gender education, some have shown improved outcomes for students … others found no advantages … and still others reported mixed results."

Others conclude that the disadvantages to single-sex education are real whilst the advantages have not been scientifically demonstrated. "Students who attend sex-segregated schools are not necessarily better educated than students who attend coeducational schools, but they are more likely to accept gender stereotypes … Liben [Lynn S. Liben, Distinguished Professor of Psychology, Human Development and Family Studies, and Education, Penn State] and her colleagues report that there is little concrete evidence to support claims that single-sex schools are a better learning environment. 'Our examination of the existing studies leads us to conclude that there is not scientific evidence for positive effects of single-sex schooling. That's not to say that academic outcomes are definitively worse, but neither are they definitively better. Advantages have not been demonstrated'" (Indivero & Messer, 2011).

In addition, as with the "middle school turn off" the important thing is whether any benefits translate to later in life. Mael, Alonso, Gibson, Rogers & Smith (2005) report "As opposed to concurrent indicators of academic achievement, any positive effects of SS schooling on longer-term indicators of academic achievement are not readily apparent.

No differences were found for postsecondary test scores, college graduation rates, or graduate school attendance rates. However, all the findings in this domain came from a pair of studies, indicating the lack of high- quality research on these important criteria. Although some studies favor single-sex education in the case of postsecondary test scores, there is a dearth of recent studies using controls. There has been a similar lack of research on other potential criteria in this domain, such as college grade point average, meritorious scholarships or funding attained, postgraduate licensure test scores, and any career achievement that could ostensibly be tied to quality of schooling."

Interestingly the snapshot poll conducted as part of this publication where responders were asked to select as many potential intervention activities as they felt were influencers, same sex classes was the lowest rated intervention for influence for both current women (11%) and the future (18%) (see Chapter 4: *The Old Approach*).

SUPPORT MECHANISMS

Key Support Mechanism factors that can influence an individual's perception of the IT industry are industry associations, groups and networks; intervention programs; and rewards and recognitions.

Industry Associations

The Queensland Government (2013) lists numerous ICT industry groups for various purposes, whose perceived benefits include "events, seminars and networking opportunities where you may be able to find suppliers, make contacts, and generate new business. Many industry organizations run training and education programs, and provide information about your industry."

Specifically for women in IT, there is a proliferation of industry associations, groups and networks (industry and company based) that already exist and ones that continue to spring up. All seek to address the issues of attraction, promotion and retention of women in technology, or related more specific areas such as improving the number of women in gaming. The advent of social media and the ease of creating an online group that is not geographically bound are resulting in a vast and ever increasing number of groups.

Traditionally associations and groups have played a significant role in designing and implementing intervention programs and networking events. Some newer initiatives illustrate how they can organically grow to extend their scope and reach according to perceived needs.

For example the initial scope of Ada Lovelace Day, first held in 2008, was "about sharing stories of women — whether engineers, scientists, technologists or mathematicians — who have inspired you to become who you are today. The aim is to create new role models for girls and women in these male-dominated fields by raising the profile of other women in STEM" (Finding Ada, 2013). By 2012 the founder described the future direction as: "There is so much that we would like to do to expand our reach, provide support for women who need it, and raise awareness of women's contributions to the STEM disciplines. Here are a few of goals:

- Create and collate teaching plans for all educational levels;
- Create an expert speakers directory for women in STEM;
- Provide media training for women interested in improving their communications skills;
- Hold events to introduce women in STEM to journalists;
- Outreach to relevant professional and student bodies;
- Curate stories of iconic women in STEM;
- Create a directory of organizations for women in STEM" (Charman-Anderson, 2012).

There is no lack of organizations or enthusiasm. However Berry & Kalessi's (2011) survey revealed that a surprising 76% of survey respondents chose not to be involved in women's networks. "This result raises questions about the effectiveness of these networks and women's attitudes towards receiving support. According to the survey, many women believe that the support provided by companies shouldn't be gender specific and do not wish to be treated differently from their male colleagues.

'I receive the same support as my male colleagues - and I would not expect to be treated differently because I am a woman.' 'I expect and hope that the support is for my performance not my gender.' 'I don't expect special support as a woman, I expect support to help me do the job I am employed to do'. (Berry & Kalessi, 2011).

Intervention Programs

The declining trend of women in technology studies and careers has prompted voluminous intervention programs designed to reverse it. These efforts and their motives and results are summed up well by Miliszewska & Moore (2011): "Initial approaches to reverse this trend centered upon notions of equality and affirmative action since the lack of significant numbers of females in the discipline was seen as inequitable. To alleviate the problem, intervention programs aimed at women have promoted information on technology-related careers, provided experience of computing work, and highlighted female role models. Other initiatives focused on helping women develop skills, attitudes, or background knowledge that they were thought to lack. Whilst the intervention strategies that university researchers produce are underpinned by one or more theoretical perspectives. They might, for example, seek to target girls at a particular age, work on dispelling myths and negative stereotypes built up around ICT, or seek to appeal to girls' interests and aspirations. Frequently, it can be seen, they seek to cover as many theoretical perspectives as possible. These affirmative action measures, while commendable in fostering gender equality, were not sufficient in that they often served to reinforce the conceptions of ICT as a masculine domain and, consequently, failed to attract women to ICT."

Miliszewska & Moore (2011) conclude we need "an alternative approach – a re-conceptualization of ICT into an environment that women would naturally embrace," and suggest that for strategies to improve female participation there are "three fundamental areas for attention: infrastructure, teacher training/attitudes, and the role of community."

I agree it is time to re-conceptualize but suggest we must go further, beyond "central planning" of structural interventions to recognizing the core of individual choice and how it might be encouraged in the current era. We cannot forget the lessons of historical initiatives, but we need to take into account the rapidly changing technology landscape and its organically evolving ecosystems.

The following two examples indicate the health of current "naturally occurring," "organically evolved" intervention activity.

A contemporary style intervention in November 2012 was the female-only XX Game Jam. This was a hack event where developers, programmers and artists who had never met before got together over 24 hours to develop games. It was primarily organized by the Women in Games group, collaboratively networked with the Ada Lovelace Day initiative.

Kleinman (2012) reports that within eight days, 40 places had been filled with another 40 on the waiting list. The female flavor was noted by participants, one stating that "Their games definitely have stories from their own lives – one group made a game about dating the cute guy from school, getting your chores done so fast so you can get to your date. Guys wouldn't make a game like that," while another said "We're all helping each other out, solving each other's problems" (Kleinman, 2012).

Another participant posted on her blog, "I took a great many things from this event, and chief amongst those was a greater respect and affection for my fellow women in the games industry. Apart from working directly with two fabulously talented people in my own team, it's been great to connect with the other participants since then. Taking men out of the equation may be a controversial move in some people's eyes, and I'm certainly a champion for equality rather than feminine superiority, but there's no denying that women *are* a minority at the moment, and the event gave *us as individuals* a chance to work with people we can feel naturally more comfortable with. By all means, sign me up for a gothic game jam, or one for retro sci-fi fans, but as a woman I'm still likely to find myself in a room with an overwhelming majority of men at either of those game jams. I'm confident that the XX Game Jam – and the media around it – will further the campaign to boost this single sector of our slowly-diversifying workforce. Games design, those of us who work at it, and even the games themselves *will* benefit from that change" (Thomson, 2012).

Another example is WitsOn (Women in Technology Sharing Online), a strong intervention support mechanism provided by a tertiary educational institution. WitsOn connects undergraduate students pursuing STEM degrees with female mentors from industry and academia who can speak from personal experience about issues of particular concern to young women. "By creating an online community of students and mentors, the sponsors of WitsOn hope that students—particularly though not exclusively young women—will better be able to envision themselves in STEM careers, thereby creating a larger pool of talented people who are ready to handle the challenges that humanity faces in the coming decades" (Garcia-Garcia, 2013).

An important point on industry association intervention programs made by Miliszewska & Moore (2011) is "Whilst not as widely cited as might be expected, the freedom from bureaucratic constraints that industry-based programs appear to enjoy has nevertheless been seen by some researchers as important to the success of smaller scale intervention strategies. Such freedom promotes flexibility, adaptation, innovation, collaboration and rapid response." This applies even more to the kinds of activities that are evolving and will evolve in #SocialEra.

In fact I see these rapid-response, organically evolved activities as part of empowering the individual using #SocialIT, rather than as intervention programs as traditionally understood. The latter attempt to generate interest in IT among a largely indifferent population, and as noted in Chapter Four: *The Old Approach*, they have failed. For example, Lyons et al. (2012) report that outreach programs for tertiary students appear to be successful but only involve 1% of the female undergraduates. 80% said the programs influenced their decision but 80% of 1% doesn't show up much overall, even ignoring the question of whether the "influence" translated into action. As noted in Chapter Four, positive feelings after intervention events are as common as they are non-predictive about actual choices.

Rewards and Recognitions (Awards)

At the launch of the ICT Portal, Neelie Kroes (Vice President of the European Commission) asked in her speech on ICT and Women, "How about awards, to recognize and celebrate women and girls working in this area?" (Kroes, 2013). Rewards and recognition programs are often proposed as motivational for women working in the industry and therefore of value to assist with retention, and also to assist with attraction by creating and publicizing role models.

However any web search will reveal that a wide variety of award programs already exist across multiple continents. There are industry association awards, research awards, company awards and government awards; they recognize girls studying technology, entrepreneurs and women working in technology in governments and research institutions.

For example, in Europe there is the DataNews ICT Woman of the Year Award, marking the culmination of an exemplary career in the ICT sector, and Young ICT Lady of the Year Award, recognizing women 30 years or younger with an impressive track record in IT (acties.datanews.knack.be/acties/datanews/she-goes-ict/index.jsp).

In the UK we have the *Everywomen in Technology Awards*, launched in 2011 and designed to showcase talented women as the role models that they are. Seven award categories currently exist (Rising star, Team leader – SME, Team leader – Corporate, Innovator, Entrepreneur, Inspiration and Woman of the Year). The aim is explicitly stated to "ultimately encourage more women into this innovative and fast moving career choice, one which rewards their talents" (www.everywoman.com/techawards). Additionally, on 14th November 2013 the *WISE Awards* presented by HRH The Princess Royal were announced (www.wisecampaign.org.uk/about-us/wise-awards/2013-wise-awards).

In Australia, the *Women in Technology Awards* is now in its 16th year and currently offering nine categories (Employer of Choice, Professional, Outstanding Achievement-Infotech and Biotech, Research-Infotech and Biotech, Rising Star, PhD Career Start and Entrepreneurial (www.wit.org.au/awards/how-to-participate).

USA examples are the *Anita Borg Women of Vision Awards* (anitaborg.org/initiatives/awards/) and the *Women in Technology International Hall of Fame*, commenced in 1996 (www.witi.com/center/witimuseum/halloffame).

In addition to award programs there are a number of scholarships and top technology "women to watch" lists, e.g. *The 10 Most Powerful Women in African Tech* (Jackson, 2012), the Huffington Post's *18 Female Founders in Tech to Watch* (Hess, 2011), *Women in Tech, 5 Start Up Founders to Watch* (Isaacson, 2013), *15 Women to Watch in Tech* (DesMarais, 2012, 2013), *The Women in Technology Generating the Most Buzz in 2013* (Zellinger, 2013) and *Women to Watch: Women Take The Lead in Technology* (Bloomberg, 2013). Whilst some of those are one-time listings, *Mass High Tech Names 2013 Women to Watch* has been running for 10 years (Resende, 2013).

Clearly there is no lack of award and recognition programs. But whilst awards are exciting and encouraging for entrants and winners, women interested in STEM are highly self-motivated (Modi et al., 2012) so whether these programs have any real influence on attraction and retention is another question. As Carola Aliaga (Project Manager, Ericsson, Japan) said, "I have not received an award, nor have I ever been part of any program... and my only mentors over the years have been Vince and my Dad, who are my expert advisors when I have to make hairy career decisions" (reported by Tandon et al., 2012).

Backlash

The dark side of #SocialEra is that if it is easy to create and coordinate collaborative activities, it is also easy to attack them. For example, Slane (2013) describes one such case as "like something out of a twisted, hi-tech superhero movie. A group of three women called the LadyCoders… join together to help women get jobs in a male-dominated tech world. While doing so, their website is hacked and they get blasted on the blogosphere… They are doing something that most people just talk about: helping women get jobs in the tech field." Perhaps most disturbing about this is where the backlash was from:

"The LadyCoders are facing backlash from feminists, who want them to change the system instead of teaching women how to adapt to the male dominated environment. In fact, many have been downright hostile, taking issue with the LadyCoders marketing materials. Shortly after that, the LadyCoders website was hacked and taken down temporarily."

Another example is from Lewis (2013): "Women who talk about loving games should expect the question: but are you a real gamer? If you write an article on the subject under a female byline… you stand a fair chance of being besieged by comments asking how you could possibly be unaware of some [very obscure game]. However deep your knowledge or enthusiasm, there's always some bloke desperate to restore what he sees as the natural order by knowing more than you. This can sometimes take a nasty turn. Last year the writer and keen gamer Anita Sarkeesian was trying to fund a video series called *Tropes vs. Women*. She planned to deconstruct some of the persistent sexist plotlines and character types in games: the damsel in distress, the huge-breasted ninja warrior. As I wrote then, it was as if her suggestion set off an 'angry misogynist Bat Signal'. She was hit with hundreds of obscene comments on her YouTube videos… As the crowd of haters expanded, Sarkeesian had her address posted on the Internet. Hackers targeted her Wikipedia page and social media accounts, and someone made a game where you could click on her face and bruises would appear. Why was the reaction against her so furious? 'The hatred directed at Anita is entirely because men (in particular) feel that gaming is their exclusive territory,' the games writer Cara Ellison told me."

I have also experienced this style of backlash, when my *Screen Goddess IT Calendar* initiative attracted not only outrage but a denial-of-service attack on the website (Hearn, 2006).

Such extreme and hostile responses to initiatives unfortunately might need to be factored into future approaches, though we can expect or hope that they are merely a symptom of a transitional time.

GOVERNMENT STRATEGY AND POLICIES

Governments have so much power in so many areas that their strategies and policies provide an overriding context. They provide information, set educational policies and procedures, make employment laws, engage in direct specific activities such as interventions, subsidies and payouts, and are themselves a very large employer using a host of IT systems.

Regarding specific policy interventions, Palmen (2011) points out that girls' engagement with IT is "usually conceived of in relation to their future participation in the labor market. This predominant approach is reflected in the majority of international literature on this subject matter. For example: Barker and Asprey's (2006) *The State of Research on Girls and IT* focuses on the US context; Gras-Valazquez et al.'s (2009) *Why are girls not attracted to ICT studies and careers?* is a comparative study looking at these issues in five European countries (Italy, Poland, UK, Netherlands and France); and, Miliszewska and Moore's [2010] *Encouraging Girls to Consider a Career in ICT: A Review of Strategies*, looks at these issues in the Australian context. This approach can be seen as embodied in specific targeted policy interventions that try to engage with girls in order to stimulate their interest in ICT and ensure that ICT is not ruled out as a viable occupational choice."

For example in the UK, a recognized skills shortage in ICT professions led to an employment policy agenda including a focus on women as able to plug the "skills gap." This led to various initiatives to encourage school-aged girls to engage with ICT so that they do not automatically rule out ICT linked professions. It included a rollout of "computer clubs for girls" (CC4G, an out of school computer club for girls 10 – 14), which aimed to change girls' perception of an IT career (www.e-skills.com).

In Australia, Government policies over the past 15 years have driven grant funding rounds specifically targeting girls and women in IT initiatives (e.g. national policies: *SET Up for Success*, *partICTipation*; Queensland Government policies: *iStar*, *Girls and ICT Framework for Action*, *Girls - Doing IT Smart in Queensland: Driving the Future for ICT 2005*). Additionally in Australia, the Federal Government's *Digital Education Revolution* (DER) (DEEWR, 2013) promises to address issues of infrastructure and teacher training in the use of ICT, through one computer per secondary school student in years nine to twelve and professional development for teachers. It also provides for high-speed broadband connection to Australian schools and should see increased incorporation of ICT into pedagogical practices (Miliszewska & Moore 2011). Both the US Government and The European Commission have also introduced a range of policies and practices to focus on STEM initiatives (education and industry).

Miliszewska & Moore (2011) flag an important point by reporting "as demonstrated in our review, policy driven initiatives can be problematic, in that they can be chaotically received and acted upon, and in that they are vulnerable to shifts in emphasis resulting from changes in government direction or institutional requirements… policy-driven initiatives are nevertheless capable of leaving gaps that can only be filled by more policy or organically produced intervention programs," and as pointed out by Faulkner & Stewart (2003) a problem is that "filling the gap frequently becomes a matter of chance." Then there is the issue of competing Government policies identified by Palmen (2011), who argues "there is a clear need for more synergies to be created between the different policy agendas and that ICT and gender equality strategies need to be mainstreamed throughout the education and employment spheres."

There are indeed problems with relying on government policies. Even assuming they choose the "right one," we have noted the disparity between academic research, intervention program design, and the rapidly changing dynamic IT industry: implementation and change of government policy are even slower. In addition we face the problems of policies that are less reasoned governance than disparate, quick fix, competing election promises; and the fact that Governments and Ministers come and go, and entire infrastructures are often discarded in the machinery of Government changes.

But the chief problem I see is that governments set their policies on the basis of advice, and as we have seen the traditional answers have never worked. In a rapidly changing world perhaps what we need is less solutions imposed from above and more solutions grown from below.

Up until now, the contexts and factors explored have largely followed traditional lines. In the next chapter we move on to a significant departure from previous analyses, when we explore the individual context and its factors and the interplay of those factors with the cultural, social and structural contexts.

REFERENCES

Adya, M., & Kaiser, K. M. (2005). Early determinants of women in the IT workforce: A model of girls' career choices. *Information Technology & People*, *18*(3), 230–259. doi:10.1108/09593840510615860

Adya, M., & Kaiser, K. M. (2006). Factors influencing girls' choice of information technology careers. In E. M. Trauth (Ed.), *Encyclopedia of gender and information technology* (Vol. 1, pp. 282–288). Hershey, PA: Idea Group Reference. doi:10.4018/978-1-59140-815-4.ch044

Albom, M. (2013, March 17). What's really behind Google's crazy offices? *Detroit Free Press*. Retrieved August 7, 2013 from http://www.freep.com/article/20130317/COL01/303170166/Mitch-Albom-What-s-really-behind-Google-s-crazy-offices-

Anderson, N., Lankshear, C., & Courtney, L. (2008a). *Girls and information communication technology (ICT) career pathways: Tackling the upper middle school turn off.* Retrieved July 21, 2013, from http://www.neilrobertanderson.com/girlsict/current%20research.html

Anderson, N., Lankshear, C., Timms, C., & Courtney, L. (2008b). 'Because it's boring, irrelevant and I don't like computers': Why high school girls avoid professionally-oriented ICT subjects. *Computers & Education*, *50*(4), 1304–1318. doi:10.1016/j.compedu.2006.12.003

Ashcraft, C., Eger, E., & Friend, M. (2012). *Girls in IT: The facts*. Boulder, CO: National Centre for Women & Information Technology (NCWIT). Retrieved August 6, 2013, from http://www.academia.edu/2283166/Girls_in_IT_The_Facts

Austin Independent School District. (2011). *Single-gender education: A review of current issues and practices*. Retrieved August 13, 2013, from http://www.austinisd.org/sites/default/files/announcements/D-White%20Paper%20Final%209.12.11.pdf

Baker, T. (2012). *Enhancing STEM education with GIS ebook released*. Retrieved July 2, 2013, from http://blogs.esri.com/esri/gisedcom/2012/09/06/advancing-stem-education-with-gis-ebook-released/

Barker, L. J., & Aspray, W. (2006). The state of research on girls and IT. In J. M. Cohoon, & W. Aspray (Eds.), *Women and information technology: Research on underrepresentation* (pp. 3–54). Cambridge, MA: MIT Press. doi:10.7551/mitpress/9780262033459.003.0001

Bartlett, B. (2012, April 17). Do small businesses create jobs? *The New York Times*. Retrieved August 7, 2013, from http://economix.blogs.nytimes.com/2012/04/17/do-small-businesses-create-jobs/

Bateman, K. (2012). *Men and women disagree on reasons why IT is less attractive to women.* Retrieved July 20, 2013, from http://www.computerweekly.com/news/2240159441/Men-and-women-disagree-on-reasons-why-IT-is-less-attractive-to-women

Bateman, K. (2013). *Is outdated terminology deterring females from roles in IT?* Retrieved July 20, 2013, from http://www.computerweekly.com/feature/Is-outdated-terminology-deterring-females-from-roles-in-IT

Beltran, D. O., Das, K. K., & Fairlie, R. W. (2008). *Home computers and educational outcomes: Evidence from the NLSY97 and CPS.* (Board of Governors of the Federal Reserve System: International Finance Discussion Papers, No. 958). Retrieved August 10, 2013, from http://www.federalreserve.gov/pubs/ifdp/2008/958/ifdp958.pdf

Bernhardt, S. (2005). *The failure of intervention programs.* Paper presented at the Girls and ICTs State Strategic Meeting. Brisbane, Australia.

Berry, M., & Kalessi, T. (2011). *Women's careers in the technology industry*. London, UK: Intellect and Women in Technology (Report). Retrieved August 1, 2013, from http://sciencewithart.ijs.si/pdf/Women's_Careers_in_the_Technology_Industry_2011_Report.pdf

Blair, R., Gill, K., & Benson, M. (2013). *Focus on the pipeline*. Alexander Mann Solutions and Everywomen. Retrieved August 1, 2013, from http://info.everywoman.com/women-in-management-focus-on-the-pipeline/

Bloomberg. (2013). *TV women to watch: Women take the lead in technology.* Retrieved August 2, 2013, from http://www.bloomberg.com/video/women-to-watch-women-take-the-lead-in-technology-4om~ml8DTCGBNcun_myleg.html

Buser, T., Niederle, M., & Oosterbeek, H. (2012). *Gender, competitiveness and career choices*. Retrieved August 13, 2013, from http://www.stanford.edu/~niederle/Gender.BNO.pdf

Castano, C., & Webster, J. (2011). Understanding women's presence in ICT: The life course perspective. *International Journal of Gender. Science and Technology*, *3*(2), 358–363.

Cave, K. (2013). Women in IT: Does the shortage matter? *IDG Connect Infographic.* Retrieved May 22, 2013, from http://www.idgconnect.com/abstract/1251/infographic-women-it-does-shortage-matter

Charman-Anderson, S. (2012). *Ada Lovelace Day fundraiser.* Retrieved August 2, 2013, from http://www.indiegogo.com/projects/ada-lovelace-day-fundraiser

Cheeseman Day, J., Janus, A., & Davis, J. (2005). *Computer and Internet use in the United States: 2003.* U.S. Census Bureau. Retrieved August 10, 2013, from http://www.census.gov/prod/2005pubs/p23-208.pdf

Clayton, K. (2007). *The influence of metropolitan Brisbane middle-school ICT experiences on girls' ICT study and career choices.* (Unpublished doctoral dissertation). Griffith University, Queensland, Australia.

Clayton, K., Beekhuyzen, J., & Nielsen, S. (2012). Now I know what ICT can do for me? *Information Systems Journal*, *22*(5), 1–16. doi:10.1111/j.1365-2575.2012.00414.x

Clayton, K. L., von Hellens, L. A., & Nielsen, S. H. (2009). Gender stereotypes prevail in ICT: A research review. In *Proceedings of the Special Interest Group on Management Information System's 47th Annual Conference on Computer Personnel Research* (SIGMIS CPR) (pp. 153-158). New York: ACM.

Cleary, P. F., Pierce, G., & Trauth, E. M. (2006). Closing the digital divide: Understanding racial, ethnic, social class, gender and geographic disparities in internet use in school age children in the United States. *Universal Access in the Information Society*, *4*, 354–373. doi:10.1007/s10209-005-0001-0

Cohoon, J. M. (2003). Just get over it or just get on with it: Retaining women in undergraduate computing. In W. Aspray, & J. M. Cohoon (Eds.), *Women and information technology: Research on the reasons for under-representation*. Cambridge, MA: MIT Press.

CONSAD Research Corp. (2009). *An analysis of the reasons for the disparity in wages between men and women* (Report for US Department of Labor). Pittsburgh, PA: CONSAD Research Corp. Retrieved August 4, 2013, from http://www.consad.com/content/reports/Gender%20Wage%20Gap%20Final%20Report.pdf

Department of Education. Employment and Workplace Relations (DEEWR). (2013). *Digital education and technology in schools*. Retrieved August 2, 2013, from http://deewr.gov.au/digital-education-and-technology-schools

DesMarais, C. (2012). *15 women to watch in tech*. Retrieved August 2, 2013, from http://www.inc.com/ss/christina-desmarais/15-women-watch-tech-startups.html#11

DesMarais, C. (2013). *10 women to watch in tech*. Retrieved August 2, 2013, from http://www.inc.com/ss/christina-desmarais/11-women-watch-tech

Dougherty, C. (2010, September 1). Young women's pay exceeds male peers. *The Wall Street Journal*. Retrieved August 4, 2013, from http://online.wsj.com/article/SB10001424052748704421104575463790770831192.html

Downes, S. (2004). *Into the new millennium: Why do students decide to study IT?* Paper presented at the Informing Science and Technology Education Joint Conference. Rockhampton, Australia.

Faulkner, W., & Stewart, J. (2003). *National ICT training for teachers: A case of 'gender blindness'?* (Deliverable DO3/Volume 1 of IST-2000-26329 SIGIS Project). Retrieved from http://www.rcss.ed.ac.uk/sigis/public/documents/SIGIS_D03_2.09_UEDIN3.pdf

Feldman, D. C. (2000). The Dilbert syndrome: How employee cynicism about ineffective management is changing the nature of careers in organizations. *The American Behavioral Scientist*, *43*(8), 1286–1300. doi:10.1177/00027640021955865

File, T. (2013). *Computer and internet use in the United States*. U.S. Census Bureau. Retrieved August 10, 2013, from http://www.census.gov/prod/2013pubs/p20-569.pdf

Finding Ada. (2013). *Ada Lovelace Day in a nutshell*. Retrieved September 22, 2013, from http://findingada.com

Fisher, A. (2006, August 15). Are you stuck in middle management hell? *CNN Money*. Retrieved August 4, 2013, from http://money.cnn.com/magazines/fortune/fortune_archive/2006/08/21/8383654/

Fisher, A. (2012, September 28). What it really takes to get that next promotion. *CNN Money*. Retrieved August 4, 2013, from http://management.fortune.cnn.com/2012/09/28/promotions-careers/

Flynn, J., Heath, K., & Holt, M. D. (2013). *Six paradoxes women leaders face in 2013*. Retrieved May 2013, from http://blogs.hbr.org/cs/2013/01/six_paradoxes_women_leaders_fa.html

Garcia-Garcia, M. (2013). *Online mentoring program for STEM fields*. Retrieved August 2, 2013, from http://www.gradschool.cornell.edu/announcement/online-mentoring-program-stem-fields

Goode, J. (2008). Increasing diversity in K-12 computer science education: Lessons from the field. *Proceedings of the 38th SIGCSE Technical Symposium on Computer Science Education*, *40*(1), 362-371.

Goode, J., Estrella, R., & Margolis, J. (2006). Lost in translation: Gender in high school computer *science*. In J. Cohoon, & W. Aspray (Eds.), *Women and information technology: Research on underrepresentation* (pp. 89–114). Cambridge, MA: MIT Press. doi:10.7551/mitpress/9780262033459.003.0003

Gras-Velazquez, A., Joyce, A., & Debry, M. (2009). *Women and ICT: Why are girls still not attracted to ICT studies and careers?* (White Paper). Brussels: European Schoolnet (EUN Partnership AISBL).

Haywood, B., Alty, C., Pearson, S., & Martin, C. (2003). *Young people's use of ICT 2002: ICT in schools research and evaluation series no. 12*. Retrieved August 2, 2013, from BECTA/DfES. http://dera.ioe.ac.uk/1646/1/becta_2002_youngpeoplesuse_report_queensprinter.pdf

Hearn, L. (2006). *Calendar girl website survives attack*. Retrieved June 2, 2013, from http://www.theage.com.au/news/biztech/calendar-girls-under-attack/2006/07/17/1152988460039.html

Heemskerk, I., Brink, A., Volman, M., & ten Dam, G. (2005). Inclusiveness and ICT in education: A focus on gender, ethnicity and social class. *Journal of Computer Assisted Learning*, *21*, 1–16. doi:10.1111/j.1365-2729.2005.00106.x

Herrick, L. K. (2009). *Same-sex schooling versus co-educational schooling and their effects on achievement, assessment and gender bias*. Project for Master in Teaching Degree, Evergreen State College. Retrieved August 11, 2013, from http://archives.evergreen.edu/masterstheses/Accession89-10MIT/Herrick_LMITthesis2009.pdf

Hess, M. (2011). *18 female founders in tech to watch*. Retrieved August 2, 2013, from http://www.huffingtonpost.com/2011/08/08/female-tech-founders_n_916751.html#s318621&title=Jess_Lee_Polyvore

Indivero, V. M., & Messer, A. E. (2011, September 22). Sex segregation in schools detrimental to equality. *Penn State News*. Retrieved August 11, 2013, from http://news.psu.edu/story/155177/2011/09/22/sex-segregation-schools-detrimental-equality

Isaacson, B. (2013). *Women in tech: 5 startup founders to watch*. Retrieved August 2, 2013, from http://www.huffingtonpost.com/2013/01/31/women-startup-founders_n_2512893.html

Jackson, T. (2012). *The 10 most powerful women in African tech*. Retrieved October 4, 2013, from http://www.ventures-africa.com/2012/08/the-10-most-powerful-women-in-african-tech/

Kenny, C. (2011, September 28). Rethinking the boosterism about small business. *Bloomberg BusinessWeek Magazine*. Retrieved August 7, 2013, from http://www.businessweek.com/magazine/rethinking-the-boosterism-about-small-business-09282011.html

Kirkup, G. (2011). Preparing women for dead-end jobs? Vocational education and training (VET) for information and communication technology (ICT) jobs. *International Journal of Gender Science and Technology*, *3*(2), 460–482.

Kleinman, Z. (2012). *Ladies first: Inside the first women-only game jam*. Retrieved August 2, 2013, from http://www.bbc.co.uk/news/technology-20186937

Koch, M. (2009). *Girls Incorporated build IT*. [Video]. Retrieved July 31, 2013 from http://www.youtube.com/watch?v=iag0Eyc0gZE

Kroes, N. (2013). *ICT and women speech*. European Commission. Retrieved July 21, 2013, from http://europa.eu/rapid/press-release_SPEECH-13-366_en.htm

Lang, C., & McKay, J. (2006). Australian IT enrollment trends and model of contributing factors. In E. M. Trauth (Ed.), *Encyclopedia of gender and information technology* (Vol. 1, pp. 50–56). Hershey, PA: Idea Group Reference. doi:10.4018/978-1-59140-815-4.ch009

Lewis, H. (2013). *Are computer games being taken over by women?* Retrieved June 4, 2013, from http://www.telegraph.co.uk/women/10086627/Are-computer-games-being-taken-over-by-women.html

Liston, C., Peterson, K., & Ragan, V. (2009). *Promising practices in informal information technology (IT) education for girls*. Paper prepared for AERA Meeting. San Diego, CA.

Lyons, T., Quinn, F., Rizk, N., Anderson, N., Hubber, P., Kenny, J., et al. (2012). *Starting out in STEM: A study of young men and women in first year science, technology, engineering and mathematics courses*. Armidale, Australia: University of New England. Retrieved August 13, 2013, from http://www.une.edu.au/simerr/pages/projects/132iris_report.pdf

Madden, M., Lenhart, A., Duggan, M., Cortesi, S., & Gasser, U. (2013). *Teens and technology 2013*. Washington, DC: Pew Research Center. Retrieved August 10, 2013, from http://www.pewinternet.org/~/media//Files/Reports/2013/PIP_TeensandTechnology2013.pdf

Mael, F., Alonso, A., Gibson, D., Rogers, K., & Smith, M. (2005). *Single-sex versus coeducational schooling: A systematic review*. Washington, DC: American Institutes for Research. Retrieved August 13, 2013, from http://www.air.org/files/Single_Sex_LitReview_091905.pdf

Margolis, J., Estrella, R., Goode, J., Holme, J., & Nao, K. (2008). *Stuck in the shallow end: Education, race and computing*. Cambridge, MA: MIT Press.

Margolis, J., & Fisher, A. (2003). *Unlocking the clubhouse: Women in computing*. Cambridge, MA: MIT Press.

Margolis, J., Jellison Holme, J., Estrella, R., Goode, J., Nao, K., & Stumme, S. (2003). The computer science pipeline in urban high schools: Access to what? For whom? *IEEE Technology and Society Magazine*, *22*(3), 12–19. doi:10.1109/MTAS.2003.1237467

Merrett, R. (2012) *Pay gap, lack of role models to blame for ICT gender imbalance: EOWA*. Retrieved August 10, 2013, from http://www.cio.com.au/article/441965/pay_gap_lack_role_models_blame_ict_gender_imbalance_eowa/

Miliszewska, I., & Moore, A. (2010). Encouraging girls to consider a career in ICT: A review of strategies. *Journal of Information Technology Education: Innovations in Practice*, *9*, 143–166.

Miliszewska, I., & Moore, A. (2011). Attracting girls to ICT studies & careers – A snapshot of strategies. *Redress*, *20*(3), 10–14.

Modi, K., Schoenberg, J., & Salmond, K. (2012). *Generation STEM: What girls say about science, technology, engineering, and math*. Girl Scouts of the USA. Retrieved August 10, 2013, from http://www.girlscouts.org/research/pdf/generation_stem_full_report.pdf

Nauert, R. (2013). *Men and women may not be so different after all*. PsychCentral. Retrieved August 4, 2013, from http://psychcentral.com/news/2013/02/05/men-and-women-may-not-be-so-different-after-all/51222.html

Newmarch, E., Taylor-Steele, S., & Cumpston, A. (2000). *Women in IT – What are the barriers?* Paper presented at the Network of Women in Further Education Conference Showcase of Strategies for Women in Education on Information Technology Conference. Adelaide, Australia.

Oblinger, D., & Oblinger, J. (Eds.). (2005). *Educating the net generation*. EDUCAUSE. Retrieved July 20, 2013, from http://www.educause.edu/educatingthenetgen

Palmén, R. (2011). Girls, boys and ICT in the UK: An empirical review and competing policy agendas. *International Journal of Gender. Science and Technology*, *3*(2), 407–423.

Parmar, B. (2013). *Women in IT*. [Video]. Retrieved July 28, 2013, from http://www.computerweekly.com/video/Women-in-IT-Belinda-Parmar-Little-Miss-Geek?videoId=eeff68e093fef310VgnVCM1000000d01c80aRCRD

Pennington, S. (2013). *Five reasons why women work in technology*. Retrieved August 2, 2013, from http://www.smh.com.au/it-pro/business-it/five-reasons-why-women-work-in-technology-20130708-2jvvd.html

Queensland Government. (2013). *Networking an ICT business*. Retrieved August 13, 2013, from http://www.business.qld.gov.au/industry/ict/connecting-ict-business/networking-ict-business

Research Career. (2013, August 6). Industry echoes call for more females. *News*. Retrieved August 7, 2013, from http://www.researchcareer.com.au/news/industry-echoes-call-for-female-engineers-researchers

Resende, P. (2013). *Mass high tech names 2013 women to watch*. Retrieved August 2, 2013, from http://www.bizjournals.com/boston/blog/techflash/2013/03/mass-high-tech-names-2013-women-to-watch.html?page=all

Selwyn, N., & Bullon, K. (2000). Primary school children's use of ICT. *British Journal of Educational Technology*, *31*(4), 321–332. doi:10.1111/1467-8535.00165

Shellenbarger, S. (2013, November 26). How one college boosted female STEM graduates–fast. *The Wall Street Journal*. Retrieved November 28, 2013, from http://blogs.wsj.com/atwork/2013/11/26/how-one-college-boosted-female-stem-graduates-fast/

Simard, C., Davies Henderson, A., Gilmartin, S. K., Schiebinger, L., & Whitney, T. (2008). *Climbing the technical ladder: Obstacles and solutions for mid-level women in technology*. Palo Alto, CA: Anita Borg Institute for Women and Technology.

Simard, C., & Gammal, D. L. (2012). *Solutions to recruit technical women*. Palo Alto, CA: Anita Borg Institute for Women and Technology.

Slane, C. (2013). *Who knew helping women get tech jobs could be so controversial?* Retrieved July 4, 2013, from http://www.huffingtonpost.com/cassie-slane/who-knew-helping-women_b_2599848.html

Tandon, N., Pritchard, S., Savelieva, V., Smith, G., & Vogt, E. (2012). *A bright future in ICTs opportunities for a new generation of women*. Geneva, Switzerland: International Telecommunication Union.

Thomson, G. (2012). *XX game jam*. Retrieved August 2, 2013, from http://www.raygun-gothic.net/blog/misc/xx-game-jam/

Timms, C., Courtney, L., & Anderson, N. (2006). Dimensions of 'boring': Secondary girls' perceptions of advanced ICT subjects. In *Proceedings of the Australian Computers in Education Conference 2006*. Cairns, Australia: ACEC.

Tobak, S. (2011, March 8). The gender pay gap is a complete myth. *CBS Moneywatch*. Retrieved August 4, 2013, from http://www.cbsnews.com/8301-505125_162-28246928/the-gender-pay-gap-is-a-complete-myth/

Turner, S. V., Brent, P. W., & Pecora, N. (2002). *Why women choose information technology careers: Educational, social, and familial influences*. New Orleans, LA: Annual Educational Research Association.

UNESCO. (2012). *Girls in STEM and ICT careers: The path toward gender equality*. New York: UNESCO.

UserExperienceWorks. (2011). *A magazine is an iPad that does not work*. [Video]. Retrieved July 29, 2013, from http://www.youtube.com/watch?v=aXV-yaFmQNk

Volman, M., van Eck, E., Heemskerk, I., & Kuiper, E. (2005). New technologies, new differences: Gender and ethnic differences in pupils' use of ICT in primary and secondary education. *Computers & Education*, *45*(1), 35–55. doi:10.1016/j.compedu.2004.03.001

Zellinger, J. (2013). *The women in technology generating the most buzz in 2013*. Retrieved August 2, 2013, from http://www.huffingtonpost.com/2013/07/10/women-in-technology-generating-most-buzz-in-2013_n_3542566.html

KEY TERMS AND DEFINTIONS

ABI: Anita Borg Institute (a USA based organisation).

ECWT: European Centre for Women and Technology.

ICT: Information and Communication Technology. Synonymous with IT.

i-STAR: ICT, Skills, Training and Role Models (an Australian program).

IT: Information Technology. Synonymous with ICT.

NCWIT: National Centre for Women and Information Technology (a USA based organisation).

#SocialEra: a term (coined by Nilofer Merchant) to describe a shift in focus from traditional methods to a more social movement, which has profound implications for business and how people work and lead.

SET: Science, Engineering and Technology. Conceptually related fields that share issues of under-representation of women. Includes IT and is a subset of STEM.

STEM: Science, Technology, Engineering and Mathematics, conceptually related fields that share issues of under-representation of women. An extension of SET to include maths.

STEMcell Model: A model designed by Sonja Bernhardt that provides a conceptual framework for viewing contexts and layers impacting STEM fields.

TTYA: Technology Takes You Anywhere (an Australian intervention program).

Chapter 7
Individual Context

ABSTRACT

The core principle derived from evaluation of the data is that the number of women in IT (or any career) is not a matter of the balance of societal forces, which we can push one way or another with the right lever. It comes down to the individual and her pursuit of happiness through her own values. This puts the individual at the core of the STEMcell Model. The influencing factors of philosophy, values, rights, assumptions, strength, self belief, interests, differences, ability, curiosity, creativity, and reality are explored in this chapter in that context. The centrality of individual choice does not mean there is nothing we can do about remaining barriers, but it does mean that empowering the individual (especially through the disruptive technologies of #SocialIT) and accepting their choices is the solution. The answer to collectivist prejudices about "women" is not collectivist actions that accept the same underlying assumption, but is instead recognising that the only differences that matter are individual ones. Contrary to beliefs that the low proportion of women in IT should be viewed through a gender or culture lens, the results and analyses in this book indicate that not only is innate interest the main driver of an IT career, but most women with that interest are perfectly capable of discovering it themselves. And that is why no single "solution" has been found, and why a wide variety of interventions have had no significant impact—because there is no generic solution to finding out "what women want"—individually.

Happiness is that state of consciousness which proceeds from the achievement of one's values.

– Ayn Rand (1961)

INTRODUCTION

The unfortunate conclusion from the years of intervention programs aimed at increasing the representation of women in IT courses and careers is that none of them have worked. There have been a few individual cases where it has made a difference, and often a short term burst in favourable thinking about IT among the participants. But none of this has produced a measurable increase.

Clearly the only way to increase the number of people pursuing a particular career is to increase the number of individuals choosing to do so. All the interventions in the world cannot achieve an increase if the individuals simply are more interested in other things. All the interventions in the

DOI: 10.4018/978-1-4666-5860-8.ch007

world and all the progress in the world regarding women's education and access to career choice *have not* achieved an increase. So perhaps we need to look more at the individual than at these external factors.

The impact of the individual has been examined in the literature by many researchers including Castano & Webster (2011), Ham, Junankar & Wells (2009), Trauth (2002) and Trauth, Huang & Quesenberry (2006). However to date it has been done from the perspective of the individual as just another societal factor. It has been under a gendered view where generally the individual is assumed to be entirely malleable, an almost blank slate absorbing cultural, social and structural influences without any free will of her own. The problem with that approach is it ignores the fundamental strength, philosophy, values and will of the individual. This is especially ironic when one thing that characterises girls interested in STEM is strong self-will and confidence (Modi, Schoenberg & Salmond, 2012).

Perhaps this is why no single "solution" has been found, and why a wide variety of solutions have had no significant impact – because there is no generic solution to finding out "what women want" – individually. What they want is what interests them, according to their individual circumstances, personalities and values.

It may appear to be an oversimplification to put the low number of women in IT down to the individual, when the individual makes her decisions in the context of the rest of her life experiences. But numerous results cited in earlier chapters indicate that most women who will be interested in fact already discovered their interest in their formative years. It is only a minority who discover it later in life through tasks assigned at work, and a much smaller minority who are influenced by interventions. That implies that the issue is not a large pool of women who would be interested "if only they knew." Most of them already know.

Therefore my conclusion is that the number of women in IT, or any career, is not a matter of the balance of societal forces, which we can push one way or another with the right lever. It comes down to values, to the individual and their pursuit of happiness through their own values. It's their choice and is highly internalised, having meaning for each individual.

That is why, in the STEMcell Model, the individual is the core and strongest element of the model. That individual core, that unique cell, may expand to an extent that it overrides and cracks the mantle of social and structural influences and the cultural crust. Figure 1 represents that individual core and outlines the factors involved.

The Individual factors and influencers in Figure 1 are those I have identified and highlighted. The literature discusses a variety of factors and some overlap or point to these, such as life events, turning points, predispositions and interests. These elements are especially represented in the "Life Course" conceptual framework initially proposed by Xie & Shauman (2003). Whilst the life course concept was developed for describing women in science it is also applicable to women in technology, and it has been cited and further enhanced in the literature since, e.g. Adya & Kaiser (2005), Ashcraft, Eger & Friend (2012), Castano & Webster (2011), Ham, Junankar & Wells (2009) and Trauth, Quesenberry & Huang (2009). The life course framework is discussed in detail in Chapter Five: *Popular Theories*.

That the individual is core and a unique cell does not mean there is nothing we can do. Though many women in IT have found their own way, not all have, and we can make the way easier to find and travel. But if the core solution is helping individuals discover their own inherent interests, then it lies in letting individuals discover themselves by letting them explore, discover and decide. Understanding individual attributes and interests, and individualising the activity for each specific person, may support this. The solution also lies in tapping into the digital disruption detailed in the next Chapter. Technology innovations and associated digital disruption empower the individual:

Figure 1. Individual factors influencing career choice

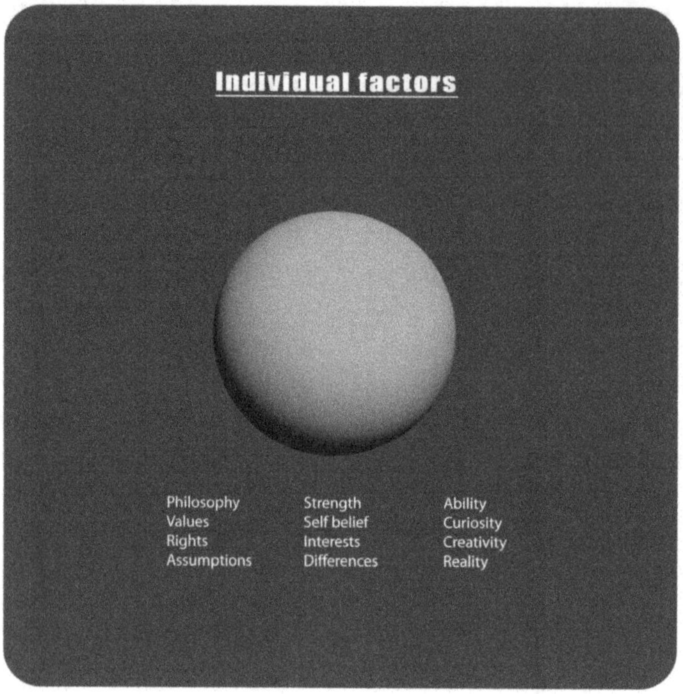

to find information, to find compatible people and to communicate. The significant impact of digital disruption is outlined by Hyek's (2011) discussion of technology innovations "blurring boundaries between industries. The power of the individual will grow and new competitors will emerge, disrupting industries and creating new business models… Google, Facebook, Twitter, smartphones, tablets and e-readers — technologies that originated in the consumer space — are now reshaping the way companies communicate and collaborate with employees, partners and customers. Through the new possibilities for 'social listening,' businesses are able to better understand what their customers and employees need and want. More change can be expected when the generation that has grown up with new technologies and instant information gratification joins the workforce."

If that is true of business it is equally true of the individuals who inhabit the IT world now and in the future. Disruptive technologies are already impacting ways of working and the expectations of all involved, and future generations will be born into a different world and grow up with new, ever more powerful technologies at their fingertips.

WE ARE ALL INDIVIDUALS

"You can't stereotype all women with respect to IT. You can't assume what women as a group want. You have to ask an individual woman," stated Dr. Eileen Trauth, Professor of Information Sciences and Technology (Hale & Fong, 2002). When discussing her *Odd Girl Out* research in an interview, Trauth further stated, "Successful women IT professionals do not all experience the same influences, nor do they all respond in the same ways… Each individual woman is shaped by the cultural assumptions of the countries which formed her, by her parents, family and teachers and by significant others and events… These findings suggest that women can best be encouraged to enter and stay in IT fields by treating them as individuals. Respecting an individual woman or girl's particular interests – what an individual woman or girl is good at – will help her resist the subtle social shaping that tells her interest in IT is normal for males but not for females" (Hale & Fong, 2002).

I agree with this focus on the individual and the need to treat women as individuals and respect their talents and interests. But frankly, I find its underlying view of women rather insulting. Is a woman really such a passive vessel, shaped by country, family, and friends, so lacking in self-direction that she needs help to resist the subtlest social shaping? Are *you?* Certainly girls interested in STEM topics see themselves as far more active determinants of their own fates (Modi et al., 2012). Is telling them they are wrong going to empower them in their life choices?

In contrast, my perspective on the individual is centred on her, not her surroundings: on her own values and rights as a human being. From a philosophical perspective, "A 'right' is a moral principle defining and sanctioning a man's freedom of action in a social context. There is only one fundamental right (all the others are its consequences or corollaries): a man's right to his own life. Life is a process of self-sustaining and self-generated action; the right to life means the right to engage in self-sustaining and self-generated action—which means: the freedom to take all the actions required by the nature of a rational being for the support, the furtherance, the fulfilment and the enjoyment of his own life. (Such is the meaning of the right to life, liberty and the pursuit of happiness.) The concept of a 'right' pertains only to action—specifically, to freedom of action. It means freedom from physical compulsion, coercion or interference by other men. Thus, for every individual, a right is the moral sanction of a positive—of his freedom to act on his own judgment, for his own goals, by his own voluntary, uncoerced choice. As to his neighbours, his rights impose no obligations on them except of a negative kind: to abstain from violating his rights" (Rand, 1963).

Perhaps that can be summed up as: leave women free to achieve, and they will achieve. In the West and increasingly throughout the world, legal barriers to female education and participation are already a thing of the past. And to the extent that prejudices remain, they are by their nature *collectivist* prejudices: "men" are more assertive and better at mathematics, "women" are more empathetic and less technical and ambitious. The best answer to collectivism is not an alternative collectivism about how good "women" are compared to "men." The best way to win that argument is to deny its assumptions outright. To recognise that everyone is an *individual*, and their talents, interests and personalities are theirs, not something they picked up by osmosis from whichever group we are talking about at the moment. It is irrelevant whether or by how much different groups differ in their averages – of anything. Whether the stereotypes are a reflection of reality or of prejudice, they are irrelevant: there will always be individual women better at IT than most men, and that simple, indisputable fact is what we need to recognise, celebrate and promote. Women are no more identical cogs from the same mold than men are. If everyone in society stopped thinking in collectives and started looking at the individual: it would be the end of prejudice in all its forms. We would all be judged for who and what we are.

Individual Strength

While it is rarely expressed in such explicit terms, numerous threads in the literature point to the centrality of individual personality and choices.

In the research conducted by Trauth (2002), respondents described themselves as "powerful people: forthright, strong, driven, ambitious, mathematical, logical and competitive. They considered these traits to be necessary for success in the IT field and also what set them apart from other women." It is interesting that these women saw themselves as different from others in those respects, and we must wonder whether their perception is accurate. Perhaps there are fewer women in IT because most women have personalities and interests that lead them to choose other careers. A possibly telling comparison to IT is raised by Sommers (2008), who relates that in the USA "Nationally, women now comprise fully 77 percent of students in veterinary schools, compared with 8 percent in the 1960s" – a penetration into a formerly male-dominated, scientific field driven not by interventions but by the natural interest of women: once it was allowed to express itself after formal educational barriers came down.

Trauth (2002) did not take that perspective. Her paper developed "a theoretical perspective on gender and information technology (IT) by examining socio-cultural influences on women who are members of the information technology profession in Australia and New Zealand. In-depth interviews with both practitioners and academics give evidence of a range of socio-cultural influences on the professional development and working lives of women IT professionals. The paper rejected the essentialist view of women and their relationship to IT that has been put forth in the information systems literature arguing, instead, the primacy of societal and structural influences. The particular contribution of this paper is a theoretical perspective of individual differences which is presented to characterize the way individual women respond in a range of specific ways to the interplay between individual characteristics and environmental influences" (Trauth, 2002). Or more briefly, Trauth's view is that "individuals experience societal influences in different ways and vary in their response to gender group biases" (Hale & Fong, 2002).

That thread is extended by Trauth, Quesenberry & Huang (2009), in which "The emergent theory of individual differences is used to focus the data analysis on the ways in which these respondents – as individual women – are responding to socio-cultural influences." They proposed a number of constructs that enable theorising on within-gender variation. These were made up of the major constructs of individual identity (personal demographics and career items), individual influences (personal characteristics and personal influences) and environmental influences (cultural, economic, policy and infrastructure). Their results lend empirical support to the individual differences theory of gender and IT as an alternative to essentialist or social construction theories.

As already noted, I think this move toward a focus on individual differences is a change in the right direction, but does not go far enough. The core is in the individual herself rather than in her reaction to external forces. That is, I propose that the individual is proactive based on her own interests, more than merely reactive to social forces. This is more consistent with the self-assertive strength of character characteristic of STEM women.

That strength is also noted by Nagey (2012), manager at a company developing software development tools. Discussing the deficiency of female coders and noting they see far fewer female than male applicants even for entry-level jobs, she suggests "The problem would appear to originate in girls at a young age just abandoning the paths that would take them to a coding career... It takes a fairly strong-minded and determined girl to decide, early on, that maths is what she loves and programming is where she wants to be. The solution has to lie in changing the attitudes of society, starting with promoting coding early on, and presenting it as a cool option to girls." A similar theme occurs in Adya & Kaiser (2005, 2006), who state "individual differences may well be similar across ethnic cultures. Every culture will have a representation of women who are determined, self-confident, and capable of taking on non-traditional careers."

But again, these interpretations assume the conventional wisdom that the reason young girls abandon (or don't take up) coding lies in the attitudes of society and the barriers they erect, not in the competing interests of those young girls themselves. Perhaps we could argue that if we removed more barriers, a wider cohort of women would be attracted to IT careers. That strong barriers select strong women to cross them, and bringing down those barriers will let the rest in. However the results of interventions and other results reported in this publication do not support the existence of any such large untapped population. Rather, the data currently available points to these characteristics being precisely those of women (and men) who are interested in STEM careers in the first place.

Individual Differences

The idea that it is specific kinds people who are interested in an IT career is supported by a number of findings. Nielsen, von Hellens, Pringle & Greenhill (1999) found that the factors of attraction relating to IT careers are attractive to certain types of people, and similarly for factors of rejection. Clayton (2007) found that a large variety of factors influence ICT career choices and that individuals perceive and react to these factors in different ways; in addition, individual attributes were more significant than socio-economic factors, a point echoed by Clayton, Beekhuyzen & Nielsen (2012). This has implications for intervention programs, at least to the extent that attendance is self-selected. As Clayton & Beekhuyzen (2004) flag, "we did consider that these programmes might be 'preaching to the converted' and not reaching those whose attitudes we wish to change." The other side to that is we should also consider how changeable those attitudes really are. It might not be surprising that if we are passionately interested in a field we wonder why other people aren't too, and think that they would be if only we could show them how fascinating it is. But perhaps the secret of the failure of interventions is not that we haven't found the right way to do it, but that the great majority of our targets are either already interested or never will be.

Factors of personal attraction are also studied in the context of the Theory of Reasoned Action (TRA) by Joshi & Kuhn (2011). They argue "TRA is an especially useful model for developing an IS-specific model of career attraction because, unlike other theories of career choice, it specifies the effect of social environment and allows for a more nuanced understanding of the factors underlying attraction to IS. Undergraduate students in an introductory IS course at a large public university were surveyed to test the study's model, providing empirical validation of a career choice model comprising IS-career relevant beliefs and values. Overall, findings reveal that intentions significantly influence actual behaviour – completion of an IS degree. IS career attitudes and social beliefs, in turn, collectively form intentions about pursuing IS careers. More specifically, attitudinal beliefs such as software/programming skill self-efficacy and technical, income, leadership, and job-variety-related work values have significant influence on favourable attitudes."

It is not surprising that this part of the equation is wider than IT and women. Investigating factors involved in occupational attainment (white collar versus blue collar), Ham et al. (2009) found that "the magnitude of the average marginal effect of parental status is small and the effect of the personality trait 'conscientiousness' is large and rivals that of education… effects differ between the genders for key variables, with personality traits in females having a relatively larger effect on their occupational outcomes due to the diminished effects of education." In terms of engaging individual concerns, an extensive report on digital inclusion ethnicity and immigration issues in France, Germany, Spain and UK found that "Evidence from the four countries shows that the most fruitful initiatives/services are those that link ICT to the substantive interests and needs of immigrants and ethnic minorities, rather than those providing generic ICT access and skilling opportunities" (Diminescu, Hepp, Welling, Maya-Jariego & Yates, 2009).

A survey of schoolgirls by Modi et al. (2012) found numerous interesting and significant results. Whilst often interpreted by conventional references to societal barriers, beneath that their data clearly highlights the centrality of individual interest and internal self-sufficiency. For example, in *Finding 3 – The DNA of a "STEM Girl" Sets Her Apart*, the report notes that the STEM girls surveyed "are less likely to say that they will become famous one day (29% vs. 40% non-STEM), likely attributing their future success to their internal abilities rather than external forces (e.g., being noticed)… STEM girls seem to be more inclined to grapple with adversity and overcome obstacles than non-STEM girls. STEM girls consider themselves hard workers (93% vs. 87% non-STEM) and feel that 'obstacles make me stronger' (91% vs. 85% of non-STEM girls). STEM girls overwhelmingly feel that 'Whatever boys can do, girls can do' (97% vs. 91% of non-STEM girls)."

Perhaps the lesson from individual choice and the failure of interventions is best reflected by Miliszewski & Moore (2011), who discovered that "young people themselves see the socialisation of technology as immensely important; that girls and women reject 'artificial' methods of recruitment into technology circles; that girls and women value technology for what it can do to advance their interests and the interests of their communities; and that the learning context or environment must incorporate the personal as well as the technical."

Believe in Yourself

Whilst not specifically an IT issue, the experience of Sheila Flavell, Chief Operating Officer at FDM Group, is relevant: "throughout her career she has always worked in a male-dominated environment. Shortly after Flavell joined the Glasgow police force, the city introduced equal pay: 'The men in the force said that women should do the same job as them. I was one of the first women to be put out on the street on foot patrol and we were given the toughest, roughest areas to patrol. We were being set up to fail but today there are thousands of female officers out on patrol. The reason I recall this particular memory is because it highlights that women are determined and resilient and will progress if they do a job well. It doesn't necessarily have to be more difficult than men; women shouldn't be compared with men and men shouldn't be compared with women. We are all individuals with our own strengths and weaknesses'" (Bateman, 2012).

Brady (2013) explains what Carly Fiorina (ex executive at AT&T, HP and Lucent) thinks of Melissa Mayer, chief executive officer of Yahoo!, halting employee telecommuting and Sheryl Sandberg, chief operating officer of Facebook, campaigning to have women "lean in" and stick with their careers: "Men disagree all the time and it's not talked about in a gender-laden context. So why is it that when women disagree, the conversation is all about gender? People have different points of view all the time… Be realistic that you'll run across some attitudes that are frustrating. But don't get a chip on your shoulder. Don't make it your problem. Just accept that people will talk about you. Don't dwell on it. Just keep going. It was more important to me to do the job I was hired to do. No matter what you do, people will talk about you." These are strong words indicating individual strengths, belief in oneself and willingness to act accordingly.

Perhaps the best advice we could give young women entering IT careers is from Lavine (2013), outlining tips from an interview with Sheryl Sandberg at the BlogHER conference: "reframe the way you think, get support, realize your right to be there." Whilst targeting improved female representation and presented with a gender lens,

Sandberg's basic premise in "*Lean In* is about believing in ourselves and reaching for any ambition. It's about each one of us, asking what we would do if we weren't afraid, and reaching for those ambitions, whatever they are." In other words: recognise what want are and go for it. Fortunately, it appears from Modi et al. (2012) that girls today already know that.

Individual Assumptions

Ann Uldridge, industry participant and ex-President of WiT, commented that "Despite some 15 years of a range of activities and effort by Women in Technology (WiT) in Queensland (in which I had a role in founding), my perception is that our activities have succeeded in attracting or retaining or returning an unknown number of *individuals* to ICT (in some cases changing their lives in the process)… but overall we have not succeeded in achieving a more balanced gender distribution in this industry. This reflects a similar lack of success by others in non-traditional roles such as engineering and science in general" (A. Uldridge, personal communication, October 17, 2012).

Some have extended the idea of individual successes to individual interventions. Ashcraft et al. (2012) quote from teachers participating in a workshop who used different individual-focused recruitment tactics. One commented, "Mostly, I... talked to girls individually in the hallway. I also put up posters. Talking to girls individually really helped. Several said they would give computing a try, and several actually joined my robotics team!" Another tried a slightly different tack: "I recruited the girls by volunteering to be the 'restroom monitor' in between classes. I talked to the girls, told them about my class, and signed them up."

An example of addressing the core individual needs versus wider group or technology aspects is in Miliszewska & Moore (2011), who note "Specifically addressing the needs of female learners also appears to have been responsible for the Amsterdam Westerpark Computers and the Internet initiative attracting almost three times as many women as men, even though that program was, like the Ardmore Network initiative, aimed at everyone in the community. If references to these projects and the WEVH initiative appear out of place in a review of strategies aimed at attracting high school girls to ICT because they happen to attract a higher proportion of mature age women than girls, their relevance should be understood in terms of what they say about the need for ICT studies and careers to meet the needs of female learners and workers." Yet it takes more than attraction to make a success. They continue that, compared to a Scottish program, "In both instances, women were provided with or made their own an environment in which they felt comfortable and secure. That the Scottish initiative was more successful than its Dutch counterpart in making women competent and enthusiastic ICT users had much more to do with its ability to build networks of local experts and informal learners than the technical prowess of instructors involved in the program. In other words, the success of the Scottish program and the relative failure of the Dutch initiative appear to lie in the first program's person-centred approach and the priority given by the second program to technology rather than people." In other words, speak to people's interests then focus on letting individuals drive what they are seeking and how they go about it, rather than imposing a one-size-fit-all approach.

The individual approach is generalised into theory by Trauth, Nielsen & von Hellens (2003) and Trauth et al. (2006). From research directed at understanding differing cross-cultural influences on female experiences in the IT workforce, they conclude by saying "These results reinforce the need to move away from monolithic analyses of gender and IT that assume a common experience for all women and toward more robust analyses that take into account the wide variation of both influences on women in the IT field and women's varied responses to them... Consequently, these results lend further support to the individual differences theory of gender and IT."

I counter that their findings lend support to the role of the individual in herself and not the assumptions of group influences and gender factors. Indeed we can go further, and suggest that theories of gender and individual malleability are themselves the result of individual predilections, that may exist more in the minds of researchers than in the world they are explaining. As Trauth (2011) herself writes, "while transparency about researcher standpoint is commonplace, if not ubiquitous, for interpretive and critical research a case can be made for its inclusion in positivist studies as well. The argument is that an individual's life experiences, biases, interests and identity will shape the assumptions one makes about a phenomenon. This is true even with positivist research. Decisions about what to include and not include in a survey, what theory to use to inform the research, and how the interpretation of findings is conducted all result from human judgments made by a human researcher. Advocates of transparency about researcher standpoint believe that the claim of an 'objective researcher' is a myth." Trauth (2011) goes on to discuss the methodological implications: "Proponents of reflexive or 'confessional' accounts of research (Kvasny, Greenhill & Trauth, 2005; Schultze, 2000) argue for greater transparency in presenting methodological details, that includes information about the researcher and how her or his identity characteristics (e.g. gender, ethnicity, nationality), philosophical orientation, disciplinary background, etc. has influenced the research. In the information systems field foundational work on methods such as that of Klein and Myers (1999) has included 'the relationship between the researcher and the researched' among the principles for conducting interpretive field studies."

CURIOUS AND CURIOUSER

"Curiosity. It's one of a few of life's assets that tends to peak during your childhood as opposed to adulthood... As you grow into your teenage years your curiosity grows with you. It evolves alongside your interests and your exposure to them in society. It's this curiosity and the resulting urge to learn and discover more that allows young people to succeed and presents them with opportunities to further their development... if you don't exercise this curiosity regularly you will lose the desire to discover, learn, and question everything in the world around you. Don't become the adult who loses curiosity and turns to the daily grind of life. Maintain your sense of curiosity and learn... that will help you with your future entrepreneurial and technological endeavours" (Hardy, 2013).

Curiosity has long been cited as a motivational factor for learning (Lowenstein, 1994). Additionally it has been recognised as a critical component of innovation in science and technology (National Science Board, 2010). It is also a motivator for interest in science and technology in the first place.

Denner's (2011) research finds "the strongest direct predictor of girls' interest in computing classes and careers was the extent to which they see value in computing, in particular their technological curiosity. The findings from this study are consistent with existing promising practices guides to engaging girls and underrepresented minorities in computing. These practices include offering hands on activities, creating opportunities to work in small groups, and allowing time for exploration. Program practices that are likely to impact values include linking activities to real world issues, exposing girls to a variety of computing careers, increasing teacher and peer encouragement, and utilizing staff members that are comfortable and positive with girls... Liston, Peterson & Ragan (2007, 2008) outline practices and hands on activities aimed at engaging curiosity."

In more detail, Denner (2011) also reports "Like others have found among high school and college women, the middle school girls in this study were more likely to express an interest in computing if they saw value in it (Anderson et al., 2008; Goode et al., 2006). Conversely, those who viewed computing as less important for their lives also reported lower interest in computing courses and careers. This finding is also consistent with decades of research by Eccles (2007) and her colleagues on math and science that suggest it is more important to help girls see how a particular career is relevant to their interests than to raise their confidence or perceived skills… However it is consistent with Dryburgh's (2000) review of research that finds the strongest motivation for both women and men to enter a computing field is interest, and that men are more motivated by self confidence, while women are more motivated by positive experiences with computing. It may also be that values are more important than expectations during middle school."

Guzdial, Ericson, McKlin & Engleman (2012) found similar results among over 1400 undergraduates in introductory computing classes in Georgia, USA. Key factors in individual participation in computing were interest in creating computer animations, enjoying working with and programming computers, interest in solving problems with computing and interest in computer games.

Of chief interest from those studies is that an individual's technological curiosity is the factor explaining most variation of interest in IT. It measures the value students place on IT as an internalization of its value to them as individuals.

The role of curiosity is supported by research by Modi et al. (2012), who report that "Girls interested in STEM like to understand how things work (87% vs. 65% non-STEM girls), solve problems (85% vs. 70% non-STEM girls), do hands-on activities (83% vs. 56% non-STEM girls), and ask questions (80% vs. 54% non-STEM girls)." It is relevant that technological curiosity and mapping to individual interests is likely to lead to the kind of experimentation and problem solving that educators rate as the most important characteristic of a computer science education (Commission on Professionals in Science and Technology, 2005). This has strong implications for course planning and intervention programs. Denner (2011) states "Problem solving is driven by curiosity about how things work. Despite the obviousness of this, technological curiosity is not commonly measured in research studies or addressed in middle school interventions. Our finding suggests the importance of providing opportunities that motivate girls to dig deeper into the technologies they already use."

It is not surprising that students pursue fields that match their interests. And those interests are individual: they are not determined by gender or any other homogeneous group identity, as demonstrated by the enormous individual variation we see. Nor is it surprising that students who want to understand how computers work are more likely to aspire to a career in computing, nor that students with high natural curiosity plus regular exposure to technology are more likely to explore studies and careers in IT and other STEM fields. We can see this in the example of Manasvi Somaiya (an Interaction Designer in Palo Alto), who states "I was immersed into a world of technology at a very early stage in my life. At the age of five I was already playing DOS games. Growing up I was aware of how technology was transforming the way we were living and doing everyday things. I was always curious and fascinated by what technology could help us achieve next. This curiosity drove me to start learning computer programming. Soon enough I was hooked, I woke up in the middle of the night with a solution of how my code could be fixed. I love working in the field of technology because it's challenging the limits and pushing the boundaries of human imagination. It's incredibly exciting to know that we are changing the way people do things… I see technology as a gushing wind bringing about changes in every field it touches whether it is in healthcare, transportation, manufacturing or education. Computers are ubiquitous, embedded everywhere around us. The unstoppable progress of technology will continue to match human imagination and will continue to transform the way we live and interact with the world outside" (Smith, 2013).

Those words will resonate with many people in IT. Many other people would be unmoved. No amount of intervention is likely to attract the latter into IT.

An example of an intervention that mapped to individual values, curiosity and interests was described by Miliszewska & Moore (2011), who report on "ITBeat, a British initiative aimed at stimulating girls' interest in ICT by appealing to their predilection for glamour, celebrity and pop culture … Centred around a competition in which girls get the opportunity to meet 'pop idols', ITBeat incorporated 'a very strong gendering process, whereby the awareness of being a girl' became 'a tool of empowerment' (Pitt, 2003, p. 9). Whilst meeting a favourite celebrity was the ultimate goal, the journey provided invaluable opportunities for girls to be 'exposed to female role models' working 'in some of the most glamorous and exciting areas of IT' (Pitt, 2003, p. 10). In this way, girls came to see how skills they already 'possess[ed] could give them access to exciting, well-paid careers in IT' (Pitt, 2003, p. 10)."

Miliszewska & Moore (2011) go on to note that "Measuring the likelihood for success of initiatives such as ITBeat in absolute terms might be difficult, but its potential to capture young girls' interest should not be underestimated (Pitt, 2003). An Internet search regrettably failed to confirm that ITBeat still exists, but as Pitt (2003) argued, the program's strength lay in its ability to conceptualise the user at the centre of the intervention – something policy makers too frequently fail to do."

Both its success and apparent failure are interesting. Appealing to girls' interests is clearly effective at attracting their attention and efforts. However perhaps attempting to "trick" them into becoming interested in IT by attracting them into IT activities via *unrelated* interests may be ineffective. This ties in to our earlier results that indicate most women who will be interested in IT already are, and only a small percentage of girls have merely failed to discover their interest.

We can expect that negative stereotypes will inhibit some girls who would otherwise be interested in IT as a career. One relevant class of stereotype is "left brain vs. right brain," "logic vs. creativity" and "science vs. art." Yet over the decades a strong correlation between curiosity and creativity has been noted in the literature. "Penney & McCann's (1964) study measured children on the Children's Reactive Curiosity Scale, noting high correlations with J. P. Guilford's divergent thinking Unusual Uses Test. Torrance (1967) noted that students who scored highly for curiosity also scored more highly for creativity than others of the same intelligence. Other studies showed significant correlations between self rated measures of curiosity and the Remote Associates Test of creativity (Torrance, 1967). One of the reasons behind this close link between curiosity and creativity might be due to curiosity's ability to stimulate both divergent and convergent thinking. In *The Nature of Human Intelligence*, psychologist J.P. Guilford identified the presence of both convergent and divergent thinking in response to a given problem" (Rowson, Young, Spence, Lindley & Gecius, 2012). Given the strong link between curiosity and interest in IT, it might be worth stressing the truly creative and problem-solving aspects of an IT career.

DECISIONS, DECISIONS AND MORE DECISIONS

There is curiosity, there is interest and there is ability, but it is a series of choices and decisions that leads to an actual career in IT.

Castano & Webster (2011), in discussing their Life Course approach, note "a major advantage of this framework is its acknowledgement of the decisions, choices and actions of individuals in the shaping of their careers. There are many accounts of women's ICT careers that reveal the decisions women have actively taken to steer a particular course. Some of these accounts have focused on women's refusal to enter or remain in the field, based on its perceived unattractiveness or the difficulties of managing such a career within the context of their non-work lives (Margolis and Fisher, 2003; Griffiths and Moore, 2010). Others, however, have drawn attention to the positive choices women have made which challenge traditional binary definitions of gender: many women enjoy technical work and define their gender identities through their facility with computers (Henwood, 1993), while others find the work engaging for other reasons, and opt for a career in the field (Kelan, 2008)." In other words, individual women make individual choices that make sense to them, and that map to their own curiosity levels and values – positive or negative.

In describing their research, Trauth et al. (2006) report "This individual variation has been categorized into differences in: *exposure, experience* and *response*. Differential *exposure* - the amount of gender bias, which a particular woman actually encounters – varies by such individual factors as her ethnicity, age or parental status, as well as by the geographic region in which she lives. Differential *experience* – a woman's consciousness of bias and the extent to which she notices and internalizes it – is influenced by such individual factors as role models, mentors and significant life experiences, as well as by an individual's personality, abilities, academic prowess, and the culture and economy of a particular geographic region. Differential *response* is affected by such individual factors as the degree of family support a woman receives, her coping mechanisms and her sense of personal agency, as well as by institutional factors such as gender and equality laws and policies of a geographic region as well as the equality climate of institutional settings." I believe this correctly identifies the factors but does not correctly apportion their degree of influence. In the STEMcell model it is the core of the individual's interests and strengths that defines where she chooses to go in life. The other factors in the structural, social and cultural layers of her environment can help or hinder, but her core itself pushes back at or embraces those factors.

Moving closer towards the STEMcell model is Liston, Peterson & Ragan's (2009) expectancy-value model of achievement-related choices:

This study supports the Expectancy Value Model of career decision making, which holds that individual beliefs, values, and goals have direct influence on choices, and are affected by inputs from the social world. Many of the respondents in this study thought of themselves as adept in working with computers. They played games, and problem solved, which increased their confidence. Their feelings of competence were much further enhanced, though, when other people provided them with positive feedback.

The respondents (N=97) who were interested in IT work by elementary school or middle school indicated higher levels of IT activities during those grades. For example, they were twice as likely to have access to a computer at school or at home in elementary and middle school. A large number of them played computer games and they were more likely to have participated in an informal IT-related education program in middle school and to have a role model or a mentor.

Although a number of women made the career decision to work in IT when they were in college or beginning work, they may have been more likely to decide earlier if they had participated in more IT-related activities. Data show that early IT-related activities and early interest in IT are highly correlated, suggesting that participating in IT-related activities early in life could influence the development of a career interest which could lead girls to pursue more IT experiences and education, and potentially careers. This research has shown a correlation, though, and it would be an interesting follow-up study to look at the causal relationship underlying the relationship of these factors (Liston et al., 2009).

That research bears a strong resemblance to the results of my snap poll (Chapter Four: *The Old Approach*) in which interest from an early age was the strongest factor followed by discovery of interest through work.

Much research has viewed results through the lens of gender or social theory, and it is interesting to see how it looks through the lens of the individual. For example, Liston et al. (2009) identify "Many similar factors, influences, and experiences are shared among the respondents, including parent support, hands-on experiences, a feeling of being adept at IT-related activities, having a positive image of those in IT, and having friends with similar interests." All of those could be considered as a result of individual choice rather than as an external force the child has adapted to: children express an interest, drawing support from their parents; interest leads to experience, ability and holding a positive image of role models; children choose their friends according to mutual compatibility and interests.

Similarly, it is unclear whether the correlation between early experience and early interest is the experience causing the interest or vice versa. In the STEMcell model, I propose it is mainly, though not exclusively, the latter. An interesting statistic in support of that is a graph in Ashcraft et al. (2012) showing the percentage of students reporting computer experience in USA High Schools from 1999 to 2011. Over those 12 years, despite the expansion in home computer ownership, the rapid spread of other computing devices through the population and numerous intervention programs, the percentages of girls reporting computer literacy and computer programming experience were virtually unchanged both as an absolute percentage and compared to boys.

Nevertheless innate interests can be nurtured or inhibited, even never discovered. While the data indicates that most girls interested in IT find that interest themselves, it also indicates that a significant minority do not. In the light of that, the research of Liston et al. (2009) has strong implications for general approaches to teaching IT (and STEM in general). It clearly shows that there is a strong need to appeal to the individual through hands-on, relevant projects. The participants "most frequently selected hands-on experiences, project-based learning opportunities, making curriculum relevant/tied to real-life issues, and opportunities to use technology to be creative and explore as the most critical elements. Overall, the most frequently selected elements that women currently working in IT experienced were hands-on activities, relevant curriculum, engaging staff, and project-based learning opportunities. More than half the respondents also experienced a challenging content level and opportunities to work together with other people" (Liston et al., 2009).

It is encouraging that career guidance has taken on board the primacy of the individual and the use of IT to empower individual choice: "Career guidance services distinctively affirm the value attached in market-based democratic societies to the rights of individuals to make free decisions about their own working lives, linking personal goals to the socioeconomic needs of the society in which they live… ICT based systems make integration of this kind easier to deliver, and also make it possible to add a diagnostic front-end to enable individuals to input their characteristics and preferences and be guided to appropriate opportunities. The National Career Information System in Australia is a good example of what can be produced… [But] while information is necessary, it is not sufficient. If individuals are to be able to find the information they need, to understand this information and relate it to their personal needs, and then to convert it into personal action, many will need some form of personal support" (Watts & Sultana, 2004).

I, I, I GENERATION

The other side of exposing children to technology in order to fire their interest is potential negative effects.

Taylor (2012) discusses the growing debate in the world of technology about its effect on children, with the view that it's not about the technology *per se* but rather, as noted by Price-Mitchell (2012): "This debate cuts to the core of who we are as individuals, families, and communities. It asks the question, 'How does technology affect the healthy development of children and teens?'" Two key messages Taylor gives are that "areas in which parents should focus their child-rearing attention include their children's self-identity, values, thinking, relationships, and physical and mental health" and "The goal for parents is not to disconnect their children, but rather to expose them to popular culture and technology when they are developmentally ready and then give them the perspectives, attitudes, and tools they need to thrive in this digital age" (Taylor, 2012). He points out that "Young people normally answer the question, 'Who am I?' during adolescence… Teens solidify their identities during adolescence, as they begin to more fully understand their personalities, values, needs, and emotions. This journey happens as they interact in their social worlds. Accelerated by technology, today's social world has expanded dramatically for teenagers. Taylor argues that this acceleration 'may be interfering with healthy development of self-identity in children.' He also suggests that technology has caused a shift from children being internally to externally driven. For example, he cites Facebook and other types of social media as facades where children must always ask two questions, 'How will others look at me? and 'How can I ensure that others view me positively?' When children are consumed with questions that propel them to be driven by external factors, Taylor believes that 'healthy self-awareness and self-expression give way to an unhealthy preoccupation with what others think, impression management, and self-promotion'" (Price-Mitchell, 2012).

However we must ask whether this is actually any different from how children interact in the playground. And whilst Taylor sounds alarm bells and warnings about tools such as Facebook and online games – and by so doing potentially scares some parents by his conclusions – there are others who write the opposite, claiming positive benefits (Rosen, 2010; Price-Mitchell, 2012). What is important is the healthy individual self and ensuring that it grows; technology is like any other tool and can help or hinder that process. Part of what we want to achieve with STEM cell and #SocialIT is children growing up liking technology while having their native self-driven confidence nurtured. And as Price-Mitchell (2012) writes, "Who will influence whether technology is good or bad for kids? Parents."

I AM NOT YOU

It is true that each one of us can be grouped with any number of collectives, from the unchosen such as race, ethnicity, generation, age, gender and sexuality, to the (more or less) chosen such as profession, religion, philosophy and club memberships. To the extent that they reflect useful facts of reality, namely qualities shared by the group that distinguish them in some useful way from other groups, such collective identifications are valid.

However it is a mistake to *define* ourselves by our membership in any group. Not only do each of us belong to many other and different groups than the one we might be looking at right now, but we differ from all other members of those groups, all the way down to our individual DNA, desires and thoughts.

That is why group stereotypes are fundamentally invalid. Group averages might be useful for some statistically based decision-making, but a stereotype, which applies the group "qualities" indiscriminately to all its members, is meaningless. For example, if a particular job requires a certain level of muscle strength, the fact that men on average are stronger than women is irrelevant to whether any particular woman (or man) can do the job. Average differences between groups say nothing about the degree of overlap between them or the ability of any individual. And the best way to fight collective stereotypes is not to accept the premise of group identity, but to celebrate the individual and her uniqueness.

Fortunately, girls are not only more independent than some theorists imply, they also know they are more than just females and their role models can cross group boundaries. "While girls need to see women like themselves in these roles, it would also be a mistake to think that girls only can relate to other girls and women (Cheryan & Plaut, 2010; Cheryan, Siy,Vichayapai, Drury & Kim, 2011). A combination of diverse male and female role models is best. Many women and girls also describe the importance of male role models, and it would be a mistake to think that people cannot relate to each other across lines of gender and race (Liston et al., 2008). One of the most important characteristics of a role model is that girls perceive these role models as 'relatable' and similar to themselves. Gender and race are most certainly important factors in perceived similarity, but they are not the only factors. This perceived similarity to people in the field and a feeling that one will 'fit in' is a major factor in choosing a major and a career (Cheryan & Plaut, 2010; Cheryan et al., 2011)" (Ashcraft et al., 2012).

For years the low proportion of women in IT has been viewed through a gender or culture lens, and for years there have been interventions on that basis that achieved nothing beyond a few individual career choices. In contrast the results and analyses reported in this book indicate that not only is innate interest the main driver of an IT career, but most women with that interest are perfectly capable of discovering it themselves. From the other end of the equation, access to education and IT has expanded substantially and cultural views of the fundamental equality of men and women have become pervasive compared to decades ago. If in the face of that there has been no significant increase in women in IT, and indeed a decline, the simplest conclusion is not that women are so sensitive to barriers that no matter how much they are reduced it has no effect. It is that the main driver of career choice and the decisions involved in persisting in it is individual interest and values: how well the career fits with their goals, taking into account all the alternatives also available. This is not to say that there are no stereotypes, no barriers or no disincentives. It is to say that their contribution is only a small part of the cause.

That does not mean that we shouldn't tell the world why we love IT. It doesn't mean that we shouldn't fight irrational prejudices wherever we find them. It doesn't mean that such efforts will have no effect. But it does mean we should understand that we are helping those women who are interested in IT and will enjoy a career in their chosen field, but nothing we can do will substantially increase that number.

Watts and Sultana (2004) wrote, "Career guidance is essentially a soft rather than a hard policy intervention. At its heart is the notion of the 'active individual': that individuals should be encouraged to determine their role in, and their contribution to, the society of which they are part. The primacy of the individual's interests is commonly a core principle in codes of practice for career guidance services." Perhaps that should be our own motto.

But however central the individual and her interests are, everyone needs information and support; and everyone can achieve more towards their own goals by working synergistically with others. That is where the second new aspect of the STEMcell model comes in, with the disruptive, enabling and empowering technologies of the #SocialIT era. We turn to that topic in the next chapter.

REFERENCES

Adya, M., & Kaiser, K. M. (2005). Early determinants of women in the IT workforce: A model of girl's career choices. *Information Technology & People*, *18*(3), 230–259. doi:10.1108/09593840510615860

Adya, M., & Kaiser, K. M. (2006). Factors influencing girls' choice of information technology careers. In E. M. Trauth (Ed.), *Encyclopedia of gender and information technology* (Vol. 1, pp. 282–288). Hershey, PA: Idea Group Reference. doi:10.4018/978-1-59140-815-4.ch044

Anderson, N., Lankshear, C., Timms, C., & Courtney, L. (2008). 'Because it's boring, irrelevant and I don't like computers': Why high school girls avoid professionally-oriented ICT subjects. *Computers & Education*, *50*, 1304–1318. doi:10.1016/j.compedu.2006.12.003

Ashcraft, C., Eger, E., & Friend, M. (2012). *Girls in IT: The facts*. Boulder, CO: National Centre for Women & Information Technology (NCWIT). Retrieved August 6, 2013, from http://www.academia.edu/2283166/Girls_in_IT_The_Facts

Bateman, K. (2012). *Industry still failing to attract female talent everywomen survey finds*. Retrieved July 20, 2013, from http://www.computerweekly.com/feature/Industry-still-failing-to-attract-female-talent-everywoman-survey-finds

Brady, D. (2013). *Carly Fiorina on Marissa, Sheryl, and women in tech*. Retrieved July 4, 2013, from http://www.businessweek.com/authors/867-diane-brady

Castano, C., & Webster, J. (2011). Understanding women's presence in ICT: The life course perspective. *International Journal of Gender. Science and Technology*, *3*(2), 358–363.

Cheryan, S., & Plaut, V. C. (2010). Explaining underrepresentation: A theory of precluded interest. *Sex Roles*, *63*(7-8), 475–488. doi:10.1007/s11199-010-9835-x PMID:20930923

Cheryan, S., Siy, J. O., Vichayapai, M., Drury, B. J., & Kim, S. (2011). Do female and male role models who embody STEM stereotypes hinder women's anticipated success in STEM? *Social Psychological and Personality Science*, *2*(6), 656–664. doi:10.1177/1948550611405218

Clayton, K. (2007). *The influence of metropolitan Brisbane middle-school ICT experiences on girls' ICT study and career choices*. (Unpublished doctoral dissertation). Griffith University, Queensland, Australia.

Clayton, K., & Beekhuyzen, J. (2004). Engaging girls in ICT: Mind the gap! In *Proceedings of the 2004 Australian Women in IT Conference* (pp. 41-47). Hobart, Australia: Academic Press.

Clayton, K., Beekhuyzen, J., & Nielsen, S. (2012). Now I know what ICT can do for me? *Information Systems Journal*, *22*(5), 1–16. doi:10.1111/j.1365-2575.2012.00414.x

Commission on Professionals in Science and Technology. (2005). *Preparing women and minorities for the IT workforce: The role of nontraditional educational pathways*. Washington, DC: American Association for the Advancement of Science.

Denner, J. (2011). What predicts middle school girls' interest in computing? *International Journal of Gender. Science and Technology*, *3*(1), 53–69.

Diminescu, G., Hepp, A., Welling, S., Maya-Jariego, I., & Yates, S. (2009). *ICT supply and demand in immigrant and ethnic minority communities in France, Germany, Spain and the United Kingdom*. Seville, Spain: European Commission.

Dryburgh, H. (2000). Underrepresentation of girls and women in computer science: Classification of 1990s research. *Journal of Educational Computing Research*, *23*(2), 181–202. doi:10.2190/8RYV-9JWH-XQMB-QF41

Eccles, J. S. (2007). Where are all the women? Gender differences in participation in physical science and engineering. In S. J. Ceci, & W. M. Williams (Eds.), *Why aren't more women in science? Top researchers debate the evidence* (pp. 199–210). Washington, DC: American Psychological Association. doi:10.1037/11546-016

Goode, J., Estrella, R., & Margolis, J. (2006). Lost in translation: Gender and high school computer science. In J. M. Cohoon, & W. Aspray (Eds.), *Women and information technology: Research on underrepresentation* (pp. 89–114). Cambridge, MA: MIT Press. doi:10.7551/mitpress/9780262033459.003.0003

Griffiths, M., & Moore, K. (2010). Disappearing women: A study of women who left the UK ICT sector. *Journal of Technology Management and Innovation*, *5*(1), 95–107. doi:10.4067/S0718-27242010000100008

Guzdial, M., Ericson, B., McKlin, T., & Engleman, S. (2012). A statewide survey on computing education pathways and influences: Factors in broadening participation in computing. In *Proceedings of ACM International Computing Education Research (ICER) Conference* (pp. 143-150). New York: ACM.

Hale, B., & Fong, V. (2002). *What do women in IT want? Ask them says Penn State researcher.* Retrieved August 6, 2013, from http://www.psu.edu/ur/2002/oddgirl.html

Ham, R., Junankar, P. N., & Wells, R. (2009). *Occupational choice: Personality matters* (IZA Discussion Paper No. 4105). Bonn: IZA.

Hardy, T. (2013). *The importance of feeding your curiosity.* Retrieved August 10, 2013, from http://teensintech.com/blog/2013/01/curiosityarticlerocketlist

Henwood, F. (1993). Establishing gender perspectives on information technology: Problems, issues and opportunities. In E. Green, J. Owen, & D. Pain (Eds.), *Gendered by design: Gender, information technology and the design of office systems* (pp. 31–52). London: Taylor and Francis.

Hyek, P. A. (2011). *Rapid technology innovation creates a smart, mobile world.* Retrieved August 16, 2013, from http://www.ey.com/GL/en/Issues/Business-environment/Six-global-trends-shaping-the-business-world---Rapid-technology-innovation-creates-a-smart--mobile-world

Joshi, K. D., & Kuhn, K. (2011). What determines interest in an IS career? An application of the theory of reasoned action. *Communications of the Association for Information Systems, 29,* Article 8.

Kelan, E. (2008). Emotions in a rational profession: The gendering of skills in ICT work. *Gender, Work and Organization*, *15*(1), 49–71.

Klein, H. K., & Myers, M. (1999). A set of principles for conducting and evaluating interpretive field studies in information systems research. *Management Information Systems Quarterly*, *23*(1), 67–93. doi:10.2307/249410

Kvasny, L., Greenhill, A., & Trauth, E. M. (2005). Giving voice to feminist projects in management information systems research. *International Journal of Technology and Human Interaction*, *1*(1), 1–18. doi:10.4018/jthi.2005010101

Lavine, L. (2013). *Sheryl Sandberg encourages women bloggers to 'lean in'.* Retrieved August 11, 2013, from http://www.entrepreneur.com/article/227596#

Liston, C., Peterson, K., & Ragan, V. (2007). *Guide to promising practices in informal technology education for girls*. Boulder, CO: National Center for Women in Information Technology.

Liston, C., Peterson, K., & Ragan, V. (2008). *Evaluating promising practices in informal information technology (IT) education for girls: Women in IT—Survey results*. Boulder, CO: National Center for Women & Information Technology.

Liston, C., Peterson, K., & Ragan, V. (2009). *Promising practices in informal information technology (IT) education for girls*. Paper prepared for AERA Meeting. San Diego, CA.

Lowenstein, G. (1994). The psychology of curiosity: A review and reinterpretation. *Psychological Bulletin, 116*, 75–98. doi:10.1037/0033-2909.116.1.75

Margolis, J., & Fisher, A. (2003). *Unlocking the clubhouse: Women in computing*. Cambridge, MA: MIT Press.

Miliszewska, I., & Moore, A. (2011). Attracting girls to ICT studies & careers – A snapshot of strategies. *Redress, 20*(3), 10–14.

Modi, K., Schoenberg, J., & Salmond, K. (2012). *Generation STEM: What girls say about science, technology, engineering, and math*. Girl Scouts of the USA. Retrieved August 10, 2013, from http://www.girlscouts.org/research/pdf/generation_stem_full_report.pdf

Nagey, H. (2012). *Why girls don't code: Musings on the gender imbalance in the developer community*. Retrieved July 10, 2013, from http://newsletters.livecode.com/october/issue141/newsletter1.php

National Science Board. (2010). *Preparing the next generation of STEM innovators: Identifying and developing our nation's human capital*. Retrieved October 14, 2010, from http://www.nsf.gov/nsb/publications/2010/nsb1033.pdf

Nielsen, S., von Hellens, L., Pringle, R., & Greenhill, A. (1999). Students' perceptions of information technology careers: Conceptualising the influence of cultural and gender factors for IT education. *GATES Journal, 5*(1), 30–38.

Penney, R. K., & McCann, B. (1964). The children's reactive curiosity scale. *Psychological Reports, 15*, 323–334. doi:10.2466/pr0.1964.15.1.323

Pitt, L. (2003). *Don't leave IT to the boys!* (Deliverable D05/Appendix 2.1 of IST-2000-26329 SIGIS Project).

Price-Mitchell, M. (2012). *Generation tech: The good, bad and scary*. Retrieved August 16, 2013, from http://www.psychologytoday.com/blog/the-moment-youth/201211/generation-tech-the-good-bad-and-scary

Rand, A. (1961). Happiness. *The Ayn Rand lexicon*. Retrieved August 2, 2013, from http://aynrandlexicon.com/lexicon/happiness.html

Rand, A. (1963). Man's rights. In H. Binswanger (Ed.), *The Ayn Rand lexicon*. Retrieved August 18, 2013, from http://aynrandlexicon.com/ayn-rand-ideas/man-rights.html

Rosen, L. (2010). *Rewired: Understanding the iGeneration and the way they learn*. New York: Palgrave Macmillan.

Rowson, J., Young, J., Spence, N., Lindley, E., & Gecius, E. (2012). *The power of curiosity – How linking inquisitiveness to innovation could help to address our energy challenges*. London, UK: RSA Social Brain Centre. Retrieved August 16, 2013, from http://www.thersa.org/__data/assets/pdf_file/0004/606829/RSA-Social-Brain-The-Power-of-Curiosity.pdf

Schultze, U. (2000). A confessional account of an ethnography about knowledge work. *Management Information Systems Quarterly, 24*(1), 1–39. doi:10.2307/3250978

Smith, P. (2013). *Manasvi Somaiya – A woman of vision at VMware on her technological curiosity to growing from an intern to fulltime employee at VMware.* Retrieved August 10, 2013, from http://blogs.vmware.com/careers/2013/08/manasvi-somaiya-a-woman-of-vision-at-vmware-on-her-technological-curiosity-to-growing-from-an-intern-to-a-full-time-employee-at-vmware.html

Sommers, C. H. (2008, March/April). Why can't a woman be more like a man? *The American.* Retrieved August 18, 2013, from http://www.american.com/archive/2008/march-april-magazine-contents/why-can2019t-a-woman-be-more-like-a-man

Taylor, J. (2012). *Raising generation tech: Preparing your children for a media-fueled world.* Naperville, IL: Sourcebooks.

Torrance, E. P. (1967). Non-test ways of identifying the creatively gifted. In J. C. Gowan, G. D. Demos, & E. P. Torrance (Eds.), *Creativity: Its educational implications*. New York: Wiley.

Trauth, E. M. (2002). Odd girl out: An individual differences perspective on women in the IT profession. *Information Technology & People*, *15*(2), 98–118. doi:10.1108/09593840210430552

Trauth, E. M. (2011). What can we learn from gender research? Seven lessons for business research methods. *The Electronic Journal of Business Research Methods*, *9*(1), 1–9.

Trauth, E. M., Huang, H., & Quesenberry, J. L. (2006). Cross-cultural influences on women in the IT workforce. In *Proceedings of ACM SIGMIS Conference on Computer Personnel Research* (pp. 12-19). Claremont, CA: ACM.

Trauth, E. M., Nielsen, S. H., & von Hellens, L. A. (2003). Explaining the IT gender gap: Australian stories for the new millennium. *Journal of Research and Practice in Information Technology*, *35*(1), 7–20.

Trauth, E. M., Quesenberry, L. L., & Huang, H. (2009). Retaining women in the U.S. I.T workforce: Theorizing the influence of organizational factors. *European Journal of Information Systems*, *18*(5), 476–497. doi:10.1057/ejis.2009.31

Watts, A. G., & Sultana, R. G. (2004). Career guidance policies in 37 countries: Contrasts and common themes. *International Journal for Educational and Vocational Guidance*, *4*, 105–122. doi:10.1007/s10775-005-1025-y

Xie, Y., & Shauman, K. (2003). *Women in science: Career processes and outcomes.* Boston, MA: Harvard University Press.

KEY TERMS AND DEFINITIONS

ICT: Information and Communication Technology. Synonymous with IT.

IT: Information Technology. Synonymous with ICT.

#SocialIT: a term coined for a layer of the STEMcell Model. It is a disruptive, penetrating force that can enhance the positive and reduce the negative aspects of the Cultural, Social, Structural and Individual contexts affecting women in IT.

STEM: Science, Technology, Engineering and Mathematics, conceptually related fields that share issues of under-representation of women. An extension of SET to include maths.

STEMcell Model: A model designed by Sonja Bernhardt that provides a conceptual framework for viewing contexts and layers impacting STEM fields.

Chapter 8
#SocialIT

ABSTRACT

The #SocialIT layer of the STEMcell Model is visualized as a layer surrounding and penetrating the other layers to interact directly with the individual core. It represents the seismic transformations where technology underpins and transforms the future. Six drivers most likely to shape the future workforce are highlighted in this chapter: longer life spans, a rise in smart devices and systems, advances in computational systems such as sensors and processing power, new multimedia technology, the continuing evolution of social media, and a globally connected world. Specific tools and potentials of #SocialIT are discussed, including big data, augmented reality and wearable technologies, crowdsourcing and the new ways for people to meet and collaborate, rapid changes in technology fracturing generations only a few years apart, and the social, educational, and career implications of substantially extended active lifespans. The #SocialIT layer implies that future programs, projects, and activities should be developed by tapping into this shifting technological landscape and actively using the tools and platforms. However, the deeper meaning is that what is happening naturally is going to rapidly overtake anything we can plan based on the present.

We are clearly living in a period of huge transformation – technological, social and economic, and while we can't know exactly what the future holds – that is we can't predict the future, neither can we assume that today's choices and assumptions will be relevant tomorrow.

– Marina Gorbis (2012),
Institute for the Future

INTRODUCTION

Castells' (1996, 1997, 1998) *Information Age* trilogy was an early herald of the shift toward a world built on technology and interconnections. He argues that technology can "unleash the power of the mind" and hence dramatically increase individuals' productivity. He examines the social dynamics of production, power and experience, how they inter-relate, and the dynamic of the self and networks in a continually changing culture. This leads to the argument that "The Information

DOI: 10.4018/978-1-4666-5860-8.ch008

Age, The Age of Consumption, and The Network Society are all perspectives attempting to describing modern life as known in the present and to depict the future of society. As Castells suggests, contemporary society may be described as 'replacing the antiquated metaphor of the machine with that of the network'" (Aragon, 2013).

That conclusion may be overstated: the network and the other technologies we depend upon are built on machines and rely on their power and precision. But we cannot doubt the transformative power of those technologies. Thus the Institute for the Future (www.iftf.org) identifies six drivers most likely to shape the future workforce (Tandon, Pritchard, Savelieva, Smith & Vogt, 2012):

- longer life spans,
- a rise in smart devices and systems,
- advances in computational systems such as sensors and processing power,
- new multimedia technology,
- the continuing evolution of social media,
- a globally connected world.

In a similar vein, Scoble & Israel (2013) declare a new era they have tagged as "age of context" and report five converging forces that "promise to change virtually every aspect of our lives: Mobile, Data, Sensors, Location Based Technology and Social Media."

The IT sector clearly underpins this future, both as underlying infrastructure and for the creation of devices and smart apps. The importance of IT in the future is reflected in the *Europe 2020* strategy establishing Information and Communication Technologies (ICTs) as a core element for five of the seven flagship initiatives to promote growth in the European Union: the European Platform Against Poverty and Social Exclusion, An Agenda for New Skills and Jobs, Youth on the Move, Digital Agenda for Europe and the Innovation Union (European Commission, 2013). Whilst these initiatives primarily focus on digital inclusion (access, skills/competencies and use) they are enablers and clearly underpin the future.

The Institute for the Future (2013) identifies a curve of incumbent practices that will slowly decline over the coming century and a second curve that will rise to shape our new human enterprises. Further, they anticipate interplay between these two curves, as second-curve innovations provoke first curve reactions, which in turn initiate adjustments in the second curve. Thus there are forces already in play, such as rapid changes in the technological landscape, continued evolution of social media and the prospect of life extension, which are rebuilding social constructs and will significantly change our ways of thinking and doing. Translating that into the context of this book, the first curve is the traditional way of thinking and acting for addressing the "problem" of declining representation of women in technology studies and careers, while the second curve is the disruptive new way of thinking and doing that is represented in the #SocialIT layer of the STEMcell Model.

The world has already changed enormously. As Richards (2013) relates, "The world is evolving and changing faster than work can keep up, warns the CIPD [Chartered Institute of Personnel and Development] as it launches debate on the future trends that will shape work and working lives. This should come as little surprise given the pace that technology is evolving. A number of 'Megatrends' over the last century have changed the world of work beyond recognition." Such Megatrends are only going to come faster. As noted by Karoly & Panis (2004), "The pace of technological change—whether through advances in information technology (IT), biotechnology, or such emerging fields as nanotechnology—will almost certainly accelerate."

We decry the relative lack of participation of women in IT. Yet it is hard for a young woman growing up today to even imagine what a woman's life was like as recently as the 1950s, only 60 years ago. A woman was expected to be a housewife and mother, serve her man and her family, and education beyond high school was a rarity (RoobixCoob, 2005). Now more women than men go to college in the USA and most young women regard their career as very important (Cave, 2013; Patten & Parker, 2012). We can only imagine what the coming decades will bring.

The research community is starting to recognise the impacts. For example, Trauth (2011) flags that "globalization, social inclusion and innovation are 21st century issues that will encourage the research community to overcome resistance to different ideas, methodologies, epistemologies and theories." I think this underestimates the impact. The wider community may well leave the researchers struggling to keep up.

#SocialIT operates within those drivers and megatrends. The #SocialIT factors may be impacted by the competing cultural crust, such as if technologies are not allowed in that culture or for some people. But its widespread nature and low barriers to entry mean that it also pushes back against that cultural crust and reaches through all layers to directly empower the individual (this tension between traditional powers and the people is noted in Wikipedia, 2013a). The #SocialIT factors influencing the model are represented in Figure 1 and explained in more detail in this chapter.

TECH TALK

Over a decade ago Herman (1999) predicted, "65% of school-aged students will work in jobs and industries that haven't been invented yet." Those school children would now be in the workforce, and with the increasing role of technology it is likely that Herman's claim has come at least partly true. Casserly (2012) discusses ten jobs that didn't exist ten years ago, including App Developer, Market Research Data Miner, Millennial Generational Expert, Social Media Manager, Chief Listening Officer (another social media-based job), Cloud

Figure 1. #SocialIT factors influencing participation in IT

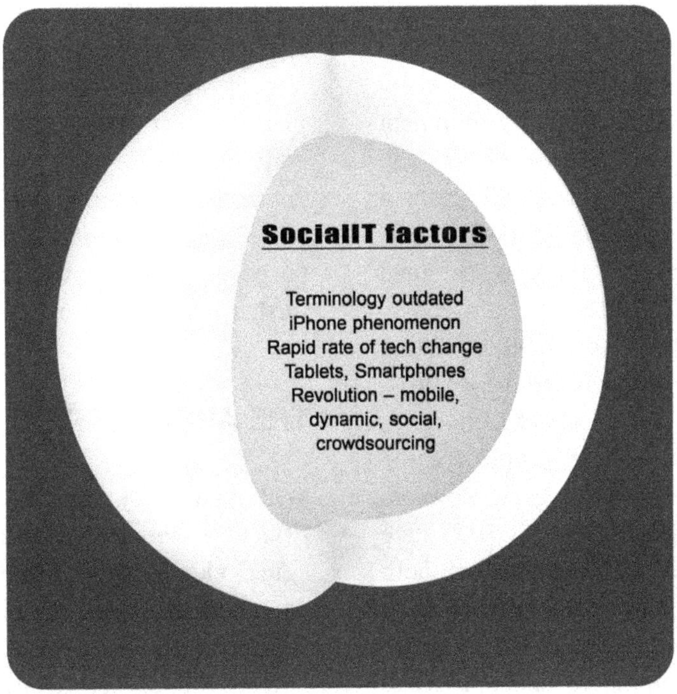

Computing Services and User Experience Design. Smalley (2013) similarly points out that "Many of today's top jobs didn't exist ten years ago," and outlines *Click your fortune* – a TED-Ed interactive, open-ended series that helps young learners find out about careers they might not have known existed but are potentially interested in. "Click Your Fortune was created in the style of 'choose-your-own-adventure'. Each video features four professionals (selected from among the awesome attendees of TEDGlobal 2013, as well as some TED speakers) reading career-related questions submitted directly by students. Once all four questions are read, the viewer can click the path that most relates to their interests" (Smalley, 2013). And in a startling turn-around from the traditional social image of geeks, the job of data scientist – analyzing big data to extract useful pieces of information and trends – has been called the "sexiest job of the 21st century" (Arnold-Smeets, 2013b).

Rapid changes mean jobs are lost as well as gained. As Barbara Tobin, industry participant, ex President of Women in Technology (WiT) (Qld), ex Chair of Australian Women in IT, Science and Engineering (AWISE) said, "I think the Technology Industry is in need of an overhaul. With Tablets and Mobility devices outselling PCs it will make several IT jobs as we know them redundant. Gaming, Software Development and Data Warehousing will be areas of survival. Unfortunately these are sections of IT that are predominately male. Project Manager will also be a survivor of the current era" (B. Tobin, personal communication, August 5, 2013).

But the jobs are lost because of changes that are leading technology, society and the job market in new directions. It's all about technology innovation and change, where people are the curious, the creative and the clever. Rowson, Young, Spencer, Lindley & Gecius (2012) state "The challenges of the 21st century require both social and technological innovation… Researchers generally agree that creativity is the 'ability to produce work that is both novel and appropriate [or useful]' (Sternberg & Lubart, 1999) while innovation is 'the successful implementation of creative ideas within an organization' (Amabile, Conti, Coon, Lazenby & Henon, 1996). Creativity involves the conception of new ideas, while innovation executes them, scaling them from rough prototype or small-scale pilot to become a widespread solution."

As stated by Ann Uldridge, industry participant and ex-president of Women in Technology (WiT) (Queensland), "The key features [of IT roles] include problem-solving, creativity and logic… things we dream up – ideas that are converted into something unique that people want to buy – things like films, business software packages, electronic games, bio-technology products, health systems, education systems and the like… ICT underpins or 'enables' activities within all other industries… from the smallest retail store to the largest enterprise – whether they be old economy, new economy or emerging economy… ICT is as fundamental a piece of the world's business infrastructure as is electricity" (A. Uldridge, personal communication, October 17, 2012).

That core of IT, creativity to imagine new ideas and logic to make them work, will not go away. It is what will keep the changes coming. People are already starting to predict the new jobs that are plausibly just around the corner, such as "alternative reality architect" for wearable technology, "personality programmer" for AI helpers like Apple's Siri, "remote drone pilot" for peacetime purposes, and so on to more speculative jobs further into the future (Arnold-Smeets, 2013a).

THE APPLE EFFECT

Without a doubt Apple products and the "Apple Effect" in personal computing, publishing, imaging, video, audio and mobility have changed the landscape. In particular the iPhone has had a significant impact on society since its introduction in 2007, when it turned smartphones into must-have products. This is described by *The Economist* (2012) as "In the past 11 years Apple has launched three products—the iPod, iPhone and iPad—that have created brand new markets, fulfilling desires that consumers did not even know they had… It shows that the Internet has come of age. The dotcom bubble of the late 1990s featured companies that were heavy on ideas but light on revenues or profits. When the bubble burst a decade ago, it was feared that the Internet would savage margins by 'commoditising' devices like phones and personal computers. Apple has so far proved that it is possible to earn high margins with brilliant design and by offering consumers ways to access the Internet effortlessly wherever they go. It has made the mobile era its own... The company is a huge beneficiary of globalisation: able not only to source its products at low cost in Asia but to sell the finished goods there as well." As described by Cave (2012), "Tablets and smartphones are the definitive accessory… and each new Apple product launch causes a quasi-religious frenzy in consumers and journalists alike… What's more, the 'Apple effect' is starting to touch other companies and products in the space." Apple's success has challenged the industry to react and there are many new developments mapping to Apple-style technologies of mobility and user-centred design.

It is this rapid change in smartphone devices and consumer patterns that was the beginning of our current mobile, dynamic, social revolution, and Apple is at the centre of technology's largest revolution ever. That revolution is highlighted above by The Institute for the Future and is reflected in KPMG's *2012 Technology Innovation Survey*, which states that "we are in a brave new global tech era. The cycle of technology innovation is speeding up, and new technologies are transforming a variety of sectors in ways that could not have been imagined even a couple of years ago. As a result, technology companies face a constant stream of change in their business and operating models. As the cloud and mobile continue to become the technology platforms for a number of industries, new business models and incremental disruptions in enterprise and consumer markets will continue to be a major trend to watch. Innovations are transforming a variety of sectors in unforeseen ways in this switched-on era: smartphones, tablets, social networking, digital media, mobile commerce and the ubiquitous cloud. All are shaking up our lifestyles and workplaces" (Matuszak & Lamoureux, 2012). This view is supported by Deloitte (2013), who explain, "Disruption used to happen occasionally… then along came the Internet… and bang everything changed… Technology has created a state of perpetual revolution, digital disruption explodes the status quo… and blurs category boundaries… pushes a business into new dimensions while questioning its very survival."

The Apple Effect is just one example of the wider phenomenon of "Digital Disruption." Reimer (2013) points out that digital disruption "can be seen as both a threat and an opportunity:

- ICT-induced change happens at a pace and scale that impacts on existing business practice in disruptive ways, threatening and invalidating existing business models.
- Digital technologies offer new opportunities for the creation of innovative business models for entrepreneurs to compete with established business practices in a wide range of industries."

Reimer (2013) further explains "Digital Disruption can occur on various levels:

- Disruptions to individual life practices (example: Mobile connectivity disrupts established work-life boundaries)
- Disruptions to work practices (example: Narrating work via microblogging in the workplace changes what counts as (valuable) work)
- Disruptions to business practices (example: Workplace social media disrupts the

way information travels in the organisation and induces shifts in power relationships)
- Disruptions to industry structures (example: Digitisation of media content and user-generated content disrupts traditional value chains of content production and delivery)
- Disruptions to societal systems (example: Social media participation disrupts traditional practices of public opinion making)."

Or as Sorman-Nilsson (2013) puts it, "Digital Disruption is having an enormous impact on business. It is a type of creative destruction which opens up the way for nimble start-ups and lowers the barriers to entry, while simultaneously destroying industry behemoths and incumbents. It is a democratising force, yet at the same time it threatens heritage, tradition, and old school business models."

These factors do not only apply to business, but to anyone wishing to accomplish something in the world. It is equally applicable to the topic at hand. Digital disruption could be viewed as a threat to traditional models, but more than that it presents an open window of opportunity. We can harness the changing technology landscape to assist with recruitment, promotion and retention strategies, applying the new rules of operating within the #SocialIT era. What McQuivey (2013) says about business is just as relevant to the cause of women in IT: "Digital disruption is not only *a* possibility for your company's future but the *only* possibility. Once you accept that premise, decisions that previously seemed courageous or outrageous will instead appear to be rational and inevitable… The only way to compete is to evolve."

BIG DATA MINING

The #SocialIT layer in the STEMcell Model proposes tapping into the shifting technological landscape and actively using its tools and platforms in the development of future programs, projects and activities. This has the potential for significant change in the processes adopted and their outcomes. An example is "big data."

A side effect of the advances in IT and elsewhere has been an explosion in the amount of data available for analysis – and one application of IT has been finding new ways to analyse it. Two signals of what is coming were presented by Bradley Kreit from The Institute for the Future when he:

1. Highlighted Foldit. For many years researchers had been grinding away at a long-standing AIDS protein-folding problem, then within two weeks of the release of the Tetris-style game Foldit the issue was solved (Bansal, 2011; Levine, 2011). Results were published recognising the multitude of co-authors (Khatib, et al., 2011). "Despite using advanced crystallography technology, scientists at the University of Washington kept encountering roadblocks while trying to discern the protein's structure. This led them, in a self-proclaimed last ditch effort, to begin an online protein folding competition. They offered several potential molecular structures on Foldit's 3-D interface, and then asked players to tweak them so that, just as in real life, they emitted the lowest possible energy… This development has huge implications for the future of crowdsourcing, or of using large groups to perform tasks typically done by individuals. In this case, gamers applied critical reasoning and spatial intelligence to a problem traditionally dominated by subject matter experts" (Bansal, 2011).
2. Discussed an analysis of malaria and how, playing a computer game with minimal training, "random folks" were able to aggregate results and analyze malaria cells to 99% accuracy, comparable to trained experts (Elmaghraby, 2013). "The no-cost game can be played by anyone around the world who has access to a computing device, such as a smartphone or a personal computer. Before

the game, players receive a brief online tutorial that uses sample images to explain what a malaria-infected red blood cell looks like. During the game, players view a screen containing several digital images of healthy and infected red blood cells. The players then use a 'syringe' tool to 'kill' the infected cells. They found that the nonexperts collectively were able to diagnose malaria-infected red blood cells with an accuracy that was within 1.25% of the diagnostic decisions made by trained medical professionals. Aydogan Ozcan – an associate professor of electrical engineering and bioengineering at UCLA and author of the study – said, 'The idea is, if you carefully combine the decisions of people – even nonexperts – they become very competitive… Also, if you just look at one person's response, it may be OK, but that one person will inevitably make some mistakes. But if you combine 10 to 20, maybe 50 non expert gamers together, you improve your accuracy greatly in terms of analysis'" (Kreit 2012).

Instead of "big data," The Institute for the Future has renamed it "abundant data": instead of implying a problem, stressing it contains interesting, valuable information that can be put to use. Whatever we call it, the years of research and interventions into women in IT has certainly accumulated it. Imagine having the opportunity to take that "abundant data" of historical women in technology research and intervention program information and tap into it. Why wait for years to mine this data for what we need to know, or as we currently stand perhaps never at all, when we could start looking at better ways to analyse it now? Instead of leaving those decades of global research unread and undervalued, perhaps with #SocialIT we can actively visualise that data, making practical, applicable sense of what is otherwise cumbersome and seemingly disconnected data flows. Perhaps we can find a way to not only release the data in accessible form but also apply the concepts of microwork and results aggregation to it. Use the tools of our trade, so to speak, and stop the guesswork and band-aid measures: to hack to the core and visually see the connections.

AUGMENTED REALITY

One possible way we will see those connections is via augmented reality and wearable technologies. We have had augmented reality technology for years and are now beginning to experience overlay data through wearable technology devices such as Google Glass. But that is just the start of this new disruptive technology, as described by Farber (2013): "Reality isn't what it used to be. With increasingly powerful technologies, the human universe is being reimagined way beyond Google Glass' photo-tapping and info cards floating in space above your eye. The future is fashionable eyewear, contact lenses or even bionic eyes with immersive 3D displays, conjuring up a digital layer to 'augment' reality, enabling entire new classes of applications and user experiences. Like most technologies that eventually reach a mass market, augmented reality, or AR, has been gestating in university labs, as well as small companies focused on gaming and vertical applications, for nearly half a century. Emerging products like Google Glass and Oculus Rift's 3D virtual reality headset for immersive gaming are drawing attention to what could now be termed the 'wearable revolution,' but they barely scratch the surface of what's to come… Augmented reality will bring to the world things beyond the graphical user interface. With sensors, computational power, storage and bandwidth, we'll see the world in a new way and make it very personal… Eventually, wearable technology will become more integrated with the human body. With advances in miniaturization and nanotechnology glasswear will be replaced with contact lens or even bionic eyes that record everything, make phone calls and allow you to use parts of your body, or even your thoughts, to navigate the world."

The future potential for development in the area of wearable devices is massive and can be expected to affect a broad range of fields. This is potentially interesting and attractive to women, not only in itself but also because of how it will assist fields traditionally attractive to women such as disabilities, health and education. Heussner (2013) flags a range of wearable devices: "Venture capitalists have been funding all kinds of wearable devices – from activity-tracking wristbands to brain-sensing headbands to armbands that let people control computers with gestures... describing it as the door to a brave new world of products and possibility."

Millar (2013) indicates how broadly this will affect the workplace, from the health industry to jobs not normally associated with heavy IT use such as forklift drivers and manual workers. "Imagine the man fixing the boiler. He is lying under a heavy device and he needs his hands, but he can still be in a computing environment. Take a sales person walking into a client's office; they might be able to access instant information in front of their eyes. 'What was the last order this company placed? Are they happy with us?' Even 'when was the client's last birthday?'... Someone driving a forklift in a warehouse can't use a PC or smartphone because they will crash into someone. But imagine if they can drive around and be able to pinpoint a pallet and then the particular box they need on that pallet" (Millar, 2013).

A theme of this book is the centrality of the individual, and augmented reality is very much about personalisation: about understanding the individual and personalising the response for the individual's interests and convenience. Skipworth (2013) discusses his experience with Google Glass as "Hands down one of the most exciting pieces of technology out there, it felt more exciting to us than picking up a new iPhone for the first time... It is likely that wearable technology will dictate gadgetry in the coming years... It's all about convenience. Wearable technology does away with the traditional need to interact with a smartphone or tablet screen, instead making the way we use the Web a more seamless experience. Google Glass does just that. The more someone uses it, the more they will become accustomed to having Internet access in the top right corner of their line of sight. It's a strange thing being able to do a Google search via your peripheral vision... This was technology at its cutting edge and something that, despite being likely a good few years away from reaching the mainstream, could become intrinsic to our everyday lives."

As noted in Chapter Three: *A New Approach*, The STEMcell Model and #SocialIT is about the new rules of operating in the #SocialEra. It is about tapping into the methods and rules of a new era and a new generation, and not bringing to it the overlays and viewpoints of the old era. In that context a salient point is made Farbar (2013), who reports "'Anyone reviewing devices like Google Glass needs to take it to their kids' school before they pass judgement,' Lorenzini (Dave Lorenzini, founder of AugmentedRealityCompany.com and former director at Keyhole.com, now known as Google Earth) added. 'This is not a device from our time, it's from theirs. They love it, use it effortlessly, and are totally unfazed by ad targeting or privacy concerns. It will be a natural part of who they are, how they learn, connect and play.'"

THERE'S AN APP FOR THAT

It is indeed a brave new world and one full of disruptive new devices and apps. Chapter Three: *A New Approach* provided recent examples of technology-enabled disruption in Egypt and the Pacific Islands. Another example is the rapid uptake of mobile payments in Africa: "East Africa is the cradle of the continent's mobile-money revolution. The three countries fill the top spots in a Gallup survey of domestic remittances via mobile phones in Africa. Mobile operators are credited with stimulating growth by helping money in the informal sector flow to the rest of the economy. Some 17m of Kenya's 19m adults are signed up to M-PESA. Cash equivalent to nearly one-third of Kenya's GDP washes through the service" (The Economist, 2013; World Bank, 2009).

These changes and others are explained by Matuszak et al. (2012), who report "Mobile and the cloud lead as most disruptive technologies of the future; the two combined will magnify the transformation of business models and many industry ecosystems around the world... Innovations are transforming a variety of sectors in unforeseen ways in this switched-on era: smartphones, tablets, social networking, digital media, mobile commerce and the ubiquitous cloud. All are shaking up our lifestyles and workplaces. We are moving to a new cycle of convergence and connectivity, led by cloud and the mobile Internet. This trend will continue to change our lifestyles, buying habits and business practices in ways that could not have been foreseen just a couple of years ago. The brisk pace of technology innovations – including mobile devices and apps, social networking and cloud – indicate a need to constantly assess the business implications of disruptive technologies. Countries that were never part of the technology innovation map are taking center stage. Tech innovative companies Apple, Google, Facebook, Microsoft, Amazon and Samsung are being joined by upstarts from emerging economies such as Tencent and Baidu from China and Yandex from Russia. Visionary technologists like Masayoshi Son from Japan and Jack Ma from China are getting in the headlines... Innovation is unfolding in other parts of the world. China, in particular, is investing to be on par with Silicon Valley. The US is respected as the world's technology innovation center, but as technology innovation becomes more global other countries are gaining momentum to become technology innovation leaders."

Gorbis (2012) explains how "new technologies are giving individuals so much power to connect and share resources that networks of individuals—not big organizations—will solve a host of problems by reinventing business, education, medicine, banking, government, and scientific research... In a time of rapid innovation, signals of change are all around us. The challenge is to see the big future trends that emerge from these weak signals. To discern these larger patterns, we need frameworks. These frameworks help us collate and categorize signals. For example, a recent *Catalysts for Change* project for the Rockefeller Foundation used a four-catalyst framework of new evidence, new capacities, new rules, and new stories. Another, *Internet human|human Internet*, developed a framework of four Internet capacities—to flow, to sense, to control, and to emerge—to interpret the multitude of signals that are likely to shape the future relationship between this vast technological network and its users. These kinds of frameworks and the signals that bring them to life can be used to create maps that make sense out complex horizons of human, technological, and environmental futures. New media tools pave the way to allow engagement of experts and non experts and to envision the future and solutions." Gorbis (2012) outlines ways to do this via "Create maps that communicate the patterns and connections in complex systems... Develop the foresight required to reveal the insights that allow for strategic action, both now and in the coming decades of disruption and uncertainty... These are unchartered waters open to creativity, innovation and entirely new ways of working, interacting and learning that should appeal to women and men alike. They require us to imagine new ways that the familiar objects of our daily life will be reinvented to adapt to futures that may be entirely unfamiliar. It's this dissonance between the familiar and the unexpected that opens our minds to possibilities we have only begun to envision."

Another person who sees this social future is Merchant (2010; also see Chapter Three: *A New Approach*), who explains the "New How" as how organisations can transform their traditional, top-down strategy planning and execution into a collaborative "stratecution." After many years of working with Apple, Adobe, HP, and many other companies, Merchant discovered the best way to create a winning strategy is to include employees at all levels, helping to create strategy they not only believe in but are also equipped to implement. She identifies that "business strategy typically has been planned by corporate chiefs in annual meetings, and then dictated to managers to carry out. *The New How* turns that notion on its head." Merchant (2010) contrasts the collaborative approach to the traditional "air sandwich" (where strategy was the top layer of bread and those told to carry it out were the bottom layer, but all the good stuff in the middle was not defined or aligned). She also discusses murderboarding as a counterbalance to whiteboarding: a way to prune ideas in order to focus on the key essential points in which a key assumption is that the future is not created, it is co-created. Such collaborative efforts in which all individuals involved have a say are part and parcel of the mobility, self-evolution and interconnectedness of #SocialIT.

The new social phenomena are also opening up opportunities or new interests for women in particular. As Porter (2011) said, "Though the cult-like world of gaming is often closely associated with computer science, there's a chance that social-media technology like Facebook which offer clearer opportunities for social impact, might have the effect of attracting more women to the field." The world of apps is also more accessible to women than the old world of obsessed hackers or male-dominated software companies. While app development is still primarily male, Meyer (2013) argues that women are too important an audience to ignore and not only do their interests demand new apps but it is relatively easy to create them once you perceive a demand. "I recently interviewed a female app creator named Carla White. Carla broke into the app scene with 'Gratitude Journal.' She had started journaling what she was grateful for after the passing of a relative, and she realized there had to be an easier way to do it. She wanted to share her experience with others and created the gratitude app. She had zero technical experience, yet she created an app that quickly rose to #1 on the lifestyle section of the Apple App Store and was even featured by Oprah Winfrey. The lesson of Carla's story is that you don't have to be tech-minded to create an app. Carla has now written a book that teaches anyone how to take a concept from 'Idea to iPhone.' Her story proves that you can create a successful app that can reap great results" (Meyer, 2013).

CROWDSOURCING

I call it #SocialIT, Papworth (2011) has "seven levels to reach people powered social media engagement," Merchant calls it "stratecution," Scoble & Israel (2013) describe it as Age of Context and Gorbis (2013) describes "Socialstructing," which is "combining initiative, passion, social connections, and the drive to build new things outside of existing institutions, ultimately with more flexible and resilient results."

Gorbis' book is summarised as providing examples of "new opportunities to create, learn, and share in this world. She also tells personal stories about these social innovators, who come together in meetups, salons, hackathons, live/work houses, clubs, and many other places that cross traditional organizational and discipline boundaries. They don't ask for permission and are often not paid for their efforts, at least not with money. They are less interested in technologies per se than in playing with established ways of doing things and conventional ways of thinking, creating, learning, and being... She outlines how individuals are socialstructing by filling gaps—doing things that previously only large institutions could do to create products and services—more efficiently and with greater ease and access than ever before. She provides practical advice based on her research for those wanting to navigate and effectively participate in this world. And she describes new kinds of network roles that are proving critical to our present and our future, such as experts, who trigger content; brokers, who trigger connection to ideas; coders, who understand new technologies and platforms; and edge surfers, who test boundaries and push the limits of networks… She describes amplified individuals who are empowered by technology and are using social connections to change the way we work, solve problems, and create value today" (Gorbis, 2013).

Crowdsourcing is basically a way to leverage the globe-spanning networks of communications and social media to perform tasks beyond the ability of the individual or even companies; a way to bring a large number of people, mostly strangers, together to achieve a shared goal.

Papworth's (2011) Stage 6: Collaborative Social Media, and Stage 7: People Powered Social Media, are of particular interest to #SocialIT. Stage 6: Collaborative Social Media is described as "the Company puts out a request – please help us design a product, please tell us how we can do XYZ better, please create an advertisement for us. The impetus may not have arisen out of the social network (it probably came from the marketing department) but it's thrown open to the online community. Or the idea came from the community but the company decided how to structure and monitor the responses. They then gave 'permission' for the community to create content around those ideas." Whilst Stage 7: People Powered Social Media is described as "Imagine a bank where the person wanting a loan puts up the request and the community analyses and responds with the interest rate and a couple of thousand members put up a dollar or two each. How much is the bank involved with producing the products and services? Or are they simply providing the social space for online community commerce to continue? That is what Prosper (prosper.com) and Zopa (uk.zopa.com) and others do. Imagine something similar for dress makers and designers and jewellers to create and transact in their vertical. That's Etsy. Artists? Redbubble. Imagine a recruitment company that allowed members to put up a job and for other members to bid on it. That's Freelancer.com, Guru.com, elance.com. You get the idea. Put up the platform then stand back and let the community do commerce. You get a clip of every sale and solve some tough problems for them (including matchmaking the one with the need to the one with the solution)."

The theme of action through social media runs through comments gained via personal interviews as well. For example, Ann Uldridge (personal communication, October 17, 2012), long time industry participant and ex-president of Women in Technology (Queensland) comments, "The power of social media to organise and empower individuals and groups is in its infancy. If we can articulate the nature of the challenge, develop a vision and an action plan, then maybe we can self-organise to start a groundswell. Where we go – the rest of the country may follow." And this from Madeleine Sanders (personal communication, August 12, 2013), co-founder of Women are IT (Victoria, South Australia, Western Australia) founding board member Australian Women in IT, Science and Engineering (AWISE): "Continue role model programs but with less expensive face to face programs and more cost-effective new social media (Facebook, Twitter) and invest in informational websites to get the message out somehow, not just to the girls themselves, but perhaps more critically, to their parents and to their teachers who remain close influencers." And Jenny Beresford (personal communication, August 7, 2013), CIO, thinks, "Social media just dramatically expands the audience and the participants in interventions and social change. This is, after all, political. The Gender (as in Arab) Spring can potentially kick-start in social media too… The breakthrough to attracting more females to STEM and ICT will come, in my opinion, from deliberate marketing and branding re-design efforts, to emphasise that (a) ICT has changed the world and (we) created the Internet, broadband, wireless, mobile devices, social media, and all that comes with it – the 'sexy' side of ICT from Google Glass to 3D printing – that it's powerful and creative and fast moving. Plus we need to promote the financial aspects – you can make an extremely good income – and that in turn gives you economic freedom and choices, to travel, to hire staff/nannies/help, to work from home, or just to have the things you love from shoes to Porsches to ???"

Beresford, Sanders, Uldridge, Gorbis, Scoble, Merchant and Papworth point to a pathway for resolving the "problem" of recruitment, promotion and retention of women in technology. It is moving the solution beyond traditional strategies, interventions and organizations to using existing and future technologies to co-create, via meetups, crowdsourcing and "hack the way through."

Tapping into the crowd by crowdsourcing for data, ideas and funding is one of those pathways worth a more detailed look. Crowdsourcing was originally termed in 2005 by editors at *Wired Magazine* and may be applied to specific requests such as crowdfunding (Wikipedia, 2013b). (Given that the existence and ongoing growth of Wikipedia is due to crowdsourced activities, it seems entirely appropriate to reference them here.)

There is an increasing number of crowdsourcing activities that span a broad range of areas. The crowd sourced does not even have to be aware they are part of the crowd. Some examples are:

- **Neal (2013):** "a tool called nEmesis, which scans millions of tweets from GPS-enabled mobile devices. The system looks for people reporting food poisoning symptoms following a restaurant visit, aggregating the data into a map of risky places to eat… Here's the gist. The tool 'listens to' millions of tweets and watches for keywords that could indicate that someone's Chinese food dinner didn't go over well—'threw up,' 'so sick omg,' 'ughhh cramps,' and that kind of thing. It then geo-locates the tweets (the ones that publish GPS data, at least) and compares that to Google Map locations of nearby restaurants that the person could have been visiting. To account for the fact that someone could tweet from a restaurant at 8 PM and at again at midnight from the bathroom floor, the tool opens up a separate data collection process that listens for new tweets from each person after they dine."
- **Merz (2013):** "WeatherSignal, a mobile app that is designed to take advantage of the potential of smartphones in meteorology... uses functions already present in smartphones to monitor light, magnetism, pressure and other conditions in order to build up a real-time weather map… With a hundred thousand people in a single city using this app, we would have a picture of the weather of unprecedented detail… Changes in light would allow the tracking of single clouds and historic data would enable precise modelling of the urban heat island effect."
- **Lynch (2013):** Outlined ten Australian crowdsourcing projects from 2012. They include marketing campaigns of major organisations (Qantas and Colgate), a political campaign, football club colours, TV show participation and voting, photography contests, Google Australia Day logo, Amnesty international T-shirt design and a car design competition.

Crowdsourcing projects have been so successful that to support their growth a number of platforms have sprung up and will no doubt continue to do so. Some well known ones are Kickstarter.com (a general crowdfunding platform that caters to various niches and is known for giving support to its users from start to finish; the project creator cannot claim the raised funds if the goal is not reached); Kiva.com (offers donation-based peer to peer lending without any interest rate charges) and IndieGoGo.com (a funding platform to open up projects to potential funders).

An interesting variant on crowdsourcing is crowdsourcing of ideas and solutions to problems. On a large scale we see this in the X PRIZE series, which offers large sums of money to the first to reach a set milestone in a major technological advance in fields such as space travel and life sciences (X Prize Foundation, 2013). A larger range of smaller incentives is available on the *Open Innovation Pavilion*, offering prizes anywhere from $5,000 to $1M for an invention or an idea (depending on the particular challenge) that meets the challenge criteria (Scientific American, 2013). Another example combines crowdsourcing with Big Data: the 2013 Geoffrey Beene Global Neuro Discovery Challenge offered $100,000 in prizes to encourage multidisciplinary teams to analyze public datasets on Alzheimer's Disease in order "to leverage large sets of clinical data and novel analytical approaches" (Comer, Freire & Russell, 2013).

The key point is crowdsourcing and crowdfunding of projects is almost commonplace now and should seriously be part of the equation for future women in IT recruitment, promotion and retention strategies. One interesting existing example from the related field of engineering is GoldieBlox, an "engineering toy for girls" which is like a poster child for the #SocialIT model, having raised its funding through Kickstarter and been sent on its way to success by "going viral" (Sterling, 2012). The motive behind the GoldieBlox story will sound familiar to many readers of this book: "GoldieBlox, Inc. is a toy company founded in 2012 by Debbie Sterling, a female engineer from Stanford University. Engineers are solving some of the biggest challenges our society faces. They are critical to the world economy, earn higher salaries and have greater job security. And they are 89% male. We believe engineers can't responsibly build our world's future without the female perspective. GoldieBlox offers a much-needed female engineer role model who is smart, curious and accessible. She has the potential to get girls interested in engineering, develop their spatial skills and build self-confidence in their problem solving abilities. This means that GoldieBlox will nurture a generation of girls who are more confident, courageous and tech-savvy, giving them a real opportunity to contribute to the progress made by engineers in our society. It's 2013. It's about time we opened our girls' minds beyond the pink aisle at the toy store. It's time to build a new story so our girls can help build our future" (CrunchBase, 2013). Where it differs is that it did not take years of research or pleading for grants to fund interventions. It took one bright mind with a good idea, the tools of #SocialIT – and some luck. Whether it will achieve its aim of increasing the number of female engineers remains to be seen. But it will certainly reach – or ignite – the interest of young girls around the world.

NANO AND MICRO GENERATIONS

The pace of change is now so fast that even the old "generation gap" is becoming fractured into differences between children only a few years apart in age.

Koschel (2013) raised some interesting points regarding this and the impacts on individuals within generations. "On the Internet, things change *fast*. What's popular one day may be gone the next. Remember when everyone was playing DrawSomething? Or when MySpace was the dominant social network? The cycle has grown so predictable that some analysts begin ringing death knells within days of a successful product launch. The quick-moving nature of the digital world means that younger users come of age in a vastly different media environment than those who were born just a few years apart... We've tied up so much of the human experience in transient things that generation gaps now occur closer and closer. Even kids two years apart will have grown up in completely different media environments: A middle schooler who spends much of their time on Tumblr speaks a different language than a high schooler who uses mostly Facebook. Throughout most of our history, technological shifts have happened gradually and without much perceptible cultural disruption. Even an event as massive as the invention of the automobile didn't cause cultural alienation — those who hadn't been in a car could still understand the basic concept… On the other hand, try explaining Facebook to someone who's never used a computer and you'll have a much harder time. The generational divide between my grandma and I, born about 60 years apart, is vaster than that between a citizen of the Roman Republic and a farm labourer in 15th-century Britain… We should avoid falling into the classic Whippersnapper/Old-Fogey Syndrome. It's natural for the older generations to yearn for the media environment of their youth, and for the younger to assume that their environment is superior due to sheer newness."

This view on different experiences across micro generations is reflected by Stone (2010) who, when discussing his then 2 year old daughter, says "My daughter and her peers will never be off the grid…My daughter's worldview and life will be shaped in very deliberate ways by technologies like the Kindle and the new magical high-tech gadgets coming out this year —Google's Nexus One phone and Apple's impending tablet among them. She'll know nothing other than a world with digital books, Skype video chats with faraway relatives, and toddler-friendly video games on the iPhone. She'll see the world a lot differently from her parents. But these are also technology tools that children even 10 years older did not grow up with, and I've begun to think that my daughter's generation will also be utterly unlike those that preceded it. Researchers are exploring this notion too. They theorize that the ever-accelerating pace of technological change may be minting a series of mini-generation gaps, with each group of children uniquely influenced by the tech tools available in their formative stages of development… One obvious result is that younger generations are going to have some very peculiar and unique expectations about the world. My friend's 3-year-old, for example, has become so accustomed to her father's multitouch iPhone screen that she approaches laptops by swiping her fingers across the screen, expecting a reaction… These mini-generation gaps are most visible in the communication and entertainment choices made by different age groups… Now in their 20s, those in the Net Generation, according to Dr. Rosen (Larry Rosen, a professor of psychology at California State University), spend two hours a day talking on the phone and still use e-mail frequently. The iGeneration — conceivably their younger siblings — spends considerably more time texting than talking on the phone, pays less attention to television than the older group and tends to communicate more over instant-messenger networks. Dr. Rosen said that the newest generations, unlike their older peers, will expect an instant response from everyone they communicate with, and won't have the patience for anything less. 'They'll want their teachers and professors to respond to them immediately, and they will expect instantaneous access to everyone, because after all, that is the experience they have growing up.'"

The major implication from this is that each micro generation is likely to have different experiences and expectations that have evolved as a result of #SocialIT and its future evolution. Whilst the trend toward ever more user-friendliness and personalisation can be expected to make future technologies increasingly accessible to everyone, the same trends will make it easier to adapt and extend the already known and familiar. Whether this leads to increasing fragmentation or instead homogenisation remains to be seen. But what is sure is that whatever is created within #SocialIT by its nature will be a moving force that will affect everyone at the individual and micro-generational level.

LIFE EXTENSION

Woody Allen famously once said, "I don't want to achieve immortality through my work. I want to achieve it through not dying." People usually consider life extension a futuristic technology, not relevant in the short term. However I propose that the impending prospect of living longer ought to be factored in when considering how to resolve the issue of attraction, promotion and retention of women in technology.

Up until now, life expectancy increases have mainly been from reducing early deaths rather than extending achievable lifespan. As outlined by Waldman (2013), "life expectancy has increased dramatically in the last century, but that's mostly because we keep doing a better and better job at preventing and treating the things that kill people when they're relatively young… Modern medicine has allowed us to live to the point where we can die of the diseases of old age, like heart disease, cancer and Alzheimer's. But the upper limit of human life span—around 120—hasn't budged in pretty much forever, and it's still reached by only a few people who seem blessed with some spectacular combination of genetics and luck."

However, even if maximum lifespan is not moving, more and more people are staying active and healthy substantially after "retirement age," so much so that governments are now moving towards increasing the retirement age to reflect the realities that imposes (e.g. Commonwealth of Australia, 2011). Similarly, reporting on the work of demographer Sanjeev Sanyal, Pethokoukis (2013) notes the societal shifts coming by increasing our active years: "With people routinely living well into their eighties, it will soon be common for people to extend their working life into their mid-seventies … Societies that cannot make the socio-political adjustment to this new reality will struggle in the 21st century and will unduly burden the shrinking base of young people entering the workforce… Thus, the main impact of aging will be the extension of active, working adulthood rather than a situation where large portions of the population are living in a prolonged geriatric twilight. In turn, this will impact consumption patterns, urban real estate and even the education system. For instance, university systems will have to be reoriented to deal with middle-aged workers who need to update their skills over a 50-year career or perhaps want to completely change their profession. In contrast, the intake of younger cohorts will ease off due to the shrinking pipeline coming out of secondary schools. This implies a big change in the way education systems are set up."

But the extension of active life is just the start. The rapid progress of technology is not confined to IT. Scientific and technological developments in other areas (often assisted by IT, as in "big data") are making substantial life extension an imminent goal. "Most of the evidence regarding genetic modification of aging and life span has been collected in the last 15 to 20 years. The results have produced a paradigm shift in the research community: The old view that aging and life span is too complicated to study has been replaced by a new and more optimistic view that the underlying processes can be dissected, analyzed, and modulated using genetic techniques" (Curtsinger, 2007).

That paradigm shift is expressed by Siegel (2013) as: "Inside the center or nucleus of a cell, our genes are located on twisted, double-stranded molecules of DNA called chromosomes. At the ends of the chromosomes are stretches of DNA called telomeres, which protect our genetic data, make it possible for cells to divide, and hold some secrets to how we age and get cancer. Telomeres have been compared with the plastic tips on shoelaces because they prevent chromosome ends from fraying and sticking to each other, which would scramble an organism's genetic information to cause cancer, other diseases or death. Yet, each time a cell divides, the telomeres get shorter. When they get too short, the cell no longer can divide and becomes inactive or 'senescent' or dies. This process is associated with aging, cancer and a higher risk of death. So telomeres also have been compared with a bomb fuse… if all processes of aging could be eliminated and oxidative stress damage could be repaired, 'one estimate is people could live 1,000 years'. Aubrey de Grey believes that the first people to live to be 1,000 have already been born (de Grey, 2009; Duncan, 2012)."

Along similar lines Keith (2009) notes, "The field is not new – anti-oxidation strategies for preventing cell aging have been proposed since at least the late 1950s. It is growing rapidly, however. There is now an International Association of Biomedical Gerontology (IABG) which has been holding annual conferences on life-extension technology for 15 years… The figurehead of the scientific longevity movement – active in research but more active in cheerleading his fellow researchers – is Aubrey de Grey of Cambridge University and the IABG. de Grey, the architect of the 'SENS (Strategies for Engineered Negligible Senescence)' movement thinks the technical challenges it presents will be met faster than critics expect… Taking a longer view, technology visionary Ray Kurzweil and longevity specialist Terry Grossman see a multi-stage procession from current, groping efforts to full control of aging and debility – what they describe as three 'bridges' to an immortal future. The first 'bridge' is life extension using the best available knowledge, to allow the current generation to last long enough to be on hand when true control of aging is finally achieved. The second bridge takes those alive at that time through the process of aging control and the revision of all life-threatening disease or degenerative processes. This would represent 'immortality' in a limited sense." As for how long this progression will take, de Grey (2009) describes a graph of doubling the efficacy of life extension research only every 42 years as "ridiculously pessimistic, it is most extraordinarily cautious… It is completely ludicrous to suggest that progress would be this slow, and yet it is still good enough to deliver longevity… It is completely inescapable that we will with the most ludicrously high probability have a genuine indefinite life span as a result of breakthroughs of what is termed at first sight to a rather modest scale, something like a couple of decades of additional life conferred on the middle age."

In addition to the unsolved scientific problems are political and perception issues. As Millar (2002) points out, "From many fronts, there is now incontrovertible evidence that aging in mammals can be decelerated and that it is not too difficult to do this… the obstacles blocking the development of the hypothetical discipline of applied gerontology are at this point about 85 percent political and 15 percent scientific, and they will not be overcome by biologists alone." Keith (2009) notes "In among the cautious engineers, sober biologists, and technologically-savvy visionaries, however, the life-extension field is rife with dreamers who range from outright cranks and opportunists to more influential figures whose intentions, and apparently sincere expectations, can give pause to the most sanguine futurist… The industry also suffers from its unwelcome association with quack medicine peddlers and scam artists who prey on the gullibility of a scientifically ignorant public, raising false hopes while touting worthless products. Fad therapies and snake-oil have flooded the 'alternative medicine' market, embarrassing researchers who do not want serious science associated with such schemes and who are afraid that funding and public acceptance for their work will be hampered by the sideshow excesses that accompany it."

But whatever critics and quacks there might be, the fact is that scientific knowledge related to life extension has grown enormously and continues to do so. The growth in knowledge so far has been exponential and there are reasons to think that will continue, though it is complicated by the differences between mature and new fields and other factors (Goodstein, 1994; He & Zhang, 2009; Tague, Beheshti & Rees-Potter, 1981). But it is no longer wildly optimistic or unrealistic to say we are already looking at a real prospect of substantially extended life spans. That could turn any solution to attracting more women into technology on its head.

The world we are heading into is going to be very different. Not only are traditional career, retirement, and social security expectations not going exist in any recognisable form, but even families will be redefined. People will marry, divorce and remarry multiple times across decades and centuries, a concept that was almost unthinkable for many from a previous time. People's perspectives will shift. As Keith (2009) comments, "What will change, if significant life-extension is achieved, is its immediacy. Generation will succeed generation as before, but with centuries, perhaps, between them; one's acquaintances will pass away as their allotted time closes, but once a decade, maybe, or once a century. Death as a near and present danger will recede."

The traditional concepts of education and career must dramatically shift too. The current concept of formal schooling from childhood to teenage years followed by tertiary education will become inapplicable. However children are educated, people are likely to have multiple careers throughout their extended adult lives, and reskilling at a variety of ages would become the norm. You're 70 and always wished you'd had a career in technology, you have decades of healthy life ahead of you and your wits are as sharp as any 20-year-old – but with the experience of decades behind you? What would stop you doing it now? Even if there were still a desire for interventions, the targets, messages and materials would be transformed. And as Pethokoukis (2013) notes, that trend is already beginning.

#ANTI-SOCIALIT?

Given the potentially transformative effect of technology in terms of what we can discover and the networks we can form, it is interesting that the rise of the Internet has actually been blamed for increasing the gap between men and women in IT.

Based on correlations between Internet use and female participation in IT degrees, Andres-Beck (2012) argues that the Internet itself is turning women off. Her proposed explanations are that "Internet culture supports a belief in a meritocratic environment, which has been linked, ironically, to an increase in biased behaviour as it provides moral cover for prejudiced beliefs. Encountering overt, covert or benevolent sexism undermines both women's performance and interest" and "the Internet encourages a sense of belonging to the masculinised culture of software development, which alienates many women by causing them to feel excluded from a camaraderie-focused profession."

I find such arguments very "no win is possible" and quite demeaning to women. Meritocracy is bad because it hides worse prejudice; women run away at any sign of covert or even benevolent "sexism"; men's camaraderie chases them away? Are girls and women really that pathetic? Whatever happened to "I am woman, hear me roar!" (Reddy, 1975)? Fortunately surveys of the actual girls and women interested in STEM indicate quite the opposite.

It is relevant that Andres-Beck dismisses the possibility that women are simply choosing for their own reasons: "I would caution against considering this support for any hypothesis relying on generalizations about the characteristics of women as a group, as the literature does not support gender as a distinguishing factor in career interest, skill or motivation. Instead, the evidence suggests we should be looking to cultural factors amplified by the Internet that affect those identified by others as women, since the one thing women have in common is being perceived as female by members of the community." The one thing women have in common is being *perceived as* female? Surely that is perceiving them as what they actually are.

As it directly addresses the thesis of this book, it is worth examining Andres-Beck's claim that the literature does not support gender as a relevant factor in career interest or motivation. That claim references Quesenberry & Trauth (2008), which addresses generic factors such as competence, challenge and security – not field-specific interest.

It is interesting that Andres-Beck (2012) concludes that "The one thing this correlation does imply is that programs to expose girls and young women to technology wouldn't be effective at boosting the number of women entering software development. In fact, they might be counterproductive if they lead to earlier encounters with the existing occupational culture. Basically, free samples only boost sales of products people find enjoyable and we are therefore unlikely to solve these problems by writing off the experiences of the current generation and placing all our chips on the next." I agree with her conclusion but for quite different reasons. Exposing girls to technology will not draw them into IT careers if they are not fundamentally interested, no matter how much fun they have on the day.

LESSONS LEARNED

Obviously the prospect of life extension and its transformative effects on society remain speculative. But that is the point. The one thing we know about the future is that we don't know what it will be. Anything is possible – and the possible might be nothing we ever imagined. #SocialIT is not about predicting the future and planning a roadmap. Any roadmap will be out of date within a decade – or less. It is about recognising that the world is entering an era of disruptive technologies that will empower the individual in ways we cannot predict, that old power bases will crumble and new things arise.

From the perspective of increasing female participation in IT, we need to ask ourselves some hard questions. If you looked with fresh eyes at this issue today and saw the increasing influence of social media and tools; the organic growth of self help groups, projects and programs; ever more disruptive technologies coming online; and the increasing prospect of life extension: what would you do if starting now? Would you even perceive there was an "issue"? Would you feel there was a pressing need to take action to address "the problem"? The perception of a problem implies a need to interfere and artificially adjust what is happening naturally. Perhaps a peek into the future tells us that what is happening naturally is going to overtake anything we can plan based on the present, let alone the past.

#SocialIT is about pursuing passions, creating amazing things with others using existing, evolving and future technologies; it is about agilely adjusting to rapidly and ever changing circumstances. Or as Gorbis (2013) says, "combining initiative, passion, social connections, and the drive to build new things outside of existing institutions, ultimately with more flexible and resilient results."

This chapter completes our look at the layers within the STEMcell Model: the cultural, social, structural, individual and #SocialIT factors that drive career choice. In the next chapter we broaden our view by looking at other industries and cultures, to see what similarities and differences there are and how they can aid our understanding of the wider, and perhaps deeper, issues.

REFERENCES

Amabile, T. M., Conti, R., Coon, H., Lazenby, J., & Henon, M. (1996). Assessing the work environment for creativity. *Academy of Management Journal, 39*(5), 1154–1184. doi:10.2307/256995

Andres-Beck, B. (2012). *The internet is convincing women not to study computer science*. Retrieved August 28, 2013, from http://blog.bethcodes.com/is-the-internet-convincing-women-not-to-study

Aragon, D. (2013). *Manuel Castells*. Retrieved November 18, 2013, from http://prezi.com/3jnj_o_zmddl/manuel-castells/

Arnold-Smeets, L. (2013a, August 19). For the horde! 10 rad jobs of the future (infographic). *PayScale*. Retrieved August 30, 2013, from http://www.payscale.com/career-news/2013/08/for-the-horde!-10-rad-jobs-of-the-future-infographic-

Arnold-Smeets, L. (2013b, December 10). Data scientist: Sexiest job of the 21st century. *PayScale*. Retrieved December 13, 2013, from http://www.payscale.com/career-news/2013/12/data-scientist-sexiest-job-of-the-21st-century

Bansal, S. (2011, September 28). One point for crowdsourcing: Gamers solve protein structure of AIDS-like protein. *Forbes*. Retrieved August 13, 2013, from http://www.forbes.com/sites/sarikabansal/2011/09/28/crowdsourcing-gamers-solve-protein/

Casserly, M. (2012, May 11). 10 jobs that didn't exist 10 years ago. *Forbes*. Retrieved August 27, 2013, from http://www.forbes.com/sites/meghancasserly/2012/05/11/10-jobs-that-didnt-exist-10-years-ago/

Castells, M. (1996). *The rise of the network society: The information age: Economy, society and culture* (Vol. 1). Oxford, UK: Blackwell.

Castells, M. (1997). *The power of identity: The information age: Economy, society and culture* (Vol. 2). Oxford, UK: Blackwell.

Castells, M. (1998). *End of millennium: The information age: Economy, society and culture* (Vol. 3). Oxford, UK: Blackwell.

Cave, K. (2012). Women: Why doesn't IT have iPad appeal? *IDG Connect Business Management*. Retrieved May 22, 2013, from http://www.idgconnect.com/blog-abstract/654/kathryn-cave-global-women-why-doesn-t-it-have-ipad-appeal

Cave, K. (2013). Women in IT: Does the shortage matter? *IDG Connect Infographic*. Retrieved May 22, 2013, from http://www.idgconnect.com/abstract/1251/infographic-women-it-does-shortage-matter

Comer, M., Freire, M. C., & Russell, A. J. (2013). Disrupting Alzheimer's disease research. *Genetic Engineering & Biotechnology News, 33*(18).

Commonwealth of Australia. (2011). *Age pension and superannuation preservation ages*. Retrieved August 30, 2013, from http://www.taxreview.treasury.gov.au/content/StrategicPaper.aspx?doc=html/Publications/Papers/Retirement_Income_Strategic_Issues_Paper/Chapter_5.htm

CrunchBase. (2013). *GoldieBlox*. Retrieved August 27, 2013, from http://www.crunchbase.com/company/goldie-blox

Curtsinger, J. W. (2007). *Clinical and health affairs – Genes, aging, and prospects of extended life spans*. Retrieved August 17, 2013, from http://www.minnesotamedicine.com/CurrentIssue/g/tabid/2307/

de Grey, A. (2009). *In pursuit of longevity*. Retrieved August 18, 2013, from http://www.youtube.com/watch?v=HTMNfU7zftQ

Deloitte. (2013). *Digital disruption – Short fuse, big bang?* Retrieved August 16, 2013, from http://www.deloitte.com/au/digitaldisruption

Duncan, D. E. (2012, August 16). *When I'm 164: The new science of radical life extension and what happens if it succeeds*. TED Conferences.

Economist. (2012). *An iPopping phenomenon.* Retrieved August 16, 2013, from http://www.economist.com/node/21551058

Economist. (2013). *Charging the mobile.* Retrieved August 16, 2013, from http://www.economist.com/news/finance-and-economics/21579870-east-african-governments-are-targeting-telecoms-firms-charging-mobile

Elmaghraby, A. (2013). *A look into the future: Citizens, communities and open data.* Retrieved August 13, 2013, from http://www.iftf.org/future-now/article-detail/a-look-into-the-future-citizens-communities-and-open-data/

European Commission. (2013). *Europe 2020.* Retrieved August 24, 2013, from http://ec.europa.eu/europe2020/index_en.htm

Farber, D. (2013). *The next big thing in tech: Augmented reality.* Retrieved August 16, 2013, from http://news.cnet.com/8301-11386_3-57588128-76/the-next-big-thing-in-tech-augmented-reality/

Goodstein, D. (1994). *The big crunch.* Paper presented at the NCAR 48 Symposium. Portland, OR. Retrieved August 30, 2013, from http://www.its.caltech.edu/~dg/crunch_art.html

Gorbis, M. (2012). *The institute for the future.* Retrieved August 10, 2013, from http://www.youtube.com/watch?v=5_EsLu4qydw

Gorbis, M. (2013). *The nature of the future: Dispatches from the socialstructured world.* New York: Free Press.

He, X., & Zhang, J. (2009). On the growth of scientific knowledge: Yeast biology as a case study. *PLoS Computational Biology*, *5*(3), e1000320. doi:10.1371/journal.pcbi.1000320 PMID:19300476

Herman, A. M. (1999). *Futurework - Trends and challenges for work in the 21st century.* Washington, DC: US Department of Labour.

Heussner, K. M. (2013). *Wearable tech VC's pan Google glass.* Retrieved August 16, 2013, from http://gigaom.com/2013/07/24/wearable-tech-vcs-pan-google-glass/

Institute for the Future. (2013). *Ten-year forecast.* Retrieved December 7, 2013, from http://www.iftf.org/fileadmin/user_upload/downloads/researchagendas/TYF_2013ResearchAgenda_01.pdf

Karoly, L., & Panis, C. (2004). *The future at work – Trends and implications.* Santa Monica, CA: RAND Corporation.

Keith, K. T. (2009). Life extension proponents, opponents, and the social impact of the defeat of death. In M. K. Bartolos (Ed.), *Speaking of death, America's new sense of morality.* Westport, CT: Praeger Publishers.

Khatib, F., & DiMaio, F.Foldit Contenders Group, Foldit Void Crushers Group, Cooper, S., Kazmierczyk, C., ... Baker, B. (2011). Crystal structure of a monomeric retroviral protease solved by protein folding game players. *Nature Structural & Molecular Biology*, *18*, 1175–1177. doi:10.1038/nsmb.2119 PMID:21926992

Koschel, J. (2013). *The growing technological generation gap.* Retrieved August 16, 2013, from http://theindustry.cc/2013/02/12/the-growing-technological-generation-gap/

Kreit, B. (2012). *Diagnosing malaria--and closing labor gaps--through games.* Retrieved August 13, 2013, from http://archive.iftf.org/node/4186

Levine, B. (2011). *Computer gamers help solve AIDS protein problem.* Retrieved August 13, 2013, from http://www.newsfactor.com/story.xhtml?story_id=10300004X4P9

Lynch, A. (2013). *10 of the best Aussie crowdsourcing projects from 2012.* Retrieved August 16, 2013, from http://www.smartcompany.com.au/start-up/053721-10-of-the-best-aussie-crowdsourcing-projects-from-2012-3.html

Matuszak, G., & Lamoureux, T. (2012). *Mobilizing innovation: The changing landscape of disruptive technologies*. KPMG Technology Innovation Center. Retrieved August 16, 2013, from http://www.kpmg.com/Global/en/IssuesAndInsights/ArticlesPublications/technology-innovation-survey/Documents/mobilizing-innovation-august-2012.pdf

McQuivey, J. (2013). *Digital disruption*. Retrieved August 16, 2013, from http://solutions.forrester.com/disruption

Merchant, N. (2010). *The new how: Creating business solutions through collaborative strategy*. Sebastopol, CA: O'Reilly Media.

Merz, T. (2013). *Weather crowdsourcing app. could track passing of single clouds*. Retrieved August 16, 2013, from http://www.telegraph.co.uk/technology/news/10244974/Weather-crowdsourcing-app-could-track-passing-of-single-clouds.html

Meyer, K. (2013, August 7). Why more women should create apps. *Forbes*. Retrieved August 27, 2013, from http://www.forbes.com/sites/85broads/2013/07/08/why-more-women-should-create-apps/

Millar, M. (2013). *How wearable technology could transform business*. Retrieved August 16, 2013, from http://www.bbc.co.uk/news/business-23579404

Millar, R. A. (2002). Extending life: Scientific prospects and political obstacles. *The Milbank Quarterly*, *80*(1), 155–173. doi:10.1111/1468-0009.00006 PMID:11933792

Neal, M. (2013). *Twitter knows which restaurants are getting people sick*. Retrieved August 16, 2013, from http://motherboard.vice.com/blog/twitter-knows-which-restaurants-are-getting-people-sick

Papworth, L. (2011). *7 levels of social media engagement*. Retrieved August 16, 2013, from http://socialmediatoday.com/laurelpapworth/277499/7-levels-social-media-engagement

Patten, E., & Parker, K. (2012). *A gender reversal on career aspirations: Young women now top young men in valuing a high-paying career*. Pew Research. Retrieved July 28, 2013, from http://www.pewsocialtrends.org/2012/04/19/a-gender-reversal-on-career-aspirations/

Pethokoukis, J. (2013, September 13). The end of global population growth may be almost here — and a lot sooner than the UN thinks. *AEIdeas*. Retrieved September 15, 2013, from http://www.aei-ideas.org/2013/09/the-end-of-global-population-growth-may-be-almost-here-and-a-lot-sooner-than-the-un-thinks/

Porter, J. (2011). *Women engineering graduates at 15-year low*. Retrieved August 26, 2013, from http://it-jobs.fins.com/Articles/SB130221786789702297/Women-Engineering-Graduates-at-15-Year-Low

Quesenberry, J. L., & Trauth, E. M. (2008). Revisiting career path assumptions: The case of women in the IT workforce. In *Proceedings of the International Conference on Information Systems*. Retrieved September 13, 2013, from http://www.eileentrauth.com/uploads/4/6/7/6/4676002/quesenberrytrauth_icis-2008.pdf

Reddy, H. (1975). *I am woman*. [Video]. Retrieved September 22, 2013, from http://www.youtube.com/watch?v=MUBnxqEVKlk

Reimer, K. (2013). *The big opportunity – What is digital disruption (part 1)*. Retrieved August 16, 2013, from http://the-big-opportunity.blogspot.com.au/2013/06/what-is-digital-disruption-part-1.html

Richards, H. (2013). *CIPD debate: The future trends that will shape work.* Retrieved August 18, 2013, from http://www.intelligenthq.com/intelligence/cipd-debatethe-future-trends-that-will-shape-work/

RoobixCoob. (2005). *A woman's role in the 1950s.* Retrieved August 27, 2013, from http://www.colorado.edu/AmStudies/lewis/1025/women1950s.pdf

Rowson, J., Young, J., Spencer, N., Lindley, E., & Gecius, E. (2012). *The power of curiosity: How linking inquisitiveness to innovation could help to address our energy challenges.* London, UK: RSA Social Brain Centre. Retrieved August 16, 2013, from http://www.thersa.org/__data/assets/pdf_file/0004/606829/RSA-Social-Brain-The-Power-of-Curiosity.pdf

Scientific American. (2013). *Open innovation pavilion.* Retrieved September 13, 2013, from http://www.scientificamerican.com/openinnovation/

Scoble, R., & Israel, S. (2013). *Age of context: Mobile, sensors, data and the future of privacy.* CreateSpace Independent Publishing Platform.

Siegel, L. J. (2013). *Are telomeres the key to aging and cancer?* Retrieved August 18, 2013, from http://learn.genetics.utah.edu/content/begin/traits/telomeres/

Skipworth, H. (2013). *Joy of tech: Google Glass, privacy and wearable technology.* Retrieved August 16, 2013, from http://www.digitalspy.com.au/tech/the-joy-of-tech/a505087/the-joy-of-tech-google-glass-privacy-and-wearable-technology.html

Smalley, L. (2013). *Click your fortune: TED-Ed's choose-your-own-adventure look at careers options.* Retrieved August 9, 2013, from http://blog.ted.com/2013/08/07/click-your-fortune-ted-eds-choose-your-own-adventure-look-at-career-options/

Sorman-Nilsson, A. (2013). *How to thrive during digital disruption.* Retrieved August 16, 2013, from http://www.mtmag.com.au/how-to-thrive-during-digital-disruption/

Sterling, D. (2012). *GoldieBlox: The engineering toy for girls.* Retrieved August 27, 2013, from http://www.kickstarter.com/projects/16029337/goldieblox-the-engineering-toy-for-girls/posts

Sternberg, R. J., & Lubart, T. I. (1999). The concept of creativity: Prospects and paradigms. In R. J. Sternberg (Ed.), *Handbook of creativity* (pp. 3–16). Cambridge, UK: Cambridge University Press.

Stone, B. (2010). *The children of cyberspace: Old fogies by their 20's.* Retrieved August 16, 2013, from http://www.nytimes.com/2010/01/10/weekinreview/10stone.html?_r=0

Tague, J., Beheshti, J., & Rees-Potter, L. (1981). The law of exponential growth: evidence, implications and forecasts. *Library Trends, 30*, 125–150.

Tandon, N., Pritchard, S., Savelieva, V., Smith, G., & Vogt, E. (2012). *A bright future in ICTs opportunities for a new generation of women.* Geneva, Switzerland: International Telecommunication Union.

Trauth, E. M. (2011). What can we learn from gender research? Seven lessons for business research methods. *The Electronic Journal of Business Research Methods, 9*(1), 1–9.

Waldman, P. (2013). *How long do you want to live?* Retrieved August 17, 2013, from http://prospect.org/article/how-long-do-you-want-live

Wikipedia. (2013a). *Internet: Social impact.* Retrieved December 7, 2013, from http://en.wikipedia.org/wiki/Internet#Social_impact

Wikipedia. (2013b). *Crowdsourcing.* Retrieved August 27, 2013, from http://en.wikipedia.org/wiki/Crowdsourcing

World Bank. (2009). *Mobile payments go viral: M-PESA in Kenya.* Retrieved August 16, 2013, from http://web.worldbank.org/WBSITE/EXTERNAL/COUNTRIES/AFRICAEXT/0,contentMDK:22551641~pagePK:146736~piPK:146830~theSitePK:258644,00.html

X Prize Foundation. (2013). *Making the impossible possible.* Retrieved September 13, 2013, from http://www.xprize.org

KEY TERMS AND DEFINITIONS

AR/Augmented Reality: Technologies that overlay digital information on what you are seeing in the real world.

Crowdsourcing: a participative online activity for obtaining needed services such as funding, ideas, or content. It solicits contributions from a large group of people, and especially from an online community, rather than from traditional employees, suppliers or investors.

Data Mining: the computational process of discovering patterns in large data sets.

IT: Information Technology. Synonymous with ICT.

#SocialIT: a term coined for a layer of the STEMcell Model. It is a disruptive, penetrating force that can enhance the positive and reduce the negative aspects of the Cultural, Social, Structural and Individual contexts affecting women in IT.

Social Media: Internet tools and sites where people interact freely, creating, sharing and discussing content and information about each other and their lives, using a multimedia mix of words, pictures, videos and audio. There are many forms including blogs, forums, social networks, wikis, virtual worlds and places to share content such as data, images and videos. See http://www.uncp.edu/home/acurtis/NewMedia/SocialMedia/SocialMediaHistory.html.

STEMcell Model: A model designed by Sonja Bernhardt that provides a conceptual framework for viewing contexts and layers impacting STEM fields.

TED: Technology, Education, Design. A series of Conferences, Talks and Conversations on "ideas worth spreading".

Chapter 9
Differences:
Industries and Ethnicity

ABSTRACT

Experiences in other industries and cultures are compared to put the issue of women in IT into a broader perspective in this chapter. The issues of low and declining participation of women are not unique to IT: similar patterns, theories, intervention programs, and results have been noted in other fields. However, in yet other fields women have risen naturally from a small minority to a substantial majority. This supports the thesis of this book that individual interest and choice are the main drivers of career choice. Among different countries and cultures, the proportion of women in IT varies from cases similar to ours, to cases where there is little difference between men and women. However, the latter represent different rather than less gender bias. It is argued that the power of #SocialIT to reach across cultural barriers directly to the individual and their personal interests will help women everywhere by showing them what is possible and giving them tools to achieve it themselves. The overall evidence is that interventions do not achieve their aims. To the extent that they have any positive effect, they do not increase numbers overall or benefit all minorities, merely rearrange the distribution. Not only have interventions had little positive effect, but the warning is made that we need to consider the unintended consequences of our well-meaning interventions.

If your culture doesn't like geeks, you are in real trouble.

– Bill Gates (Riddell, 2010)

INTRODUCTION

Over my years of involvement in the issues of recruitment, promotion and attraction of women into technology fields, I have seen the perspective expand. Initially the interest was specifically in computing or more generally IT, then over time it became increasingly bundled with the related fields of Science and Engineering, which had been seeing similar issues. This occurred almost across the board in the literature, government policies and campaigns, gathering acronyms as it went: first with SET (Science, Engineering and Technology) and then STEM (Science, Technology, Engineering and Maths).

DOI: 10.4018/978-1-4666-5860-8.ch009

It is not surprising that we first see our own environment and then broaden our viewpoint to related fields experiencing similar issues. From the other side of that, we can learn from the experiences of people outside our own environment: both in other fields and other cultures. So in this chapter we compare issues of female involvement in industries other than IT and in non-Western or specific ethnic cultures.

INDUSTRIAL REVOLUTIONS

Scientific Analysis

Issues of low and declining participation of women are far from unique to IT. Similar patterns, intervention programs and results have been noted in other fields. Indeed the arguments presented in a United Nations report about the low and falling percentage of women in science are eerily similar to those regarding IT noted earlier in this book: "The participation of women in science can increase their contribution to society, because, among other things, they could influence the agenda for science and technology (S&T) research and development (R&D). However, at present a gender imbalance is observed in S&T education, which favours boys/men in three out of four countries worldwide that report on intake ratios. This is often due to barriers such as inappropriate school environments for girls, safety concerns, teaching methods that favour boys, and varying levels of access to technical and vocational education. Some of these problems can be addressed by promoting gender-relevant teaching methods and materials, and providing funds to promote girls and women in S&T education… To increase the participation of women in science, it would be necessary to promote women role models in STI [Science, Technology and Innovation], allow flexible working conditions, and support women's recruitment, retention, advancement and leadership in this area" (UNCTAD, 2011).

Asian Scientist (2013) reports that "researchers have found that the number of women in scientific fields is alarmingly low in the world's leading economies, including the United States, and are actually on the decline in others. The Elsevier Foundation funded study mapped the opportunities and obstacles faced by women in science in Brazil, South Africa, India, the Republic of Korea, Indonesia, the US, the EU. It was led by Dr. Sophia Huyer, Executive Director of Women in Global Science & Technology (WISAT), and Dr. Nancy Hafkin, Senior Associate of WISAT, and experts in international gender, science and technology issues from the Organization for Women in Science for the Developing World (OWSD). Despite efforts by many of the countries in this study to give women greater access to science and technology education, research shows negative results in the areas of engineering, physics, and computer science… the numbers of women actually working in these fields are declining across the board – only 12 percent of the science and engineering workforce in India was female in 2010. South Korea ranks last of the countries in the study in female economic status, access to resources, supportive policy, and participation in the knowledge and STI sectors. In South Korea, less than 15 percent of women are enrolled in degree programs for science and technology fields – a figure lower than the 30 percent in most countries. Only 11 percent of science and engineering enrolments (including bio and health sciences) are women, lower than the average of 21 percent in most countries."

In Chapter Four – *The Old Approach,* the suggestion was made of calculating the amount of financial investment into research and intervention programs for women in IT. It seems a further multiplier effect can be applied to include other industries with similar issues. This further stresses how much money has been invested in addressing the issue with no real solution and no significant improvement. In any of them.

Factors studied in research by Udeani (2012) have a clear correspondence to the IT industry and the factors identified there. For example, Udeani (2012) used a "modified adaptation of the Science Career Predictor Scale (SCPS) to assess eight factors involved with science career choices: Interest, Enrolment, Masculine image of science, Social barriers, Role Model, School factor, Teacher factor and Parental factor. The instrument was administered to a sample of 375 females enrolled in a general studies programme in the 2010/2011 academic session at the University of Lagos, Nigeria. The sample was then sub divided into female science major and female non-science major groups. Results indicated that the group means were significant for enrolment, social barriers and role models. The group means for interest, masculine image of science, school, teacher and parental factors were found not to be significant. The paper concludes that ... females and males appear to possess equal potential to develop the skills required for the pursuit of science." This could have been research into IT, as the factors, methods and results are similar.

Eccles (2007) comments, "The president of Harvard University, Lawrence Summers, gave a speech in 2005 that set off a firestorm of discussion about the relatively low numbers of women researchers in the fields of science, engineering and math. I found this debate particularly interesting because I have been studying exactly this issue for the past 35 years." Eccles then proposes an expectancy value model looking at psychological and social factors that might underlie the gender differences, and talks about frustrations with the many disconnected theories that had emerged to explain the situation. Eccles further goes on to explain her achievement-related choices model by saying, "In summary, my colleagues and I assume that educational and occupational choices... are guided by (a) individuals' expectations for success on (sense of personal efficacy at) the various options, and well as their sense of competence for various tasks; (b) the relations of options to their short and long term range goals, to their core personal and social identities, and to their basic psychological needs; (c) individuals' culturally based schemas lined to gender, social class, and ethnic group; and (d) the potential cost of investing time in one activity rather than another." In so many ways – the length of time it has been studied, the theories proposed, the ever-growing abundance of models – it is like holding up a mirror to the circumstances, explanations and issues in IT.

We also find that issues identified in IT such as lack of visibility and reduced conference presentations also appear in the science field. For example, Carpenter (2013) reports "Women who have beaten the odds to find themselves in the upper echelons of science face a further hurdle—visibility. Female scientists are less likely to sit on science advisory boards, receive awards, and give invited talks at conferences. However, a new study suggests that the reasons women appear less often on the podium are complicated... The dearth of women is not because they aren't being invited. Instead, female scientists were twice as likely as their male counterparts to turn down an invitation to talk in slots reserved for presenting original and important work. At the same time, the number of female presenters of posters and uninvited talks was almost at parity with men." A wide variety of personal internalized reasons are given for why women have turned down such invitation. So again, there is a dearth of women – without obvious external causes to account for it.

Some very interesting data is presented by Angier (2013): "Over the past few years, the pool of applicants [for a renowned science and mathematics magnet program] had included nearly as many girls as boys, and the acceptance rate — based largely on test scores and grades — had followed suit. Yet when it came to which of the invitees ended up choosing Blair's magnet option over other offerings in the area, the scales tilted male. In 2012, for example, 80 percent of the eligible boys said yes, but only 70 percent of the girls. In 2010, the figures had been 93 percent and 56 percent." An attempt to pitch specifically to girls, by girls, extolling the wonders of the program and dispelling the myths, had little effect, with enrolment remaining almost two-thirds male. The difference is not in ability, classroom performance, aptitude or confidence. But fascinatingly, "aptitude is one thing, aspiration another. In answer to the question 'Are you likely to pursue a scientific career?' some 2,300 students — 11 percent of the total — said yes. Among the ninth-grade yea-sayers, 61 percent were male. Mr. Derriso admits to bafflement. 'If boys and girls are equally interested in math and science and feel equally confident about their abilities,' he wondered, 'why this humongous difference in intent? I don't have an answer for that.' The division marches off to college. Connie Chow, the executive director of the non-profit group Science Club for Girls, pointed out that 29 percent of male college students major in math or science, compared with only 15 percent of female ones. Boys who ace science embrace science, but female mathletes keep their skills at arm's length. Researchers have found that, among students with high scores on the math portion of the SAT, boys cited their desire to major in the physical sciences, engineering or computers, while the girls preferred fields like economics, political science or medicine. One reason for the disparity may be that girls with high math scores, unlike their male counterparts, also tend to have high verbal scores and so may feel their career options are wide open. But still, given the choice, why do so many girls walk away from science and math?"

Perhaps that question has answered itself. Statistically they are more interested in other possibilities.

A further clue can be gleaned from comparisons within science in the USA. The proportion of women drops from Bachelor's to Master's to Doctorates in biology, chemistry and mathematics/statistics. Nevertheless, women outnumber men in biology even in doctorates. Interestingly, the proportion of women goes up from Bachelor's to Master's then back down in Doctorates (to roughly equal to Bachelor's) in earth sciences, engineering, physics and computer science. The percentage of doctorates awarded to women is over 50% in biology, about 40% in chemistry and earth sciences, 30% in maths/statistics and around 20% in physics, engineering and computing (Matson, 2013). I suggest that it would be hard to explain these differences and trends by reference to factors outside of women's own interests and ambitions.

Whilst both male and female academics in the sciences (biology, physics and chemistry) show similar, statistically significant differences their evaluation of male and female job applicants (Moss-Racusin, Dovidio, Brescoll, Graham & Handelsman, 2012), its significance for actual outcomes is unclear. Nature Cell Biology (2009) noted that at least for tenure-track positions, women were more likely to be interviewed and even more likely to receive an offer. In addition, whatever structural issues are also involved, the clearest differences between men and women lay in their own choices, for example the positions they would consider, their persistence in pursuing them and the relative value placed on family considerations (Nature Cell Biology, 2009).

Engineering the Outcome

If we turn our attention to engineering fields we find echoes of the same situation. In a Society of Women Engineers study, Hussein (2012) reports that "The term 'leaky pipeline' is used to describe the trend of women leaving the engineering workforce shortly after obtaining positions as engineers … However, despite the occupation's higher-than-national-average salary, availability of scholarships for engineering students, greater job security and efforts of schools and employers to recruit female engineers, female engineering jobs numbers are stagnant, and studies show the numbers continuing to fall… Maj Mirmirani, Dean of the engineering program at Embry-Riddle Aeronautical University in Daytona Beach, said the 'lack of females in the workforce is problematic because women have inherent abilities they can offer in the field, which translate to more innovation, greater business opportunities and a more competitive economic environment'… And, Cheri Maboudou-Tchao, president of the Central Florida section of the Society of Women Engineers, said 'even after recruiting women to join engineering, there is a problem of keeping them in the job… The problem is partially in messaging.'" Again very strong feelings of déjà vu are invoked. All interviewees in Hussein's (2012) study agreed that "girls' false perceptions of engineering contribute to the problem… In the past, the image of engineers has been focused mostly on males. A Stanford University study also showed that female students' low confidence, negative perceptions and stereotypes of the engineering field are some of the issues that keep females from entering the engineering workforce."

The decline of female participation in engineering courses also reflects the situation in IT. For example, Casallas, Hernandez, Rodriguez, & Ortega (2012) report "The participation of women in undergraduate program of Systems and Computing Engineering at the University of los Andes, Colombia, has been declining over the past years, and today it is only about 11%. This phenomenon has been evidenced in many universities around the world and there are several collaborative projects and networks trying to understand the causes to find mitigation actions in the future." Johnson & Jones (2006) flag "The numbers of students studying engineering have declined in recent years, both in the United States and in Western European countries. Many factors have contributed to this decline – including the difficulty of the curriculum, the attractiveness of alternate paths to good technical jobs, and the lack of attractiveness of projected employment paths for engineering graduates."

When discussing why it is important to have female participation, Porter (2011) presents similar arguments as those in IT discussions when she reports that Karen Panetta, editor-in-chief of Women in Engineering magazine said "Women are large consumers…If you want to appeal to them, you need to understand what their needs and requirements are. Having women design the products many of them consume is one sure-fire way to make certain a female perspective goes into their design." For achieving that, Porter notes that "To change the perception of less popular branches of engineering and make them relevant to women, schools are overhauling their outreach and programs." She reports that Christine Valle, director of the Women in Engineering Program from Georgia Institute of Technology, revealed that "students now use simulations of the collapsed Minneapolis Bridge and a levee in New Orleans to study bridge forces and water pressure. We've revamped the curriculum to show how what they are studying has a very clear connection to improving people's lives." Porter also points to "At MIT, the Women's Technology Program that started in 2002 brings rising high-school senior girls to campus for a four-week immersion program to encourage young women to pursue engineering. 'You have to get them at K through 12,' said Associate Provost Barbara Lisko. 'We've lost a lot of them before they ever get here.'"

There are also growing reports of a decline in women in architecture. Jett (2012) flags that "According to The Architect's Journal's first Women in Architecture Survey the percentage of women in architecture has fallen over the past few years" (from 28% in 2009 to 21% in 2011). And the pattern is also similar to that in IT, if with higher numbers: "Whilst the number of female architecture students has grown – now 44%, we can't seem to retain them in the profession. Just

34% officially qualified chartered architects are women. And the drop-off continues into senior levels: 22% of senior architects are women, 19% of associates and just 12% partners or shareholder directors" (Duncan, 2013).

It almost sounds like a broken record here. However one unique engineering outcome may be a light towards the future. Debbie Sterling, a graduate of Stanford University, developed toys for girls aged 5 to 11, called "GoldieBlox." Orsini (2013) explains how GoldieBlox went from Kickstarter to one of Amazon's top 20 toys: "The toy, which teaches engineering skills through the adventures of kid inventor Goldie, is available in 600 Toys 'R' Us stores, and 400 other toy stores nationwide. But it's not the sales that make Sterling proudest. Instead, it's the messages from the parents that pour in every day. Stories about little girls that sing songs about building and engineering, or are inspired to build their own toys after playing with GoldieBlox." Orsini (2013) explains "Sterling designed the GoldieBlox kit in 2012, writing and illustrating the picture books herself while looking for a manufacturer to mass produce the toy. Before the Kickstarter, she invested her entire life savings into production. Luckily for her, the Kickstarter was funded in just four days. By October 2012, Sterling had over 5,000 backers and over $280,000 in funds." This different approach that lets children discover if they have a personal interest at a young age shows high promise. Research presented in Chapters Three and Four shows that personal interest is the highest ranking reason for progression into a field, therefore early exposure and encouragement can be expected to help girls discover and/or strengthen that interest.

A potentially unique and thought provoking "experiment" on women in engineering is presented by Barabanova (2013), who points out that "Since the Communist Revolution of 1917 and during the ensuing Soviet times, the role of women in engineering and engineering education was strong with almost 60% of the engineers being women. Since the fall of the Soviet Union, Russian women in these engineering careers has fallen to below 40% of the engineering workforce with a continuing downward trend. As a point of reference, the representation of women in the U.S. engineering workforce has remained around 9% with a very large attrition and departure of women from engineering professions during college and their early professional life." The historically high percentage of women in the USSR may have been more due to an absence of men than greater interest or accessibility to women: "At many periods of Russian history there have been fewer men in Russia than women. Primary reasons for this include the high death rates in the two World Wars, the October Revolution, the war campaigns in Afghanistan and Chechnya, in addition to the high incidence of drug and alcohol addiction" (Barabanova, 2013). Perhaps this reflects the finding that women are more likely to seek lucrative careers when men are relatively scarce (Durante, Griskevicius, Simpson, Cantu & Tybur, 2012). However as well as high military death rates we also need to consider how many men who did not die were still drawn out of the workforce into the armed forces. The actual cause of the high female participation would be fascinating to know, but even more fascinating is the fact of its apparently precipitous decline. Even in the absence of a full understanding, it should make us take a hard look at critical mass and other theories.

Constructing the Difference

Moving to the construction industry, an extensive report by the Construction Sector Council (2010) in Canada states, "Most industry experts observed that social biases at work, such as negative career stereotyping and gender stereotyping, are persistent barriers to growth in the rate of women's participation in construction… Despite successful initiatives to increase the numbers of women in the construction industry, the rate of their participation, particularly in the trades and onsite construction management, has not grown significantly over time." International data shows similar results across countries, where female participation in 2005 ranged from 8.8% in the Netherlands to 13.1% in Australia, with even more extreme disparities seen in specific jobs (e.g. cabinetmakers, glaziers and welders). The failure to improve matters leads to the conclusion that "to address this problem, questions about the challenges and barriers women face must be reopened" (Construction Sector Council, 2010).

Interventions in the construction industry are also similar to those in IT and science:

- Employers and industry association representatives actively promote careers in construction by giving presentations at high schools, colleges and trade fairs.
- Programs have been developed to expose girls to work in trades and technology, including the Saskatchewan Girls Exploring Trades and Technology camps and the Toronto Discover Engineering program.
- Employers and industry associations provide funds for scholarships for women entering or advancing in construction careers.
- Pre-apprenticeship programs provide training to prepare women for entry to the construction trades, for example the British Columbia Institute of Technology Trades Discovery Program.
- In Alberta, employers have partnered with community organizations to provide significant funding to support the preparation of women for the skilled trades. Examples include the Women Building Futures program and the Vermilion/YWCA Skills Training Centre.
- Various toolkits are being developed and made available via the Internet to support the spread of good industry practices and standards. Two examples are the Construction Owner's Association of Alberta (COAA) Respect in the Workplace toolkit – a standardized policy that enables companies to assess worksites, promote awareness, training and communication, and develop mechanisms to address bullying, harassment and violence – and the human resources toolkit under development in Saskatchewan to improve the hiring and retention of women employees.

The theories too are similar to those applied to women in IT, e.g. critical mass theory: "For the construction industry, critical mass theory suggests two key questions. First, is there a particular number or percentage of women required in the construction industry for these sorts of changes to be achieved, and if so, what might that percentage be? In other words, what is the target number of women necessary to maintain an increased rate of women's participation in the construction trades and onsite management? Second, could the changes described above be expected if a critical mass of women in construction trades and onsite management were achieved?" (Construction Sector Council, 2010).

Construction has its own leaky pipeline too, with not only recruitment but also retention an issue. "The third reason that the rate of women's participation in construction trades/management has not increased more significantly is the problem of retention. Key informants reported that most women do not stay in the trades longer than five years. Many leave to start families and then are unable to return because of inflexible work policies that make it difficult to fulfil parenting responsibilities" (Construction Sector Council, 2010). This leaky pipeline or "opt out" is experienced across all industries, with Catalyst (2013) describing it as "women are in the labour force but their employment patterns may be different than men," though not surprisingly there are occupational differences: "Working after a birth varies by occupation: for example, healthcare practitioners and technicians were less likely than construction labourers to take time off without pay. Management, business, and financial occupations had the highest rates of new mothers working part time or dropping out of the labour force" (Cheeseman Day & Downs, 2009). It is interesting that in the Cheeseman Day & Downs (2009) study, computing, engineering and science had the second highest probability (84%) of working after having a birth, while construction had the lowest probability (52%). Yet the descriptions and proposed solutions are much the same.

Such considerations lead the Construction Sector Council (2010) to make an important point about the depth of the issue and the inherent risk of isolated intervention activities: "This review of literature about the barriers to women's participation in the construction trades and strategies to overcome them produced two key findings. The first is that, to succeed, the interventions that have been developed to provide women with supportive training opportunities, to help women secure and maintain employment, and to improve workplaces must all function in tandem. For example, training women for work in construction will not, on its own, boost the rate of their participation in industry unless supports are in place to help them overcome the hiring and other workplace barriers. Women need support in securing and maintaining employment and in dealing with the obstacles they face in the industry. Furthermore, even if all of these interventions were implemented, it is unlikely that they would solve all of the issues women in construction face."

However, in the light of the many interventions and programs at all levels, perhaps the answer lies elsewhere. The experience of the construction industry may bear out the warning in Chapter Six: *Cultural & Social Context* about the futility of attracting women into IT only to find they weren't really interested. While from 1996 to 2007 the proportion of women in registered apprenticeships grew by from 7.5% to 10.6% (an increase of over 40%), the increase in female apprenticeship *completions* was insignificant, rising from 1.7% to only 1.8% (Construction Sector Council, 2010).

Whilst most of the above report concerns Canada, its comparative data shows similar issues elsewhere. The factors behind the low participation rate for women in construction in the UK are reviewed by Amaratunga, Haigh, Lee, Shanmugam & Elvitigala (2006), who identified the same barriers as in IT and science: "image of the industry, career knowledge, culture and working environment, family commitments, male dominated training course and recruitment practices were the major barriers to women in construction." Amaratunga et al. (2006) further report, "Women who choose careers in non-traditional occupations such as the construction industry have to face many challenges in order to enter and retain in the industry... major barriers [are] faced by construction women in terms of entry, career development and retention. Mainly the male dominated image and culture of the construction industry strongly deter women from entering it... it would be illogical not to include money as a reason for women leaving the industry. In general women earn less than men do. In other words, women's lifetime earnings are below than those of an equivalently skilled and educated man. Finally, the over emphasis on 'male values' of the industry which include long working hours, working away from home and geographical instability, and a highly competitive culture; alternative working arrangements such as part time working, career breaks, and job sharing are considered as feminine and unfeasible in the industry." These findings are echoed in another UK study by Worrall, Harris Stewart, Thomas & McDermott (2010), who find that "male-dominated organisational cultures and inflexible working practices are the main barriers to women in the UK construction industry, irrespective of job role or profession." Much the same is reported for Nigeria: "Despite the fact that women possess the required knowledge, skills, competencies, training and experiences to perform effectively and efficiently in construction industry, they experience entry and career advancement barriers" (Kolander & Kehinde, 2013). The conclusions again match those regarding women in IT: "Considering these barriers, it is felt that the reduction or elimination of most of such barriers is an important step which leads to recruit and to retain more women into construction industry" (Amaratunga et al., 2006).

Yet while the barriers are perceived from the outside, at least some appear less daunting to the women who have proceeded to make successful careers. For example on the competing demands of work and personal life, the Catalyst (2013) report finds that "73% of executive women surveyed in Catalyst's Women in U.S. Corporate Leadership study said they were comfortable with the trade-offs they have made between career and personal goals," with similar results reported by Accenture (2013).

Thus across countries, years and careers, we see the same pattern as in IT and more generally STEM. Women have the same abilities yet there are far fewer of them. Negative stereotyping and gender barriers are blamed, the same theories are invoked, and the same interventions are made with metrics indicating success; but little improvement ensues, and the response to failure is more of the same.

In science, theories generate experiments whose results mean the theories are supported, revised or dropped. In the issue of women in male-dominated careers, we have the same theories and experiments across industries and across the globe, the same "experiments," the same results, but little effect on the theories. Perhaps the true lesson is that it is time to reconsider the theories and approaches taken.

Women Rule

The dire tales of women apparently fleeing everything from STEM to construction must make us wonder where they are all going. It is not that they are leaving the workforce in general. For example, in the USA women comprised 47% of the labour force in 2010 and are projected to contribute 51% of labour force growth up to 2018. Nor are they just doing menial jobs: over 40% worked in management, professional and related occupations (Women's Bureau, 2010). The trends over the years are equally interesting. From 1962 to 2012, the percentage of women in the workforce rose from 32% to 46%, while the percentage in management positions rose from 15% to 41%; both these increases plateaued after 2002 (Cohen, 2013). Whilst Cohen (2013) views those trends through the traditional sociology paradigms of gender unfairness and the need for government funding of childcare, perhaps discarding those old lenses will give us clearer vision.

Thus if the "experiments" in increasing female participation in male-dominated industries have so universally failed, perhaps we should start looking at the successes.

In the 1960s, women comprised only 8% of veterinary students in the USA, a number that rose to 77% by 2008 (Sommers, 2008).

At Harvard University, which displays lower gender bias (in both directions) than the USA average, anthropology shows very low male participation (dropping from 22% in 2011 to 17.5% in 2012), while sociology and psychology are only about 30% male; interestingly, between 2006 and 2010 the proportion of men in the department of government dropped from 63% to only 48% (Kansra & Mohamed, 2012). Curiously, explanations for such differences continue to cite gender stereotypes, suggest that existing imbalances may be self-perpetuating, and dismiss a role for any "innate difference" between men and women

(Kansra & Mohamed, 2012). I suggest that the data shows otherwise, and that stereotypes are having more of an influence on the theories than on the facts.

The US Healthcare industry presents a very interesting case study (American College of Healthcare Executives, 2006). Even back in 1990, women achieved CEO positions at about 40% of the male rate, rising to 63% in 2006. In addition, by 2006 women were moving up their organizational hierarchy at about the same rate as men. Yet fascinating differences in attitudes remain. Between 73 and 85 percent of men, depending on the study year, were willing to move to advance their careers, compared to less than 60% of women. While approximately equal proportions of women and men planned to work in hospitals or health systems in the short term (5 years), looking forward 15 years 52% of men but only 31% of women did. And about twice as many men as women aspired to a CEO position in 5, 10 or 15 years.

In psychology, men are considered a shrinking minority, with women earning doctoral degrees outnumbering men three to one (Willyard, 2011). The history of that trend is illuminating: "In psychology, women began earning more PhDs than men in the late 1980s… 'When I got my doctorate in 1976 and I first started to go to professional meetings, it was a handful of women and sea of white men,' says Dorothy W. Cantor, PsyD, a former APA president and chair of the task force set up to look at this issue. Over the next 15 years, however, more and more women entered the field. Cantor says there was a fear that as the profession became increasingly 'feminized,' salaries would fall and the field would lose prestige, but the task force found little evidence to support that idea. In 1996, Cantor and the other task force members wrote, 'There appears to be no evidence that women's increased participation eroded psychology's status…'" (Willyard, 2011).

These are just a few examples. As Willyard (2011) points out, "The phenomenon is not unique to psychology. Other fields such as law and education have seen an influx of women as well."

It is true that decades ago, there were severe structural and social impediments to women seeking almost any kind of career. But it is readily apparent that the resulting male domination has not always presented an impediment to a "female takeover" in less than one generation. Yet we find persistently low numbers in fields like IT. My challenge to researchers in the field is to defend their theories in the light of that. If all the barriers, biases and excuses proposed for IT were so easily swept aside in other fields: are they really the cause, or are they a distraction?

In Shakespeare's *Julius Caesar*, Cassius says "The fault, dear Brutus, is not in our stars, But in ourselves, that we are underlings." Perhaps our cause is not in our social milieu, but in ourselves. There are not fewer women than men in IT because faced with insuperable obstacles they are dropping out to become housewives or shop assistants. They are choosing other careers, for reasons of their own.

THE RACE AGAINST RACE

In the STEMcell Model, cultural impacts are depicted as an outer crust that contracts and expands depending on the prevailing influence of other factors, including individual choices and ambitions. Studying other cultures gives us a greater insight into this. There is a remarkable variety among cultures. In some non-Western countries there are plenty of female coders with no perceived technology gender barriers; in others it is at a stage of first enabling access to ICT before further development is possible; in others, even access to technology is a difficult issue; while many others closely map to the issues we have seen in

Western societies. Both the ethnic-specific and overall collective results are intriguing.

This remarkable variation was highlighted by Galpin (2002), who compared and contrasted women's participation in computing in more than 30 countries, focusing on the undergraduate level. Whilst overall participation was low there was a wide range, from 10-40% in most countries, with some below 10% and a few where women were the majority. Furthermore, some levels were falling and some rising. Galpin (2002) identified a bewildering array of cultural and societal factors and attitudes involved and concluded that "there is no clear indication that this will improve in the near future. Ongoing research is required to determine causes and solutions."

We do need to remember one key point. Differences between countries and cultures are determined by women's choices with what is possible to them. That is determined not merely by factors that might pull them into our push them out of one career (such as IT), but by all the other factors that might pull them into or push them out of competing career choices. Thus we have to be careful interpreting higher participation in IT in other countries: in the absence of good data about why women choose what they do, it could indicate greater freedom – or less.

Whatever the differences, one near constant is the spread of recognising an issue with women in IT and governments jumping to "do something," usually gender based. Thus UNCTAD (2011) report that developing countries have begun to include a gender perspective in their STI [Science, Technology and Innovation] policies, as indicated in these examples:

- "The Republic of Korea has been supporting the participation of women in its STI sector at all levels, including through its 'Women's Informatization' programme. In 2003, the country passed legislation fostering and supporting women scientists and technicians, and in support of this the Ministry of Education, Science, and Technology implemented a recruitment target system through its National Science and Technology Council with the aim of increasing the percentage of women hired in its 98 national and governmental S&T institutes to 30 per cent.
- Rwanda has committed to reforming its public sector to ensure that 'women shall be empowered to participate fully in S&T development and management'.
- The Government of India's S&T policy identifies as one of its objectives: 'To promote the empowerment of women in all science and technology activities and ensure their full and equal participation', and refers to the need to provide women with opportunities for higher education and skills to pursue careers in R&D.
- Brazil is one of the few countries where the Ministry of Policy for Women has adopted S&T as one of its programme areas.
- Gambia has a gender policy which emphasizes the promotion of science education for both girls and boys."

India

In some countries the situation is very different from Western cultures, at least in the details. Misra (2004) describes the circumstances in India: "Information and communication technologies have created new types of work that favour women because the technology enables work to be brought to homes and allows for better accommodation of work and family schedules. Women have also been able to capture a large proportion of jobs in ICT-enabled services because of the worldwide shortage of skills necessary for work in this sector. Many women are software programmers, but very few are in hardware design." That last comment is interesting. Whereas increasing the number of female programmers is a key objective in other countries, it is not an issue in India and the calls are for more hardware design roles.

Misra (2004) further states, "New ICT jobs for women especially in India are in the service industries in information processing, banking, insurance, printing and publishing. So far, the most promising potential for women is in the creation of new jobs at 'Call Centres' and in work involving data processing. The International Labour Organisation reports that 'telecentres and fax booths have created a quarter of a million jobs in India in the last four years alone, a huge proportion of which have gone to women'. While specific gender data on the networking profession in India were not available, fewer women are employed in networking compared to software occupations."

Despite the differences, we start to see barriers and obstacles analogous to those in the West when Misra (2004) reports: "This is attributed to the preconceptions that the physical aspects of the work are too difficult for women such as the long, erratic hours and travelling. The lack of mobility is cited as one of the major constraints to women's ability to participate in the IT work force in India." Specific cultural influences play a role here: "If women want to work in the IT sector, they have to relocate themselves. However, living alone away from home is not the norm for young, single women because of security issues and the traditional view that women's role is in the home with the family. As a result, the current IT employment opportunities in large cities like Hyderabad or Mumbai are often not appealing or feasible for many women, particularly those from the other parts of the country. So, there are many cases where women have sufficient IT education and training, but do not work in the field because they lack the essential mobility to go to where the jobs are" (Misra, 2004). Though strength of personality or interest can override such cultural norms to achieve a career of choice.

Despite the successful entry of women into some areas of IT in India, Misra's comments on the norms for young women indicate that the cultural factors in India probably remain stronger than in the West. The difference is not in a more female-friendly culture, but in how IT jobs are perceived by men and women compared to the other careers open to them. This is reflected in the Indian government's policy to promote the empowerment of women in technology fields (UNCTAD, 2011, quoted above).

Indeed it is almost amusing to read that "Female lawyers have a huge role to play in the effective administration of justice, India's top judges have said, adding that encouraging more women to join the profession is 'vital for the transformation of future society'. Despite the small number of women lawyers in the Indian Bar … there is an equivalent ratio of men and women in law school, but the ratio swings greatly towards men further up the ladder." (Barnes, 2013). It is like reading about women in IT in Australia or the USA.

Malaysia

Like India, Malaysia has good representation of women in IT. At the University of Malaysia, women made up 53% of undergraduates in computer science and 64% in specialised IT programmes (Othman & Latih, 2006). This reflects a culture where "The dominant Western perception of the relationship between gender and computer science codes the latter as 'masculine' and the low number of women is seen at least partly as an effect of that coding, is not the case in Malaysia" (Lageson, 2008). In contrast, "There are large numbers of women in computer science, and computer science is not perceived as 'masculine.' Rather, it is deemed as providing suitable jobs and good careers for women. This reflects an understanding of gender where femininities are constructed by association to office work, commonly recognized as a woman-friendly space because it is seen as more safe and protected than, for example, construction sites and factories" (Lageson, 2008).

This intriguing twist, in which computer work is considered 'safe' and thus attracts women, echoes Spender (2011): "There are always issues associated with non-traditional jobs (such as engineering, trades etc) where girls are put off by dirt and grease, along with ugly protective clothing and the prospect of broken finger nails: but these arguments aren't relevant when it comes to IT. It's clean, can be very creative, well paid etc – with a range of options for specialisation. So much so that in certain Asian countries, IT is considered a good job for a girl, (possibly for much the same reasons as office work and accountancy are also considered appropriate)."

That raises the question of why, given the same qualities of the job, there is such a difference between Western countries and Malaysia. Some of the issues are the same. For example, Goh (2013) reports "The latest ICT Job Market Outlook study revealed that male ICT (information and communications technology) professionals in Malaysia tend to earn a median monthly salary of RM5,201 (US$1,641), while females earn a median salary of only RM3,855 (US$1,216), which works out to a 35% difference. The annual report, produced by national ICT association Pikom and conducted in collaboration with recruitment portal Jobstreet.com which provided the salary data, and KPMG, which analysed the data in the report – noted the pay disparity between genders." Yet this disparity has not deterred female entrants (possibly because it is no worse than elsewhere).

As with India, this is not a reflection of less bias against Malaysian women, who suffer greater cultural and legal barriers to equality than in the West (Wikigender, 2013).

The Middle East

In the Middle East to date, the majority of research and activity appears primarily focused on an earlier stage of participation in IT: access and use rather than careers. But of course access and use are the starting point and of definite value, as other research shows.

The importance of IT for women in Arab countries is expressed by Mathew (2010), who notes "in order [to] develop women entrepreneurship for economic growth there must be [a] strong move by all stakeholders. ICT enables women entrepreneurs to extend equal participation compared to the male in the growth and development of the nation's economy. The extended use of ICT will help the entrepreneur for creating advantage [and] research; participate in the global world of business for technology transfer, training, collaboration, and development [of] initiatives at the global level."

Unfortunately they have a fair way to go. Elnaggar (2007) writes, "Women in the Arab Gulf region in general and in Oman in particular are at a higher risk of being marginalized from today's knowledge based economy, due to … a traditionally male-dominated ICT sector, unequal access to training, the lack of 'Arabized' Internet content and training, and the lack of awareness and policy advocacy, among others… women's access and utilization of ICT among Arab countries continue to lag behind men creating a widening gender digital gap… women [are] as low as 4% of Internet users in Arab countries." However as identified in Chapter Three – *The New Approach,* the "Arab Spring" is not only an indicator that this is changing, but is part of the change itself.

Elnaggar (2007) identifies the usual suspects of gender stereotyping, cultural norms and other obstacles, e.g. "Females are still responding to gender stereotyping of ICT jobs. Few are attempting to enter the non-conventional engineering and hardware-based ICT space, and even fewer fight their way to the top positions of the ICT scale… Socio-cultural norms are perceived and constantly expected by females to be a barrier discouraging them from joining the ICT areas when studying and working… Statistics indicate that there is a huge market of females to train in ICT, but the challenge is how to reach them." Elnaggar (2007) concludes that "ICT is a tool that can either be used to transform and liberate or to continue reproducing traditional ways of life that exclude women. Female users may come to ICT with goals that fit rigidly within the confines of socially defined gender roles but it is possible that, once they are exposed to ICT, they can undergo a process of empowerment. For this to happen, ICT should be promoted within the larger goal of enhancing the capabilities of women and empowering them through information and knowledge gain."

That is exactly what we hope for from the STEMcell Model and #SocialIT. Defined gender roles that attempt to suppress individual interests cannot long survive the knowledge of what is possible and the power to achieve that modern IT is bringing around the world. And for all that we criticise certain aspects of our own culture, in many ways it shows what is possible.

South Africa

In South Africa, a relatively strong female presence in courses is not reflected in careers, with WISAT (2013) reporting "while South Africa sees 45% representation of females in Science and Engineering enrolments, the numbers of women actually working in these fields is 16%, with 36% representation in the technician workforce." As we find in Western nations, this is not explained by a gender difference in ability, at least when access to computers is roughly equivalent. Research by Gudmundsdottir (2010) at four primary schools in South Africa found "months of observation of computer sessions in the disadvantaged schools clearly showed that learners' ICT use and skill level varied greatly by school. Numerous earlier studies have revealed gender differences in ICT use and skills. However, the results from this study showed no gender differences. This finding may possibly be explained by the relatively limited home computer use by the participants (by both girls and boys) and/or the possible equalising effect of school use where every learner had access regardless of gender."

These results indicate the strong influence of basic access and factors that affect it, such as socio-economic circumstances. Of course this is not limited to Africa, for example similar results for poorer ethnic minorities are reported by Volman, van Eck, Heemskerk & Kuiper (2005) in The Netherlands and Calvert, Rideout, Wollard, Barr & Strouse (2005) in the USA. However while we can expect it to be true anywhere, whether it disproportionately affects girls is probably more a factor of culture than socio-economic status per se.

Korea

In overall workforce participation, Korea lags behind the West, with concerns that only about half of women are participating in economic activity. Hence the importance of full capitalization of women's resources has been emphasised.

Korea has a history of strong government-backed campaigns. Lee (2010) relates that "In the 1970s, the Korean government launched a program called Stop at Two and Raise Them Well to encourage newly-weds to regulate the size of their families. As a result, Korea has the world's second lowest birth-rate (United Nations Populations Fund [UNFPA], 2009)." Whether that is truly the dominant cause or not, possibly based on such success "In 2002, the Korean government legislated to strengthen the capacity of women in SET and to improve the retention within SET of qualified women scientists and engineers. In Korea it is accepted that the competitiveness of SET-based industries is crucial in terms of the nation's overall competitiveness in global markets. In the past 10 years, Korea's competitiveness in SET-based industries has grown remarkably (IMD, 2009). Interestingly, this increasing trend in SET competitiveness is almost parallel to the increasing ratio of women scientists and engineers within the SET workforce, even though women are still less than 20% of the SET workforce" (Lee, 2010).

Numerous interventions resulted. "The WISE (Women Into Science and Engineering) program was started in 2001 with a mentoring program to encourage young women to major in science and engineering. To promote women engineers and technicians, the WIE (Women in Engineering) project developed a gender recognized education system in engineering schools. The WATCH21 (Women's Academy for Technology Changer in the 21st Century) program provided high-school girls with experience in engineering research laboratories. The ISWIST (Institute for Supporting Women in Science and Technology) was established by the Act on Fostering and Supporting Women" (Lee, 2010), and so on.

Here we see the familiar pattern, where an issue is noted and the response is an array of theories and interventions: and what are the results? Lee (2010) concludes, "there certainly is a move towards gender-mainstreaming in SET in Korea. The number of young women researchers is increasing, and the concept of gender equality is widely disseminated. An important matter seems to be time. Does Korea have enough time to wait for a natural transition from male-domination to gender equality in SET within Korea?" I suggest that we have no choice about that. Once a certain level of access and removal of structural barriers is achieved, any gender equality will happen in its own time according to the interests of all the women involved.

European Subcultures

The issue of ethnicity is not just about the dominant culture of a country, but also about immigrants and minorities within it.

In Europe, there appears to be little difference between the majority and ethnic minorities. In an extensive study for the European Commission, Diminescu, Hepp, Welling, Maya-Jariego & Yates (2009) state "In our view, the first important empirical finding, supported by data on three out of four countries (excluding France due to lack of data), is that with respect to ICT awareness, attitudes towards ICT (especially acknowledged importance), and ICT basic access and use, IEM (immigrants and ethnic minorities) are not too dissimilar from the host population. In fact, in some respects, they are ahead of it. Although in different ways and with different nuances, the German, Spanish and UK country reports converge in affirming that at a basic level ICT awareness, attitudes, access and use are not a function of ethnicity at all. Differences and barriers emerge when considering the process of appropriation (how ICT are used and for what purpose) and its social context in more detail."

While Diminescu et al. (2009) reported some difficulties comparing countries due to the different ways ethnic data is available (for example, with France being assimilationist versus the UK encouraging distinct ethnic identities), overall they found "ICT skills are clearly perceived by immigrants and ethnic minorities as crucial for enhancing their job prospects and they play an important role in many businesses they run, and found that ethnicity does not shape the propensity to consume ICT products and services."

The Netherlands provide a partial exception, with Volman et al. (2005) reporting that their "empirical research studied issues related to the use of ICT in which gender and ethnic differences have been identified in the literature, namely computer use in and out of school, computer skills, learning outcomes when ICT is used, pupils' attitudes towards ICT and their way of working with computers. In primary education, gender differences regarding all these points are small. Ethnic differences, however, do exist. First and foremost, fewer pupils from an ethnic-minority background have a computer and an Internet connection at home than pupils from the majority population." However four years is a long time in IT and the difference may simply reflect the earlier date of their study.

It is interesting that Volman et al. (2005) did find gender differences in later years: "Unlike primary education, the gender differences found in secondary education were considerable. Girls use the computer less at home than boys and programming and games in particular are unpopular. At school, both genders use computers equally intensively but girls e-mail more frequently, while boys play games more. There are few gender differences in ICT skills but many in ICT attitude, especially interest in computers and self-confidence in computer use. Girls and boys also differ in their approach to working with ICT, with girls preferring an explanation to trying something themselves and boys the other way round."

It would be fascinating to see a follow-up study when those primary age students are in secondary school, to see if the change in attitude of girls is due to changing interests as they get older or to different experiences across the micro-generations. Given the overriding importance of personal interest in career choice, that would tell us a lot about the whole issue of women in IT.

USA Subcultures

A growing body of research covers African-Americans and Hispanics in the USA. Mostly the findings and interventions map closely to what we have already seen. For example, "While the ethnic breakdown of computer science undergraduate degrees is consistent with the population as a whole, the number of African-American students pursuing advanced degrees in computing is alarmingly low… Nationwide, black students account for 1.3 percent of graduates of computer science master's and doctorate programs and 1.2 percent of tenure-track faculty at doctoral-granting institutions" (Anderson, 2013).

Specifically among women, the issue, response and even criteria of success are familiar. Only 3% of Computer Science Graduates in the USA are African-American women, prompting the formation of *Black Girls Code* specifically to encourage young female African-Americans to join the IT industry. Kimberly Bryant, head of *Black Girls Code*, said in an interview, "I'm positive that one of the girls from our programs in the next twenty years is going to be one of those people we read about in the papers. If we are going to have a pipeline we are going to have to create it" (Burnett, 2013).

The research in this field covers areas previously discussed, such as access to computers and the Internet, parental influence, personal interest etc.: the classic structural and social issues, but explored within cultural contexts. For example, Guzdial, Ericson, McKlin & Engleman (2012) study the connections between stages of computing education pathways, and how factors that influence students' pursuit of computing differ between genders and majority/minority group students. In their survey of 1,434 undergraduates (31% female and 69% male; 59% White, 15% Asian, 15% Black, 5% Hispanic, less than 1% Native American, and 5% Multiracial), they found that "encouragement was the driving factor in how likely female students were to complete a computing major/minor and to choose a computing career — more important than girls' confidence in and perceptions of their ability. This was also true for Black students (not disaggregated by gender). For White males, both perceptions of ability and encouragement were important factors." Somewhat in contrast, Zarrett, Malanchuk, Davis-Kean & Eccles (2006) found that expectations for success predicted interest in a computing career among African American and white high school students. However, Cohoon & Aspray (2006) feel that more research is needed to confirm the connection between expectations and interest in computing.

The role of computer access, or rather low socio-economic status and lack of access, comes into play in research by Calvert et al. (2005): "About 75% of parents reported that their families had a computer and 88% of those had Internet access. However, this study finds a socioeconomic and racial divide in access to computers and the Internet in early childhood. Consistent with prior research, families with higher incomes, higher educational levels, and in two-parent families were more likely to own computers and to have Internet access. Regardless of income, education, and family structure, African American and Latino families were less likely to have Internet access, and Latino families were less likely than Caucasian families to report that they owned a computer." Though as noted earlier, whether this affects girls more than boys is a separate question. In addition we can expect the computer access statistics to have already changed.

The role of parental support was examined by Denner (2011) in a study of 140 girls (primarily Latina). She found that perceived parental support had a direct influence on the extent to which girls value computing (see it as important and relevant), which in turn had a powerful impact on their interest in computing. Qualitative data from this study indicated that girls consider their parents and other family members as the greatest influence on their career interests (Denner, 2009). The role and impact of parental support has appeared in many other studies; the difference here is the implication that support results in interest, versus interest first followed by support in following it. In addition, Gándara & Contreras (2009) suggest that confidence plays a critical role in shaping the academic performance and aspirations of Latino students. Taken together, the results of Denner (2009, 2011) and Gándara & Contreras (2009) suggest the importance of getting messages to parents about IT in general and IT careers in particular, and for them to encourage their children's interests and confidence.

Modi, Schoenberg & Salmond (2012) found a significant ethnic difference, where "African American and Hispanic girls have high interest in STEM, high confidence, and a strong work ethic, but have had less exposure to STEM, less adult support for pursuing STEM fields, lower academic achievement, and greater awareness of gender barriers in STEM professions. However, their confidence and ability to overcome obstacles are high, pointing to the strong role of individual characteristics in STEM interest and perceived ability in these subjects." Given the earlier statistic that only 3% of tech graduates are African-American women, perhaps this reduced support is a key contributing factor to lower IT engagement, despite the high level of interest and personal strength reported.

An intriguing aspect of the Modi et al. (2012) findings is the ethnic differences in subsets of IT work. For example, they found that "although interest in STEM is high for all ethnic groups (73% of Caucasian girls, 76% of African American girls, 74% of Hispanic girls), interest in some aspects of STEM is higher for African American and Hispanic girls. African American and Hispanic girls are more interested in:

- How things work (African American – 82%, Hispanic – 83%, Caucasian – 73%)
- Building things/putting things together (African American – 58%, Hispanic – 67%, Caucasian – 56%)
- Creating an iPhone app or designing a computer or video game (African American – 67%, Hispanic – 68%, Caucasian – 55%)."

It is hard to predict how the conflicting factors found by Modi et al. (2012) would play out. Whilst "African American and Hispanic girls are more cognizant of gender barriers in STEM fields," they also have "strong internal assets such as confidence and the ability and desire to overcome obstacles, which appear to complement and support their high levels of interest in STEM despite reported lower levels of adult support, exposure, and academic achievement." In addition, "African American and Hispanic girls have financial motivations in choosing a career path, fuelled by their parents, and are less likely to say they want to be stay-at-home moms."

Given the greater interest of African American and Hispanic girls in some aspects of computing, their equal drive and higher motivation to seek well-paid jobs, we might expect higher entry into IT careers. But current representation in the Silicon Valley workforce (both sexes) does not reflect that: "African Americans/Blacks and Hispanics/Latinos(as) are underrepresented in the technical workforce. African American technical workers comprise just 1.8 percent of our sample, as compared to 12.7 percent of the U.S. population, 11.4 percent of computer science bachelor's degrees, and 5.2 percent of engineering bachelor's degrees. Hispanic/Latino(a) technical employees make up just 3.5 percent of our sample, versus 12.6 percent of the U.S. population, 6.8 percent of computer science bachelor's degrees, and 7.5 percent of engineering bachelor's degrees" (Simard, Davies Henderson, Gilmartin, Schiebinger & Whitney, 2008).

Other than that, Simard et al. (2008) find that technical employees in Silicon Valley are very ethnically diverse. In their study only 53.9 percent of respondents were White, while a large proportion of technical employees were Asian (39.1%) This includes Asian American, South Asian, Southeast Asian, East Asian, and "other" Asian. Of key interest here is that in this Silicon Valley survey, technical women were more ethnically diverse than were technical men. Perhaps that reflects a higher individual drive, fewer opportunities at home, or greater attraction to Silicon Valley culture.

The representation of women within the minority groups varies. "There is no difference in the proportion of Hispanic/Latino(a) women and men among our respondents; however, technical women are more likely to be African American/Black than are technical men (3.2% versus 1.0%)… Asian women represent the second-largest racial/ethnic category in our sample of technical women. This broad Asian category includes many different cultures and countries. Mid-level technical women are more likely to be Asian and less likely to be White than mid-level technical men. Hispanic or Latina technical women are completely absent from the highest level technical jobs. The proportion of African American women falls from 4.6 percent at the entry level to 1.6 percent at the high level (though the decline is not statistically significant). Further, entry level women are more likely than men to be African American" (Simard et al., 2008).

Such differences indicate that personal interests and/or social pressures vary among different ethnic groups in the same country, which implies that any interventions might need to be tailored for specific circumstances. On the other hand, the Advanced Placement Computer Science 2012 Exam national statistics show a surprising uniformity in gender makeup among ethnic groups. The outliers were Asian (32% female) and White (17%), with all other groups including American Indian, Black and Hispanic around 22-25% women (Exploring Computer Science, 2013). The relative uniformity across ethnicities may be telling us something fascinating. In either case, the power of #SocialIT to reach across cultural barriers directly to the individual and their personal interests might make such issues and circumstances less relevant.

One step back from the numbers, Varma (2010) found significant ethnic differences in students' opinions on why so few women enrol in IT: a "large majority of students believe either gendered socialization (stereotypes, parental influence etc) or technical anxiety (confidence, level of difficulty etc.) is a prime reason. White students, more than any other groups tend to blame genderized socialization and Asian American students lean towards roles played by technical anxiety. Ethnicity showed significant differences amongst females but not males. Native American female students did not believe in either and had entirely different reasons." However we learned from Modi et al. (2012) that girls identify barriers as discouraging other girls, not themselves. So we must ask whether such opinions reflect the reality or are just repeating the conventional wisdom.

Warning Bells Toll

Similar worries, theories and actions in diverse industries provide us with comparative data on the effectiveness of programs to "correct" the situation.

Some warning bells have already tolled and ought to be heard. For example Myers & Fealing (2012) were interested in whether diversity programs aimed at increasing the representation of one group had the unintentional effect of alienating another. Their results revealed that five decades of policies to increase the representation of minority groups in biology, chemistry, and medicine have benefitted some people at the cost of others. The study examined the effects of diversity efforts in two eras: 1968 to 1989, when institutions employed race-conscious admissions policies, and 1990 to 2009, when institutions shifted to purportedly race-neutral policies that placed economic disadvantage on the same footing as characteristics including gender, race, and ethnicity. The study labelled the two periods "the affirmative-action era" and "the diversity era" respectively.

Myers & Fealing (2012) used data from the Current Population Survey March Supplement (a product of the U.S. Census Bureau and the Bureau of Labour Statistics that tracks race, ethnicity, and employment) to compute the representation ratios of persons employed in biology, chemistry, and medicine from 1968 to 2009 (inclusive). They calculated the ratios of racial, gender, and ethnic groups working as biologists, chemists, or physicians. They derived the representation ratios by computing the ratio of the conditional probability that a member of a given group is employed in a specific skilled science field to the overall probability of employment in that field. Their analysis tested for differences in representation ratios among racial, gender, and ethnic groups and across time among those employed as biologists, chemists, and medical doctors.

Zeilinska (2012) summarises the findings: "The results showed that the ratio of white women in medicine increased more than any other group, and the representation of African Americans increased more in biology than the other two fields. However, the ratios of Hispanics fell across all three fields. 'Successful diversity initiatives in one science field can have the unintended effect of reducing representation in other science fields,' the authors concluded, thereby 'creating competition for the same students.' The authors call for new approaches to improving diversity in science and medical fields."

NCWIT found correspondingly mixed results. The overall number of women in the computing workforce decreased markedly between 2000 and 2009, and the racial/ethnic diversity of technical women shifted. The proportions of women in computing occupations who are African American/Black or Latina/Hispanic increased gradually between 2000 and 2009, while the percentages of White and Asian/Pacific Islander women decreased (US Department of Labour) (DuBow, 2011). Nevertheless it is interesting that for full-time enrolment among all undergraduates (2010 figures), the percentages of women enrolling among each group (White, Asian and Minorities [Blacks, Hispanics and American Indians]) was only slightly less than the percentages of men (and more in numbers), and the differences between the ethnic groups were also minor with less than a 10% spread (National Science Foundation, 2013).

The simple interpretation of such results is that attempts to attract women or minorities into particular technical careers are not increasing their numbers in technical careers per se, just rearranging the distribution. Nor are they benefitting all minorities: just increasing some at the expense of others. The creation of new jobs, new technologies and new opportunities increases the size of the pie and does more to achieve those ends than telling people how to slice it.

More bells are tolling re quota systems. These not only tend to alienate the people we are relying on to create the jobs, by telling them who they can hire, they can even alienate the people they are trying to help. Dainty, Bagilhole & Neale (2001) noted that "many women are leaving the industry as they feel they have been hired because of their gender rather than their abilities." Having a stated quota can marginalize the recruitment reasons for the people, such as women in technology, who fit within the quota bounds. So it is not surprising that women who want to achieve something out of their own efforts and have a strong sense of personal worth and achievement will leave if they feel their gender is the only reason they were hired.

More generally, it seems as soon as we identify "something" as an issue there is a rush by Governments, Associations and activists to "do something" about it to artificially adjust the situation, with little to show for it. For example, Court and Moralee (1995) noted "the under-representation of women in construction only became an issue in the 1980s. In 1988, less than 7% of the full time construction industry workforce in Britain were women. The Equal Opportunities Commission (1995) stated in its annual publication that 'women continue to be significantly underrepresented in the primary sector (agriculture and energy and water), in most manufacturing, in transport and communications and, in particular, in the construction industry." There have been a number of other studies carried out by various researchers on the under-representation within the construction industry, then and since (Gale, 1994; Fielden, Davidson, Gale & Davey, 2000). As a result of all the concern and doing, female participation in construction in the UK was 9.9% in 2000 and 10.2% in 2005 (Construction Sector Council, 2010).

We also need to consider the unintended consequences of our well-meaning interventions. We noted above the success of Korea's program to reduce its birth-rate and the confidence it engendered in the power of government interventions. Yet now the "implications of this low birth-rate and the shift towards an 'aging society', both of which may lead to a decrease in economically active human resources, have become a key issue within Korean society" (Lee, 2010). To an extent that problem reflects the effects of quotas and other interventions aimed at minorities in achieving partial, localized success at the expense of negative effects on other groups or endeavours. In focusing on one issue and attempting to force a solution, we often have no idea what damage we might be doing elsewhere.

This survey across fields and cultures completes the data analysis. The next chapter looks at where we can go from here, presenting conclusions and recommendations for future activity both overall and for the various stakeholder groups.

REFERENCES

Accenture. (2013). *Defining success: 2013 global research results*. Retrieved September 1, 2013, from http://www.accenture.com/SiteCollectionDocuments/PDF/Accenture-IWD-2013-Research-Deck-022013.pdf

Amaratunga, D., Haigh, R., Lee, A., Shanmugam, M., & Elvitigala, G. (2006). *Construction industry and women: A review of the barriers*. Salford, UK: The University of Salford.

American College of Healthcare Executives. (2006). *A comparison of the career attainments of men and women healthcare executives*. Retrieved September 6, 2013, from http://www.ache.org/pubs/research/gender_study_full_report.pdf

Anderson, M. (2013). *UA part of national alliance to spur African-American computer science graduate students*. UA News. Retrieved September 7, 2013, from http://uanews.ua.edu/2013/05/ua-part-of-national-alliance-to-spur-african-american-computer-science-graduate-students/

Angier, N. (2013, September 2). Mystery of the missing women in science. *The New York Times*. Retrieved September 7, 2013, from http://www.nytimes.com/2013/09/03/science/mystery-of-the-missing-women-in-science.html

Asian Scientist. (2013). *Elsevier: Lack of women scientists in South Korea, India*. Retrieved August 24, 2013, from http://www.asianscientist.com/academia/elsevier-lack-women-scientists-south-korea-india-2013/ also from http://wisat.org/home/new-gender-benchmarking-study-finds-women-greatly-under-represented-in-south-korean-science-technology-innovation/

Barabanova, S. V. (2013). *The decline of women in Russian engineering education*. Paper presented at 120th ASEE Annual Conference & Exposition – Frankly we do give a D*MN. New York, NY.

Barnes, J. (2013, March 18). Women lawyers in India 'vital for future society'. *The Global Legal Post*. Retrieved September 25, 2013, from http://www.globallegalpost.com/global-view/women-lawyers-in-india-vital-for-future-society-46922508

Biology, N. C. (2009). Attracting women [editorial]. *Nature Cell Biology*, *11*, 915. doi:10.1038/ncb0809-915 PMID:19648973

Burnett, E. (2013). *Black girls code and the digital divide*. Retrieved August 24, 2013, from http://Ed.cnn.com/video/data/2.0/video/bestoftv/2013/08/22/exp-erin-pkg-simon-idea-black-girls-code-bridges-digital-divide.cnn.html

Calvert, S. L., Rideout, V. J., Wollard, J. L., Barr, R. F., & Strouse, G. A. (2005). Age, ethnicity, and socioeconomic patterns in early computer use. *The American Behavioral Scientist*, *48*(5), 590–607. doi:10.1177/0002764204271508

Carpenter, J. (2013). *Study finds women biologists more likely to avoid spotlight at conferences*. Retrieved August 28, 2013, from http://news.sciencemag.org/people-events/2013/06/study-finds-women-biologists-more-likely-avoid-spotlight-conferences

Casallas, R., Hernandez, J. T., Rodriguez, D. H., & Ortega, M. F. (2012). Understanding the women participation decline in systems & computing engineering: Case study at the University of Los Andes, Colombia. In *Proceedings of Informatica (CLEI), 2012 XXXVIII Conferencia Latinoamericana En*. IEEE. Retrieved August 26, 2013, from http://ieeexplore.ieee.org/xpl/login.jsp?tp=&arnumber=6427243

Catalyst. (2013). *Catalyst quick take: Women leaving and re-entering the workforce*. New York: Catalyst. Retrieved August 26, 2013, from http://www.catalyst.org/knowledge/women-leaving-and-re-entering-workforce

Cheeseman Day, J., & Downs, B. (2009). *Opting-out: An exploration of labor force participation of new mothers*. Paper presented at the Population Association of America 2009 Annual Meeting. Detroit, MI.

Cohen, P. N. (2013, November 23). How can we jump-start the struggle for gender equality? *The New York Times*. Retrieved November 26, 2013, from http://opinionator.blogs.nytimes.com/2013/11/23/how-can-we-jump-start-the-struggle-for-gender-equality/

Cohoon, J. M., & Asprey, W. (Eds.). (2006). *Women and information technology: Research on underrepresentation*. London: MIT Press. doi:10.7551/mitpress/9780262033459.001.0001

Construction Sector Council. (2010). *The state of women in construction in Canada*. Ontario, Canada: Construction Sector Council.

Court, G., & Moralee, J. (1995). *Balancing the building team: Gender issues in the building professions*. London: Institute for Employment Studies/CIOB, University of Sussex.

Dainty, A. R. J., Bagilhole, B. M., & Neale, R. H. (2001). Male and female perspectives on equality measures for the UK construction sector. *Women in Management Review*, *16*(6), 297–304. doi:10.1108/EUM0000000005820

Denner, J. (2009). The role of the family in the IT career goals of middle school Latinas. In *Proceedings of AMCIS 2009*. AMCIS.

Denner, J. (2011). What predicts middle school girls' interest in computing? *International Journal of Gender. Science and Technology*, *3*(1), 53–69.

Diminescu, G., Hepp, A., Welling, S., Maya-Jariego, I., & Yates, S. (2009). *ICT supply and demand in immigrant and ethnic minority communities in France, Germany, Spain and the United Kingdom*. Seville, Spain: European Commission.

DuBow, W. M. (2011). *NCWIT scorecard: A report on the status of women in information technology*. Boulder, CO: NCWIT.

Duncan, J. (2013, August 7). Why are so many women leaving architecture? *Guardian Professional*. Retrieved September 6, 2013, from http://www.theguardian.com/women-in-leadership/2013/aug/07/women-leaving-architecture-profession

Durante, K. M., Griskevicius, V., Simpson, J. A., Cantu, S. M., & Tybur, J. M. (2012). Sex ratio and women's career choice: Does a scarcity of men lead women to choose briefcase over baby? *Journal of Personality and Social Psychology*, *103*(1), 121–134. doi:10.1037/a0027949 PMID:22468947

Eccles, J. S. (2007). Where are all the women? Gender differences in participation in physical science and engineering. In S. J. Ceci, & W. M. Williams (Eds.), *Why aren't more women in science? Top researchers debate the evidence* (pp. 199–210). Washington, DC: American Psychological Association Books. doi:10.1037/11546-016

Elnaggar, A. (2007). The status of Omani women in the ICT sector. *International Journal of Education and Development using Information and Communication Technology*, *3*(3), 4-15.

Equal Opportunities Commission. (1995). Job segregation linked to gender bias. *Equal Opportunities Review, 60*.

Exploring Computer Science. (2013). *CS education statistics*. Retrieved September 22, 2013, from http://www.exploringcs.org/resources/cs-statistics

Fielden, S. L., Davidson, M. J., Gale, A. W., & Davey, C. L. (2000). Women in construction: The untapped resource. *Construction Management and Economics*, *18*, 113–121. doi:10.1080/014461900371004

Gale, A. W. (1994). Women in non-traditional occupations: the construction industry. *Women in Management Review*, *9*(2), 3–14. doi:10.1108/EUM0000000003989

Galpin, V. (2002). Women in computing around the world. *ACM SIGCSE Bulletin*, *34*(2), 94–100. doi:10.1145/543812.543839

Gándara, P., & Contreras, F. (2009). *The Latino education crisis: The consequences of failed social policies*. Cambridge, MA: Harvard University Press.

Goh, G. (2013). *Why women in the ICT industry are paid less than men.* Retrieved August 24, 2013, from http://www.digitalnewsasia.com/digital-economy/why-women-in-the-ict-industry-are-paid-less-than-men

Gudmundsdottir, G. (2010). From digital divide to digital equity: Learners' ICT competence in four primary schools in Cape Town, South Africa. *International Journal of Education and Development using Information and Communication Technology, 6*(2), 84-105.

Guzdial, M., Ericson, B., McKlin, T., & Engleman, S. (2012). A statewide survey of computing education pathways and influences: Factors in broadening participation in computing. In *Proceedings of ACM International Computing Education Research (ICER) Conference* (pp. 143-150). New York: ACM.

Hussein, F. (2012). *Female engineers in short supply, declining.* Retrieved August 26, 2013, from http://www.news-journalonline.com/article/20121028/BUSINESS/310269984

IMD. (2009). *World competitiveness yearbook 2009*. Lausanne, France: IMD Publications.

Jett, M. (2012, March 14). Infographic: Women in architecture. *ArchDaily.* Retrieved Aug 28, 2013, from http://www.archdaily.com/216844/infographic-women-in-architecture/

Johnson, W. C., & Jones, R. C. (2006). *Declining interest in engineering studies at a time of increased business need.* Retrieved August 28, 2013, from http://www.worldexpertise.com/Declining_Interest_in_Engineering_Studies_at_a_Time_of_Increased_Business_Needs.htm

Kansra, N., & Mohamed, S. A. (2012, October 4). Gender imbalances persist in academics. *The Harvard Crimson.* Retrieved September 1, 2013, from http://www.thecrimson.com/article/2012/10/4/gender-imbalance-social-sciences/

Kolander, O. J., & Kehinde, O. (2013). Glass ceiling and women career advancement: Evidence from Nigerian construction industry. *Iranian Journal of Management Studies*, *6*(1), 77–97.

Lagesen, V. A. (2008). A cyberfeminist utopia? Perceptions of gender and computer science among Malaysian women computer science students and faculty. *Science, Technology & Human Values*, *33*(1), 5–27. doi:10.1177/0162243907306192

Lee, K. J. B. (2010). Women in science, engineering and technology (SET) in Korea: Improving retention and building capacity. *International Journal of Gender. Science and Technology*, *2*(2), 236–248.

Mathew, V. (2010). Women entrepreneurship in Middle East: Understanding barriers and use of ICT for entrepreneurship development. *International Entrepreneurship Management*, *6*, 163–181. doi:10.1007/s11365-010-0144-1

Matson, J. (2013, May). Women are earning greater share of STEM degrees, but doctorates remain gender-skewed. *Scientific American.* Retrieved September 1, 2013, from http://www.scientificamerican.com/article.cfm?id=women-earning-greater-share-stem-degrees-doctorates-remain-gender-skewed

Misra, K. D. (2004). Information & communication technology for women's empowerment in India. *Information Technology in Developing Countries IFIP Working Group 9.4, 14*(2).

Modi, K., Schoenberg, J., & Salmond, K. (2012). *Generation STEM: What girls say about science, technology, engineering, and math*. Girl Scouts of the USA. Retrieved August 10, 2013, from http://www.girlscouts.org/research/pdf/generation_stem_full_report.pdf

Moss-Racusin, C. A., Dovidio, J. F., Brescoll, V. L., Graham, M. J., & Handelsman, J. (2012). Science faculty's subtle gender biases favor male students. *Proceedings of the National Academy of Sciences of the United States of America, 109*(41), 16474–16479. doi:10.1073/pnas.1211286109 PMID:22988126

Myers, S. L., & Fealing, K. H. (2012). Changes in the representation of women and minorities in biomedical careers. *Academic Medicine, 87*(11), 1525–1529. doi:10.1097/ACM.0b013e31826d7189 PMID:23018333

National Science Foundation. (2013). *Women, minorities, and persons with disabilities in science and engineering: Enrollment*. Retrieved December 8, 2013, from http://www.nsf.gov/statistics/wmpd/2013/digest/theme1.cfm

Orsini, L. (2013). *How an engineering toy for girls went from Kickstarter to bestseller*. Retrieved July 30, 2013, from http://readwrite.com/2013/07/12/how-an-engineering-toy-for-girls-went-from-kickstarter-to-bestseller

Othman, M., & Latih, R. (2006). Women in computer science: No shortage here! *Communications of the ACM, 49*(3), 111–114. doi:10.1145/1118178.1118185

Porter, J. (2011). *Women engineering graduates at 15-year low*. Retrieved August 26, 2013, from http://it-jobs.fins.com/Articles/SB130221786789702297/Women-Engineering-Graduates-at-15-Year-Low

Riddell, M. (2010, October 20). Bill Gates: If you don't like geeks, you're in trouble. [Interview]. *The Telegraph*. Retrieved August 2, 2013, from http://www.telegraph.co.uk/technology/bill-gates/8073946/Bill-Gates-If-you-dont-like-geeks-youre-in-trouble.html

Simard, C., Davies Henderson, A., Gilmartin, S. K., Schiebinger, L., & Whitney, T. (2008). *Climbing the technical ladder: Obstacles and solutions for mid-level women in technology*. Palo Alto, CA: Anita Borg Institute for Women and Technology.

Sommers, C. H. (2008, March/April). Why can't a woman be more like a man? *The American*. Retrieved August 18, 2013, from http://www.american.com/archive/2008/march-april-magazine-contents/why-can2019t-a-woman-be-more-like-a-man

Spender, D. (2011). *Girls and IT – What's changed?* Retrieved July 27, 2013, from http://dalespender.com.au/~dalespen/wp-content/uploads/2011/05/GIRLS-AND-IT.pdf

Udeani, U. (2012). Increasing female participation in science and technology careers: Problems and suggested interventions from Nigeria. *Developing Country Studies, 2*(5), 87–95.

United Nations Conference on Trade and Development (UNCTAD). (2011). *Applying a gender lens to science, technology and innovation*. New York: United Nations.

UNPFA. (2009). *State of the world population: Facing a changing world: Women, population and climate*. Retrieved from http://www.unfpa.org/swp/

Varma, R. (2010). Why so few women enroll in computing? Gender and ethnic differences in students' perception. *Computer Science Education, 20*(4), 201–316. doi:10.1080/08993408.2010.527697

Volman, M., van Eck, E., Heemskerk, I., & Kuiper, E. (2005). New technologies, new differences: Gender and ethnic differences in pupils' use of ICT in primary and secondary education. *Computers & Education, 45*(1), 35–55. doi:10.1016/j.compedu.2004.03.001

Wikigender. (2013). *Gender equality in Malaysia.* Retrieved September 6, 2013, from http://www.wikigender.org/index.php/Gender_Equality_in_Malaysia

Willyard, C. (2011, January). Men in psychology: A growing minority? *gradPSYCH Magazine.* Retrieved September 6, 2013, from http://www.apa.org/gradpsych/2011/01/cover-men.aspx

WISAT. (2013). *New gender benchmarking study: South Africa ranks low on women participation in STI.* Retrieved August 24, 2013, from http://wisat.org/home/new-gender-benchmarking-study-south-africa-ranks-low-on-women-participating-in-sti/

Women's Bureau. (2010). *Women in the labor force in 2010.* United States Department of Labor. Retrieved September 6, 2013, from http://www.dol.gov/wb/factsheets/Qf-laborforce-10.htm

Worrall, L., Harris, K., Stewart, R., Thomas, A., & McDermott, P. (2010). Barriers to women in the UK construction industry. *Engineering, Construction, and Architectural Management, 17*(3), 268–281. doi:10.1108/09699981011038060

Zarrett, N., Malanchuk, O., Davis-Kean, P. E., & Eccles, J. (2006). Examining the gender gap in IT by race: Young adults' decisions to pursue an IT career. In J. M. Cohoon, & W. Aspray (Eds.), *Women and information technology: Research on underrepresentation* (pp. 55–88). Cambridge, MA: MIT Press. doi:10.7551/mitpress/9780262033459.003.0002

Zeilinska, E. (2012). *Diversity in life science proves elusive.* Retrieved August 1, 2013, from http://www.the-scientist.com/?articles.view/articleNo/32713/title/Diversity-in-Life-Science-Proves-Elusive/

KEY TERMS AND DEFINITIONS

ICT: Information and Communication Technology. Synonymous with IT.

IT: Information Technology. Synonymous with ICT.

NCWIT: National Centre for Women & Information Technology (a USA based organisation).

SET: Science, Engineering and Technology. Conceptually related fields that share issues of under-representation of women. Includes IT and is a subset of STEM.

STEM: Science, Technology, Engineering and Mathematics, conceptually related fields that share issues of under-representation of women. An extension of SET to include maths.

STEMcell Model: A model designed by Sonja Bernhardt that provides a conceptual framework for viewing contexts and layers impacting STEM fields.

WISAT: Women in Global Science & Technology (a USA based organisation).

Chapter 10
Conclusions and Recommendations

ABSTRACT

The focus of this chapter is recommendations. Overall and individual chapter conclusions are summarized; then 3 overarching and 35 detailed recommendations are presented of relevance to all stakeholders from governments to theorists to individuals. The primary recommendation is simple: Stop.

No sensible decision can be made any longer without taking into account not only the world as it is, but the world as it will be.

– Isaac Asimov
(Notable Quotes, 2013)

CONCLUSION

For decades, we have been worried about how few women there are in IT and other technical fields. Based at least partly on the historical bias against women having any career at all, we have generated theories and interventions relating to surmised barriers that keep women out of IT or drive them from it after they enter it. We have achieved nothing.

But instead of questioning our assumptions, we have held them inviolable and linked them to increasingly subtle and insidious barriers. It gives the impression of women as a herd of frightened deer, ready to run at the mere sniff of a man.

Yet that is not how women in IT or girls interested in STEM see themselves: they see themselves as interested, competent and above all as people who regard obstacles as a challenge to be met and overcome.

That there are statistical differences between men and women is considered controversial in some contexts, but in fact is widely accepted implicitly or explicitly. "It is widely acknowledged that women bring a different mix of skills to the workplace – the area of contention seems to be whether these differences are good or bad" (Cave, 2013). For example, "Both women and men believed that women affected the organizational culture in a positive manner: by encouraging more collaboration, more participative decision-making and hence more collegial workplaces" (Soe & Yakura, 2008). Similarly, "A wealth of research

DOI: 10.4018/978-1-4666-5860-8.ch010

in the past decade shows that diversity improves problem-solving, productivity, innovation, and ultimately, the bottom line" (Ashcraft, Eger & Friend, 2012).

Indeed, that there are relevant differences between men and women is implicit in many explanations in the literature for the shortfall of women – by the fact that they affect girls specifically. For example, Ashcraft et al.'s (2012) argument that "Computing is often taught in the abstract... This lack of relevancy is troubling because making relevant connections is particularly important for increasing girls' interest in computing courses and careers," and Miliszewska & Moore's (2011) conclusion that we need "an alternative approach – a re-conceptualization of ICT into an environment that women would naturally embrace."

At school, it is considered that boys and girls have different learning styles and boys are more assertive in the classroom (Herrick, 2009), and "While boys and girls have very similar levels of academic ability, boys are substantially more likely than girls to choose more prestigious profiles" (Buser, Niederle & Oosterbeek, 2012). It is interesting that this difference extends into adulthood: Cohen (2013) relates that generally women do not appear motivated by the prestige and self gratification of presentation, so when approaching female speakers TED adjust their requests to reflect the social impact of the presentation.

Research into gender differences including how wide they are and to the degree to which they are innate or learned has produced varying results. The results are complicated by human complexity itself: measurements can be affected not only by primary causes but by such self-referential factors as expectations. Nevertheless it is clear that there are varied and significant innate average differences between males and females (Yoshida, 2013). Indeed, recent research indicates significant differences in the neural wiring of male and female brains (Lewis & LiveScience, 2013), though what it means remains a matter of debate (Jarrett, 2013).

Perhaps the best example of the widespread acceptance of average psychological differences between the sexes is from a discussion on why there are too few men in psychology itself. "The most obvious problem is that the field doesn't represent the diversity of people it's meant to serve… Guys are built differently. They have different brains and different ways of being emotional… We [male therapists] understand male issues differently than females do… But the feminization of the field is probably having an impact — perhaps even on the types of theories that gain traction, says Kathryn Anderson, PhD, a social psychologist at Our Lady of the Lake University in San Antonio. Many of the classic theories in social psychology, which were developed by men, focus on the individual, she says. 'It's kind of a swashbuckling cavalier 'pull yourself up by the bootstraps' orientation, where you're responsible for yourself,' she says. Women tend to be more 'collectivistic,' focused on serving the family and the community, research suggests. 'So if more women are developing the research questions and developing theory, [the field] might become more collectivistically oriented,' Anderson says" (Willyard, 2011).

The failure of interventions and the stagnant level of female participation in IT while in other fields it has soared from a small minority to a large majority of its own accord, point to the answer lying within women not outside them. It is certainly not that women aren't as good at the subject as men. It isn't even the case that women aren't interested in it: many girls are interested in STEM fields. But career choice takes more than ability and interest. It takes being *more interested than in any of the other choices available.*

I believe that is the whole secret. Women are under-represented in some fields and over-represented in others because statistically, their interests differ from those of men. It doesn't matter how much we tell girls how much *we* enjoy IT, all that matters to them is what *they* are interested in.

However, while personal interest is the main driver, not all girls have an equal ability to discover their interest; and while interest can drive someone to a career, there may still exist barriers such as prejudice that make it an unhappy experience. That is where the power of the STEMcell model and #SocialIT comes in, to break down old traditions and build new ones.

And the fundamental solution to it is the same as the other: women are unique individuals. It is by promoting the idea that it is the individual who matters, the individual who thinks and has talent, which will one day mean people are judged as individuals on their own merits, not according to prejudices based on gender or ethnicity. It is not up to us to decide what other people should be interested in. But it is up to us to do what we can to empower all individuals, whoever they are and whatever their interests are. To let them choose their own path, not the path someone else thinks they should.

CHAPTER CONCLUSIONS

Each chapter of this book has its own specific conclusions, which lead to the overall message. These are noted below.

- **Chapter 1** finds that throughout history there have been women in technology who have made key contributions, but they have been few and far between. It concludes that past pervasive social and cultural contexts hindered and practically suppressed female involvement in such fields, and it took exceptionally resilient, strong individuals to identify their interests and come to excel in those fields.
- **Chapter 2** highlights the rise of social media and other pervasive, disruptive, empowering technologies. These changes suggest that a new model of career choice is needed, one that incorporates the influence of these technologies and the centrality of the individual. We need to adapt to the rules of the new social era or lose relevance.
- **Chapter 3** looks at traditional approaches to increasing the number of women in IT. Over the past twenty years much has been done to encourage female students to choose computing courses and computing careers. Yet while some instances of positive effects have been reported the proportional disparity in gender continues to grow. From research presented it is concluded that the great majority of women in IT are there because of personal interest and very few as a result of interventions. The conclusion is that there is little value in the traditional approaches and further massive spending is unwarranted. It is time to embrace the new era instead.
- **Chapter 4** looks at popular theories on the dearth of women in IT. It concludes that the leaky pipeline, critical mass and other historical theories do not apply in the new social era and ought to be cast aside. That is not to say they have had no value, nor that superseding them implies there are no cultural, social or structural contexts that affect career choice. It simply implies that it is time for a new approach.
- **Chapter 5** examines the cultural and social contexts identified in past models and how they are incorporated into the new. These contexts and their influencing factors feature strongly in the literature on women in technology and are often blamed for deterring women from choosing IT education or careers. However it is concluded that in freer societies their influence is much less

than often claimed and ameliorating interventions are correspondingly ineffective.

- **Chapter 6** examines the structural context and factors referenced in the literature. This context is another recurring theme of women in technology research, with numerous factors identified as deterrents to women choosing IT education or careers. However again the conclusion is that they are not significant factors today and interventions to address them have had minimal effects.
- **Chapter 7** looks at the individual and her influencing factors and concludes that the number of women in IT, or any career, is not a matter of them being pushed this way or that by the balance of societal forces, which we can adjust with the right lever. Rather it comes down to each individual's choice based on her own values and what she wants out of life and her career. That is why no single "solution" has been found, and why a wide variety of solutions have had no significant impact – because there is no generic solution to finding out "what women want" – individually. What they want is what interests them, according to their individual circumstances, personalities and values; and they are not so ignorant that most of them need interventions to know.
- **Chapter 8** examines the #SocialIT layer of the model and concludes that we are in a period of seismic transformations where technology underpins the future. We must tap into the shifting technological landscape to actively use its tools and platforms in the development of future programs, projects and activities. We must realise that all targets are shifting and the future will overtake anything we plan based on the present.
- **Chapter 9** compares other fields and cultures. Issues of low and declining participation of woman are far from unique to IT, with similar patterns, intervention programs and results noted in other fields such as science, engineering and construction. Yet other fields such as sociology and psychology have experienced the opposite. This supports the contention that it is not social forces but individual choice that drives career participation. There is also remarkable variety among cultures with some non-Western cultures having substantially higher female participation in IT. However this does not reflect any greater female freedom, just different cultural evaluations and opportunities. A further conclusion from the research is that attempts to attract women or minorities into particular technical careers do not increase numbers overall or benefit all minorities, but merely rearrange the distribution.

These conclusions lead to this book's recommendations.

RECOMMENDATIONS

Studies on the issue of women in IT typically produce recommendations that run to many pages. My primary recommendation is much simpler.

Stop.

Stop reinventing past intervention programs. Stop bringing historical viewpoints and issues into today's world. Stop viewing the issue through a gender or social lens that sees the individual as putty molded by the world. See the individual as the core. Stop pushing *your* solutions and let individuals and society organically evolve *their* solutions.

What does a shift from a "collective social forces" view to an "individual core" view mean?

Figure 1. Recommendation Categories

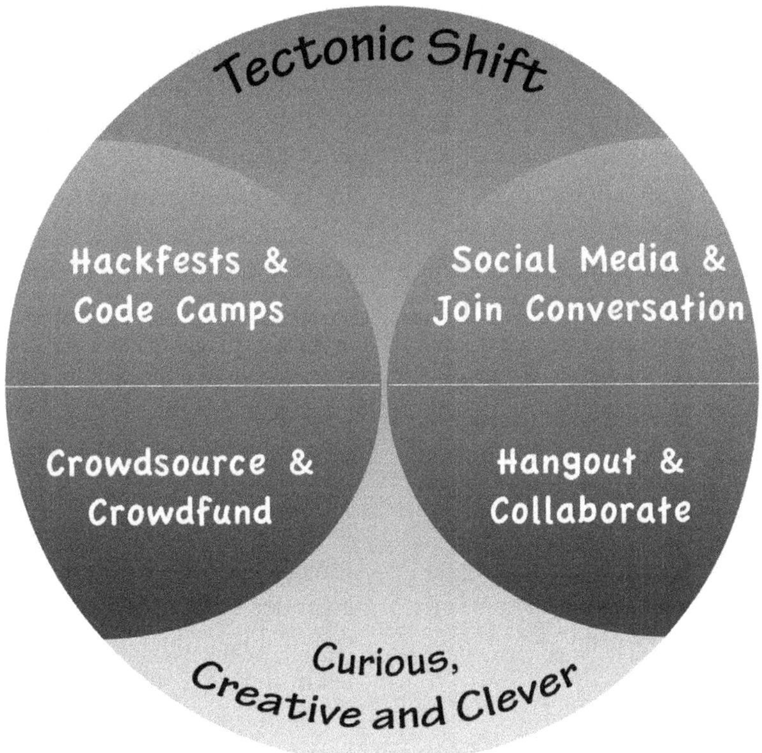

It means shift from *"we need to encourage more women"* to *"we need to engage more curious, creative and clever* ***people****."* Focus on individual interests. Treat people as individuals, as unique cells. There is already a shift in the research away from a social constructionism and gender lens toward a focus on the differences within genders. Extend that to realise that there are statistical differences between genders – but that none of us are defined by our gender. The differences within genders are much greater than the differences between them. Stop thinking collectively and start thinking individually.

My second recommendation is equally simple, if ironic.

Don't stop.

It is an enthusiastic: continue to be passionate and inspired. But the world is changing more rapidly than ever before. Shift to methods that belong in the tectonically changing world we inhabit. Embrace the disruptive technologies and increasingly pervasive social media with its multiple interest groups and activities. Collaborate and move towards hands on code workshops and hackfests. Focus on efforts to create new models and activities that incorporate crowdsourcing, open innovation, transparency, co-creation and collaboration.

In other words, embrace our collective differences and individual uniqueness and move on. Moving into a new era with new rules of operating.

Ultimately though, those very forces make any recommendations provisional and short term and we could therefore raise a third recommendation:

Don't bother.

If everything will change under our feet and it's impossible to keep up, what can we actually achieve? And further disruptive changes such as life extension will render any approach void. Furthermore, the individual empowerment and networking power of the new technologies imply that very soon we won't have to "do" anything: it will do itself without our driving it. And take itself in directions we cannot imagine or control.

But having said that we are not there yet, and 35 detailed recommendations follow. I believe there is something in these recommendations for many interest groups and individuals: feminists, gender theorists and researchers; governments, policy makers and taxpayers; parents, educators (primary, secondary, trade and tertiary), the media and content developers; individual activists and advocates, traditional women in IT associations and their sponsors and supporters, and new social media-style women in tech associations and specialist groups; employers and recruiters; and above all for the individual women and men in technology.

The recommendations are structured into logical groupings that work within the STEMcell Model: Hackfests & Code Camps, Crowdsourcing & Crowd Funding, Social Media & Join the Conversation, and Hangout & Collaborate: all framed by the changing Tectonic Shift environment and with the overall goal to foster a Curious, Creative & Clever culture (Figure 1). The recommendations are also summarised in the Appendix – Table of Recommendations.

Stakeholders should address each of the categories and recommendations listed below.

TECTONIC SHIFT

To deliver different outcomes it is time for dramatic change and fundamental shifts in thinking. Digital disruption is the only possible future: it is time to accept that premise (and reality) and act accordingly. It is time to discard traditional beliefs and practices: not struggle to adapt old ideas to the new realities, but instead leap over that struggle into active adoption of newer methods, tools – and aims.

We are in an era of tectonic shift with multiple influencing factors. This has the potential to disrupt all of society including the education system, governments and social structures. And in addition to the tectonic shifts in technology outside of us, we need a tectonic shift in our own thinking. This leads to the following recommendations.

Viewing Lens

A primary shift we need if we are to make a difference to is to move from a *"why we need to encourage more women"* to a *"we need to engage more curious, creative and clever* ***people****"* approach. As such we should stop viewing this as a gender based problem or issue, and therefore stop re-inventing traditional gender based intervention programs.

Historical gender based viewpoints and issues have proved unsuccessful. We need to stop bringing them into today's world. Instead it is about leaving individuals, their areas of interest and the market (of ideas as much as activities) to organically evolve. As such the primary **Recommendation T1** is remove the gender lens and replace it with an individual lens. If researchers and feminists find it impossible to remove a social constructionism and gender lens then at least shift the focus from differences between genders to differences between the individuals within them.

Removing or refocusing the gender lens may help reduce the classically perceived issues such as "fixing women" and "making women a diversity target." It would assist with providing a pivot point for the growing "lean in" trends and "shifting the conversation from what can't be done to what can be done" (Sandberg, 2013).

This corresponds with the findings in Chapter 4: *The Old Approach*, that women enter IT careers primarily because of who they are, not because of interventions. If IT is an interesting and a satisfying career, show that and individual choice will follow – in those in whom the message resonates. What can be done is showcase what is good and interesting about IT. What can be done is sparking interest in the minds of receptive listeners. What cannot be done is creating that interest to achieve our numerical ideals. If we make women or women in technology a gender diversity target then we risk marginalizing them in the view of the public and demoralising those who were already interested. It is ultimately damaging to view this issue with a gender lens. It is a lens more likely to inflame than illuminate.

Removing the gender lens implies the associated **Recommendation T2** of ensuring that any future intervention programs are done without one. Making something an issue can keep it alive. Rather than designing programs specifically to raise female participation rates in IT studies and/or careers, design them to help people enjoy their existing interest – or discover their latent interest. Rather than presenting technology and role models, keep that secondary to *experiencing* what it means to work in IT. Rather than starting from behind, bemoaning the paucity of women in IT and the dread barriers they face, start afresh on the assumptions that gender doesn't matter and barriers won't last: show what IT is and why might be interesting for anyone, regardless of gender. And even within genders one size does not fit all: perhaps one reason large scale female-focused interventions miss their targets is their aim is too broad and their focus too general. We need to focus on the individual, on their interests and values, not on technology as such nor on their gender. In addition, some research indicates that inexpensive career fairs may accomplish as much as expensive intervention programs. Which leads to a further **Recommendation T3** that perhaps the most radical lesson is to stop women in technology career fairs as such, and instead focus on highlighting IT in general career fairs.

The implications are similar for workplace reforms. Stop gender targets and diversity techniques and discussions, and instead focus on areas of individual interest. Whilst this might go against the grain: *realise that they don't actually help*. Appeal to a person, not a "target" or a target group.

Recommendation T4 is that we all accept that it is past time to realise that in reality only a certain number of women will ever be interested in technology careers. Accept it, and work within that to recruit from that circle. We know from the literature review there is not an issue with women's abilities; it's just how it is. We are often told we should celebrate diversity, and so we should. Perhaps it is time to celebrate diversity in career choices as well.

Education

Five key areas within educational frameworks are presented, and explained below along with their recommendations:

1. Introduce technology theme-based schools.
2. In other schools, when IT is taught tap into online code classes instead of teachers.
3. Expand collaboration, mentoring and hands-on experience.
4. Teach children innovation and entrepreneurship.
5. Focus career guidance primarily on the individual.

All of these recommendations ultimately lead to questioning the entire general school based system as it currently stands. They also raise flags about the traditional structure of physical schools, classrooms, and universities. The details are worthy of their own book, and beyond the scope of this publication. But the revolution is coming; it is only a matter of how soon and how well we adapt (Friedman, 2013; Olds, 2013).

Introduce Technology Theme-Based Schools

Most children have little idea of what future career they might follow. Most children also think school is boring and irrelevant (Bryner, 2007). Yet my snapshot poll shows that most women in IT are there because they were interested from an early age.

In line with the shift in perspective from gender representation to personal interest, **Recommendation T5** is not single-sex classes or schools, but theme-based schools where technology is the specific focus. Such schools would not only focus on their specialist theme but also attempt a well-rounded education. Nor would they replace more general schools. But they would provide a superior solution for those children who have identified their interests and have a passion for a particular field, allowing them to explore it more widely and deeply.

There have been calls for Computer Science teacher certification and the adoption of CS curriculum standards in order to make CS an established part of the curriculum (Ashcraft et al., 2012). But I endorse the opposite: fewer rules, less imposition of uniformity, more choice. The option of themed schools; not the imposition of the same thing on everyone, most of whom aren't interested and don't care.

This recommendation goes one step further than the career academies discussed by Tandon, Pritchard, Savelieva, Smith & Vogt (2012): "One promising approach is the development of 'career academies'. Schools of 100 to 150 students within larger high schools offering a curriculum that mixes academic coursework with hands-on technical courses designed to build work skills. Studies show that career academy students develop firmer roots in the job market than their peers." The difference is one of focus. In a themed school the theme is the main focus not a minor add-on to an otherwise standard curriculum.

Tap into Online Code Classes

Not all schools can be technology themed and most will remain generalist. For these, **Recommendation T6** is not to train teachers or worse, throw them into technology subjects beyond their own interests or skills. Rather, tap into the many online code classes, thus accessing a depth of ability and passion unlikely to be equalled otherwise.

Again this is counter to prior calls. For example Ashcraft et al. (2012) suggest we "advocate for or host teacher professional development workshops for a range of teachers. Both computer science and teacher education faculty can offer professional development for teachers who wish to learn about computing and how they might incorporate computing lessons into their classrooms. These workshops are useful for math, science, and CS teachers but also can be useful for art, music, language arts, social science, and other kinds of teachers who may wish to incorporate computing lessons into their classrooms."

IT is important, but perhaps such calls overstate the case. Imagine if every field demanded the same explicit penetration into other subjects. Whilst IT underlies a huge part of the modern world we should remember that in terms of careers, IT comprises only a small percentage of total jobs. To put it in grim perspective, in 2011 only 4.8 million people were employed in IT jobs in the USA, which was less than half the number of the *unemployed* (Milfort, 2012).

This recommendation also helps educators better manage the key issue that IT and STEM more generally are changing too quickly. There is a severe inherent problem in the field's pace of change compared to the time it takes to develop, let alone approve and implement, curriculum changes. I suggest it is impossible to keep up and therefore a new paradigm is necessary. There are universal principles and concepts in science and technology: formal curricula should concentrate on those, tapping into more agile and contemporary sources for practical learning and application of those concepts. Tapping into the growing online code classes immediately shifts this issue into the hands of the people who focus specifically on what is happening now.

Then education would not be a slow-moving behemoth forever struggling to stay five years behind the present; it would be a stable launch pad into the future.

The implication is that educators must move beyond the traditional thinking that only pedagogically trained educators can bring value to the field. We need to accept that online code classes and related agile resources are the best way to teach the practical elements of a dynamic subject area.

And that is just the start. Massively online courses are already appearing in which thousands of students can do the same course at once, and even the chief weakness of such systems – lack of fast, tailored feedback – is beginning to be addressed using AI systems (Hodson, 2013). A theme of this book is that old systems will give way to new ones whether we like it or not. Educators too need to not resist the changes, but work out how to work with them to improve outcomes. In line with that theme, this is not a formal recommendation, but a simple acknowledgement of what *will* happen.

Expand Collaboration, Mentoring And Hands-On Experience

Recommendation T7 is that educational institutions lend their physical infrastructure and technology resources to host hands-on computing code clubs and activities for younger groups. For example, university campuses could offer this to local schools, which also lets the school students experience campus life and helps promote the university to that target group.

An extension of this is perhaps that the students can become teachers themselves (**Recommendation T8**). For example, a component of secondary school code camps could be hosting hands-on activities for primary schools. Given that children as young as toddlers are now gaining exposure to technology and with the rise of code tools such as Scratch, this concept might even extend to primary schools hosting code camps and game clubs for earlier classes or preschools. This ties in with the suggestion that "multi-level mentoring has been shown to be particularly effective. Having many mentors and individuals supporting and encouraging participation can help girls increase interest in computing... provide mentoring across stages; for example, professors mentor graduate or undergraduate students who mentor 'near peer' high school girls" (Ashcraft et al., 2012). In addition, such a leadership role for interested older students could only increase their depth of understanding and confidence.

A further dimension to that is combining the value of increased responsibility with that of hands-on activities and real world relevance. **Recommendation T9** is that schools and tertiary institutions consider encouraging interested students to set up and look after the school/university network and other aspects of its IT systems.

Teach Children Innovation and Entrepreneurship

Traditionally children are brought up thinking of a career as getting a job with an employer, and the general focus of the education system tends to be acquiring the knowledge and skills to become job-worthy. **Recommendation T10** is to teach children innovation and entrepreneurship. Shift the focus from job-seeking alone to more awareness that you can create technologies and businesses yourself. This recognises not only the importance of innovation and business creation but also the fact that the barriers to doing so are rapidly dropping as a result of the tectonic shifts in technology.

Again there are an abundance of existing programs in this field that schools may tap into instead of needing to retrain teachers.

Career Guidance Strategies

Recommendation T11 is for career guidance practitioners to focus on the primacy of the individual rather than a collective approach and generic career advice, echoing Watts & Sultana (2004). Appeal to the individual's internal strengths, interests and needs. In addition, doing is more compelling than being told, so where possible career fairs and information programs should include hands-on activities on real world questions.

Where Do We Go From Here?

The above education recommendations may be combined. For example, themed schools might be small, distributed "meeting points." Or they might be multiple modules in a more traditional school providing an overall education along with multiple themes for different interest groups. In either case the bulk of the material used could be accessed electronically from centralised resources.

The recommendations allow for varying levels of risk takers and change adopters. Meaning they can be adopted in small, easily bitten off moves such as shifting to online code classes, all the way to sweeping changes to overhaul the entire education system. Naturally the latter would take time and collaborative efforts and might be dismissed by some as too sweeping. However it needs to be taken in light of the rapid rate of change and tectonically shifting landscape we are experiencing. As such it ought to be viewed using the #SocialEra rules as noted by Merchant (2012) and tagged in Chapter 3 – *A New Approach.* In other words, the future is coming whether we like it or not, and we can choose to embrace it or miss it.

Let it Drive Itself

There is some rationale in taking my essential recommendation literally: stop. **Recommendation T12** would be just that: totally stopping, and leaving things alone.

It is indeed quite possible that we don't have to "do" anything: it will do itself without our driving it. There is already evidence that the situation is starting to sort itself out, with younger generations' increasing technology exposure and interests, the increasing career-mindedness of young women and the pace of other changes in society. Those elements could be interpreted as implying "why bother": everything will change, it's impossible to keep up and so it is a waste of time and effort. And if we have hints of that already: imagine the effect of looming changes just a little further in the future such as life extension and who knows what else, that will render any approach we think of now void.

Perhaps we should just jump on the train and enjoy the ride with everyone else.

HACKFESTS AND CODE CAMPS

The potential of tapping into the trending activity of hackathons and hackfests produces two key focus areas, presented here with associated recommendations and explained below:

1. Hack historical women in IT research.
2. Hack to build a global IT information portal.

Hack Historical Women in IT Research

The primary **Recommendation H1** here is for a hackfest-style collaborative activity to maximise the value of the substantial volume of existing research. It would access the existing data sets of women in technology research and intervention programs to make them more accessible and valuable: creating not only improved access but also something new through visualization techniques, which would in turn contribute to deeper understanding. It could be as small as local and national events whose results are later combined in further hackfests, or as large as a combined international effort sweeping the world.

Hack events are supported by **Recommendation H2** to add further value by encouraging young girls themselves to form hacker teams and contribute to the outcomes. Perhaps even age-varied hackfests, where children as young as year 4 and 5 could be given the opportunity to contribute; it would be fascinating to see what sort of use and what apps would be developed across the different age groups. Potential outcomes are:

- Enhanced relevance of the research via mashups and visualization techniques;
- Hands-on code development by the hacker teams;
- Participants see the value of what they, their team and the other teams create within a short timeframe, showing them that coding is relevant and not just abstract;
- Empowerment and pride of work via hackathon rewards and recognition.

This will need universities, research organisations and other knowledge holders to relinquish any pre-#SocialEra proprietary policies in favour of an open data mining approach. If their reason for existing is the generation and dissemination of knowledge, then they should: hacking the research would breathe life into old research, add amazing tools for new research, and may itself reveal patterns pointing to influences, issues, obstacles and solutions not yet seen.

Hack the Existing IT Information and Portals

While intervention activities have failed to deliver their desired outcomes, nevertheless they have reached some women. A focus on the individual is all about empowering her, and improving access to quality information can only be good for everyone. This then leads to **Recommendation H3** of conducting a hackathon or similar activity aimed at creating an exciting, information packed, user friendly portal. This could provide a good conceptual framing of IT careers and allow people to drill down to whatever detail they want to pursue, in whatever direction or aspect that grabs their interest.

We know from the many historical activities and ongoing programs that there is an abundance of information out there: let's get it together into a truly global, easily located source; let's stop the fragmentation and duplicated efforts as people struggle to reinvent information. Or worse, repeat the old mistakes. Let differing age groups hack what is of interest to them and design the information and access in a commensurate style. This no longer needs to be the controlled domain of educational institutions, governments and industry associations. Open it up and let the hackers come and build. Make it open-ended so it continues to evolve with us.

Again a further **Recommendation H4** is encouragement for varied aged groups and possibly girl-only hack teams, which may enhance the outcomes and stories. Or why not the opposite: girl-only groups, boy-only groups and mixed groups – whatever the individuals prefer. The comparative results themselves would be illuminating. And why not both different ethnic groups and mixtures – again, whatever the participants themselves want. Freedom from gender stereotypes and cultural prejudices is an issue noted in the literature. We can do it, just by doing it. We will learn fascinating things not only from the results but from the activity itself.

Capitalise on the 'Code Camps' Trend

We learned in Chapter 5 – *Popular Theories* that personal interest can be fired up by exposure to technology as part of one's job. We also learned that a significant minority of women don't find out they are interested until they are already in the workforce: yet interventions, popular culture and personal advice do little to catch them before that. We can conclude that showing and explaining have some effect but *doing* and *experiencing* are far more important. Which forms the basic **Recommendation H5** in this section: focus on hands-on individual experiences. Move beyond generic "talkfests" to focus on providing relevant, interesting activities. Yes, that is harder to do. But there is little point taking an easier option if it fails to achieve your goals.

We learned in Chapter 6 – *Cultural & Social Contexts and Influencing Factors* about school based computer clubs. UNESCO (2012) notes "Develop specialized training. This is considered essential if girls and young women are to develop ICT skills commensurate with their needs as full-fledged participants in knowledge-based societies. Some nations take advantage of digital literacy initiatives such as summer camps for girls and adolescents in math, science and technology, operated by public-private partnerships." More recently there has been a marked increase in code camps, both virtual ones and physical, face-to-face weekend camps. On any week, even day, on Twitter you will see numerous classes run by STEMettes, BlackGirlsCode and the like. This is a powerful movement we can tap into to maximise hands-on exposure and activities.

So a further **Recommendation H6** is to capitalise on the code camp trend. Why design new computer clubs in the traditional sense, when you can explore the existing ones and those that will continue to crop up online?

Recruiters also need to pay attention. The code camp trend attracts participants who represent a pool of enthusiastic, actively engaged people with a demonstrable interest and talent in technology. Sponsorship, other support and placement of recruiters at code camps is a logical, highly targeted tactic to adopt. One in which everyone wins. Which is the essence of the #SocialIT world.

CROWDSOURCE AND CROWDFUND

There's enormous potential for tapping into the "crowd" for ideas, content and funding. Crowdsourcing harnesses information and volunteers to work together on a problem or project, whilst crowdfunding is a pathway to assist funding of activities via a large number of small donations from interested people.

Four key crowdsourced and crowdfunded projects are proposed and outlined below:

1. Role Models and Leaders.
2. Awards & Recognition.
3. IT Jingle.
4. "Up Series" style longitudinal study.

UNESCO (2012) notes that it's important to "Break the leadership mold. In a field in which women don't fit the 'standard template' of leadership, there's great value in creating a class of women STEM leaders. There may be beneficial economic and social consequences for companies that seek the increased participation of women in STEM."

But as discussed in Chapter 6 – *Cultural & Social Contexts and Influencing Factors*, despite ongoing calls for more there is in fact no shortage of role models, role model initiatives or named role models, either historical or new. Thus the issue is more about visibility. This leads to **Recommendation C1** being a crowdsourcing project to bring the wealth of existing role model and technology leaders information into better public view.

In addition to many recent initiatives we have 20 years of role model events and building up of achiever and leader profiles. They are from a multitude of organisations, most conducted in fragmented ways and as single efforts. This recommendation is about collecting those stories, combining them together and making the information readily and freely available in the public space. Information could be collected via crowdsourcing and costs paid by crowdfunding. Potentially the combination and presentation of the information could be via another hackfest.

The same logic applies to information on awards and recognition programs. As Modi, Schoenberg & Salmond (2012) suggest, role modelling and award programs help "expose girls to people who have careers in STEM, so they can observe firsthand what these careers are, and what they can offer. Girls can see the kinds of people who are in these careers, and begin to develop relationships with them. Girls can recognize how women in these fields have succeeded and overcome obstacles."

Thus **Recommendation C2** is that all the relevant award and recognition programs could be made visible via crowdsourcing the information and crowdfunding a project to hack the data and build associated apps and websites. This would bring global visibility and build a significant and valuable database with global stories to tell.

An aim would be to include differing views and layers to the information on role models and awards and recognition. As Ashcraft et al. (2012) note, role models need to be people we relate to in some way. And more, multiple views and layers are more likely to appeal to the wide variety of individual interests that are the true core of the issue. It is our individual interests that grab our attention and ignite our enthusiasm. We should do all we can to enable that.

Poor branding has been identified as an issue with IT careers. The image of the smelly, pizza-gobbling nerd is still trotted out even by people who know or should know better. **Recommendation C3** is that in the era of #SocialIT, the branding issue has a readily available solution through a crowdsourcing project to rename and rebadge the industry and its various acronyms, plus develop catchy promotional materials such as jingles and videos. The promotional materials could then be presented via #SocialIT tools such as YouTube.

Recommendation C4 is to seek community funding and resources to design and create an *Up Series* (Wikipedia, 2013) style longitudinal study of people in technology. The aim of this series is to digitally capture people in IT progressively across years of their lives, thus demonstrating the reality and individualism of those who inhabit the IT world, and the variety and impact of their work.

An element of interest for participants in some crowdsourced projects is rewards (financial and otherwise). As such there is an embedded link between the proposed crowdsourced projects and an earlier step of crowdfunding. Traditionally projects have been funded via government grants, corporate sponsorship, organization fundraising or individual philanthropy. Crowdfunding is a way to widen the funding pool, building it up from smaller amounts of money where people donate according to their specific areas of interest. Traditional funding sources could continue to actively participate as part of the crowdsourced pool, for example by encouraging people to donate by offering to match funds raised.

SOCIAL MEDIA AND JOIN THE CONVERSATION

Social Media are tools that women in technology activists can and should use to mobilise the wider community of politicians, educators, students, those in the industry and women in general into action, and engage their energy, interests, sponsorship and support. We already know from examples presented in Chapter 3 – *A New Approach* and Chapter 9 - *#SocialIT* that social media tools are already beginning to be actively used. This is not only in the West but also among women in developing countries, where they are used to communicate and spread information in general, address issues, voice opinions, debate politics, mobilize action in times of crisis, and discover connections and like minds across the Internet, where it is all about interaction and sharing. This presents a powerful opportunity "to create awareness and advocate for girls to be engaged in STEM opportunities. Become part of the conversation to get more girls involved and interested in STEM in order to improve their chances of engaging in a STEM career and to make STEM careers more accepting of women" (Modi et al., 2012). Social media tools are ideal to kick off and engage in the conversation, with the added value of being able to extend our reach enormously.

As such **Recommendation S1** is that advocates, activists and interested parties actively engage in social media campaigns and conversations. The essence of #SocialIT is that this can be *any way you want.* Activities may be anything from well thought out, structured, planned and coordinated programs, to ad hoc "chatter." With its global reach and opportunities for #SocialIT activities like the hackfests and crowdsourcing discussed above, this may well supplant traditional industry associations for connecting, networking, raising issues and influencing.

Key to this is identifying your audience and utilizing the appropriate social media forums, tools and approaches. Extend your reach directly to the people that matter, taking the advice of Ashcraft et al. (2012) to engage "key influencers in girls' lives—parents, teachers, school counsellors—about … why girls should consider a technical career … about why they should consider a computing career … point out the ways that computing can be used in a variety of fields to solve important problems. Highlight that these jobs are well-paying and likely to be quite plentiful." UNESCO (2012) suggest "Resonate with students… relate to girls and young women by talking about science and technology in ways that resonate and relate to their lives and aspirations. Girls are more likely to be attracted to technology education if STEM curricula and ICT projects are tied to the real world beyond school and domestic contexts."

As an individual you could seek to become an expert in your own right by blogging or posting to comments on blogs or online articles. Learn to leverage social and online media to become relevant on the topics you care about. Take to social media with specific critical thinking campaigns. For example, "talk with girls and others about unconscious biases like stereotype threat, its effects, and what can be done about it. Make girls aware of this phenomenon; recognizing it is the first step to overcoming it… Have informal conversations with girls (and others) about media and popular culture representations of technology and computing. As appropriate, strike up informal conversations with youth and others about media portrayals regarding technology and technology professionals... Have discussions about media representations and unconscious biases with your children or children you know" (Ashcraft et al., 2012). Encourage others to post the images they see and critically analyze the representations. This will help bring the conversation into the general public and provide people with the analytical insight required to deal with future material.

The conversation may be started outside social media itself with people who may then take it into their own social media circles. For example, Ashcraft et al. (2012) suggest "When watching television shows, reading magazines, or coming across advertisements related to technology, strike up informal conversations with children about the kinds of representations they are seeing. Ask for their opinions about these representations and offer your own… Talk with your children or children you know, particularly girls, about why they should consider computing careers. Remember that girls often know very little about or have significant misconceptions about technical careers. Make them aware of the benefits of these careers."

A secondary **Recommendation S2** is to consider using traditional media such as radio, newsletters, magazines and newspapers (specific, local, state and national) to publish comments and findings gathered through social media. Consider starting your own traditional media avenues, creating them yourself or submitting proposals to established providers. UNESCO (2012) suggests "Take it to the airways. The power of television can be used to attract girls to ICTs and STEM. The Argentine government has created a public television station dedicated to science and technology, and is commissioning programming on girls and ICTs." In my own backyard I volunteered as resident "geek girl" on ABC radio for over a decade covering interesting bits and bytes about technology, and one of my women in technology colleagues (Ann Uldridge) organised a series of role model profiles and stories that were presented over 8 episodes on community TV.

The global potential of harnessing these ideas and bringing them into reality is here, enhanced with the ease of social media connectivity. However a down side discussed in Chapter 7 – *Structural Context and Influencing Factors* is the corresponding ease of hostile reactions, not merely verbal but actual attacks on infrastructure. Unfortunately the possibility of such extreme and hostile responses to initiatives might need to be factored into future approaches. I suggest that a focus on the individual, rather than promoting one collective at the (real or imagined) expense of another, may help minimize such hostility.

Active use of social media is not just recommended for activists and advocates: there is value for educators, parents, governments and recruiters as well. For example, the extended networks through social media present an opportunity for employers and recruiting agencies to reach a wider pool of potential employees, and vice versa. Additionally **Recommendation S3** is that employers extend their recruitment reach via the social media networks of existing and past employees.

Similarly, the problem of the (in)visibility of female presenters and attendees at conferences has been noted (Donald, 2013). **Recommendation S4** is that social media could be used by organizers, other presenters and attendees to recommend and seek out female presenters.

HANGOUT AND COLLABORATE

Recommendations in this category are about collaborative activities that people as individuals and groups may undertake.

That many women *love* their careers in IT – not because or in spite of being women, but because as individuals they are good at it and like doing it – provides a platform of natural enthusiasm and interest whose influence could be extended using hangout techniques. **Recommendation G1** is that you consider what you can do to tap into these enthusiastic passionate women, whether searching for existing hangouts or creating your own – female only or mixed gender. As Modi et al. (2012) suggest, "Show girls that what they want out of their careers can be achieved through STEM. Showing girls that they can change the world and help people through STEM, while also making a good salary, will help make STEM more of a priority for girls as they begin to think about and narrow down their college majors and career choices. Girls need more exposure to and understanding of what STEM careers entail to see that some of the ways of work they are already interested in—such as designing technologies, asking questions, and solving problems are the foundations of many STEM professions." Tapping into the hangout culture will help provide that greater exposure. It will also help dispel common myths and misperceptions, such as the natural work culture of STEM professions being isolating rather than inclusive. And in real life, how much opportunity do schoolgirls get to have ongoing personal conversations with women enjoying the career they might be thinking about?

Being involved in technology hangouts may also help to address an issue noted by Modi et al. (2012) re needing to "keep girls interested and engaged in STEM over time and beyond transition points. While past research shows that girls' interest in STEM drops in middle school, this study points out another transition point—that girls' interest in STEM may be challenged by competing opportunities and interests as girls move from high school to college years and beyond. Providing college and career counselling for teen girls is important in bridging STEM interest in high school to a STEM major in college, eventually leading to a STEM career. Many high school girls say they are interested in STEM subjects and careers, but a much lower percentage say that a STEM career is their number one choice."

These points overlap the issue of mentoring. As Ashcraft et al. (2012) note, multi-level mentoring and encouragement is particularly valuable, and "mentoring does not only have to take place in person. Telementoring or e-mentoring can be an effective method to bring mentors or role models to girls who may not have any."

It's not just about hangouts using virtual meeting tools – it's also about meetups (organizing face to face meetings) of interest groups. Meetup tools extend our social reach, allowing us to find and meet people we otherwise wouldn't.

This leads us to recommendations stemming from the fact that for all the benefits of the virtual world, we should not neglect the vital importance of personal interaction in the real world. "Hanging out" in the original sense.

For parents and teachers, I propose **Recommendation G2** that you hang out with your children and/or students: talk with them and discuss their thoughts about technology and careers. As suggested by Modi et al. (2012), "Support and encourage STEM interests. When supportive adults, such as parents, relatives, teachers, and mentors show an interest in STEM careers for girls, they make those fields seem much more realistic and feasible, rather than something untouchable or unreachable." Indeed, one of the recurring themes among the pioneering women in technology (Chapter 2: *Women in Technology – Background*) was having parents who encouraged them.

But more valuable than talking is doing. For parents who may harbour an anti technology viewpoint I strongly endorse **Recommendation G3** that parents consider hanging out with their children by playing *Minecraft*. Parents could look at setting up their own Minecraft server together with your children, building your own worlds and characters and sharing the Minecraft experience. Understand more about this phenomenon and share it with your children. Using computers doesn't have to be an isolating experience; it can be a bonding one. The same applies to other creative games and virtual worlds, now and in the future.

Recommendation G4 is that schools and industry continue to hang out together, building closer ties by schools inviting industry representatives to visit them, engage the students in discussions and look at student placements. This is about local micro and small businesses, not just about giant brand name firms. Actively encourage closer engagement, with businesses not only visiting schools but where practical, students visiting businesses to see what life in the workplace is really like. With the rapid pace of change, work experience with current tools is becoming increasingly important, and perhaps we even need to consider some kind of "apprenticeship" style system instead of formal education followed by job-seeking. And we also need to think about how to exploit the tools of technology, e.g. virtual visits and remote work experience, in order to maximize the benefits and minimize the difficulties and costs.

CURIOUS, CREATIVE, AND CLEVER

Modi et al. (2012) sum up the chief purpose of this section well by stating in their recommendations,

"Encourage young girls to ask questions about the world, to problem solve, and to use natural creativity through play, creativity, and experimentation. This inquisitiveness can lead to innovative work in the future. It is important to continue this growth in developmentally appropriate ways throughout childhood and adolescence—the phase where typically STEM interest has dropped… Foster girls' internal assets such as confidence, self-esteem, initiative, and a work ethic. This can make girls feel successful and capable when it comes to interest in STEM fields—and anything else they set their minds to and have traditionally been steered away from. When girls feel capable and confident in their abilities, they will be more likely to challenge themselves and obstacles along the way."

Knowing how to use technology is important but uncreative: like knowing how to use a chisel compared to carving a sculpture. **Recommendation I1** is that policymakers and school curriculum developers acknowledge that the technology curriculum should not just be about using technology. It should be about engendering a spirit of innovation and curiosity about how to create and design technologies: how to *do* things and *why* to do them. This complements my earlier recommendation T6 to use online code classes rather than teachers for keeping abreast of the latest technologies and tools: instead the teacher should concentrate on principles and fostering a critical thinking environment.

Fostering curiosity and critical thinking should start in the home with parents, relatives and friends: encourage children to raise questions, solve problems and critically analyze information such as book storylines, media information and people's comments. Build curiosity by providing girls with early technology and computing experiences. **Recommendation I2** is that toy makers and children's authors ought to be encouraged to include critical thinking elements in their products, where a prime example is GoldieBlox (Sterling, 2012). As Ashcraft et al. (2012) point out, "quite a bit of research shows the importance of early exposure to technology and computing, and familial encouragement to pursue these interests."

It follows that if you as a school or parent cannot or do not want to have computer or Internet access, it is important for your children to have the opportunity by other means. Not only can it ignite their curiosity and interest, but having at least basic computer skills is important for life today and in the future. As such **Recommendation I3** is that other avenues, such as free facilities in public libraries and community centres, be explored to ensure that children have the chance to become familiar with computers.

There is a further implication for programs (intervention or otherwise) showcasing IT. Whilst they should demonstrate its creative and problem solving aspects in a hands-on way, they need to go further. Leading to **Recommendation I4** that designers of such activities target individual interests: focus on letting the individual participants drive what they are seeking and how they go about it, rather than assuming a one size solution fits all.

But my primary recommendation in this section is **Recommendation I5**: Foster an environment of critical thinking and questioning curiosity. Promote critical thinking classes and activities in schools. Cultivate curiosity by encouraging forms of mental attention, including mindfulness, that make us more curious about things we previously hadn't noticed or took for granted. Teach children to not just accept things as they are but to ask, "Why is that?" and "Must it be so?" Teach them *how to think:* how to work out the answers to those questions. Use high quality lesson preparation to engage students in creative problem solving with real world data and issues.

These suggestions go far beyond the narrow focus of IT, or even STEM. They will help educate our children for living, for whatever they choose to do with their lives.

Authors Log, 31 August, 2013: I asked my 10-year old daughter, "Why do you think some girls don't like computers?" Her instantaneous response: "It's just how they are."

REFERENCES

Ashcraft, C., Eger, E., & Friend, M. (2012). *Girls in IT: The facts*. Boulder, CO: National Centre for Women & Information Technology (NCWIT). Retrieved August 6, 2013, from http://www.academia.edu/2283166/Girls_in_IT_The_Facts

Bryner, J. (2007, February 28). Most students bored at school. *LiveScience*. Retrieved September 17, 2013, from http://www.livescience.com/1308-students-bored-school.html

Buser, T., Niederle, M., & Oosterbeek, H. (2012). *Gender, competitiveness and career choices*. Retrieved August 13, 2013, from http://www.stanford.edu/~niederle/Gender.BNO.pdf

Cave, K. (2013). Women in IT: Does the shortage matter? *IDG Connect Infographic*. Retrieved May 22, 2013, from http://www.idgconnect.com/abstract/1251/infographic-women-it-does-shortage-matter

Cohen, J. (2013). *We're frustrated too! The challenge of finding women presenters*. Retrieved September 15, 2013, from http://tedxcanberra.org/2013/08/were-frustrated-too-the-challenge-of-finding-women-presenters/

Donald, A. (2013). *Invited speakers, role models and women*. Retrieved August 2, 2013, from http://blogs.royalsociety.org/inside-science/2013/06/24/invited-speakers-role-models-and-women

Friedman, T. L. (2013, January 26). Revolution hits the universities. *The New York Times*. Retrieved September 17, 2013, from http://www.nytimes.com/2013/01/27/opinion/sunday/friedman-revolution-hits-the-universities.html

Herrick, L. K. (2009). *Same-sex schooling versus co-educational schooling and their effects on achievement, assessment and gender bias*. Project for Master in Teaching Degree, Evergreen State College. Retrieved August 11, 2013, from http://archives.evergreen.edu/mastersthesesIAc-cession89-10MIT/Herrick_LMITthesis2009.pdf

Hodson, H. (2013). AI to watch over you. *New Scientist, 220*(2944), 21. doi:10.1016/S0262-4079(13)62730-X

Jarrett, C. (2013, December 4). Getting in a tangle over men's and women's brain wiring. *Wired*. Retrieved December 5, 2013, from http://www.wired.com/wiredscience/2013/12/getting-in-a-tangle-over-men-and-womens-brain-wiring/

Lewis, T., & LiveScience. (2013, December 2). How men's brains are wired differently than women's. *Scientific American*. Retrieved December 4, 2013, from http://www.scientificamerican.com/article.cfm?id=how-mens-brains-are-wired-differently-than-women

Merchant, N. (2012). 11 rules for creating value in the #SocialEra. Boston, MA: Harvard Business School (HBR Singles).

Milfort, M. (2012). *An examination of the information technology job market*. Jobs for the Future. Retrieved September 17, 2013, from http://www.jff.org/sites/default/files/CTW_ExaminationInfo-TechnJobMarket_071212_0.pdf

Miliszewska, I., & Moore, A. (2011). Attracting girls to ICT studies & careers – A snapshot of strategies. *Redress, 20*(3), 10–14.

Modi, K., Schoenberg, J., & Salmond, K. (2012). *Generation STEM: What girls say about science, technology, engineering, and math*. Girl Scouts of the USA. Retrieved August 10, 2013, from http://www.girlscouts.org/research/pdf/generation_stem_full_report.pdf

NotableQuotes. (2013). *Isaac Asimov quotes*. Retrieved August 2, 2013, from http://www.notable-quotes.com/a/asimov_isaac.html

Olds, K. (2013, January 27). Memo to Trustees re: Thomas Friedman's 'revolution hits the universities'. *Inside Higher Ed*. Retrieved September 17, 2013, from http://www.insidehighered.com/blogs/globalhighered/memo-trustees-re-thomas-friedman's-'revolution-hits-universities'

Sandberg, S. (2013). *Lean in women, work, and the will to lead*. New York: Knopf.

Soe, L., & Yakura, E. K. (2008). What's wrong with the pipeline? Assumptions about gender and culture in IT work. *Women's Studies. An Inter-Disciplinary Journal*, *37*(3), 176–201.

Sterling, D. (2012). *GoldieBlox: The engineering toy for girls*. Retrieved August 27, 2013, from http://www.kickstarter.com/projects/16029337/goldieblox-the-engineering-toy-for-girls/posts

Tandon, N., Pritchard, S., Savelieva, V., Smith, G., & Vogt, E. (2012). *A bright future in ICTs opportunities for a new generation of women*. Geneva, Switzerland: International Telecommunication Union.

UNESCO. (2012). *Girls in STEM and ICT careers: The path toward gender equality*. New York: UNESCO.

Watts, A. G., & Sultana, R. G. (2004). Career guidance policies in 37 countries: Contrasts and common themes. *International Journal for Educational and Vocational Guidance*, *4*, 105–122. doi:10.1007/s10775-005-1025-y

Wikipedia. (2013). *Up series*. Retrieved September 20, 2013, from http://en.wikipedia.org/wiki/Up_Series

Willyard, C. (2011, January). Men in psychology: A growing minority? *gradPSYCH Magazine*. Retrieved September 6, 2013, from http://www.apa.org/gradpsych/2011/01/cover-men.aspx

Yoshida, K. S. (2013). *Forget Venus and Mars, we're beginning to understand gender behavior on Earth*. Retrieved October 1, 2013, from http://arstechnica.com/science/2013/09/forget-venus-and-mars-were-beginning-to-understand-gender-behavior-on-earth/

APPENDIX

Table 1. Table of Recommendations

Group	Ref	Summary Recommendation
Tectonic	T1	Remove the gender lens and replace it with an individual lens.
	T2	Ensure that any future intervention programs are done without a gender focus.
	T3	Instead of specific women in technology career events, focus on highlighting IT in general career activities.
	T4	Accept that only a certain number of women will ever be interested in technology careers and focus on reaching them.
	T5	Theme-based schools focused on technology, rather than single-sex classes or one-size-fit all universal curricula.
	T6	Schools embrace online courses such as code classes instead of relying on their own teachers.
	T7	Educational institutions lend their physical infrastructure and technology resources to host hands-on computing code clubs and activities for younger groups.
	T8	Secondary school code camps could host hands-on activities for primary schools.
	T9	Schools and tertiary institutions consider encouraging interested students to set up and look after their networks and other aspects of their IT systems.
	T10	Teach children innovation and entrepreneurship. Shift the focus from job-seeking alone to more awareness that you can create technologies and businesses yourself.
	T11	Career guidance practitioners to focus on the primacy of the individual rather than a collective approach and generic career advice.
	T12	Totally stop and leave things alone. It is quite possible that we don't have to "do" anything: it will do itself without our driving it.
Hackfests & Code Camps	H1	Build a hackfest-style collaborative activity to maximise the value of the substantial existing formal and informal research. It would access the data sets of women in technology research and intervention programs to make them more accessible and valuable.
	H2	Add further value to the research hackfest by encouraging young girls themselves to form hacker teams and contribute to the outcomes.
	H3	Conduct a hackathon or similar activity aimed at creating an exciting, information packed, user friendly portal on IT careers and pathways.
	H4	In the portal hack, enhance the outcomes and stories by encouraging varied age and gender teams.
	H5	Move beyond generic "talkfests" to focus on providing relevant, interesting activities, especially hands-on individual experiences.
	H6	Capitalise on the code camp trend: tap into the world's enthusiasm rather than reinventing your own solution.
Crowdsourcing & Crowdfunding	C1	Create a crowdsourcing project to bring the wealth of existing role model and technology leaders information into better public view.
	C2	Create a crowdsourcing and crowdfunding project to hack the relevant award and recognition programs data and build associated apps and websites.
	C3	Design a crowdsourcing project to rename and rebadge the industry and its various acronyms, plus develop catchy promotional materials such as jingles and videos.
	C4	Seek community funding and resources to design and create an *Up Series* style longitudinal portrait of people in technology.

continued on following page

Table 1. Continued

Group	Ref	Summary Recommendation
Social Media & Join the Conversation	S1	Advocates, activists and interested parties should actively engage in social media campaigns and conversations.
	S2	Utilise traditional media such as radio, newsletters, magazines and newspapers to publish comments and findings gathered through social media.
	S3	Employers to extend their recruitment reach via the social media networks of existing and past employees.
	S4	Social media to be used by organizers, other presenters and attendees to recommend and seek out female presenters for conferences.
Hangout & Collaborate	G1	Consider what you can do to tap into the enthusiastic passionate women in IT, whether searching for existing hangouts or creating your own – female only or mixed gender
	G2	Hang out with your own children and/or students: talk with them and discuss their thoughts about technology and careers.
	G3	Parents consider hanging out with their children by playing Minecraft. Parents could look at setting up their own Minecraft server together with your children, building your own worlds and characters and sharing the Minecraft experience.
	G4	Schools and industry continue to hang out together, building closer ties.
Curious, Creative & Clever	I1	For policymakers and school curriculum developers, the technology curriculum should not just be about using technology. It should be about engendering a spirit of innovation and curiosity about how to create and design technologies: how to *do* things and *why* to do them.
	I2	Toy makers and children's authors ought to be encouraged to include critical thinking elements in their products.
	I3	Explore the free computer facilities in public libraries and community centres to ensure that all children have the chance to become familiar with computers.
	I4	Whilst programs (intervention and otherwise) should demonstrate technology's creative and problem solving aspects in a hands-on way, they need to go further to target individual interests: focus on letting the individual participants drive what they are seeking and how they go about it, rather than assuming a one size solution fits all.
	I5	Foster an environment of critical thinking and questioning curiosity. Promote critical thinking classes and activities in schools.

Compilation of References

Accenture. (2013). *Defining success: 2013 global research results*. Retrieved September 1, 2013, from http://www.accenture.com/SiteCollectionDocuments/PDF/Accenture-IWD-2013-Research-Deck-022013.pdf

Adam, A. (2002). Exploring the gender question in critical information systems. *Journal of Information Technology*, *17*, 59–67. doi:10.1080/02683960210145959

Advincula, F. (2012). *A letter for new engineers: You will be different and that's OK*. Retrieved July 10, 2013, from http://women2.com/a-letter-for-new-engineers-you-will-be-different-and-thats-ok/

Adya, M., & Kaiser, K. M. (2005). Early determinants of women in the IT workforce: A model of girls' career choices. *Information Technology & People*, *18*(3), 230–259. doi:10.1108/09593840510615860

Adya, M., & Kaiser, K. M. (2006). Factors influencing girls' choice of information technology careers. In E. M. Trauth (Ed.), *Encyclopaedia of gender and information technology* (Vol. 1, pp. 282–288). Hershey, PA: Idea Group Reference. doi:10.4018/978-1-59140-815-4.ch044

Ahuja, M. K. (2002). Women in the information technology profession: A literature review, synthesis, and research agenda. *European Journal of Information Systems*, *11*(1), 20–34. doi:10.1057/palgrave.ejis.3000417

Akst, J. (2013). *Some girls better at science*. Retrieved July 2, 2013, from http://www.the-scientist.com/?articles.view/articleNo/34284/title/Some-Girls-Better-at-Science/

Albom, M. (2013, March 17). What's really behind Google's crazy offices? *Detroit Free Press*. Retrieved August 7, 2013 from http://www.freep.com/article/20130317/COL01/303170166/Mitch-Albom-What-s-really-behind-Google-s-crazy-offices-

Alic, M. (1986). *Hypatia's heritage: A history of women in science from antiquity to the late nineteenth century*. London, UK: The Women's Press.

Allen, M. W., Armstrong, D. J., Riemenschneider, C. K., & Reid, M. F. (2006). Making sense of the barriers women face in the information technology workforce: Standpoint theory, self-disclosure, and causal maps. *Sex Roles*, *54*, 831–844. doi:10.1007/s11199-006-9049-4

Alper, J. (1993). The pipeline is leaking women all the way along. *Science*, *260*, 409–411. doi:10.1126/science.260.5106.409 PMID:17838262

Amabile, T. M., Conti, R., Coon, H., Lazenby, J., & Henon, M. (1996). Assessing the work environment for creativity. *Academy of Management Journal*, *39*(5), 1154–1184. doi:10.2307/256995

Amaratunga, D., Haigh, R., Lee, A., Shanmugam, M., & Elvitigala, G. (2006). *Construction industry and women: A review of the barriers*. Salford, UK: The University of Salford.

American College of Healthcare Executives. (2006). *A comparison of the career attainments of men and women healthcare executives*. Retrieved September 6, 2013, from http://www.ache.org/pubs/research/gender_study_full_report.pdf

Anderson, M. (2013). *UA part of national alliance to spur African-American computer science graduate students*. UA News. Retrieved September 7, 2013, from http://uanews.ua.edu/2013/05/ua-part-of-national-alliance-to-spur-african-american-computer-science-graduate-students/

Anderson, N. (2003). *Making the link: Three successful university, industry and community collaborations around ICT development*. Paper presented at Higher Education without Borders – Sustainable Development in Education. Khon Kaen, Thailand. Retrieved August 3, 2013, from http://eprints.jcu.edu.au/834/

Anderson, N., Lankshear, C., & Courtney, L. (2008a). *Girls and information communication technology (ICT) career pathways: Tackling the upper middle school 'turn off'*. Retrieved July 21, 2013, from http://www.neilrobertanderson.com/girlsict/current%20research.html

Anderson, N., Lankshear, C., Courtney, L., & Timms, C. (2006). Girls and ICT survey: Initial findings. *Curriculum Leadership, 4*(12).

Anderson, N., Timms, C., & Courtney, L. (2006). If you want to advance in the ICT industry, you have to work harder than your male peers: Women in ICT industry survey: Preliminary findings. In *Proceedings of the 2006 Australian Women in IT Conference AusWIT 2006 10th Australian Women in IT Conference: Participation One Year On*. Adelaide, Australia: AusWIT.

Anderson, N., Lankshear, C., Timms, C., & Courtney, L. (2008b). 'Because it's boring, irrelevant and I don't like computers': Why high school girls avoid professionally-oriented ICT subjects. *Computers & Education, 50*(4), 1304–1318. doi:10.1016/j.compedu.2006.12.003

Andres-Beck, B. (2012). *The internet is convincing women not to study computer science*. Retrieved August 28, 2013, from http://blog.bethcodes.com/is-the-internet-convincing-women-not-to-study

Angier, N. (2013, September 2). Mystery of the missing women in science. *The New York Times*. Retrieved September 7, 2013, from http://www.nytimes.com/2013/09/03/science/mystery-of-the-missing-women-in-science.html

Anita Borg Institute. (2013). *Famous women in computer science*. Retrieved November 15, 2013, from http://anitaborg.org/news/profiles-of-technical-women/famous-women-in-computer-science/

Aragon, D. (2013). *Manuel Castells*. Retrieved November 18, 2013, from http://prezi.com/3jnj_o_zmddl/manuel-castells/

Armstrong, D. J., Riemenschneider, C. K., Reid, M., & Allen, M. (2007). Advancement, voluntary turnover and women in IT: A cognitive study of work–family conflict. *Information & Management, 44*, 142–153. doi:10.1016/j.im.2006.11.005

Arnold-Smeets, L. (2013a, August 19). For the horde! 10 rad jobs of the future (infographic). *PayScale*. Retrieved August 30, 2013, from http://www.payscale.com/career-news/2013/08/for-the-horde!-10-rad-jobs-of-the-future-infographic-

Arnold-Smeets, L. (2013b, December 10). Data scientist: Sexiest job of the 21st century. *PayScale*. Retrieved December 13, 2013, from http://www.payscale.com/career-news/2013/12/data-scientist-sexiest-job-of-the-21st-century

Ashcraft, C., Eger, E., & Friend, M. (2012). Girls in IT: The facts. Boulder, CO: National Centre for Women & Information Technology (NCWIT).

Asian Scientist. (2013). *Elsevier: Lack of women scientists in South Korea, India*. Retrieved August 24, 2013, from http://www.asianscientist.com/academia/elsevier-lack-women-scientists-south-korea-india-2013/ also from http://wisat.org/home/new-gender-benchmarking-study-finds-women-greatly-under-represented-in-south-korean-science-technology-innovation/

Austin Independent School District. (2011). *Single-gender education: A review of current issues and practices*. Retrieved August 13, 2013, from http://www.austinisd.org/sites/default/files/announcements/D-White%20Paper%20Final%209.12.11.pdf

Australian Mentor Centre. (2008). *What is mentoring?* Retrieved August 10, 2013, from http://www.australian-mentorcentre.com.au/what+is+mentoring

Baker, T. (2012). *Enhancing STEM education with GIS ebook released.* Retrieved July 2, 2013, from http://blogs.esri.com/esri/gisedcom/2012/09/06/advancing-stem-education-with-gis-ebook-released/

Bansal, S. (2011, September 28). One point for crowdsourcing: Gamers solve protein structure of AIDS-like protein. *Forbes*. Retrieved August 13, 2013, from http://www.forbes.com/sites/sarikabansal/2011/09/28/crowd-sourcing-gamers-solve-protein/

Barabanova, S. V. (2013). *The decline of women in Russian engineering education.* Paper presented at 120th ASEE Annual Conference & Exposition – Frankly we do give a D*MN. New York, NY.

Barker, L. J., & Aspray, W. (2006). The state of research on girls and IT. In J. M. Cohoon, & W. Aspray (Eds.), *Women and information technology: Research on under-representation* (pp. 3–54). Cambridge, MA: MIT Press. doi:10.7551/mitpress/9780262033459.003.0001

Barnes, J. (2013, March 18). Women lawyers in India 'vital for future society'. *The Global Legal Post*. Retrieved September 25, 2013, from http://www.globallegalpost.com/global-view/women-lawyers-in-india-vital-for-future-society-46922508

Barron, B. (2004). Learning ecologies for technological fluency: Gender and experience differences. *Journal of Educational Computing Research*, *31*(1), 1–36. doi:10.2190/1N20-VV12-4RB5-33VA

Barry, D. (2012). *Geena Davis wants to give Hollywood a heads up that female characters need way more speaking roles.* Retrieved August 4, 2013, from http://jezebel.com/5963090/geena-davis-wants-to-give-hollywood-a-heads-up-that-female-characters-need-way-more-speaking-roles

Bartlett, B. (2012, April 17). Do small businesses create jobs? *The New York Times*. Retrieved August 7, 2013, from http://economix.blogs.nytimes.com/2012/04/17/do-small-businesses-create-jobs/

Bartlett, D. (2013, September 30). ICT's masculine identity. *CIO*. Retrieved October 1, 2013, from http://www.cio.com.au/blog/comfort-zone/2013/09/30/icts-masculine-identity/

Bateman, K. (2012). *Industry still failing to attract female talent everywomen survey finds.* Retrieved July 20, 2013, from http://www.computerweekly.com/feature/Industry-still-failing-to-attract-female-talent-everywoman-survey-finds

Bateman, K. (2012). *Men and women disagree on reasons why IT is less attractive to women.* Retrieved July 20, 2013, from http://www.computerweekly.com/news/2240159441/Men-and-women-disagree-on-reasons-why-IT-is-less-attractive-to-women

Bateman, K. (2013). *Is outdated terminology deterring females from roles in IT?* Retrieved July 2, 2013, from http://www.computerweekly.com/feature/Is-outdated-terminology-deterring-females-from-roles-in-IT

Beekhuyzen, J. (2013). *Tech girls are superheroes.* [Video]. Retrieved November 15, 2013, from http://www.kickstarter.com/projects/1891407856/tech-girls-are-superheroes

Beekhuyzen, J., Nielsen, S., & von Hellens, L. (2006). *Making IT fit: Research and action in Queensland.* Paper presented at the AusWIT Australian Women in IT Conference. Adelaide, Australia.

Beekhuyzen, J., Nielsen, S., & von Hellens, L. (2003). Challenging dualisms in female perceptions of IT work. *Australian Journal of Information Systems*, *10*(2), 105–114.

Beltran, D. O., Das, K. K., & Fairlie, R. W. (2008). *Home computers and educational outcomes: Evidence from the NLSY97 and CPS.* (Board of Governors of the Federal Reserve System: International Finance Discussion Papers, No. 958). Retrieved August 10, 2013, from http://www.federalreserve.gov/pubs/ifdp/2008/958/ifdp958.pdf

Bernhardt, S. (2001). *WIT real women unreal jobs: Post event analysis report.* Brisbane, Australia: Unpublished report.

Bernhardt, S. (2002). *ICT skills, training and role model (i-STAR) program: Final report women to stars (W2*.)* Brisbane, Australia: Unpublished Report.

Bernhardt, S. (2005). *The failure of intervention programs.* Paper presented at the Girls and ICTs State Strategic Meeting. Brisbane, Australia.

Bernhardt, S. (2006). *Go girl go for IT event analysis.* Paper presented at the ACEC Conference. Cairns, Australia.

Bernhardt, S. (2006). The global failure of intervention programs. In *Proceedings of ACEDC Conference*. Cairns, Australia: ACEDC. Retrieved July 29, 2013, from http://conferences.acce.edu.au/item.asp?pid=7493

Bernhardt, S. (2006). Boards need women with IT. In E. M. Trauth (Ed.), *Encyclopedia of gender and information technology* (Vol. 1, pp. 70–76). Hershey, PA: Idea Group Reference. doi:10.4018/978-1-59140-815-4.ch012

Berry, M., & Kalessi, T. (2011). *Women's careers in the technology industry*. London, UK: Intellect and Women in Technology (Report). Retrieved August 1, 2013, from http://sciencewithart.ijs.si/pdf/Women's_Careers_in_the_Technology_Industry_2011_Report.pdf

Berryman, S. E. (1983). *Who will do science? Minority and female attainment of science and mathematics degrees: Trends and causes*. New York: Rockefeller Foundation.

Beyer, K. W. (2009). *Grace Hopper and the invention of the information age*. Cambridge, MA: MIT Press.

Biology, N. C. (2009). Attracting women (editorial). *Nature Cell Biology, 11*, 915. Retrieved October 9, 2013, from http://www.nature.com/ncb/journal/v11/n8/full/ncb0809-915.html

Blair, R., Gill, K., & Benson, M. (2013). *Focus on the pipeline*. Alexander Mann Solutions and Everywomen. Retrieved August 1, 2013, from http://info.everywoman.com/women-in-management-focus-on-the-pipeline/

Bloomberg. (2013). *TV women to watch: Women take the lead in technology.* Retrieved August 2, 2013, from http://www.bloomberg.com/video/women-to-watch-women-take-the-lead-in-technology-4om~ml8DTCGBNcun_my-leg.html

Bobe, A. (2013). *Meet a 13 year old programmer excited to change the world.* Black Girls CODE. Retrieved July 17, 2013, from http://women2.com/meet-a-13-year-old-programmer-excited-to-change-the-world/

Bogart, N. (2013). *How the role of social media has evolved since Egypt's last upheaval.* Retrieved July 18, 2013, from http://globalnews.ca/news/693614/how-the-role-of-social-media-has-evolved-since-egypts-last-upheaval/

Boyd, S. (2011). *Revolution – Messiness at scale, again.* Retrieved July 18, 2013, from http://stoweboyd.com/post/3105227293/revolution-messiness-at-scale-again

Brady, D. (2013). *Carly Fiorina on Marissa, Sheryl, and women in tech.* Retrieved July 4, 2013, from http://www.businessweek.com/authors/867-diane-brady

BrainyQuote. (2013). *Albert Einstein quotes.* Retrieved August 2, 2013, from http://www.brainyquote.com/quotes/authors/a/albert_einstein.html

BrainyQuote. (2013). *Hypatia quotes.* Retrieved August 2, 2013, from http://www.brainyquote.com/quotes/authors/h/hypatia.html

Bryner, J. (2007, February 28). Most students bored at school. *LiveScience.* Retrieved September 17, 2013, from http://www.livescience.com/1308-students-bored-school.html

Burnett, E. (2013). *Black girls code and the digital divide.* Retrieved August 24, 2013, from http://Ed.cnn.com/video/data/2.0/video/bestoftv/2013/08/22/exp-erin-pkg-simon-idea-black-girls-code-bridges-digital-divide.cnn.html

Buser, T., Niederle, M., & Oosterbeek, H. (2012). *Gender, competitiveness and career choices*. Retrieved August 13, 2013, from http://www.stanford.edu/~niederle/Gender.BNO.pdf

Calvert, S. L., Rideout, V. J., Wollard, J. L., Barr, R. F., & Strouse, G. A. (2005). Age, ethnicity, and socioeconomic patterns in early computer use. *The American Behavioral Scientist, 48*(5), 590–607. doi:10.1177/0002764204271508

Carbone, A., & Sheard, J. (2001). *Go girl, go for IT 2001 expo: Analysis of student and teacher surveys*. Unpublished report.

Carbone, A., & Sheard, J. (2006). *Go girl, go for IT 2006 evaluation report*. Unpublished report.

Carpenter, J. (2013). *Study finds women biologists more likely to avoid spotlight at conferences*. Retrieved August 28, 2013, from http://news.sciencemag.org/people-events/2013/06/study-finds-women-biologists-more-likely-avoid-spotlight-conferences

Carrington, B., Tymms, P., & Merrell, C. (2008). Role models, school improvement and the gender gap – Do men bring out the best in boys and women bring out the best in girls? *British Educational Research Journal*, *34*(3), 1–13. doi:10.1080/01411920701532202

Casallas, R., Hernandez, J. T., Rodriguez, D. H., & Ortega, M. F. (2012). Understanding the women participation decline in systems & computing engineering: Case study at the University of Los Andes, Colombia. In *Proceedings of Informatica (CLEI), 2012 XXXVIII Conferencia Latinoamericana En*. IEEE. Retrieved August 26, 2013, from http://ieeexplore.ieee.org/xpl/login.jsp?tp=&arnumber=6427243

Casserly, M. (2012, May 11). 10 jobs that didn't exist 10 years ago. *Forbes*. Retrieved August 27, 2013, from http://www.forbes.com/sites/meghancasserly/2012/05/11/10-jobs-that-didnt-exist-10-years-ago/

Castano, C., & Webster, J. (2011). Understanding women's presence in ICT: The life course perspective. *International Journal of Gender. Science and Technology*, *3*(2), 358–363.

Castells, M. (1996). *The rise of the network society: The information age: Economy, society and culture* (Vol. 1). Oxford, UK: Blackwell.

Castells, M. (1997). *The power of identity: The information age: Economy, society and culture* (Vol. 2). Oxford, UK: Blackwell.

Castells, M. (1998). *End of millennium: The information age: Economy, society and culture* (Vol. 3). Oxford, UK: Blackwell.

Catalyst. (2013). *Catalyst quick take: Women leaving and re-entering the workforce*. New York: Catalyst. Retrieved August 26, 2013, from http://www.catalyst.org/knowledge/women-leaving-and-re-entering-workforce

Cave, K. (2012). Women: Why doesn't IT have iPad appeal? *IDG Connect Business Management*. Retrieved May 22, 2013, from http://www.idgconnect.com/blog-abstract/654/kathryn-cave-global-women-why-doesn-t-it-have-ipad-appeal

Cave, K. (2013). Women in IT: Does the shortage matter? *IDG Connect Infographic*. Retrieved May 22, 2013, from http://www.idgconnect.com/abstract/1251/infographic-women-it-does-shortage-matter

Cave, D. (2012). *Digital islands: How the Pacific's ICT revolution is transforming the region*. Sydney, Australia: Lowy Institute.

Chang, A. (2013). *Record number of women give tech talks at PYCON 2013*. Retrieved August 8, 2013, from http://women2.com/5-great-talks-by-women-software-engineers-at-pycon-2013/

Charman-Anderson, S. (2012). *Ada Lovelace Day fundraiser*. Retrieved August 2, 2013, from http://www.indiegogo.com/projects/ada-lovelace-day-fundraiser

Cheeseman Day, J., & Downs, B. (2009). *Opting-out: An exploration of labor force participation of new mothers*. Paper presented at the Population Association of America 2009 Annual Meeting. Detroit, MI.

Cheeseman Day, J., Janus, A., & Davis, J. (2005). *Computer and Internet use in the United States: 2003*. U.S. Census Bureau. Retrieved August 10, 2013, from http://www.census.gov/prod/2005pubs/p23-208.pdf

Cherry, K. (2013). What is the actor observer bias? *About.com: Psychology*. Retrieved July 21, 2013, from http://psychology.about.com/od/aindex/g/actor-observer.htm

Cheryan, S., Meltzoff, A. N., & Kim, S. (2011). Classrooms matter: The design of virtual classrooms influences gender disparities in computer science classes. *Computers & Education*, *57*(2), 1825–1835. doi:10.1016/j.compedu.2011.02.004

Cheryan, S., & Plaut, V. C. (2010). Explaining underrepresentation: A theory of precluded interest. *Sex Roles*, *63*(7-8), 475–488. doi:10.1007/s11199-010-9835-x PMID:20930923

Cheryan, S., Plaut, V. C., Handron, C., & Hudson, L. (2013). The stereotypical computer scientist: Gendered media representations as a barrier to inclusion for women. *Sex Roles*, *69*(1), 58–71. doi:10.1007/s11199-013-0296-x

Cheryan, S., Siy, J. O., Vichayapai, M., Drury, B. J., & Kim, S. (2011). Do female and male role models who embody STEM stereotypes hinder women's anticipated success in STEM? *Social Psychological and Personality Science*, *2*(6), 656–664. doi:10.1177/1948550611405218

Childs, S., & Krook, M. L. (2006). Should feminists give up on critical mass? A contingent yes. *Politics & Gender*, *2*, 522–530. doi:10.1017/S1743923X06251146

Clark Blickenstaff, J. (2005). Women and science careers: Leaky pipeline or gender filter? *Gender and Education*, *17*(4), 369–386. doi:10.1080/09540250500145072

Clayton, K. (2007). *The influence of metropolitan Brisbane middle-school ICT experiences on girls' ICT study and career choices*. (Unpublished doctoral dissertation). Griffith University, Queensland, Australia.

Clayton, K. L., von Hellens, L. A., & Nielsen, S. H. (2009). Gender stereotypes prevail in ICT: A research review. In *Proceedings of the Special Interest Group on Management Information System's 47th Annual Conference on Computer Personnel Research* (SIGMIS CPR) (pp. 153-158). ACM.

Clayton, K., & Beekhuyzen, J. (2004). Engaging girls in ICT: Mind the gap! In *Proceedings of the 2004 Australian Women in IT Conference* (pp. 41-47). Hobart, Australia: Academic Press.

Clayton, K., Beekhuyzen, J., & Nielsen, S. (2012). Now I know what ICT can do for me? *Information Systems Journal*, *22*(5), 1–16. doi:10.1111/j.1365-2575.2012.00414.x

Cleary, P. F., Pierce, G., & Trauth, E. M. (2006). Closing the digital divide: Understanding racial, ethnic, social class, gender and geographic disparities in internet use in school age children in the United States. *Universal Access in the Information Society*, *4*, 354–373. doi:10.1007/s10209-005-0001-0

Cohen, J. (2013). *We're frustrated too! The challenge of finding women presenters*. Retrieved September 15, 2013, from http://tedxcanberra.org/2013/08/were-frustrated-too-the-challenge-of-finding-women-presenters/

Cohen, P. N. (2013, November 23). How can we jump-start the struggle for gender equality? *The New York Times*. Retrieved November 26, 2013, from http://opinionator.blogs.nytimes.com/2013/11/23/how-can-we-jump-start-the-struggle-for-gender-equality/

Cohoon, J. M. (2012). *Different genders, different worlds*. Open Thoughts 2012: Universitat Oberta de Catalunya. Retrieved August 17, 2013, from http://openthoughts.blogs.uoc.edu/2012/11/different-genders-different-worlds.html

Cohoon, J. M. (2003). Just get over it or just get on with it: Retaining women in undergraduate computing. In W. Aspray, & J. M. Cohoon (Eds.), *Women and information technology: Research on the reasons for under-representation*. Cambridge, MA: MIT Press.

Cohoon, J. M., & Asprey, W. (Eds.). (2006). *Women and information technology: Research on underrepresentation*. London: MIT Press. doi:10.7551/mitpress/9780262033459.001.0001

Comer, M., Freire, M. C., & Russell, A. J. (2013). Disrupting Alzheimer's disease research. *Genetic Engineering & Biotechnology News, 33*(18).

Commission on Professionals in Science and Technology. (2005). *Preparing women and minorities for the IT workforce: The role of nontraditional educational pathways*. Washington, DC: American Association for the Advancement of Science.

Commons Select Committee. (2013). *Women in STEM careers*. Retrieved July 26, 2013, from http://www.parliament.uk/business/committees/committees-a-z/commons-select/science-and-technology-committee/inquiries/parliament-2010/women-in-stem-careers/

Commonwealth of Australia. (2011). *Age pension and superannuation preservation ages*. Retrieved August 30, 2013, from http://www.taxreview.treasury.gov.au/content/StrategicPaper.aspx?doc=html/Publications/Papers/Retirement_Income_Strategic_Issues_Paper/Chapter_5.htm

Computerworld. (2011). *Moth in the machine: Debugging the origins of 'bug'*. Retrieved November 11, 2013, from http://www.computerworld.com/s/article/9183584/Moth_in_the_machine_Debugging_the_origins_of_bug_

CONSAD Research Corp. (2009). *An analysis of the reasons for the disparity in wages between men and women* (Report for US Department of Labor). Pittsburgh, PA: CONSAD Research Corp. Retrieved August 4, 2013, from http://www.consad.com/content/reports/Gender%20Wage%20Gap%20Final%20Report.pdf

Construction Sector Council. (2010). *The state of women in construction in Canada*. Ontario, Canada: Construction Sector Council.

Copeland, J. (Ed.). (2006). *Colossus: The secrets of Bletchley Park's codebreaking computers*. Oxford, UK: Oxford University Press.

Court, G., & Moralee, J. (1995). *Balancing the building team: Gender issues in the building professions*. London: Institute for Employment Studies/CIOB, University of Sussex.

Cozza, M. (2011). Bridging gender gaps, networking in computer science. *Gender, Technology and Development*, *15*(2), 319–337. doi:10.1177/097185241101500207

Crabb, A. (2012). Publication of Germaine Greer's the female eunuch. *ABC Personalities Tell Us Which Days Changed Their Lives*. Retrieved August 2, 2013, from http://www.abc.net.au/archives/80days/stories/2012/01/19/3411580.htm

Craig, A. (2008). *Attracting women to computing, a framework for evaluating intervention programs.* (Unpublished doctoral dissertation). Monash University, Melbourne, Australia.

Craig, A., Dawson, L., & Fisher, J. (2009). *Measuring the success of intervention programmes designed to increase the participation rate by women in computing*. Paper presented at the European Conference on Information Systems 2009. Verona, Italy.

Craig, A., Fisher, J., & Dawson, L. (2011). Women In ICT: Guidelines for evaluating intervention programmes. In *Proceedings of European Conference on Information Systems* (pp. 1-13). Aalto University School of Economics.

Craig, A., Fisher, J., & Lang, C. (2007). ICT and girls: The need for a large scale intervention programme. In *Proceedings of the 18th Australasian Conference on Information Systems* (pp. 761-769). Toowoomba, Australia: University of Southern Queensland.

Craig, A., Lang, C., & Fisher, J. (2008). Twenty years of girls into computing days: Has it been worth the effort? *Journal of Information Technology Education*, *7*, 339–353.

CrunchBase. (2013). *GoldieBlox*. Retrieved August 27, 2013, from http://www.crunchbase.com/company/goldie-blox

Curtis, A. (2013). *The brief history of social media*. Retrieved July 12, 2013, from http://www.uncp.edu/home/acurtis/NewMedia/SocialMedia/SocialMediaHistory.html

Curtsinger, J. W. (2007). *Clinical and health affairs – Genes, aging, and prospects of extended life spans.* Retrieved August 17, 2013, from http://www.minnesotamedicine.com/CurrentIssue/g/tabid/2307/

D'Mello, M. (2006). Gendered selves and identities of information technology professionals in global software organizations in India. *Information Technology for Development*, *12*(2), 131–158. doi:10.1002/itdj.20031

Da Silva Reis, S., & Schulze, E. (2012). *Policy department citizens rights and constitutional affairs – Women in ICT*. Brussels: European Parliament.

Dahlerup, D. (2006). The story of the theory of critical mass. *Politics & Gender*, *2*, 511–522. doi:10.1017/S1743923X0624114X

Dainty, A. R. J., Bagilhole, B. M., & Neale, R. H. (2001). Male and female perspectives on equality measures for the UK construction sector. *Women in Management Review*, *16*(6), 297–304. doi:10.1108/EUM0000000005820

de Grey, A. (2009). *In pursuit of longevity*. Retrieved August 18, 2013, from http://www.youtube.com/watch?v=HTMNfU7zftQ

Deloitte. (2013). *Digital disruption – Short fuse, big bang?* Retrieved August 16, 2013, from http://www.deloitte.com/au/digitaldisruption

Denner, J. (2009). The role of the family in the IT career goals of middle school Latinas. In *Proceedings of AMCIS 2009*. AMCIS.

Denner, J. (2011). What predicts middle school girls' interest in computing? *International Journal of Gender. Science and Technology*, *3*(1), 53–69.

Department of Education. Employment and Workplace Relations (DEEWR). (2013). *Digital education and technology in schools*. Retrieved August 2, 2013, from http://deewr.gov.au/digital-education-and-technology-schools

DesMarais, C. (2012). *15 women to watch in tech*. Retrieved August 2, 2013, from http://www.inc.com/ss/christina-desmarais/15-women-watch-tech-startups.html#11

DesMarais, C. (2013). *10 women to watch in tech*. Retrieved August 2, 2013, from http://www.inc.com/ss/christina-desmarais/11-women-watch-tech

DEST. (2002). *Australian selected higher education statistics, table 2: All students with user specified field of study by gender, 1989 to 2000*. Canberra, Australia: Department of Education Science and Training.

Dickason, E. (1992). *Remembering Grace Murray Hopper: A legend in her own time*. Retrieved November 11, 2013, from http://www.history.navy.mil/bios/hopper_grace.htm

Diminescu, G., Hepp, A., Welling, S., Maya-Jariego, I., & Yates, S. (2009). *ICT supply and demand in immigrant and ethnic minority communities in France, Germany, Spain and the United Kingdom*. Seville, Spain: European Commission.

Donald, A. (2013). *Invited speakers, role models and women*. Retrieved August 2, 2013, from http://blogs.royalsociety.org/inside-science/2013/06/24/invited-speakers-role-models-and-women

Dougherty, C. (2010, September 1). Young women's pay exceeds male peers. *The Wall Street Journal*. Retrieved August 4, 2013, from http://online.wsj.com/article/SB10001424052748704421104575463790770831192.html

Downes, S. (2004). *Into the new millennium: Why do students decide to study IT?* Paper presented at the Informing Science and Technology Education Joint Conference. Rockhampton, Australia.

Dryburgh, H. (2000). Underrepresentation of girls and women in computer science: Classification of 1990s' research. *Journal of Educational Computing Research*, *23*(2), 181–202. doi:10.2190/8RYV-9JWH-XQMB-QF41

DuBow, W. M. (2011). *NCWIT scorecard: A report on the status of women in information technology*. Boulder, CO: NCWIT.

Duliba, K. A., & Barouid, J. (1991). *IS personnel: Do they form an occupational community?* New York: Stern School of Business, New York University. doi:10.1145/111084.372748

Duncan, D. E. (2012, August 16). *When I'm 164: The new science of radical life extension and what happens if it succeeds*. TED Conferences.

Duncan, J. (2013, August 7). Why are so many women leaving architecture? *Guardian Professional*. Retrieved September 6, 2013, from http://www.theguardian.com/women-in-leadership/2013/aug/07/women-leaving-architecture-profession

Durante, K. M., Griskevicius, V., Simpson, J. A., Cantu, S. M., & Tybur, J. M. (2012). Sex ratio and women's career choice: Does a scarcity of men lead women to choose briefcase over baby? *Journal of Personality and Social Psychology*, *103*(1), 121–134. doi:10.1037/a0027949 PMID:22468947

Eccles, J. S. (2007). Where are all the women? Gender differences in participation in physical science and engineering. In S. J. Ceci, & W. M. Williams (Eds.), *Why aren't more women in science? Top researchers debate the evidence* (pp. 199–210). Washington, DC: American Psychological Association. doi:10.1037/11546-016

Economist. (2012). *An iPopping phenomenon*. Retrieved August 16, 2013, from http://www.economist.com/node/21551058

Economist. (2013). *Charging the mobile*. Retrieved August 16, 2013, from http://www.economist.com/news/finance-and-economics/21579870-east-african-governments-are-targeting-telecoms-firms-charging-mobile

Elder, G. H., Jr. (1999). Children of the great depression: Social change in life experience (25th anniversay Ed.). Boulder, CO: Westview Press.

Elmaghraby, A. (2013). *A look into the future: Citizens, communities and open data*. Retrieved August 13, 2013, from http://www.iftf.org/future-now/article-detail/a-look-into-the-future-citizens-communities-and-open-data/

Elnaggar, A. (2007). The status of Omani women in the ICT sector. *International Journal of Education and Development using Information and Communication Technology, 3*(3), 4-15.

Eltahawy, M. (2008). *Arab bloggers keep watch over government – and each other*. Retrieved August 1, 2013, from http://newsweek.washingtonpost.com/postglobal/mona_eltahawy/2008/05/arab_bloggers_keep_watch_over.html

Empson, R. (2012). *Learn to code, get a job: Treehouse offers free courses to 2,500 college students*. Retrieved January 10, 2013, from http://techcrunch.com/2012/09/14/learn-to-code-get-a-job-treehouse-offers-free-courses-to-2500-college-students/

Engineer. (2011). *Decline in government support for women in engineering*. Retrieved August 26, 2013, from http://www.theengineer.co.uk/channels/skills-and-careers/news/decline-in-government-support-for-women-in-engineering/1006869.article

Equal Opportunities Commission. (1995). Job segregation linked to gender bias. *Equal Opportunities Review, 60*.

European Commission. (2013). *Europe 2020*. Retrieved August 24, 2013, from http://ec.europa.eu/europe2020/index_en.htm

Exploring Computer Science. (2013). *CS education statistics*. Retrieved September 22, 2013, from http://www.exploringcs.org/resources/cs-statistics

Falub, M. (2013). *Fix the leaky pipeline – A career building program for women in science*. Retrieved July 26, 2013, from http://www.fix-the-leaky-pipeline.ch/

Fang, I. (1997). *A history of mass communication: Six information revolutions*. Boston: Focal Press.

Farber, D. (2013). *The next big thing in tech: Augmented reality*. Retrieved August 16, 2013, from http://news.cnet.com/8301-11386_3-57588128-76/the-next-big-thing-in-tech-augmented-reality/

Faulkner, W., & Stewart, J. (2003). *National ICT training for teachers: A case of 'gender blindness'?* (Deliverable DO3/Volume 1 of IST-2000-26329 SIGIS Project). Retrieved from http://www.rcss.ed.ac.uk/sigis/public/documents/SIGIS_D03_2.09_UEDIN3.pdf

Feldman, D. C. (2000). The Dilbert syndrome: How employee cynicism about ineffective management is changing the nature of careers in organizations. *The American Behavioral Scientist*, *43*(8), 1286–1300. doi:10.1177/00027640021955865

Fielden, S. L., Davidson, M. J., Gale, A. W., & Davey, C. L. (2000). Women in construction: The untapped resource. *Construction Management and Economics*, *18*, 113–121. doi:10.1080/014461900371004

File, T. (2013). *Computer and internet use in the United States*. U.S. Census Bureau. Retrieved August 10, 2013, from http://www.census.gov/prod/2013pubs/p20-569.pdf

Finding Ada. (2013). *Ada Lovelace Day in a nutshell.* Retrieved September 22, 2013, from http://findingada.com

Firth, N. (2013). Power at their fingertips. *New Scientist, 220*(2943), 22–23. doi:10.1016/S0262-4079(13)62682-2

Fisher, A. (2006, August 15). Are you stuck in middle management hell? *CNN Money.* Retrieved August 4, 2013, from http://money.cnn.com/magazines/fortune/fortune_archive/2006/08/21/8383654/

Fisher, A. (2012, September 28). What it really takes to get that next promotion. *CNN Money.* Retrieved August 4, 2013, from http://management.fortune.cnn.com/2012/09/28/promotions-careers/

Fitzpatrick, K. (2011). *Planned obsolescence: Publishing, technology, and the future of the academy.* New York: New York University Press. Abstract retrieved November 23, 2013, from http://www.amazon.com/gp/product/0814727883

Flynn, J., Heath, K., & Holt, M. D. (2013). *Six paradoxes women leaders face in 2013.* Retrieved May 2013, from http://blogs.hbr.org/cs/2013/01/six_paradoxes_women_leaders_fa.html

Frankincense. (2012). *Really, no girls play Minecraft? What do you think?* Retrieved August 3, 2013, from http://www.minecraftforum.net/topic/1262129-really-no-girls-play-minecraft-what-do-you-think/

Fried, I. (2013). *Stanford students hope posting documentary online will get more women to code.* Retrieved July 17, 2013, from http://allthingsd.com/20130717/stanford-pair-hopes-posting-documentary-online-will-get-more-women-to-code/

Friedman, T. L. (2013, January 26). Revolution hits the universities. *The New York Times.* Retrieved September 17, 2013, from http://www.nytimes.com/2013/01/27/opinion/sunday/friedman-revolution-hits-the-universities.html

Gale, A. W. (1994). Women in non-traditional occupations: the construction industry. *Women in Management Review, 9*(2), 3–14. doi:10.1108/EUM0000000003989

Gal-Ezer, J., Shahak, D., & Zur, E. (2009). Computer science issues in high school: Gender and more…. *Inroads SIGCSE Bulletin, 41*(3), 278–282. doi:10.1145/1595496.1562963

Galpin, V. (2002). Women in computing around the world. *ACM SIGCSE Bulletin, 34*(2), 94–100. doi:10.1145/543812.543839

Gándara, P., & Contreras, F. (2009). *The Latino education crisis: The consequences of failed social policies.* Cambridge, MA: Harvard University Press.

Garcia-Garcia, M. (2013). *Online mentoring program for STEM fields.* Retrieved August 2, 2013, from http://www.gradschool.cornell.edu/announement/online-mentoring-program-stem-fields

Garratt, P. (2012). *Minecraft - Why I stopped playing it with my kids.* Retrieved August 3, 2013, from http://www.vg247.com/2012/08/07/minecraft-why-i-stopped-playing-it-with-my-kids/

Giddens, A. (1984). *The constitution of society: Outline of the theory of structuration.* Cambridge, UK: Polity Press.

Gladwell, M. (2001). *The tipping point: How little things can make a big difference.* London, UK: Abacus.

Goh, G. (2013). *Why women in the ICT industry are paid less than men.* Retrieved August 24, 2013, from http://www.digitalnewsasia.com/digital-economy/why-women-in-the-ict-industry-are-paid-less-than-men

Goode, J. (2008). Increasing diversity in K-12 computer science education: Lessons from the field. *Proceedings of the 38th SIGCSE Technical Symposium on Computer Science Education, 40*(1), 362-371.

Goode, J., Estrella, R., & Margolis, J. (2006). Lost in translation: Gender in high school computer science. In J. Cohoon, & W. Aspray (Eds.), *Women and information technology: Research on underrepresentation* (pp. 89–114). Cambridge, MA: MIT Press. doi:10.7551/mitpress/9780262033459.003.0003

Goodreads. (2013). *Jules Verne > Quotes > Quotable quote*. Retrieved August 2, 2013, from https://www.goodreads.com/quotes/51047-we-see-that-science-is-eminently-perfectible-and-that-each

Goodreads. (2013). *Richard Buckminster Fuller > Quotes*. Retrieved August 2, 2013, from https://www.goodreads.com/author/quotes/165737.Richard_Buckminster_Fuller

Goodstein, D. (1994). *The big crunch*. Paper presented at the NCAR 48 Symposium. Portland, OR. Retrieved August 30, 2013, from http://www.its.caltech.edu/~dg/crunch_art.html

Goodwin, B. (2006). *Better networking keeps me in the top IT jobs, research suggests*. Retrieved June 2, 2013, from http://www.computerweekly.com/news/2240076516/Better-networking-keeps-men-in-the-top-IT-jobs-research-suggests

Gorbis, M. (2012). *The institute for the future*. Retrieved August 10, 2013, from http://www.youtube.com/watch?v=5_EsLu4qydw

Gorbis, M. (2013). *The nature of the future: Dispatches from the socialstructured world*. New York: Free Press.

Gordon, C. (2012). *Randi Zuckerberg: The controversial ambassador for women in tech*. Retrieved July 4, 2013, from http://jobs.aol.com/articles/2012/11/02/randi-zuckerberg-the-controversial-ambassador-for-women-in-tech/

Gras-Velazquez, A., Joyce, A., & Debry, M. (2009). *Women and ICT: Why are girls still not attracted to ICT studies and careers?* (White Paper). Brussels: European Schoolnet (EUN Partnership AISBL).

Gratton, L. (2012). *Could Steve Jobs have been a woman?* Open Thoughts 2012: Universitat Oberta de Catalunya. Retrieved August 17, 2013, from http://openthoughts.blogs.uoc.edu/2012/05/could-steve-jobs-have-been-woman.html

Greenfield, S., Peters, J., Lane, N., Rees, T., & Samuels, G. (2002). *SET fair – A report on women in science, engineering and technology*. London: UK Government.

Greer, G. (1970). *The female eunuch*. London, UK: Paladin.

Griffiths, M., & Moore, K. (2010). 'Disappearing women': A study of women who left the UK ICT sector. *Journal of Technology Management and Innovation*, *5*(1), 95–107. doi:10.4067/S0718-27242010000100008

Groom, D. (2012). *Why won't she get off Minecraft?* Retrieved August 3, 2013, from http://deangroom.wordpress.com/2012/11/28/why-wont-she-get-off-minecraft/

Gudmundsdottir, G. (2010). From digital divide to digital equity: Learners' ICT competence in four primary schools in Cape Town, South Africa. *International Journal of Education and Development using Information and Communication Technology, 6*(2), 84-105.

Gutelle, S. (2012). *Google to profile powerful women in the tech industry via hangout*. Retrieved July 10, 2013, from http://www.tubefilter.com/2012/11/01/google-developers-live-women-techmakers/

Guzdial, M., Ericson, B., McKlin, T., & Engleman, S. (2012). A statewide survey of computing education pathways and influences: Factors in broadening participation in computing. In *Proceedings of ACM International Computing Education Research (ICER) Conference* (pp. 143-150). New York: ACM.

Guzman, I., & Stanton, J. (2009). IT occupational culture: The cultural fit and commitment of new information technologists. *Information Technology & People*, *22*(2), 157–187. doi:10.1108/09593840910962212

Guzman, I., Stanton, J., & Eischen, D. (2006). Female perceptions of the information technology culture. In E. M. Trauth (Ed.), *Encyclopedia of gender and information technology* (Vol. 1, pp. 304–309). Hershey, PA: Idea Group Reference. doi:10.4018/978-1-59140-815-4.ch047

Hale, B., & Fong, V. (2002). *What do women in IT want? Ask them says Penn State researcher.* Retrieved August 6, 2013, from http://www.psu.edu/ur/2002/oddgirl.html

Ham, R., Junankar, P. N., & Wells, R. (2009). *Occupational choice: Personality matters* (IZA Discussion Paper No. 4105). Bonn: IZA.

Harding, S. (1986). *The science question in feminism*. Ithaca, NY: Cornell University Press.

Harding, S. (1991). *Whose science? Whose knowledge?* Ithaca, NY: Cornell University Press.

Harding, S. (1998). *Is science multicultural? Postcolonialisms, feminisms, and epistemologies*. Bloomington, IN: Indiana University Press.

Hardy, T. (2013). *The importance of feeding your curiosity*. Retrieved August 10, 2013, from http://teensintech.com/blog/2013/01/curiosityarticlerocketlist

Haskins, J. (2013). *Natalie Portman and Marvel team up to get girls into science*. Retrieved October 7, 2013, from http://www.healthline.com/health-news/women-natalie-portman-and-marvel-host-girls-contest-100613

Hayes, E. (2005). Women, video gaming, and learning: Beyond stereotypes. *TechTrends*, *49*(5), 23–28. doi:10.1007/BF02763686

Hayes, E. (2008). Girls, gaming and trajectories of IT expertise. In Y. B. Kafai, C. Heeter, J. Denner, & J. Y. Sun (Eds.), *Beyond Barbie and Mortal Kombat: New perspectives on gender and gaming* (pp. 217–230). Cambridge, MA: MIT Press.

Haywood, B., Alty, C., Pearson, S., & Martin, C. (2003). *Young people's use of ICT 2002: ICT in schools research and evaluation series no. 12*. Retrieved August 2, 2013, from BECTA/DfES.http://dera.ioe.ac.uk/1646/1/becta_2002_youngpeoplesuse_report_queensprinter.pdf

Hearn, L. (2006). *Calendar girl website survives attack*. Retrieved June 2, 2013, from http://www.theage.com.au/news/biztech/calendar-girls-under-attack/2006/07/17/1152988460039.html

Heemskerk, I., Brink, A., Volman, M., & ten Dam, G. (2005). Inclusiveness and ICT in education: A focus on gender, ethnicity and social class. *Journal of Computer Assisted Learning*, *21*, 1–16. doi:10.1111/j.1365-2729.2005.00106.x

Henwood, F. (1993). Establishing gender perspectives on information technology: Problems, issues and opportunities. In E. Green, J. Owen, & D. Pain (Eds.), *Gendered by design: Gender, information technology and the design of office systems* (pp. 31–52). London: Taylor and Francis.

Herman, A. M. (1999). *Futurework - Trends and challenges for work in the 21st century*. Washington, DC: US Department of Labour.

Herrick, L. K. (2009). *Same-sex schooling versus co-educational schooling and their effects on achievement, assessment and gender bias*. Project for Master in Teaching Degree, Evergreen State College. Retrieved August 11, 2013, from http://archives.evergreen.edu/masterstheses/Accession89-10MIT/Herrick_LMITthesis2009.pdf

Hess, M. (2011). *18 female founders in tech to watch*. Retrieved August 2, 2013, from http://www.huffingtonpost.com/2011/08/08/female-tech-founders_n_916751.html#s318621&title=Jess_Lee_Polyvore

Heussner, K. M. (2013). *Wearable tech VC's pan Google glass*. Retrieved August 16, 2013, from http://gigaom.com/2013/07/24/wearable-tech-vcs-pan-google-glass/

HEXUStv. (2009). *Bletchley Park code breakers – Mr and Mrs Lawn*. [Video]. Retrieved November 12, 2013, from http://www.youtube.com/watch?v=FVE5K89EMe0

He, X., & Zhang, J. (2009). On the growth of scientific knowledge: Yeast biology as a case study. *PLoS Computational Biology*, *5*(3), e1000320. doi:10.1371/journal.pcbi.1000320 PMID:19300476

Higher Education Statistics Agency. (2013). *Students and qualifiers data tables*. Retrieved September 21, 2013, from http://www.hesa.ac.uk/index.php/content/view/1973/239/

Hodkinson, P., & Sparkes, A. C. (1997). Careership: A sociological theory of career decision making. *British Journal of Sociology of Education, 18*(1), 29-44.

Hodson, H. (2013). AI to watch over you. *New Scientist*, *220*(2944), 21. doi:10.1016/S0262-4079(13)62730-X

Howard, K. (2013). *Women codebreakers*. Bletchley Park Research. Retrieved November 12, 2013, from http://www.bletchleyparkresearch.co.uk/research-notes/women-codebreakers/

Howcroft, D., Adam, A., & Richardson, H. (2004). A decade of neglect: reflecting on the gender and IS field. *New Technology, Work and Employment*, *19*, 222–240. doi:10.1111/j.1468-005X.2004.00139.x

Hussein, F. (2012). *Female engineers in short supply, declining*. Retrieved August 26, 2013, from http://www.news-journalonline.com/article/20121028/BUSINESS/310269984

Hutchison, E. D. (2008). *Dimensions of human behavior: The changing life course*. Los Angeles, CA: Sage.

Hyek, P. A. (2011). *Rapid technology innovation creates a smart, mobile world*. Retrieved August 16, 2013, from http://www.ey.com/GL/en/Issues/Business-environment/Six-global-trends-shaping-the-business-world---Rapid-technology-innovation-creates-a-smart--mobile-world

IMD. (2009). *World competitiveness yearbook 2009*. Lausanne, France: IMD Publications.

Indivero, V. M., & Messer, A. E. (2011, September 22). Sex segregation in schools detrimental to equality. *Penn State News*. Retrieved August 11, 2013, from http://news.psu.edu/story/155177/2011/09/22/sex-segregation-schools-detrimental-equality

Institute for the Future. (2013). *Ten-year forecast*. Retrieved December 7, 2013, from http://www.iftf.org/fileadmin/user_upload/downloads/researchagendas/TYF_2013ResearchAgenda_01.pdf

Isaacson, B. (2013). *Women in tech: 5 startup founders to watch*. Retrieved August 2, 2013, from http://www.huffingtonpost.com/2013/01/31/women-startup-founders_n_2512893.html

Jackson, T. (2012). *The 10 most powerful women in African tech*. Retrieved October 4, 2013, from http://www.ventures-africa.com/2012/08/the-10-most-powerful-women-in-african-tech/

Janack, M. (2004). Feminist epistemology. *Internet Encyclopedia of Philosophy*. Retrieved November 17, 2013, from http://www.iep.utm.edu/fem-epis/

Jarrett, C. (2013, December 4). Getting in a tangle over men's and women's brain wiring. *Wired*. Retrieved December 5, 2013, from http://www.wired.com/wiredscience/2013/12/getting-in-a-tangle-over-men-and-womens-brain-wiring/

Jett, M. (2012, March 14). Infographic: Women in architecture. *ArchDaily*. Retrieved Aug 28, 2013, from http://www.archdaily.com/216844/infographic-women-in-architecture/

Johnson, W. C., & Jones, R. C. (2006). *Declining interest in engineering studies at a time of increased business need*. Retrieved August 28, 2013, from http://www.worldexpertise.com/Declining_Interest_in_Engineering_Studies_at_a_Time_of_Increased_Business_Needs.htm

Joshi, K. D., & Kuhn, K. (2011). What determines interest in an IS career? An application of the theory of reasoned action. *Communications of the Association for Information Systems, 29*, Article 8.

Kafai, Y. B. (2008). Considering gender in digital games: Implications for serious game designs in the learning sciences. In *Proceedings of the 8th International Conference on Learning Sciences* (vol. 1, pp. 422-429). ICLS.

Kafai, Y. B., Heeter, C., Denner, J., & Sun, J. Y. (Eds.). (2008). *Beyond Barbie and Mortal Kombat: New perspectives on gender and gaming*. Cambridge, MA: MIT Press.

Kansra, N., & Mohamed, S. A. (2012, October 4). Gender imbalances persist in academics. *The Harvard Crimson*. Retrieved September 1, 2013, from http://www.thecrimson.com/article/2012/10/4/gender-imbalance-social-sciences/

Karoly, L., & Panis, C. (2004). *The future at work – Trends and implications*. Santa Monica, CA: RAND Corporation.

Kaskey, V. (2012). An investigation into a career day on a student's choice of profession. *International Journal of Business and Social Science*, *3*(14), 53–58.

Keith, K. T. (2009). Life extension proponents, opponents, and the social impact of the defeat of death. In M. K. Bartolos (Ed.), *Speaking of death, America's new sense of morality*. Westport, CT: Praeger Publishers.

Kelan, E. (2008). Emotions in a rational profession: The gendering of skills in ICT work. *Gender, Work and Organization*, *15*(1), 49–71.

Kenny, C. (2011, September 28). Rethinking the boosterism about small business. *Bloomberg BusinessWeek Magazine*. Retrieved August 7, 2013, from http://www.businessweek.com/magazine/rethinking-the-boosterism-about-small-business-09282011.html

Khatib, F., & DiMaio, F.Foldit Contenders Group, Foldit Void Crushers Group, Cooper, S., Kazmierczyk, C., ... Baker, B. (2011). Crystal structure of a monomeric retroviral protease solved by protein folding game players. *Nature Structural & Molecular Biology*, *18*, 1175–1177. doi:10.1038/nsmb.2119 PMID:21926992

Kirkup, G. (2011). Preparing women for dead-end jobs? Vocational education and training (VET) for information and communication technology (ICT) jobs. *International Journal of Gender Science and Technology*, *3*(2), 460–482.

Kirkup, G., Zalevski, A., Maruyama, T., & Batool, I. (2010). *Women and men in science, engineering and technology: The UK statistics guide 2010*. Bradford: UKRC.

Klawe, M. (2002). Girls, boys and computers. *SIGCSE Bulletin*, *34*(2), 16–17. doi:10.1145/543812.543818

Klawe, M., Whitney, T., & Simard, C. (2009). Women in computing – Take 2. *Communications of the ACM*, *52*, 68–76. doi:10.1145/1461928.1461947

Klein, H. K., & Myers, M. (1999). A set of principles for conducting and evaluating interpretive field studies in information systems research. *Management Information Systems Quarterly*, *23*(1), 67–93. doi:10.2307/249410

Kleinman, Z. (2012). *Ladies first: Inside the first women-only game jam*. Retrieved August 2, 2013, from http://www.bbc.co.uk/news/technology-20186937

Kniveton, B. (2004). The influences and motivations on which students base their choice of career. *Research in Education*, *72*, 47–59. doi:10.7227/RIE.72.4

Koch, M. (2009). *Girls Incorporated build IT*. [Video]. Retrieved July 31, 2013 from http://www.youtube.com/watch?v=iag0Eyc0gZE

Kolander, O. J., & Kehinde, O. (2013). Glass ceiling and women career advancement: Evidence from Nigerian construction industry. *Iranian Journal of Management Studies*, *6*(1), 77–97.

Koons, S. (2012). *iDream play encourages young women to consider IT careers*. Retrieved August 2, 2013, from http://ist.psu.edu/news/idream-play-encourages-young-women-to-consider-it-careers

Koschel, J. (2013). *The growing technological generation gap*. Retrieved August 16, 2013, from http://theindustry.cc/2013/02/12/the-growing-technological-generation-gap/

Kramer, V. W., Konrad, A. M., & Erkut, S. (2006). *Critical mass on corporate boards: Why three or more women enhance governance*. Wellesley, MA: Wellesley Centers for Women's Publications Office.

Krause, K. W. (2013, March 13). The progressive war on science. *eSkeptic*. Retrieved August 2, 2013, from http://www.skeptic.com/eskeptic/13-03-13/

Kreit, B. (2012). *Diagnosing malaria--and closing labor gaps--through games*. Retrieved August 13, 2013, from http://archive.iftf.org/node/4186

Kroes, N. (2013). *ICT and women speech – European commission*. Retrieved July 21, 2013, from http://europa.eu/rapid/press-release_SPEECH-13-366_en.htm

Kvasny, L., Greenhill, A., & Trauth, E. M. (2005). Giving voice to feminist projects in management information systems research. *International Journal of Technology and Human Interaction*, *1*(1), 1–18. doi:10.4018/jthi.2005010101

Lagesen, V. A. (2008). A cyberfeminist utopia? Perceptions of gender and computer science among Malaysian women computer science students and faculty. *Science, Technology & Human Values*, *33*(1), 5–27. doi:10.1177/0162243907306192

Lang, C., Craig, A., Fisher, J., Bennetts, K., & Forgasz, H. (2010). Dualisms: What women say about working in ICT. In *Proceedings of ACIS 2010*. ACIS.

Lang, C., Fisher, J., & Craig, A. (2007). *Digital divas: Computer clubs for girls trial*. Brentwood Secondary College, Swinburne University of Technology Women in ICT Group and Victorian ICT for Women Network. Retrieved August 1, 2013, from http://www.swinburne.edu.au/ict/wict/documents/Report%20on%20Brentwood%20Computer%20Club%20Trial.pdf

Lang, C., & McKay, J. (2006). Australian IT enrolment trends and model of contributing factors. In E. M. Trauth (Ed.), *Encyclopedia of gender and information technology* (Vol. 1, pp. 50–56). Hershey, PA: Idea Group Reference. doi:10.4018/978-1-59140-815-4.ch009

Lanzer, F. (2009). Attracting girls to engineering & technology: Reach them before they're turned off. In *Proceedings of the 2009 Mid-Atlantic Section Conference of the American Society for Engineering Education*. Baltimore, MD: AACC. Retrieved August 5, 2013, from http://ola3.aacc.edu/fplanzer/documents/Attracting%20Girls%20to%20Technology%20Reach%20Them%20Before%20Turnoff.doc

Lavine, L. (2013). *Sheryl Sandberg encourages women bloggers to 'lean in'*. Retrieved August 11, 2013, from http://www.entrepreneur.com/article/227596#

Lee, K. J. B. (2010). Women in science, engineering and technology (SET) in Korea: Improving retention and building capacity. *International Journal of Gender. Science and Technology*, *2*(2), 236–248.

Leonard, J. S. (1989). Women and affirmative action. *The Journal of Economic Perspectives*, *3*(1), 61–75. doi:10.1257/jep.3.1.61

Lerner, A. W. (2013). *Bletchley Park*. Espionage Encyclopaedia. Retrieved November 12, 2013, from http://www.faqs.org/espionage/Bl-Ch/Bletchley-Park.html

Levine, B. (2011). *Computer gamers help solve AIDS protein problem*. Retrieved August 13, 2013, from http://www.newsfactor.com/story.xhtml?story_id=10300004X4P9

Lewis, H. (2013). *Are computer games being taken over by women?* Retrieved June 4, 2013, from http://www.telegraph.co.uk/women/10086627/Are-computer-games-being-taken-over-by-women.html

Lewis, J. J. (2013a). *Ada Lovelace*. About.com Women's History. Retrieved November 11, 2013, from http://womenshistory.about.com/cs/sciencemath1/a/bio_lovelace.htm

Lewis, J. J. (2013b). *Hypatia of Alexandria*. About.com Women's History. Retrieved November 11, 2013, from http://womenshistory.about.com/od/hypati1/a/hypatia.htm

Lewis, T., & LiveScience. (2013, December 2). How men's brains are wired differently than women's. *Scientific American*. Retrieved December 4, 2013, from http://www.scientificamerican.com/article.cfm?id=how-mens-brains-are-wired-differently-than-women

Light, J. S. (1999). When computers were women. *Technology and Culture*, *40*(3), 455–483.

Liston, C., Peterson, K., & Ragan, V. (2007). *Guide to promising practices in informal technology education for girls*. Boulder, CO: National Center for Women in Information Technology.

Liston, C., Peterson, K., & Ragan, V. (2008). *Evaluating promising practices in informal information technology (IT) education for girls: Women in IT—Survey results*. Boulder, CO: National Centre for Women & Information Technology.

Liston, C., Peterson, K., & Ragan, V. (2009). *Promising practices in informal information technology (IT) education for girls*. Paper prepared for AERA Meeting. San Diego, CA.

Lovgren, S. (2004). *CSI effect is mixed blessing for real crime labs*. Retrieved August 4, 2013, from http://news.nationalgeographic.com/news/2004/09/0923_040923_csi.html

Lowenstein, G. (1994). The psychology of curiosity: A review and reinterpretation. *Psychological Bulletin*, *116*, 75–98. doi:10.1037/0033-2909.116.1.75

Lynch, A. (2013). *10 of the best Aussie crowdsourcing projects from 2012*. Retrieved August 16, 2013, from http://www.smartcompany.com.au/start-up/053721-10-of-the-best-aussie-crowdsourcing-projects-from-2012-3.html

Lyons, T., Quinn, F., Rizk, N., Anderson, N., Hubber, P., Kenny, J., et al. (2012). *Starting out in STEM: A study of young men and women in first year science, technology, engineering and mathematics courses*. Armidale, Australia: University of New England. Retrieved August 13, 2013, from http://www.une.edu.au/simerr/pages/projects/132iris_report.pdf

Madden, M., Lenhart, A., Duggan, M., Cortesi, S., & Gasser, U. (2013). *Teens and technology 2013*. Washington, DC: Pew Research Center. Retrieved August 10, 2013, from http://www.pewinternet.org/~/media//Files/Reports/2013/PIP_TeensandTechnology2013.pdf

Mael, F., Alonso, A., Gibson, D., Rogers, K., & Smith, M. (2005). *Single-sex versus coeducational schooling: A systematic review*. Washington, DC: American Institutes for Research. Retrieved August 13, 2013, from http://www.air.org/files/Single_Sex_LitReview_091905.pdf

Mainwaring, S. (2011). *Exactly what role did social media play in the Egyptian revolution?* Retrieved July 18, 2013, from http://www.fastcompany.com/1727466/exactly-what-role-did-social-media-play-egyptian-revolution

Maisel, M., & Smart, L. (1997). *Women in science*. San Diego, CA: San Diego Supercomputer Centre. Retrieved November 11, 2013, from http://www.sdsc.edu/ScienceWomen/GWIS.pdf

Margolis, J., Estrella, R., Goode, J., Holme, J., & Nao, K. (2008). *Stuck in the shallow end: Education, race and computing*. Cambridge, MA: MIT Press.

Margolis, J., & Fisher, A. (2003). *Unlocking the clubhouse: Women in computing*. Cambridge, MA: MIT Press.

Margolis, J., Jellison Holme, J., Estrella, R., Goode, J., Nao, K., & Stumme, S. (2003). The computer science pipeline in urban high schools: Access to what? For whom? *IEEE Technology and Society Magazine*, *22*(3), 12–19. doi:10.1109/MTAS.2003.1237467

Mason, M. A., & Mason Ekman, E. (2007). *Mothers on the fast track: How a new generation can balance family and careers*. New York: Oxford University Press. doi:10.1093/acprof:oso/9780195182675.001.0001

Mathew, V. (2010). Women entrepreneurship in Middle East: Understanding barriers and use of ICT for entrepreneurship development. *International Entrepreneurship Management*, *6*, 163–181. doi:10.1007/s11365-010-0144-1

Matic, J. (2012). *Women and girls in ICT information session - Side event @ WRC-12*. Retrieved August 4, 2013, from http://www.youtube.com/watch?v=RIWB0jF9kxE

Matson, J. (2013, May). Women are earning greater share of STEM degrees, but doctorates remain gender-skewed. *Scientific American*. Retrieved September 1, 2013, from http://www.scientificamerican.com/article.cfm?id=women-earning-greater-share-stem-degrees-doctorates-remain-gender-skewed

Matuszak, G., & Lamoureux, T. (2012). *Mobilizing innovation: The changing landscape of disruptive technologies*. KPMG Technology Innovation Center. Retrieved August 16, 2013, from http://www.kpmg.com/Global/en/IssuesAndInsights/ArticlesPublications/technology-innovation-survey/Documents/mobilizing-innovation-august-2012.pdf

McCaskill, S. (2012). *Geena Davis named ITU special envoy for women in ICT*. Retrieved August 4, 2013, from http://www.techweekeurope.co.uk/news/itu-geena-davis-women-i-82154

McQuivey, J. (2013). *Digital disruption*. Retrieved August 16, 2013, from http://solutions.forrester.com/disruption

Meister, J. (2012). Job hopping is the 'new normal' for millennials: Three ways to prevent a human resource nightmare. *Forbes*. Retrieved July 28, 2013, from http://www.forbes.com/sites/jeannemeister/2012/08/14/job-hopping-is-the-new-normal-for-millennials-three-ways-to-prevent-a-human-resource-nightmare/

MentorSET. (2008). *What is mentoring?* Retrieved August 10, 2013, from http://www.mentorset.org.uk/pages/mentoring.htm

Merchant, N. (2012). 11 rules for creating value in the #SocialEra. Boston, MA: Harvard Business School (HBR Singles).

Merchant, N. (2012b). Stop talking about social and do it. *HBR Blog Network*. Retrieved September 16, 2012, from http://blogs.hbr.org/cs/2012/03/stop_talking_about_social_and_do_it.html

Merchant, N. (2012c). The social era is more than social media. *FastCompany*. Retrieved September 24, 2012, from http://www.fastcompany.com/3001505/social-era-more-social-media

Merchant, N. (2010). *The new how: Creating business solutions through collaborative strategy*. Sebastopol, CA: O'Reilly Media.

Merrett, R. (2012) *Pay gap, lack of role models to blame for ICT gender imbalance: EOWA*. Retrieved August 10, 2013, from http://www.cio.com.au/article/441965/pay_gap_lack_role_models_blame_ict_gender_imbalance_eowa/

Merz, T. (2013). *Weather crowdsourcing app. could track passing of single clouds*. Retrieved August 16, 2013, from http://www.telegraph.co.uk/technology/news/10244974/Weather-crowdsourcing-app-could-track-passing-of-single-clouds.html

Meszaros, P. S., Lee, S., & Laughlin, A. (2007). Information processing and information technology career interest and choice among high school students. In C. J. Burger, E. G. Creamer, & P. S. Meszaros (Eds.), *Reconfiguring the firewall: Recruiting women to information technology across cultures and continents* (pp. 77–95). Wellesley, MA: AK Peters, Ltd. doi:10.1201/b10634

Meyer, K. (2013, August 7). Why more women should create apps. *Forbes*. Retrieved August 27, 2013, from http://www.forbes.com/sites/85broads/2013/07/08/why-more-women-should-create-apps/

Milfort, M. (2012). *An examination of the information technology job market*. Jobs for the Future. Retrieved September 17, 2013, from http://www.jff.org/sites/default/files/CTW_ExaminationInfoTechnJobMarket_071212_0.pdf

Miliszewska, I., & Moore, A. (2010). Encouraging girls to consider a career in ICT: A review of strategies. *Journal of Information Technology Education: Innovations in Practice*, *9*, 143–166.

Miliszewska, I., & Moore, A. (2011). Attracting girls to ICT studies & careers – A snapshot of strategies. *Redress*, *20*(3), 10–14.

Millar, M. (2013). *How wearable technology could transform business*. Retrieved August 16, 2013, from http://www.bbc.co.uk/news/business-23579404

Millar, R. A. (2002). Extending life: Scientific prospects and political obstacles. *The Milbank Quarterly*, *80*(1), 155–173. doi:10.1111/1468-0009.00006 PMID:11933792

Miller, L., & Hayward, R. (2006). New jobs, old occupational stereotypes: Gender and jobs in the new economy. *Journal of Education and Work*, *19*(1), 67–93. doi:10.1080/13639080500523000

Misa, T. J. (Ed.). (2010). *Gender codes: Why women are leaving computing*. Hoboken, NJ: John Wiley. doi:10.1002/9780470619926

Misra, K. D. (2004). Information & communication technology for women's empowerment in India. *Information Technology in Developing Countries IFIP Working Group 9.4, 14*(2).

Mitchell, R. L. (2013). *Women computer science grads: The bump before the decline*. Retrieved August 28, 2013, from http://blogs.computerworld.com/it-careers/21993/women-computer-science-visual-trendline

Mkbschmid. (2009). *Jean Valentine explains the Bombe*. [Video]. Retrieved November 12, 2013, from http://www.youtube.com/watch?v=oex-9IkQRcg

Modi, K., Schoenberg, J., & Salmond, K. (2012). *Generation STEM: What girls say about science, technology, engineering, and math*. Girl Scouts of the USA. Retrieved August 10, 2013, from http://www.girlscouts.org/research/pdf/generation_stem_full_report.pdf

Moss-Racusin, C. A., Dovidio, J. F., Brescoll, V. L., Graham, M. J., & Handelsman, J. (2012). Science faculty's subtle gender biases favour male students. *Proceedings of the National Academy of Sciences of the United States of America*, *109*(41), 16474–16479. doi:10.1073/pnas.1211286109 PMID:22988126

Munro, K. (2011, June 13). More women than men taking the plunge into small business. *The Sydney Morning Herald*. Retrieved July 28, 2013, from http://www.smh.com.au/business/more-women-than-men-taking-the-plunge-into-small-business-20110612-1fzbj.html

Myers, S. L., & Fealing, K. H. (2012). Changes in the representation of women and minorities in biomedical careers. *Academic Medicine*, *87*(11), 1525–1529. doi:10.1097/ACM.0b013e31826d7189 PMID:23018333

Nagey, H. (2012). *Why girls don't code: Musings on the gender imbalance in the developer community.* Retrieved July 10, 2013, from http://newsletters.livecode.com/october/issue141/newsletter1.php

National Congress of Inventor Organizations. (1997). Great inventors: 1940's film goddess Hedy Lamarr responsible for pioneering spread spectrum. *America's Inventor Online Ed.* Retrieved November 30, 2013, from http://inventionconvention.com/americasinventor/dec97issue/section2.html

National Institute of Forensic Science. (2001). *Career information.* Retrieved August 16, 2013, from http://www.nifs.com.au/F_S_A/FSA_frame.html?Careers.asp&1

National Science Board. (2010). *Preparing the next generation of STEM innovators: Identifying and developing our nation's human capital.* Retrieved October 14, 2010, from http://www.nsf.gov/nsb/publications/2010/nsb1033.pdf

National Science Foundation. (2013). *Women, minorities, and persons with disabilities in science and engineering: Enrollment.* Retrieved December 8, 2013, from http://www.nsf.gov/statistics/wmpd/2013/digest/theme1.cfm

Nauert, R. (2013). *Men and women may not be so different after all.* PsychCentral. Retrieved August 4, 2013, from http://psychcentral.com/news/2013/02/05/men-and-women-may-not-be-so-different-after-all/51222.html

Neal, M. (2013). *Twitter knows which restaurants are getting people sick.* Retrieved August 16, 2013, from http://motherboard.vice.com/blog/twitter-knows-which-restaurants-are-getting-people-sick

NetHope. (2013). *Women's TechConnect.* Retrieved August 17, 2013, from http://nethopeacademy.org/womens-techconnect/

Newman, K. M. (2013). *Code fellows to hold Ruby on Rails bootcamp for women only.* Retrieved August 4, 2013, from http://tech.co/code-fellows-ruby-on-rails-bootcamp-for-women-only-2013-05

Newmarch, E., Taylor-Steele, S., & Cumpston, A. (2000). *Women in IT – What are the barriers?* Paper presented at the Network of Women in Further Education Conference Showcase of Strategies for Women in Education on Information Technology Conference. Adelaide, Australia.

Ng, C., & Mitter, S. (2005). *Gender and the digital economy: Perspectives from the developing world.* Thousand Oaks, CA: Sage. doi:10.4135/9788132103622

Nielsen, S., & von Hellens, L. (2006). The social construction of Australian women in IT. In E. M. Trauth (Ed.), *Encyclopedia of gender and information technology* (Vol. 2, pp. 1105–1111). Hershey, PA: Idea Group Reference. doi:10.4018/978-1-59140-815-4.ch174

Nielsen, S., von Hellens, L., Pringle, R., & Greenhill, A. (1999). Students' perceptions of information technology careers: Conceptualising the influence of cultural and gender factors for IT education. *GATES Journal*, *5*(1), 30–38.

NotableQuotes. (2013). *Isaac Asimov quotes.* Retrieved August 2, 2013, from http://www.notable-quotes.com/a/asimov_isaac.html

O'Connor, J. J., & Robertson, E. F. (1999). *Hypatia of Alexandria.* University of St Andrews Scotland. Retrieved November 12, 2013, from http://www-history.mcs.st-and.ac.uk/Printonly/Hypatia.html

O'Dell, J. (2013). *Tackling tech's gender problem the right way: Teaching women to code.* Retrieved June 2, 2013, from http://venturebeat.com/2013/01/10/hackbright/#gO5dqOMhKArT1l7p.99

Oblinger, D., & Oblinger, J. (Eds.). (2005). *Educating the net generation.* EDUCAUSE. Retrieved July 20, 2013, from http://www.educause.edu/educatingthenetgen

OECD. (2007). *ICTs and gender, working party on the information economy report, DSTI/ICCP/IE(2006)9/final.* Paris: Organisation for Economic Co-Operation and Development.

Olds, K. (2013, January 27). Memo to Trustees re: Thomas Friedman's 'revolution hits the universities'. *Inside Higher Ed.* Retrieved September 17, 2013, from http://www.insidehighered.com/blogs/globalhighered/memo-trustees-re-thomas-friedman's-'revolution-hits-universities'

Onwurah, C. (2013). *Women in IT: Reclaim the byte.* [Video]. Retrieved July 28, 2013, from http://www.computerweekly.com/video/Women-in-IT-Chi-Onwurah-Labour-Shadow-Cabinet-Office-Minister?videoId=2b0b3dc9692ef310VgnVCM1000000d01c80aRCRD

Orsini, L. (2013). *How an engineering toy for girls went from Kickstarter to bestseller*. Retrieved July 30, 2013, from http://readwrite.com/2013/07/12/how-an-engineering-toy-for-girls-went-from-kickstarter-to-bestseller

Othman, M., & Latih, R. (2006). Women in computer science: No shortage here! *Communications of the ACM*, *49*(3), 111–114. doi:10.1145/1118178.1118185

Palmén, R. (2011). Girls, boys and ICT in the UK: An empirical review and competing policy agendas. *International Journal of Gender. Science and Technology*, *3*(2), 407–423.

Papworth, L. (2011). *7 levels of social media engagement*. Retrieved August 16, 2013, from http://socialmediatoday.com/laurelpapworth/277499/7-levels-social-media-engagement

Parmar, B. (2013). *Women in IT*. [Video]. Retrieved July 28, 2013, from http://www.computerweekly.com/video/Women-in-IT-Belinda-Parmar-Little-Miss-Geek?videoId=eeff68e093fef310VgnVCM1000000d01c80aRCRD

Patten, E., & Parker, K. (2012). *A gender reversal on career aspirations: Young women now top young men in valuing a high-paying career*. Pew Research. Retrieved July 28, 2013, from http://www.pewsocialtrends.org/2012/04/19/a-gender-reversal-on-career-aspirations/

Penney, R. K., & McCann, B. (1964). The children's reactive curiosity scale. *Psychological Reports*, *15*, 323–334. doi:10.2466/pr0.1964.15.1.323

Pennington, S. (2013). *Five reasons why women work in technology*. Retrieved August 2, 2013, from http://www.smh.com.au/it-pro/business-it/five-reasons-why-women-work-in-technology-20130708-2jvvd.html

Pethokoukis, J. (2013, September 13). The end of global population growth may be almost here — and a lot sooner than the UN thinks. *AEIdeas*. Retrieved September 15, 2013, from http://www.aei-ideas.org/2013/09/the-end-of-global-population-growth-may-be-almost-here-and-a-lot-sooner-than-the-un-thinks/

Pitt, L. (2003). *Don't leave IT to the boys!* (Deliverable D05/Appendix 2.1 of IST-2000-26329 SIGIS Project).

Porter, J. (2011). *Women engineering graduates at 15-year low*. Retrieved August 26, 2013, from http://it-jobs.fins.com/Articles/SB130221786789702297/Women-Engineering-Graduates-at-15-Year-Low

Powell, R. (2013). *Learnable opens $10 million in online coding education for young people as fears mount Australia is falling behind*. Retrieved August 19, 2013, from http://www.startupsmart.com.au/growth/business-advice-and-education/learnable-donates-10-million-worth-of-coding-training-to-school-students/2013081910498.html

Powell, A., Bagilhole, A., & Dainty, A. (2006). The problem of women's assimilation into UK engineering cultures: Can critical mass work? *Equal Opportunities International*, *25*, 688–699. doi:10.1108/02610150610719146

Price-Mitchell, M. (2012). *Generation tech: The good, bad and scary*. Retrieved August 16, 2013, from http://www.psychologytoday.com/blog/the-moment-youth/201211/generation-tech-the-good-bad-and-scary

Queensland Government. (2013). *Networking an ICT business*. Retrieved August 13, 2013, from http://www.business.qld.gov.au/industry/ict/connecting-ict-business/networking-ict-business

Quesenberry, J. L., & Trauth, E. M. (2008). Revisiting career path assumptions: The case of women in the IT workforce. In *Proceedings of the International Conference on Information Systems*. Retrieved September 13, 2013, from http://www.eileentrauth.com/uploads/4/6/7/6/4676002/quesenberrytrauth_icis-2008.pdf

Rand, A. (1961). Happiness. *The Ayn Rand lexicon*. Retrieved August 2, 2013, from http://aynrandlexicon.com/lexicon/happiness.html

Rand, A. (1963). Man's rights. In H. Binswanger (Ed.), *The Ayn Rand lexicon*. Retrieved August 18, 2013, from http://aynrandlexicon.com/ayn-rand-ideas/man-rights.html

Ratcliffe, R. (2013, January 30). The gender gap at universities: Where are all the men? *The Guardian*. Retrieved September 21, 2013, from http://www.theguardian.com/education/datablog/2013/jan/29/how-many-men-and-women-are-studying-at-my-university

Rathgeber, E.-M., & Ofwona Adera, E. (2000). *Gender and the information revolution in Africa*. Ottawa, Canada: International Development Research Centre.

Reddy, H. (1975). *I am woman.* [Video]. Retrieved September 22, 2013, from http://www.youtube.com/watch?v=MUBnxqEVKlk

Reimer, K. (2013). *The big opportunity – What is digital disruption (part 1).* Retrieved August 16, 2013, from http://the-big-opportunity.blogspot.com.au/2013/06/what-is-digital-disruption-part-1.html

Research Career. (2013, August 6). Industry echoes call for more females. *News.* Retrieved August 7, 2013, from http://www.researchcareer.com.au/news/industry-echoes-call-for-female-engineers-researchers

Resende, P. (2013). *Mass high tech names 2013 women to watch.* Retrieved August 2, 2013, from http://www.bizjournals.com/boston/blog/techflash/2013/03/mass-high-tech-names-2013-women-to-watch.html?page=all

Rice, C. (2012a). *Science: It's a girl thing! A viral fiasco.* Retrieved July 14, 2013, from http://curt-rice.com/2012/07/28/science-its-a-girl-thing-a-viral-fiasco/

Rice, C. (2012b). *Science: It's your thing! 3 steps to a crowdsourcing success.* Retrieved July 14, 2013, from http://curt-rice.com/2013/01/03/science-its-your-thing-3-steps-to-a-crowdsourcing-success/

Richards, H. (2013). *CIPD debate: The future trends that will shape work.* Retrieved August 18, 2013, from http://www.intelligenthq.com/intelligence/cipd-debatethe-future-trends-that-will-shape-work/

Riddell, M. (2010, October 20). Bill Gates: If you don't like geeks, you're in trouble. [Interview]. *The Telegraph.* Retrieved August 2, 2013, from http://www.telegraph.co.uk/technology/bill-gates/8073946/Bill-Gates-If-you-dont-like-geeks-youre-in-trouble.html

Rincon, P. (2005). *CSI shows give 'unrealistic view'.* Retrieved August 4, 2013, from http://news.bbc.co.uk/2/hi/science/nature/4284335.stm

Rommes, E. (2003). *I don't know how to fit it into my life: Courses computers and the internet for everybody in Amsterdam* (Deliverable D03/ Appendix 2.4 of IST-2000-26329 SIGIS Project).

RoobixCoob. (2005). *A woman's role in the 1950s.* Retrieved August 27, 2013, from http://www.colorado.edu/AmStudies/lewis/1025/women1950s.pdf

Rosen, R. (2013). *A simple suggestion to help phase out all-male panels at tech conferences.* Retrieved August 2, 2013, from http://www.theatlantic.com/technology/archive/2013/01/a-simple-suggestion-to-help-phase-out-all-male-panels-at-tech-conferences/266837/

Rosen, L. (2010). *Rewired: Understanding the iGeneration and the way they learn.* New York: Palgrave Macmillan.

Rowson, J., Young, J., Spence, N., Lindley, E., & Gecius, E. (2012). *The power of curiosity – How linking inquisitiveness to innovation could help to address our energy challenges.* London, UK: RSA Social Brain Centre. Retrieved August 16, 2013, from http://www.thersa.org/__data/assets/pdf_file/0004/606829/RSA-Social-Brain-The-Power-of-Curiosity.pdf

Salowey, C. A. (2004). *Great lives from history: The ancient world, prehistory-476 C.E. Hypatia – Egyptian scientist.* Pasadena, CA: Salem Press. Retrieved November 15, 2013, from http://salempress.com/store/samples/great_lives_from_history_ancient_world/great_lives_from_history_ancient_world_hypatia.htm

Samarji, A. (2013). *Get real, forensic scientists: The CSI effect is waning.* Retrieved August 4, 2013, from http://theconversation.com/get-real-forensic-scientists-the-csi-effect-is-waning-13260

Sandberg, S. (2013). *Lean in women, work, and the will to lead.* New York: Knopf.

Satterfield, L. (2013). *TechWomen collaborate, code and connect in Jordan.* Retrieved June 2, 2013, from http://blogs.state.gov/stories/2013/02/14/techwomen-collaborate-code-and-connect-jordan

Satz, D. (2011). Feminist perspectives on reproduction and the family. In E. N. Zalta (Ed.), *The Stanford encyclopedia of philosophy* (Summer 2011 Ed.). Retrieved August 18, 2013, from http://plato.stanford.edu/archives/sum2011/entries/feminism-family/

Schultze, U. (2000). A confessional account of an ethnography about knowledge work. *Management Information Systems Quarterly, 24*(1), 1–39. doi:10.2307/3250978

Scientific American. (2013). *Open innovation pavilion.* Retrieved September 13, 2013, from http://www.scientificamerican.com/openinnovation/

Scoble, R., & Israel, S. (2013). *Age of context: Mobile, sensors, data and the future of privacy*. CreateSpace Independent Publishing Platform.

Selwyn, N., & Bullon, K. (2000). Primary school children's use of ICT. *British Journal of Educational Technology*, *31*(4), 321–332. doi:10.1111/1467-8535.00165

Sexton, M. (2010). *Gillian Armstrong meets up with old friends*. Retrieved July 19, 2013, from http://www.abc.net.au/7.30/content/2010/s2903068.htm

Shadbolt, N. (2013). Time to let it all out. *New Scientist*, *220*(2943), 29.

Shellenbarger, S. (2013, November 26). How one college boosted female STEM graduates–fast. *The Wall Street Journal*. Retrieved November 28, 2013, from http://blogs.wsj.com/atwork/2013/11/26/how-one-college-boosted-female-stem-graduates-fast/

Shen, K. N., Zhang, P., & Tarmizi, H. (2009). The role of culture in women interacting with ICT. *University of Wollongong Research Online*. Retrieved August 16, 2013, from http://ro.uow.edu.au/cgi/viewcontent.cgi?article=1049&context=dubaipapers

Siegel, L. J. (2013). *Are telomeres the key to aging and cancer?* Retrieved August 18, 2013, from http://learn.genetics.utah.edu/content/begin/traits/telomeres/

Simard, C., Davies Henderson, A., Gilmartin, S. K., Schiebinger, L., & Whitney, T. (2008). *Climbing the technical ladder: Obstacles and solutions for mid-level women in technology*. Palo Alto, CA: Anita Borg Institute for Women and Technology.

Simard, C., & Gammal, D. L. (2012). *Solutions to recruit technical women*. Palo Alto, CA: Anita Borg Institute for Women and Technology.

Simmonds, M. (2013). *Girls in ICT: Little or no progress in 30 years*. Retrieved July 1, 2013, from http://chionwurahmp.com/2013/04/girls-in-ict-little-or-no-progress-in-30-years/

Skipworth, H. (2013). *Joy of tech: Google Glass, privacy and wearable technology*. Retrieved August 16, 2013, from http://www.digitalspy.com.au/tech/the-joy-of-tech/a505087/the-joy-of-tech-google-glass-privacy-and-wearable-technology.html

Slane, C. (2013). *Who knew helping women get tech jobs could be so controversial?* Retrieved July 4, 2013, from http://www.huffingtonpost.com/cassie-slane/who-knew-helping-women_b_2599848.html

Smalley, L. (2013). *Click your fortune: TED-Ed's choose-your-own-adventure look at careers options*. Retrieved August 9, 2013, from http://blog.ted.com/2013/08/07/click-your-fortune-ted-eds-choose-your-own-adventure-look-at-career-options/

Smange. (2013). *The women of Bletchley Park*. Retrieved November 12, 2013, from http://www.squidoo.com/women-bletchley-park

Smith, L. (2011). *Should kids play Minecraft?* Retrieved August 3, 2013, from http://thecybersafetylady.com.au/2011/05/should-kids-be-playing-minecraft/

Smith, P. (2013). *Manasvi Somaiya – A woman of vision at VMware on her technological curiosity to growing from an intern to fulltime employee at VMware*. Retrieved August 10, 2013, from http://blogs.vmware.com/careers/2013/08/manasvi-somaiya-a-woman-of-vision-at-vmware-on-her-technological-curiosity-to-growing-from-an-intern-to-a-full-time-employee-at-vmware.html

Soe, L., & Yakura, E. K. (2008). What's wrong with the pipeline? Assumptions about gender and culture in IT work. *Women's Studies. An Inter-Disciplinary Journal*, *37*(3), 176–201.

Solberg, C. A. (2002). *Culture and industrial buyer behavior: The Arab experience*. Paper presented at the 18th IMP Conference. Retrieved August 16, 2013, from http://impgroup.org/uploads/papers/522.pdf

Sommers, C. H. (2008, March/April). Why can't a woman be more like a man? *The American*. Retrieved August 18, 2013, from http://www.american.com/archive/2008/march-april-magazine-contents/why-can2019t-a-woman-be-more-like-a-man

Sorman-Nilsson, A. (2013). *How to thrive during digital disruption*. Retrieved August 16, 2013, from http://www.mtmag.com.au/how-to-thrive-during-digital-disruption/

Soubbotina, T. P. (2004). *Beyond economic growth: An introduction to sustainable development* (2nd ed.). Washington, DC: The World Bank. doi:10.1596/0-8213-5933-9

Spender, D. (2011). *Girls and IT – What's changed?* Retrieved July 27, 2013, from http://dalespender.com.au/~dalespen/wp-content/uploads/2011/05/GIRLS-AND-IT.pdf

Sterling, D. (2012). *GoldieBlox: The engineering toy for girls*. Retrieved August 27, 2013, from http://www.kickstarter.com/projects/16029337/goldieblox-the-engineering-toy-for-girls/posts

Sternberg, R. J., & Lubart, T. I. (1999). The concept of creativity: Prospects and paradigms. In R. J. Sternberg (Ed.), *Handbook of creativity* (pp. 3–16). Cambridge, UK: Cambridge University Press.

Stirland, S. L. (2013). *Kimberly Bryant wants black girls code to be girl scouts of technology*. Retrieved July 24, 2013, from http://techpresident.com/news/23974/kimberly-bryant-wants-black-girls-code-be-girl-scouts-technology

Stone, B. (2010). *The children of cyberspace: Old fogies by their 20's*. Retrieved August 16, 2013, from http://www.nytimes.com/2010/01/10/weekinreview/10stone.html?_r=0

Suriya, M., & Craig, A. (2003). Gender issues in the career development of IT professionals: A global perspective. In S. Spencer (Ed.), *AusWIT 2003 - Participation, progress and potential* (pp. 97–108). Hobart, Tasmania: University of Tasmania.

Svinth, L. (2006). *Leaky pipeline – To be or not to be a useful metaphor in understanding why women to a disproportional degree exit from scientific careers*. Paper presented at the 6th European Gender Research Conference – UPGEM. Retrieved July 27, 2013, from http://www.dpu.dk/upgem/conferencesandseminars/europeangenderresearchconference/

Swade, D. (2008). *The Babbage engine*. Computer History Museum. Retrieved November 11, 2013, from http://www.computerhistory.org/babbage/

Tague, J., Beheshti, J., & Rees-Potter, L. (1981). The law of exponential growth: evidence, implications and forecasts. *Library Trends*, *30*, 125–150.

Tandon, N., Pritchard, S., Savelieva, V., Smith, G., & Vogt, E. (2012). *A bright future in ICTs opportunities for a new generation of women*. Geneva, Switzerland: International Telecommunication Union.

Taylor, J. (2012). *Raising generation tech: Preparing your children for a media-fueled world*. Naperville, IL: Sourcebooks.

TechWomen. (2013a). *Meet the 2013 emerging leaders*. Retrieved August 10, 2013, from https://www.techwomen.org/participants/2013-techwomen

TechWomen. (2013b). *What is TechWomen?* Retrieved August 17, 2013, from https://www.techwomen.org

Thomson, G. (2012). *XX game jam*. Retrieved August 2, 2013, from http://www.raygun-gothic.net/blog/misc/xx-game-jam/

Thornton, M. (2007). *Who's minding the gender gap in IT?* Retrieved June 10, 2013, from http://searchcio-midmarket.techtarget.com/magazineContent/Whos-Minding-the-Gender-Gap-in-IT

Timms, C., Courtney, L., & Anderson, N. (2006). Dimensions of 'boring': Secondary girls' perceptions of advanced ICT subjects. In *Proceedings of the Australian Computers in Education Conference 2006*. Cairns, Australia: ACEC.

Tobak, S. (2011, March 8). The gender pay gap is a complete myth. *CBS Moneywatch*. Retrieved August 4, 2013, from http://www.cbsnews.com/8301-505125_162-28246928/the-gender-pay-gap-is-a-complete-myth/

Torrance, E. P. (1967). Non-test ways of identifying the creatively gifted. In J. C. Gowan, G. D. Demos, & E. P. Torrance (Eds.), *Creativity: Its educational implications*. New York: Wiley.

Trauth, E. M., & Quesenberry, J. (2006). Are women an underserved community in the information technology profession? In *Proceedings of the International Conference on Information Systems* (pp. 1757-1770). Milwaukee, WI: University of Wisconsin.

Trauth, E. M., Huang, H., & Quesenberry, J. L. (2006). Cross-cultural influences on women in the IT workforce. In *Proceedings of ACM SIGMIS Conference on Computer Personnel Research* (pp. 12-19). Claremont, CA: ACM.

Trauth, E. M. (2002). Odd girl out: An individual differences perspective on women in the IT profession. *Information Technology & People*, *15*(2), 98–118. doi:10.1108/09593840210430552

Trauth, E. M. (2006). Theorizing gender and information technology research using the individual differences theory of gender and IT. In E. M. Trauth (Ed.), *Encyclopedia of gender and information technology* (Vol. 2, pp. 1154–1159). Hershey, PA: Idea Group Reference. doi:10.4018/978-1-59140-815-4.ch182

Trauth, E. M. (2011). What can we learn from gender research? Seven lessons for business research methods. *The Electronic Journal of Business Research Methods*, *9*(1), 1–9.

Trauth, E. M. (Ed.). (2006). *Encyclopedia of gender and information technology*. Hershey, PA: Idea Group Reference. doi:10.4018/978-1-59140-815-4

Trauth, E. M., Nielsen, S. H., & von Hellens, L. A. (2003). Explaining the IT gender gap: Australian stories for the new millennium. *Journal of Research and Practice in Information Technology*, *35*(1), 7–20.

Trauth, E. M., Quesenberry, L. L., & Huang, H. (2009). Retaining women in the U.S. I.T workforce: Theorizing the influence of organizational factors. *European Journal of Information Systems*, *18*(5), 476–497. doi:10.1057/ejis.2009.31

Turner, E. (2005). New Europe – New attitudes? Some initial findings on women and computing in the Czech Republic. In J. Archibald, J. Emms, F. Grundy, J. Payne, & E. Turner (Eds.), *The gender politics of ICT* (pp. 133–148). London: Middlesex University Press.

Turner, S. V., Brent, P. W., & Pecora, N. (2002). *Why women choose information technology careers: Educational, social, and familial influences*. New Orleans, LA: Annual Educational Research Association.

Udeani, U. (2012). Increasing female participation in science and technology careers: Problems and suggested interventions from Nigeria. *Developing Country Studies*, *2*(5), 87–95.

UNESCO. (2012). *Girls in STEM and ICT careers: The path toward gender equality*. New York: UNESCO.

United Nations Conference on Trade and Development (UNCTAD). (2011). *Applying a gender lens to science, technology and innovation*. New York: United Nations.

UNPFA. (2009). *State of the world population: Facing a changing world: Women, population and climate*. Retrieved from http://www.unfpa.org/swp/

UserExperienceWorks. (2011). *A magazine is an iPad that does not work*. [Video]. Retrieved July 29, 2013, from http://www.youtube.com/watch?v=aXV-yaFmQNk

Valenduc, G., Vendramin, P., Guffens, C., Wagner, I., Birbaumer, A., & Tolar, M. et al. (2005). *Widening women's work in information and communication technology: Synthesis report of European project*. Namur: Fondation-Travail Université.

Varma, R. (2010). Why so few women enroll in computing? Gender and ethnic differences in students' perception. *Computer Science Education*, *20*(4), 201–316. doi:10.1080/08993408.2010.527697

Victoria Police. (2013). *Is forensic science really like the television show CSI?* Retrieved August 10, 2013, from http://www.police.vic.gov.au/content.asp?Document_ID=699

Volman, M., van Eck, E., Heemskerk, I., & Kuiper, E. (2005). New technologies, new differences: Gender and ethnic differences in pupils' use of ICT in primary and secondary education. *Computers & Education*, *45*(1), 35–55. doi:10.1016/j.compedu.2004.03.001

von Hellens, L. A., Pringle, R., Nielsen, S. H., & Greenhill, A. (2000). People, business, and IT skills: The perspective of women in the IT industry. In W. Nance (Ed.), *Proceedings of the ACM SIGCPR Special Interest Group on Computer Personnel Research* (pp. 152-157). Chicago, IL: Association for Computing Machinery.

von Hellens, L. A., & Nielsen, S. N. (2001). Australian women in IT. *Communications of the ACM*, *44*(7), 46–52. doi:10.1145/379300.379310

von Hellens, L., Trauth, E., & Fisher, J. (2012). Editorial. *Information Systems Journal*, *22*, 343–353. doi:10.1111/j.1365-2575.2012.00412.x

Wajcman, J. (2010). Feminist theories of technology. *Cambridge Journal of Economics*, *34*, 143–152. doi:10.1093/cje/ben057

Waldman, P. (2013). *How long do you want to live?* Retrieved August 17, 2013, from http://prospect.org/article/how-long-do-you-want-live

Watts, A. G., & Sultana, R. G. (2004). Career guidance policies in 37 countries: Contrasts and common themes. *International Journal for Educational and Vocational Guidance*, *4*, 105–122. doi:10.1007/s10775-005-1025-y

Waugh, P. (2013a). *Pia Waugh: Director of coordination and gov 2.0 for technology & procurement division, department of finance and deregulation*. Retrieved July 22, 2013, from http://www.linkedin.com/pub/pia-waugh/0/a7b/990

Waugh, P. (2013b). *GovHack 2013 report – How the beast went national*. Retrieved July 22, 2013, from http://www.govhack.org/govhack-2013-report-how-the-beast-went-national/

Whitney, T. (2013). *The White House tech inclusions champions of change!* Retrieved August 16, 2013, from http://anitaborginstitute.tumblr.com/post/56988102023/the-white-house-tech-inclusion-champions-of-change?utm_source=15+August+2013+Newsletter+ABI&utm_campaign=2013+Aug+15+Newsletter&utm_medium=email

Wikigender. (2013). *Gender equality in Malaysia*. Retrieved September 6, 2013, from http://www.wikigender.org/index.php/Gender_Equality_in_Malaysia

Wikipedia. (2013). *Up series*. Retrieved September 20, 2013, from http://en.wikipedia.org/wiki/Up_Series

Wikipedia. (2013a). *Ada Lovelace*. Retrieved November 11, 2013, from http://en.wikipedia.org/wiki/Ada_Lovelace

Wikipedia. (2013a). *Internet: Social impact*. Retrieved December 7, 2013, from http://en.wikipedia.org/wiki/Internet#Social_impact

Wikipedia. (2013b). *Crowdsourcing*. Retrieved August 27, 2013, from http://en.wikipedia.org/wiki/Crowdsourcing

Wikipedia. (2013b). *ENIAC*. Retrieved November 12, 2013, from http://en.wikipedia.org/wiki/ENIAC

Wikipedia. (2013c). *Hypatia*. Retrieved November 12, 2013, from http://en.wikipedia.org/wiki/Hypatia

Willyard, C. (2011, January). Men in psychology: A growing minority? *gradPSYCH Magazine*. Retrieved September 6, 2013, from http://www.apa.org/gradpsych/2011/01/cover-men.aspx

WISAT. (2013). *New gender benchmarking study: South Africa ranks low on women participation in STI*. Retrieved August 24, 2013, from http://wisat.org/home/new-gender-benchmarking-study-south-africa-ranks-low-on-women-participating-in-sti/

WIT. (2010). *Women in technology win with board readiness program.* Retrieved July 20, 2013 from http://www.wit.org.au/news/women-in-technology-win-with-board-readiness-program

Wittenberg-Cox, A. (2013). *What Cisco CEO John Chambers needs to know about gender balance.* Retrieved June 4, 2013 from http://blogs.hbr.org/cs/2013/03/what_cisco_ceo_john_chambers_n.html

Women's Bureau. (2010). *Women in the labor force in 2010.* United States Department of Labor. Retrieved September 6, 2013, from http://www.dol.gov/wb/factsheets/Qf-laborforce-10.htm

World Bank. (2009). *Mobile payments go viral: M-PESA in Kenya.* Retrieved August 16, 2013, from http://web.worldbank.org/WBSITE/EXTERNAL/COUNTRIES/AFRICAEXT/0,contentMDK:22551641~pagePK:146736~piPK:146830~theSitePK:258644,00.html

Worrall, L., Harris, K., Stewart, R., Thomas, A., & McDermott, P. (2010). Barriers to women in the UK construction industry. *Engineering, Construction, and Architectural Management, 17*(3), 268–281. doi:10.1108/09699981011038060

X Prize Foundation. (2013). *Making the impossible possible.* Retrieved September 13, 2013, from http://www.xprize.org

Xie, Y., & Shauman, K. (2003). *Women in science: Career processes and outcomes.* Boston, MA: Harvard University Press.

Yoshida, K. S. (2013). *Forget Venus and Mars, we're beginning to understand gender behavior on Earth.* Retrieved October 1, 2013, from http://arstechnica.com/science/2013/09/forget-venus-and-mars-were-beginning-to-understand-gender-behavior-on-earth/

Zandt, D. (2013). *Top reasons why the #SocialEra changes everything.* Retrieved July 18, 2013, from http://www.speakers.ca/2013/07/top-reasons-the-socialera-changes-everything/

Zarrett, N., Malanchuk, O., Davis-Kean, P. E., & Eccles, J. (2006). Examining the gender gap in IT by race: Young adults' decisions to pursue an IT career. In J. M. Cohoon, & W. Aspray (Eds.), *Women and information technology: Research on underrepresentation* (pp. 55–88). Cambridge, MA: MIT Press. doi:10.7551/mitpress/9780262033459.003.0002

Zeilinska, E. (2012). *Diversity in life science proves elusive.* Retrieved August 1, 2013, from http://www.the-scientist.com/?articles.view/articleNo/32713/title/Diversity-in-Life-Science-Proves-Elusive/

Zellinger, J. (2013). *The women in technology generating the most buzz in 2013.* Retrieved August 2, 2013, from http://www.huffingtonpost.com/2013/07/10/women-in-technology-generating-most-buzz-in-2013_n_3542566.html

About the Author

Sonja Bernhardt is CEO of the award-winning software development firm ThoughtWare, Australia, and has been awarded three degrees: a Bachelor of Arts majoring in Abstract Algebra and Psychology (1987), Graduate Diploma in Human Resource Management (1989), and MBA (Masters of Business Administration) (1992). For decades, she has tirelessly volunteered to passionately encourage women into technology studies and careers. This has included multiple industry-related activities such as executive committees and board membership over a period of 20 years, judging appointments in a wide variety of innovation and technology awards over a period of 15 years, and taking to the airwaves as resident "geek girl" on ABC Radio over a period of 7 years. In addition, she has been an occasional contributor and/or sponsor for government and university research and is a published author of book chapters and articles in industry magazines. Her prestigious honours are that she was the first Australian inducted into the WITI (Women in Technology International) Hall of Fame in 2005, winner of the Industry and Business Award in the Our Women, Our State Awards in 2009, and first Queensland woman to be awarded the prestigious Medal of the Order of Australia (OAM) for services to Information Technology in 2011. She bases her life and all activities on a reality- and reason-based philosophy.

Index

T

U

V

W

www.ingramcontent.com/pod-product-compliance
Lightning Source LLC
LaVergne TN
LVHW080527300926
849162LV00007B/1551